The Records
of Ming Scholars

明儒學案選譯

馮友大題

The Records of Ming Scholars

by
Huang Tsung-hsi

A Selected Translation
edited by Julia Ching

with the collaboration of
Chaoying Fang

University of Hawaii Press • Honolulu

Library of Congress Cataloging-in-Publication Data

Huang, Tsung-hsi, 1610–1695.
  The records of Ming scholars.

  Translation of: Ming ju hsüeh an.
  Bibliography: p.
  Includes indexes.
  1. Learning and scholarship—China. 2. Scholars—
China. I. Ching, Julia. II. Fang, Chao-ying,
1908–   . III. Title.
AZ791.H7982513 1987   001.2'0951   86–27257
ISBN 0-8248-1028-7

Frontispiece calligraphy by Fung Yu-lan

The editor wishes to dedicate this book
to Tsen-chüeh Tsao and Wing-tsit Chan

Contributors

Irene Bloom

Anne Ch'ien

Edward Ch'ien

Julia Ching

Mark Cummings

Ronald Dimberg

Chaoying Fang

Joanna Handlin

John Langlois

Rodney Taylor

Contents

Part Three: Epilogue 265

Acknowledgments

A selected translation of Huang Tsung-hsi's *Ming-ju hsüeh-an* would not have seen the light of day without the inspiration and collaboration of a number of persons, many of them associated with Columbia University and its Regional Seminar in Neo-Confucianism. The original proposal came appropriately from W. Theodore de Bary, who had himself worked on Huang Tsung-hsi, obtaining an initial grant from the American Council of Learned Societies in 1974 to support the work. As it now has taken form, this volume is the work of ten persons whose contributions—including the labor divided between the two editors—are explained in the Editor's Note. Fortunately some of these contributors had prepared doctoral dissertations on specific thinkers included in this volume, such as Chiao Hung and Kao P'an-lung, so that the translations might be said to have benefited from these specialized studies.

Several other individuals deserve special mention. Wing-tsit Chan read over the explanatory introduction and gave various suggestions. Liu Ts'un-yan and T. C. Tsao shed light on several difficult passages, especially those dealing with Buddhism. Yamanoi Yū pointed out the direction in the very beginning. Yü Ying-shih gave friendly support and encouragement, as did the former chairman of the Regional Seminar in Neo-Confucianism, David Dilworth, and its executive secretary, Irene Bloom. Special thanks are also due to Willard G. Oxtoby of the University of Toronto and David Mungello of Coe College. Willard's help has been especially crucial in bringing about a final manuscript. And then, we are very honored to possess a title page in the Chinese calligraphy of the famous contemporary Chinese philosopher and historian of philosophy, Fung Yu-lan.

After word of the acceptance of the manuscript by the University of Hawaii Press came the sad news of the passing away in Peking, China of Dr. Chaoying Fang (April 28, 1985), our beloved coeditor and the teacher of us all. Many a book in Chinese studies bears a note of acknowledgment to him, the wise and self-effacing scholar. This book would not be what it is without him. It is indeed our privilege that, with his permission, the book should bear his name on its title page. He also insisted that it be made clear that while he offered collaboration, he was not the author of the Editor's Note, or of the book's Introduction and Epilogue. Also with Dr. Fang's knowledge and support, this book is dedicated to Dr. T. C. Tsao, his friend and the father of the editor, as well as to Dr. Wing-tsit Chan, our guide in the field of Chinese philosophy.

We wish to conclude by thanking Mr. Stuart Kiang, our editor at the University of Hawaii Press, for his collaboration, which has made the publication of this book such a pleasant effort.

JULIA CHING

Editor's Note

THE difficulties of rendering in good and proper English the title of the book, *Ming-ju hsüeh-an,* illustrate for us the difficulties of translating such a work altogether. The problems are *ju* and *hsüeh-an. Ju* refers to a scholar (or scholars) and stands usually for the Confucian, to distinguish him from the Taoist and the Buddhist. In this book, however, one also meets such *ju* (albeit exceptionally) as ignorant potter(s) and woodcutter(s), hardly exemplars of conventional scholarship. *Hsüeh-an* refers to "records of scholarship" or "records of schools," the latter being preferable as the "scholars" are presented in groupings organized by the author and compiler of the work, Huang Tsung-hsi (1610–95). However, many of these groupings are not autonomous schools of thought in themselves but rather branches of the Wang Yang-ming school. There was, for example, the T'ai-chou branch itself, which produced a wise potter and a woodcutter deserving of mention in such a classic as this work of Huang's. In order to keep intact the intended meaning of the original title of the book, we are calling this selected translation *The Records of Ming Scholars.* We presume the understanding of our readers that potters and woodcutters may very well be Confucian "scholars," provided they really seek after wisdom and acquire real insights into its nature. Such, certainly, was the reason Huang Tsung-hsi included them in this work while excluding those figures for whom he had less respect, such as Yen Chün and Ho Hsin-yin.

These considerations may help also to explain the character of the book itself. Although the reference is to "scholars," the book is concerned with those persons—in all, two hundred—who were seekers of wisdom or at least claimed to have been such. In this sense, it is also concerned with "philosophers," or lovers of wisdom, although we should point out that all two hundred can hardly be described as having great philosophical minds. Nevertheless and without doubt, there were some keen philosophical minds among them, the greatest of whom was Wang Yang-ming.[1] But their philosophies never lost sight of wisdom and, particularly, of a wisdom inseparable from a life of virtue.

The exigencies of such a wisdom are that, in every case, a thinker-scholar's life becomes the ultimate testing ground for the genuineness of his philosophy. This explains the important place biographies hold in any account of the evolution of thought—those of eminent monks or, as in our case, of Confucian thinkers and scholars. We learn from biographies how various persons grappled with life's problems in developing their philosophies, in both the outer and inner realms of human existence. In this context, a man could hardly have been called a moral or social philosopher without having also had a definite commitment to the improvement of the social order—a commitment that led him into social-political action whenever possible or kept him from it in the interest of protest. Moreover he could hardly make metaphysical or even mystical claims unless he had personally exercised his faculties in the contemplation of truth, as, for example, in reflective reading of the classics accompanied by meditations designed to purify his mind and make it more attentive to the silent voice of truth according to these exigencies.

Huang's *Records* are not of "armchair philosophers," secure in their government positions or in institutions of higher learning, perpetuating the Confucian profession by the production of students who would pass civil examinations. Rather they tell of men living in difficult circumstances, called sometimes to heroic self-sacrifice, as in the cases of Fang Hsiao-ju and Liu Tsung-chou, or, more usually, to prove their convictions by frequent risk of life and honor. Thus the soul-stirring tales of greatness they present serve also as an indictment of the times and the governments under which these thinkers and scholars had to live and struggle. The *Ming-ju hsüeh-an* becomes in this sense a complement to Huang's other work, the *Ming-yi tai-fang lu* (Plan for a Prince), an outspoken critique of political despotism that could not be published until the late nineteenth century.

This book offers only a selected translation of the original. Of the clear tripartite division in the original work, all the prefaces (to the various schools of thought) are translated here in their entireties, but only forty-two biographies have been singled out for translation and annotation, while none of the excerpts from the scholars' sayings and writings are included. These last exclusions are the more comprehensible for the reason that they are themselves excerpts and have therefore an ad hoc character.[2] The selection of only certain scholars for translation is determined by definite criteria: all the major creative thinkers of the period are included—such giants as Wang Yang-ming, Ch'en Hsien-chang, Wang Chi, Kao P'an-lung, and the rest. We have also done what we can to assure that each school or branch of a school is represented by at least one man, even though this person might be considered a less creative thinker or scholar in comparison with some other person belonging to another school with a larger following. Here we are consoled by the thought that biographies do exist, in the *Dictionary of Ming Biography*, of certain "next to major" thinkers that have been excluded from this collection. And then, we have also done what we can to see that the entire period of the Ming dynasty is represented; in other words, that the thinkers and scholars selected represent also various generations of Ming thought and scholarship. This criterion has led to the choice of some later figures in preference to certain earlier ones.

The *Ming-ju hsüeh-an* is a massive work. One does not expect that it will ever be translated in toto into English. There is actually no such need, since probably no one outside of the Chinese circle could be interested in all two hundred scholars included in the original work, many of whom could hardly be called original thinkers.

We have singled out for translation the biographies of these forty-two persons and believe that this choice gives us an adequate introduction to the text itself and even to the character and flavor of the history of Ming thought. Some readers might wish that more had been included, but considerations of space and cost preclude this now. As to the selection made, the editor is quite aware that Huang regards the Kiangsi (Chiang-yu) branch as bearing the orthodox transmission of the Yang-ming school. For this reason he gives it the most coverage (8 ch.), yet only five of its representatives are included; whereas the T'ai-chou branch (5 ch.), considered almost heretical, is represented by ten. The reasons for such partiality are as follows:

(i)   The Chiang-yu branch is being represented by several of its principal thinkers. But while regarded by Huang as orthodox, it has not produced the most outstanding persons nor the most influential. Besides, several others, not included here, have biographies in the *DMB*.

(ii) The T'ai-chou branch is far more colorful and in many ways exercised a more important influence in late Ming thought and society. The biographies included are frequently short, giving information not available anywhere else, whether in Chinese or in translation.

Provided, therefore, that Huang's own judgments and interpretations are faithfully rendered (as we believe has been done in the Introduction and throughout the translations), the editor feels this somewhat uneven selection is justified and perhaps more useful to would-be readers than otherwise. After all, no major thinker of the period has been overlooked, and each school or branch is represented by at least one person.

A few procedural details:

(i)   Names given are usually the formal ones *(ming)*, frequently converted from the original text. However, wherever the text gives both *ming* and *hao,* both remain in the translation, and wherever the text gives the *hao,* this is indicated in the notes.

(ii) Dates given are usually of the Western calendar, as is age as well (by Western computation wherever possible). In the case of direct discourse, both the Chinese cyclical years and the Western equivalents are given.

(iii) Geographical names are made precise whenever possible; for example, Nanking is indicated where the text gives the Southern Capital (Nan-tu), Shao-hsing is indicated where the text gives Yüeh, and so on. Ming administrative provinces are often indicated in parentheses in the first sentence of each biography introducing the person involved, such as Ch'ang-chou Prefecture (Nan Chihli), although later place references are usually followed by indications in parentheses of modern province names.

(iv) References to classical texts and other sources are given wherever possible, but notes are intentionally brief, presenting only matters of interest to the intellectual historian or philosopher. When certain references are repeated frequently, bibliographical indications are not added every time. A lengthy bibliographical note explaining certain Chinese collections or series precedes the bibliographical entries at the end of this book.

Huang Tsung-hsi makes frequent mention of various works by persons whose biographies and ideas are included in this book. An effort has been made to trace these texts; for example, by finding the books themselves and consulting available bibliographical dictionaries. Whenever information from these texts has been used, the titles are included in the Bibliographies. In some cases, they are either no longer extant or not available in North America. In other cases, certain treatises are actually included in the collected or complete works of the person in question.

There is also the problem of variant translations of book titles, such as of the Five Classics. We have consistently translated *Shih-ching* as *Book of Poetry,* even though it is also known as *Odes,* and *Shu-ching* as *Book of History,* even though it is also known as *Book of Documents* or *Book of Historical Documents.*

(v) Wherever the Chinese text gives only an abbreviated form of a name or reference which does not make sense in English, such as Hsi for Huang Tsung-hsi or the "four beginnings" *(ssu-tuan)* for the four beginnings of virtue *(Mencius* 2A: 6), the translation usually spells out the entire meaning contained implicitly, not always using parentheses, in order to make the reference clear for readers of English. The same holds for the insertion of function words in English such as conjunctions, conjunctional phrases, and the like, which the Chinese text does not always provide.

(vi) In questions of style—capitals, italics, romanizations, and the like—the usage in the *Dictionary of Ming Biography* is usually followed.[3]

This volume is presented to its readers, most of whom are specialists or specialists-to-be in Ming thought, some of whom may be intellectual historians or philosophers of a more general orientation. We hope that it will serve not only as an aid in reading the original—which is obscure and difficult enough even for those who read Chinese well—but also as a work in itself. For this reason, the editor has provided a lengthy introduction, and each translation is supplied with critical annotations. Technical terms and expressions are rendered into English whenever possible, according to their semantic and syntactic usages and expressions in a language so different from Chinese—English, with its own philosophical vocabulary. *Hsin* becomes, therefore, "mind" or "mind and heart" or "consciousness"; *hsin-t'i* becomes the "substance" of mind or "mind-in-itself"; while *liu-hsing* becomes "flow" or "process" or "flow of consciousness."[4] It is our hope that the richness of thought and vitality of expression may appear all the more obvious with such minor shifts in translations and that the English translation may be rendered as clear and uncumbersome as possible and even sometimes illuminated. Those responsible for this volume have not sought to adorn the prose itself; Huang Tsung-hsi, the prolific author, was himself much less the stylist that Wang Yang-ming had been. But we have striven for clarity and simplicity and hope that these qualities will enable Huang Tsung-hsi to speak for himself.

As this is a work of translation, the selections included do not represent the original work of the contributors. Yet it should be said that without the laborious work of the collaborators, the translation could not have appeared. Although we worked separately, we agreed to use the standard text, based on the Mo edition (first published 1821). The page numbers given are from the SPPY text, which is available to all.

Following is a list of the specific contributions which have made this translation possible. We shall begin with the biographies, following the order of the book itself:

Wu Yü-pi (Chaoying Fang)
Hu Chü-jen (Anne Ch'ien)
Lou Liang (Julia Ching)
Ch'en Hsien-chang (Edward Ch'ien)
Hsüeh Hsüan (Edward Ch'ien)
Wang Shu (Julia Ching)
Wang Shou-jen (John Langlois)
Hsü Ai (Julia Ching)
Ch'ien Te-hung (Julia Ching)
Wang Chi (Julia Ching)

Tsou Shou-yi (Julia Ching)
Ou-yang Te (Julia Ching)
Nieh Pao (Julia Ching)
Lo Hung-hsien (Julia Ching)
Hu Chih (Rodney Taylor)
T'ang Shun-chih (Julia Ching)
Chiang Hsin (Edward Ch'ien)
Mu K'ung-hui (Julia Ching)
Hsüeh K'an (Julia Ching)
Li Ts'ai (Julia Ching)
Wang Ken (Mark Cummings)
Wang Pi (Julia Ching)
Chu Shu (Julia Ching)
Han Chen (Julia Ching)
Hsü Yüeh (Edward Ch'ien)
Lo Ju-fang (Joanna Handlin)
Keng Ting-hsiang (Ronald Dimberg)
Keng Ting-li (Ronald Dimberg)
Chiao Hung (Edward Ch'ien)
Chou Ju-teng (Edward Ch'ien)
Chan Jo-shui (Edward Ch'ien)
Hsü Fu-yüan (Julia Ching)
Fang Hsiao-ju (Edward Ch'ien)
Ts'ao Tuan (Edward Ch'ien)
Lo Ch'in-shun (Irene Bloom)
Lü K'un (Joanna Handlin)
Hao Ching (Joanna Handlin)
Ku Hsien-ch'eng (Rodney Taylor)
Kao P'an-lung (Rodney Taylor)
Sun Sheng-hsing (Rodney Taylor)
Huang Tsun-su (Julia Ching)
Liu Tsung-chou (Julia Ching)

Julia Ching has translated other parts of the work, including Huang Tsung-hsi's general preface, his introductory remarks and prefaces to the individual schools of thought, as well as the *Shih-shuo,* with the excerpts from Liu Tsung-chou. She has also written the introduction to this book. Both she and Chaoying Fang have gone over all the translations, sometimes adjusting and in a few cases rewriting the drafts in an effort to give greater unity and consistency to this book—which is, after all, a selected translation of one book and not a collection of original contributions. In general, it has been Chaoying Fang's responsibility to verify the translations in the light of Ming history, and Julia Ching's responsibility to assure a consistent and coherent interpretation of Ming thought. Julia Ching has also been responsible for the organization and overall presentation of the book in its final form. Despite these efforts, we are aware that the published book will exhibit some of the predictable inconsistencies and unevenness of a cooperative work, and we shall appreciate corrections and criticisms in the same cooperative spirit.

As this work goes to press, we hear of the project at the Zhejiang (Chekiang) Academy of Social Sciences, in Hangchow, China, to publish a complete edition of Huang Tsung-hsi's writings. Volume 1, including parts of *Ming-yi tai-fang lu* that have never seen print, has just appeared. We also hear of the conference to take place in Ningpo (Chekiang) in October 1986. It is another signal that the work of Huang Tsung-hsi continues to be regarded as significant and perhaps relevant, even today.

Julia Ching
March 1986

NOTES

1. Except in the case of Wang Yang-ming (Wang Shou-jen), the names given are usually the *ming,* the private or formal names of the persons concerned. But Wang Yang-ming is already well known even in the West under his *hao* (courtesy name).

2. It may also be mentioned that, from time to time, the entire *Ming-ju hsüeh-an* displays a certain ad hoc character. Huang Tsung-hsi gives us no reasons why some of his prefaces (to the individual schools) are longer, others are shorter, and why he provides here and there lists of names without further explanation of their contributions to the schools. There are also occasional errors in the book, of fact or of misquotation. One has the impression that Huang wrote partly from memory—for example, of books he once read but possibly did not check again, perhaps because he no longer had access to them. These errors cannot, however, vitiate the importance of the work itself, which is without doubt a classic.

3. The transliteration *yi* is used instead of *i,* since, for those unfamiliar with transliterations, *i* is difficult to pronounce.

4. The words "flow" and "flow of consciousness" offer examples of the living and vital character of the Chinese philosophical vocabulary, which has kept a certain closeness to nature itself. The English word "process" also recalls to us the philosophy of A. N. Whitehead. Whitehead's position does exhibit some marked resemblances to the overall aspects of Chinese thought; in technical detail, however, Whitehead's usage addresses a different set of specific questions. Where Whitehead speaks, for example, of *cosmic* change and becoming, the corresponding Chinese terms usually refer to the realm of inner consciousness, and the activities of the mind and heart.

Abbreviations

CTCS	*Chang-tzu chüan-shu* (Complete Works of Chang Tsai)
CYTC	*Cheng-Yi-t'ang ch'üan-shu* (*Cheng Yi-t'ang* series edition)
DMB	*Dictionary of Ming Biography,* edited by L. Carrington Goodrich and Chaoying Fang
ECCP	*Eminent Chinese of the Ch'ing Period,* edited by Arthur Hummel
ECCS	*Erh-Ch'eng ch'üan-shu* (Complete Works of Ch'eng Hao and Ch'eng Yi)
ESWS	*Erh-shih-wu shih* (Twenty-five Dynastic Histories)
HCCC	*Hsin-chai ch'üan-chi* (Complete Works of Wang Ken)
KTYS	*Kao-tzu yi-shu* (Surviving Works of Kao P'an-lung)
LTCS	*Liu-tzu ch'üan-shu* (Complete Works of Liu Tsung-chou)
MJHA	*Ming-ju hsüeh-an* (The Records of Ming Scholars)
MS	*Ming-shih* (Ming Dynastic History)
NCL	National Central Library
NLP	National Library of Peking
SK	*Ssu-k'u ch'üan-shu tsung-mu t'i-yao* (*Essentials of the Catalog of the Four Libraries* series)
SBE	*Sacred Books of the East* series, edited by F. Max Müller
SPPY	*Ssu-pu pei-yao* (*Essentials of the Four Libraries* series edition)
SPTK	*Ssu-pu ts'ung-k'an* (*Four Libraries* series edition)
SS	*Sung-shih* (Sung Dynastic History)
SYHA	*Sung-Yüan hsüeh-an* (Records of Sung and Yüan Scholars)
TSCC	*Ts'ung-shu chi-ch'eng* (*Collected Writings* series edition)
TSD	*Taishō shinshū daizōkyō* (*Taishō* edition of the Buddhist canon)
WLHC	*Wang Lung-hsi ch'üan-chi* (Complete Works of Wang Chi)
WWKC	*Wang Wen-ch'eng kung ch'üan-shu* (Complete Works of Wang Yang-ming)

Part One
Introduction

I. The Author and the Work

FOLLOWING the metaphysical heights attained during the Sung dynasty (960–1279), the Ming period (1338–1644) marks the second great climax of thought for the later development of Confucian philosophy. For those who wish to discover in some depth the philosophical ideas and intellectual movements of that time, *The Records of Ming Scholars (Ming-ju hsüeh-an)* remains an indispensable source of knowledge. It is one of the best-known and in some ways the best history of Chinese thought of its genre. Its superiority is better appreciated when the work is compared with two others: *The Orthodox Transmission of the Doctrine of Sages (Sheng-hsüeh tsung-chuan)*, compiled by Chou Ju-teng (1547–1629) and *The Orthodox Transmission of the Philosophy of Principle (Li-hsüeh tsung-chuan)*, compiled by Sun Ch'i-feng (1585–1675), an older contemporary and friend of the author of *The Records of Ming Scholars* itself.[1] The Chou volume, a work of 18 *chüan*, traces the succession of sages and their disciples, concluding with Lo Ju-fang (1515–88), Chou's own mentor. It reflects Chou's own fusion of Confucian and Buddhist thought as well as his desire to trace a lineal transmission of ideas from the legendary sages to his teacher and himself—an impossible task, because there was no such direct, lineal transmission. The Sun work, with 26 *chüan*, embraces the schools of thought of both Sung and Ming times as well as other historical and biographical accounts based on geographical regions and case studies. This represents much better scholarship and greater objectivity of viewpoint. While Sun's grandfather had been a disciple of Tsou Shou-yi (1491–1562), a direct disciple of Wang Yang-ming, Sun himself points out carefully the merits of both the schools of Chu Hsi and of Wang Yang-ming, taking the position of conciliator without defending one against the other. He finished this work in 1666 and presented a copy of it to Huang Tsung-hsi (1610–95), the compiler of the *Ming-ju hsüeh-an*, in the following year. Huang benefited from these earlier works for his own writing and compiling, as he also profited from exchanges with another scholar, Ku Yen-wu (1613–82),[2] author of *The Record of Daily Learning (Jih-chih lu)*, a result of thirty years' work and a collection in 32 *chüan* of encyclopedic scope.[3] Ku's manifest dissatisfaction with Ming philosophy also could have performed some kind of dialectical function in preparing Huang for his own philosophical reflections and writings.

Huang Tsung-hsi has left behind his own judgments of both Chou Ju-teng's *Sheng-hsüeh tsung-chuan* and Sun Ch'i-feng's *Li-hsüeh tsung-chuan*. This is what he has to say:

> . . . every school has its own principal doctrines, [but] Chou preferred Ch'an Buddhist doctrines, melting gold, silver, copper and iron into one vessel. This was his own idea, not that of all the schools. As to Sun, he collected information indiscriminately without careful discernment and classification. His own comments are not necessarily to the point. His information is like Chou's. Scholars only have to read *my* book, to recognize the coarseness and negligence of the other two works.[4]

This may appear to be self-centered and boastful. But for those who know Huang's superb historical knowledge, careful research, and keen insight, the statement is fair enough. Huang was, by comparison with both Chou and Sun, the better philosopher, scholar, and historian; his own work, *The Records of Ming Scholars,* stands as a classic of historical and philosophical scholarship, which has rendered the other two books largely obsolete, except for the curious specialist.

Huang Tsung-hsi (*tzu* Nan-lei, *hao* Li-chou),[5] the author and compiler of *The Records of Ming Scholars,* was a man of many parts—a colorful figure whose long life (1610–95) spanned the last three and a half decades of the Ming and the first five decades of the Ch'ing dynasty (1644–1911). He combined in himself the gifts and training of a scholar, an official, a philosopher, and a historian, with the fiery ardor of a filial son, a devoted disciple, and a lifelong patriot and Ming loyalist. His father, Huang Tsun-su (1584–1626), a scholar of the Tung-lin school,[6] had held a post at Peking as a censor (1623), and the eldest son, Tsung-hsi, had ample opportunity for education and for making scholarly contacts at an early age. Huang Tsun-su's denunciation of the powerful eunuch Wei Chung-hsien and his faction cost him his official post (1625) and led to his imprisonment and death (1626). His three sons[7] attached themselves to their father's friend, Liu Tsung-chou (1578–1645), who became their teacher as well as a second father. Liu was a man of remarkable independence. He was close to the Tung-lin movement but deplored its partisan politics. He was also a follower of Wang Yang-ming's school of thought but criticized its latter-day disciples. The highest government position he occupied was that of senior censor-in-chief, although for only a year (1642), as his outspoken disapproval of various measures, including the government's employment of the Jesuit Adam Schall and his cannons in guarding the northern frontiers, incurred imperial displeasure. He responded to the call of the southern

Ming government (1644) but resigned shortly afterwards, disgusted with its politically corrupt leaders. After the Manchus overran Nanking and Hangchow, Liu decided on death as an ultimate expression of his political loyalty and patriotism. He refrained from food and drink for twenty days and died on July 30, 1645. His example and his teachings were to leave an indelible imprint on the consciousness of his disciple Huang Tsung-hsi, and through Huang, on *The Records of Ming Scholars,* in which Liu figures as the final, shining example of Ming thought and scholarship.

Liu's philosophy is characterized by the words *shen-tu* (vigilance in solitude), a teaching derived from the two Confucian texts, the *Great Learning* (ch. 6) and the *Doctrine of the Mean* (ch. 1). In the former text, *shen-tu* is associated with "making the intention sincere," an important tenet of Wang Yang-ming's philosophy. In the latter, it is situated in the larger context of Heaven and human nature, of the Way (Tao) and its cultivation. In both, it follows the paradoxical assertion that the hidden is also the manifest:

> "What is truly within will be manifested without." Therefore the gentleman must be watchful over himself when he is alone. *(Great Learning)*[8]
>
> There is nothing more visible than what is hidden, nothing more manifest than what is subtle *(wei)*. Therefore the gentleman is watchful over himself, when he is alone. *(Doctrine of the Mean)*[9]

This teaching of vigilance in solitude is an instance of the depth of Confucian ethics and cultivation, that which was part of the Chinese tradition even before the introduction of Buddhism. It is basically an exhortation to interiorize the exterior concepts of morality and rituals, with which the entire Confucian ethical system has sometimes been exclusively identified. The Neo-Confucian thinkers had contributed to the clarification and elaboration of this dimension of interiority. Liu regarded it as the goal and substance of the quest of sagehood, while earlier thinkers had taken it to be mainly an exercise in self-examination.

If this teaching carries strong resonances of Wang Yang-ming's philosophy, it should be pointed out that Liu took an entire lifetime to develop it. He moved from an initial, youthful opposition to Wang Yang-ming, a position based on his distaste for Yang-ming's doctrine that "the mind is neither good nor evil" as being conducive to ethical nihilism, to a position of appreciation for Yang-ming. The change of heart occurred around the age of fifty, when Liu decided that Yang-ming had been poorly represented by his disciple Wang Chi, who had injected a strong dose of Buddhist teaching into his master's philosophy.[10] In his old age, as he deepened his understanding of Yang-ming's core teaching, that of the sincerity of the intention, Liu developed an enthusiasm for Yang-ming, one that he shared with his own disciple Huang Tsung-hsi.[11]

The young Huang had been pained and shocked by the arrest and death of his father. In 1628, at the accession of a new emperor (Ssu-tsung), he had set out for Peking from his native Chekiang with an awl in his sleeve and a memorial in his hand, intending to avenge his father's death and vindicate his good name. Before he reached the city, however, the eunuch Wei Chung-hsien had already died and his principal followers had been punished, while their victims were given posthumous honors. But Huang Tsung-hsi personally stabbed the jailors at whose hands his father had died. The emperor was touched by his filial piety and refrained from punishing him. He was then eighteen years old.[12]

Huang Tsung-hsi was accepted early into the literary and political circles of his day. He joined the group called "Fu-she" in 1630 during a sojourn in Nanking, becoming thereby part of a nationwide movement having literary as well as political importance and recognized sometimes as a continuation of the Tung-lin movement itself,[13] although its followers lacked the philosophical propensities of the earlier Tung-lin scholars. Huang also began a detailed study of Chinese history, in deference to a last wish expressed by his father. In two years he covered the Veritable Records of the first fifteen reigns of the Ming dynasty as well as the entire *corpus* of the twenty-one Dynastic Histories. In 1644, on hearing the news of the fall of Peking, he followed his teacher Liu Tsung-chou to Hangchow in Chekiang. They tried to raise volunteer troops for the Ming cause against the peasant rebels who had overtaken the capital. Together with his two younger brothers and several hundred volunteers, he assisted in battle against the Manchus as they pushed south to the Ch'ien-t'ang River. He was later made a censor and a secretary in the ministry of war by the prince of Lu, administrator of the realm (1646). That same year, together with five hundred others, Huang Tsung-hsi set up barricades in the Ssu-ming Mountains in Chekiang that served as guerrilla headquarters for the Ming loyalists gathered under Wang Yi. In 1649 he joined Prince Lu on the Chusan Islands but decided to retire from active politics and return home when he perceived that he could do little to advance the prince's cause and because his mother's life was being jeopardized by his own activities. It appears that Huang might have undertaken a journey to Nagasaki, Japan, in the company of an official, Feng Ching-ti, to request military aid for the Ming cause, but the exact circumstances of this mission and Huang's part in it remain unclear.[14]

From 1649 on, Huang Tsung-hsi lived in Yüyao and devoted himself wholly to the work of teaching and scholarship. He showed remarkable productivity. Today the Imperial Catalogue *(ssu-k'u)* lists only fifteen of his works, of which six were copied into the Imperial Manuscript Library.[15] But about one hundred titles, either extant or included in various catalogs, are attributed to him.[16] He also displayed an astonishing versatility. His writings on the Classics—especially on the *Book of Changes*—show a keen sense of discernment in matters regarding documentary evidence. He attacked the so-called "Yellow River Chart" and "Lo River Writing," attributed respectively to the sages Fu-hsi and the emperor Yü, as lacking in historical authenticity. In his political treatise, *Ming-yi tai-fang lu* (1662) (which antedated Rousseau's *Social Contract* [1762] by a century), he gives a critique of despotic government and his own ideas for institutional reform. It was much praised by his friend Ku Yen-wu, who differed otherwise from him on ideas of philosophy. A forbidden book during the Ch'ien-lung period (1736–95),[17] it was privately published in Canton in the mid-nineteenth century. Later it was circulated by Liang Ch'i-ch'ao and his friends and exerted a strong influence in promoting reformist and constitutional ideas.[18] Huang's anthology of Ming literature—actually a collection of biographies and selected texts—remains incomplete with 482 *chüan*. He also began anthologies of Sung and Yüan literature. His own poetry and short prose pieces reveal his literary gifts and his highly diversified interests. Huang had, besides, a remarkable understanding of mathematics and astronomy, having produced learned treatises on these subjects and a calendar for the use of one of the southern Ming princes.[19] He has also left behind a work on musical theory that has been highly regarded. He refused to accept the *po-hsüeh hung-ju* degree offered him by the Manchu government (1679) and declined the official invitation to work on the Ming dynastic history. But his works were assembled at the bureau of historiography where several of his disciples worked, consulting him frequently in cases of doubt. The present *Ming Dynastic History* itself is derived mostly from the draft version compiled by his most famous disciple, Wan Ssu-t'ung.[20]

It is important to mention here that Huang Tsung-hsi did not see any need for the *Ming Dynastic History* to contain the separate category of biographies entitled *Tao-hsüeh* (Followers of the Way) as did the *Sung Dynastic History*, in order to present the lives of the Neo-Confucian thinkers in a distinct way. Rather he criticized the *Sung Dynastic History* for having created this category. He preferred to have the broader category, the *Ju-lin* (Confucian Scholars), go on in order to emphasize the continuity of the Confucian school and to leave to later scholars any judgments regarding doctrinal similarities and differences. In this regard, he was affected by the sentiment voiced by many of his contemporaries, which he himself shared, that too much metaphysical speculation on the part of the latter-day followers of Wang Yang-ming had contributed to a certain scholarly impracticality. This mentality, some would even say, was responsible for the downfall of the Ming dynasty, just as the school of Lu Chiu-yüan allegedly also paved the way for the fall of the Sung dynasty. While remaining himself a philosopher and an admirer of Sung and Ming philosophical speculation, indeed, especially of the Lu-Wang school, Huang Tsung-hsi was careful to acknowledge the contributions of the textual and philological tradition—the so-called school of Han learning *(Han-hsüeh).*[21] He himself represented the integration of both philosophical reflection and textual and historical scholarship. Presumably, it was also for this reason that he entitled his own anthology of Ming thinkers the *Ming-ju hsüeh-an—Records of Ming* [Confucian] *Scholars.* Today, we might do well to remember that the English term "Neo-Confucian" is only useful to the extent that its users are aware of the same continuity in the Confucian tradition.

There could have been another, secondary, consideration. Since the anthology gives such importance to the many schools of thought that sprang up under the influence of Wang Yang-ming, it could scarcely have claimed to represent *Li-hsüeh* (the school of Principle), and yet the term *Hsin-hsüeh* (the school of Mind) was hardly acceptable to those conscious of the demands of orthodoxy.

What about *hsüeh-an?* Why did Huang Tsung-hsi select this term to designate the book, rather than other terms, such as possibly *hsüeh-p'u* (intellectual biography)?

The answer may lie in the associative meaning of this term, *hsüeh-an,* since the second word suggests "official dossiers" or even "judicial records." Confucian writings have always been didactic. Confucius himself allegedly compiled the *Spring-Autumn Annals* to teach later generations, for which reason he has been hailed as a judge of history, even an uncrowned king. In *The Records of Ming Scholars,* Huang Tsung-hsi has not hesitated to praise or blame—albeit subtly—the persons whose lives and ideas he discusses. The book, actually, has a hidden agenda written into its very structure. It is to this subject that we shall soon turn our attention.

Since Huang, philosopher and historian of philosophy, was at the same time an accomplished classicist and historian, political theorist, mathematician and astronomer, a man of letters as well as of music, he was, in a real sense, the last universalist of his generation. Many of the Ch'ing Confucian scholars might possess, in their own ways, the competencies of philologist and classicist, of documentary historian and poet-essayist. Few of them, however, engaged in deep philosophical reflection. Ironically, the Manchu government—and the subsequent political establishments—preferred devotion to textual minutiae even when this was allied to philosophical sterility, since such scholarly immersion was less likely to provoke political protest. Interestingly also, the late nineteenth-century reformers rediscovered Huang Tsung-hsi—

his critique of despotic power, his advocacy of political reform and change, as well as his speculative insights. This very fact can serve as a corrective to the simplistic view that philosophical speculation is in itself socially useless and politically unhealthy.

In his *History of Chinese Philosophy,* the modern Confucian philosopher Fung Yu-lan explains how Westerners have written histories of philosophy in what he calls a narrative style, whereas the Chinese have produced "histories of selected anthologies" with the compiler's comments on the philosophical ideas represented. Huang Tsung-hsi's work falls in this second category. Fung himself sees a certain advantage in this kind of historical work, which permits the reader to come into direct contact with the philosopher's words, although he acknowledges that such a genre suffers from a certain lack of systematization. His own *opus magnum,* representing a conscious fusion of both styles,[22] is an example of how Huang Tsung-hsi's model still has its modern emulators.

How does a compilation of selected anthologies permit the expression of the compiler's own views? Here the selection and ordering of the material in the anthologies represented becomes very important. In the case of *The Records of Ming Scholars,* Huang Tsung-hsi would forgo the strictly chronological order that had been followed by his predecessors Chou Ju-teng and Sun Ch'i-feng. Rather he organized the book in such a way as to focus on two central figures: Wang Yang-ming, around whose philosophy the entire work revolves, and Liu Tsung-chou, Huang's own teacher and Wang's reinterpreter. This allows Huang Tsung-hsi himself to give his own ideas and evaluations indirectly, through the selection he makes of the thinkers, through his accounts of their lives and his presentation of their texts. It is an example of Chinese "indirectness," with biographies replacing philosophical exposition, and the lives of their thinkers exemplifying the greatness or limitations of their thought systems. It is all the more appropriate for a philosophy claiming to unite knowledge with action, metaphysics with ethics and politics. And it imposes upon readers the duty of not merely reading the words and the sentences, which is frequently difficult enough, but also of understanding the meaning hidden "between the lines," and written into the entire structure of the book itself.

Speaking generally, one might characterize the book as comprising three sub-genres: prefaces—both the general preface standing at the head of the book and the individual preface heading the record of each particular school of thought; biographies—of individual thinkers grouped according to their schools; and selected texts, usually following each biography. Huang Tsung-hsi gives his own ideas and impressions of Ming thought as a whole in his general preface, a brief introduction to each school of thought in the individual prefaces, and his assessment and interpretation of each thinker in the biographies, usually toward the end of the accounts. Some of the minor thinkers and scholars included are given only a few brief lines of description—without any selection from their writings.

Let us present here in outline form the structure of the book:

Introductory Section:
Author's Preface
(*Tzu-hsü,* dated 1693, apparently the latest inclusion in the book, dictated by Huang Tsung-hsi before his death.)
A brief statement of his philosophy, of his association with Liu Tsung-chou, and of the genesis of the book.
The Teacher's Sayings
(*Shih-shuo,* not dated)
Quotations from Liu Tsung-chou on certain chosen Ming thinkers. This section actually marks the beginning of the formal content of the book.
Author's Introduction[23]
(*Fa-fan,* not dated)
This gives his reasons for compiling the book and situates it in relation to existing histories of thought.

Records of the Schools:
A total of seventeen records, the length of which varies from one to eight *chüan.* Each record includes the following:
Preface: usually, an interpretation of the school, sometimes including remarks and comments on thinkers excluded from the records, as is especially the case with the preface to the T'ai-chou school.
Biographies: usually several, sometimes a whole multitude, and always following a standard format: the person's official career (if any), the highest positions attained, and then a few salient facts from his life followed by comments upon him voiced by other thinkers, as well as Huang Tsung-hsi's own evaluation of these comments and of the thinker or scholar in question.
Selected Texts: usually following each important thinker or scholar. Some of these selected texts are from works no longer extant.

In the 62-*chüan* work that is the *Ming-ju hsüeh-an,* the schools of Wang Yang-ming and his disciples take up 27 *chüan,* almost two-fifths of the entire book. The chapters preceding the discussion of Wang Yang-ming himself, especially those dealing with Wu Yü-pi and his disciples, actually lead up to Wang Yang-ming, an heir to Wu's school through association with Wu's disciple, Lou Liang. The few chapters following the discussion proper of Wang Yang-ming himself concern the many schools of transmission developed by his disciples and their followers, usually grouped according to regional loyalties, and here the school of Chiang-yu (Kiangsi) is given special prominence (8 ch.) as the most faithful to Wang's teachings. Considerable space is devoted to the controversial debates on mind and human nature, goodness and evil, aroused by Wang's teachings, which continued long after his death. The school of Chan Jo-shui (6 ch.), a contemporary and friend of Wang's, and the Tung-lin school (4 ch.) are important particularly on account of their participation in such debates and their efforts—in collaboration with the Chekiang and Kiangsi schools of Wang's disciples—to bring about a more rational and balanced response to these questions that had generated so much emotional heat.

II. The Philosophical Horizons

HUANG begins his own preface to the book with a definite philosophical assertion:

> That which fills Heaven and Earth is Mind *(hsin)*. Its transformations . . . assume myriad forms. The mind has no original substance *(pen-t'i)* except what is achieved by its activity *(kung-fu)*. To exhaust and comprehend principles is to exhaust and comprehend Mind's myriad manifestations, rather than the myriad manifestations of all things.[24]

The language employed here is ambiguous and difficult, although his general position is unmistakable. Huang is assuming that "mind" represents something more than individual consciousness or, rather, that one can move from the myriad forms of individual consciousness to the principles of the myriad things. He is presenting a definite philosophical position, his own, but one that is supported by the entire thrust of Ming thought, that is even its very culmination. He is conducting us into an entire universe of thoughts and intentions, through which we should be better able to understand the entire Ming dynasty. For Ming thought represents a continuation of the Sung legacy—especially in its orthodox form in the school of Ch'eng Yi and Chu Hsi—as well as a protest against this orthodoxy, which is given expression in the school of Wang Yang-ming. Indeed it is better to say that in both its orthodox and protest forms, Ming thought demonstrates its own character, which is at the same time dependent upon and yet significantly different from Sung Confucianism. For the Ming Confucians are more inner-oriented, almost always starting with the questions of mind and human nature and moving from these to an understanding of the wider world; whereas Sung thinkers, from Chou Tun-yi to Ch'eng Yi and Chu Hsi, take as their starting point the external universe, especially questions of cosmology, before moving to the personal universe of mind and nature. For this opinion we have the support of Ku Yen-wu, the inveterate critic of Ming thought, as well as of Huang Tsung-hsi himself. Ku says:

> It is a matter of great regret to me for the past hundred-odd years, scholars have devoted so much discussion to mind and human nature, all of it vague

and incomprehensible. . . . The gentlemen of today . . . set aside broad knowledge and concentrate upon a search for a single, all-inclusive method; they say not a word about the distress and poverty of the world within the four seas, but spend their days lecturing on theories of "the weak and subtle," "the refined and undivided" . . .[25]

and Huang Tsung-hsi asserts elsewhere in his book:

In letters as well as in exterior accomplishments, the Ming dynasty was inferior to the earlier ones. Only in philosophy *(li-hsüeh)* is it superior. Every nuance, be it fine as the ox's hair and the cocoon's silk, has been carefully discerned and analyzed. What the former scholars did not develop has been done for them.[26]

Whether criticizing Ming thought for its emptiness and petty preoccupations or praising it for its depth and subtlety, Ku and Huang agree that it is essentially concerned with problems of mind and nature—and they see this concern as marking out an important difference between Ming thought and its Sung model, a difference that does not overlook certain underlying continuities but points to a significant development, a movement toward increasing interiorization and subjectivity. This development spells no absolute opposition, whether that of the Ming against the Sung or that of the subject against the object. On the contrary, the changes are of a subtle nature, focusing greater attention upon the meaning of sagehood and the way of achieving it. What emerges is a more personalist emphasis, an increasing pragmatic orientation, developed against a wider perspective of an older cosmology and metaphysics, but which does not risk the danger of fossilization through a process of objectification brought about by state control and the blessings of orthodoxy. But then, if the Sung period witnessed an impressive array of thinkers, the Ming was largely dominated by one single thinker: Wang Yang-ming. No other philosopher exerted as much influence over a period, and the imprint he left upon it would mark the whole movement of Confucian thought as it continued to spread from China to Japan and Korea.

The philosophy of Wang Yang-ming was nothing else than the quest for wisdom and its meaning, a quest involving self-knowledge and self-transcendence, formulated in terms of relationships between mind and human nature and the relevance of each or both to the quest itself, a quest that was supposed to involve a certain methodology. Wang Yang-ming's great discovery was nothing other than the paradoxical character of this quest: that wisdom was to be found in the seeking because the seeds of wisdom were always present in the mind, that the method of acquiring wisdom and sagehood was also, in itself, no method, since it could hardly be defined but must assume diverse forms according to the variegated manifestations of the mind itself. He set the tone for Ming thought, giving a deeper, more introvertive dimension to its inherent mysticism[27]—inherited, as this was, from Mencius as well as from Ch'an Buddhism. He did not neglect the external universe; indeed, he sought all the more to unite the inner and the outer, the theoretical and the practical, through his assimilation of the concept of *li,* principle, especially the principles of things, to that of *hsin,* the mind. His philosophy came to be known as the school (or learning) of the mind *(hsin-hsüeh),*[28] in contradistinction to that of the Sung thinkers' school (or learning) of principle or reason *(li-hsüeh),* sometimes referred to as the school of nature and principle *(hsing-li hsüeh).*

With this greater emphasis upon mind rather than nature—whether human or of things—comes also a stronger affirmation of *ch'i* (vital force, matter-energy), the principle of individuation and of concretization, that which gives to mind and emotions their dynamism. This distinction between *li* and *ch'i,* which resembles in some ways the Aristotelian form-matter dichotomy, provided for the Sung philosophers a basis for their new explanation of both the world and man—with the capacities for good and evil present in human nature. Where moral nature in itself is apprehended in terms of *li* as the principle of goodness almost inaccessible to evil, physical nature, which comes with *ch'i,* is the source of human emotions, the excess of which results in evil intentions and behavior. But the Ming philosophers, by giving more prominence to mind over nature, state their preference for the dynamic principle over the static, bringing also into greater focus the problem of the ubiquitous *ch'i,* that which is at once vital and changing, the existential as seen against the essential *(li).* In the case of Wang Yang-ming, a follower of Chu Hsi's rival Lu Chiu-yüan, "mind" becomes also *liang-chih,* a Mencian term that receives metaphysical overtones without losing its ethical implications. And "mind-in-itself" *(hsin-t'i)* is described as neither good nor evil—in a statement that became the occasion for centuries of controversy. Much of *The Records of Ming Scholars* following upon *chüan* 10 *(Yao-chiang hsüeh-an)* is given to interpretations and reinterpretations of this statement, which Liu Tsung-chou, Huang Tsung-hsi's master, ascribes to Wang Chi rather than to Wang Yang-ming himself.

The philosophy of mind proposes to overcome the tension between self and the world while also offering a method for the achievement of sageliness, which is said to consist in the very realization of self-transcendence through a consciousness of the oneness of all things. This method refers back to the self-determining power of the mind, or *liang-chih,* based upon the presence of the seeds of sagehood within the self. It is said that one need merely discover this truth to find it realized. But such a method does not offer a systematic approach toward such realization. It merely indicates that ultimate reality *(pen-t'i)* is already present in the quest for the ultimate, a quest that involves self-exertion *(kung-fu)*

—a life of personal discipline usually including some form of meditation. The great Ming philosophers, such as Wang Yang-ming[29] and Liu
Tsung-chou, all emphasize the interaction of activity *(tung)* and passivity or tranquility *(ching)* in one's spiritual quest. The careful reader of
The Records of Ming Scholars cannot but be impressed by the pervading
concern for finding wisdom through a life of virtuous action, which
honors man's social and political responsibilities whenever possible and
is balanced by the practice of meditation or quiet-sitting *(ching-tso).* The
unity of the inner-outer dimension is usually recommended, although
emphases differ regarding the importance of the gradual cultivation
(hsiu) or of the sudden experience of enlightenment *(wu)*—which is supposed to reveal to the heart the meaning of Tao or *pen-t'i.*[30] Interestingly
enough, there is no particular association of action with cultivation or
of meditation with enlightenment. Many followers of the T'ai-chou
branch of the Yang-ming school advocate the finding of an enlightenment experience without particular reliance on meditation. They frequently seek for enlightenment in activity. This appears also as an
expression of their belief in the dynamic power of the mind itself to
achieve wisdom in action. It became the duty of the followers of the
Kiangsi branch, as well as of the Kan-ch'üan school and of the Tung-lin
school, to restore the balance between activity and tranquility by a
return to the practice of quiet meditation.

This explains also the influence of Buddhism, especially of Ch'an or
Zen Buddhism, both in its gradualist or Ts'ao-tung form, and in its
subtilist or Lin-chi form, upon the evolution of Ming Confucianism.
True, Sung Confucianism began as a rationalist movement reacting
against the nonrational and antisocial teachings of the Buddhist religion. But it did so in part with what it had learned from Buddhist logic
and metaphysics, reconstituting a lost Confucian heritage and its teaching of sagehood with the assistance of Buddhist methods of cultivation
and near-monastic discipline.[31] Ming Confucianism continued to criticize Buddhism and Taoism, while developing further a philosophy of
immanence and a method of inner concentration centered more and
more on enlightenment. The influence of Pure Land Buddhism is also
felt in the philosophy of Wang Chi, a follower of Wang Yang-ming, who
advocates the achievement of enlightenment through faith in *liang-
chih.*[32] The continued decline of the Buddhist religion in Ming times
is accompanied by the increasing religiosity of Confucianism itself.
Huang Tsung-hsi speaks himself of accusations laid against Confucian
philosophers for being "Buddhists in disguise." Later scholars of the
Ch'ing times would especially focus upon this development, associating
it with Wang Yang-ming's teaching of the mind-in-itself as being "neither good nor evil." For them, this was responsible in large part for the
individualism and factionalism that characterized the behavior of late

Ming intellectuals and allegedly led to the eventual disintegration of
Ming state and society. The Ch'ing period became a time when metaphysical interests were discouraged while classical philology experienced its great revival.

Liu Tsung-chou and the *Ming-ju hsüeh-an*

The *Shih-shuo*

Shih-shuo refers literally to "The Teacher's Words," and expresses
Huang Tsung-hsi's deference to Liu Tsung-chou. It includes Liu's
comments on over twenty Ming thinkers and scholars, with Fang
Hsiao-ju leading the group and Hsü Fu-yüan, Liu's own teacher, at the
end. The lengths of the comments are irregular. While Wang Yang-
ming was given a long appraisal, Lo Ch'in-shun received an even
longer—but much less favorable—one. The comments also appear random in character. Liu discusses not merely each man's philosophical
contributions and metaphysical insights but also his personality and his
character.

Our first question is: where did the *Shih-shuo* come from? Did Huang
Tsung-hsi quote from memory—from what he heard from Liu's own
lips—or from Liu's writings, whether published or unpublished?

Obviously, the *Shih-shuo* is not derived from the two known collections
of Liu's extant writing; we refer here to the 40-*chüan Complete Writings of
Liu Tsung-chou (Liu-tzu ch'üan-shu)* and its 24-*chüan* supplement. There
is, however, evidence that it was taken out of another work by Liu,
entitled *Ming Tao-t'ung lu* (The Orthodox Transmission of the Way in
Ming Times) (ch. 7), which seems to be no longer extant. We base this
judgment on Liu's biography *(Hsing-chuang)*, written by another disciple, Tung Yang, as well as on Liu's *Chronological Biography (Nien-p'u)*,
where it is recorded of the year 1627, when Liu was in his fiftieth year,
that:

> The *Huang Ming Tao-t'ung lu* is completed. The Master compiled the *Tao-
> t'ung lu* in 7 *chüan*, modeling it upon Chu Hsi's *Ming-ch'en yen-hsing lu* (Words
> and Deeds of Famous Ministers). It first records their lives and deeds, then
> gives [selected] dialogues, and at the end concludes with the compiler's judg-
> ments. . . . His appraisals and critiques are all unique. Such scholars as
> Hsüeh Hsüan, Ch'en Hsien-chang, Lo Ch'in-shun, Wang Chi, whom the
> world regards as great, are criticized by Liu. Fang Hsiao-ju . . . and Wu
> Yü-pi [on the other hand], are especially praised. . . .[33]

All this is supported by the *Shih-shuo*. Liu praises Fang Hsiao-ju for
his scholarship and character, lamenting that others had lauded his
political martyrdom while overlooking his intellectual contributions.
Liu is even warmer in his appraisals of Wu Yu-pi, whom he considers to

be superior to both Hsüeh Hsüan and Ch'en Hsien-chang, as an example of personal cultivation. Liu also voices special approval of Wang Yang-ming, identifying the teaching of *liang-chih,* as already mentioned, with his teaching on vigilance in solitude. He quotes Yang-ming's words, that "the knowledge of good *(liang-chih)* is the knowledge of the self in solitude."[34] He compares him favorably with Chu Hsi, saying that while both taught vigilance in solitude, Yang-ming understood it better as the fundamental doctrine of the *Great Learning.* For where Chu explains this text as a systematic account of cultivation, which moves from investigation of things and extension of knowledge to sincerity of intention, Yang-ming identifies investigating things and extending knowledge with sincerity of intention—that is, with vigilance in solitude. In extravagant language, Liu likens Yang-ming to the "thunderbolt that awakens people from sleep, the blazing sun that pierces through obscurity,"[35] indeed, "a hero among men in an extraordinary epoch."[36] His only defect—if that could be called one—was his premature death. Should he have lived longer, Liu says, he would have entered into the realms of sagehood, integrating the teachings of Chu Hsi and Lu Chiu-yüan as well as mediating between them.

In the light of such enthusiasm for Wang Yang-ming, one can hardly be surprised by Liu's criticism of Lo Ch'in-shun: that Lo wasted several decades of time in investigating things, rather than concentrating his efforts on mind and nature.[37]

The *Chi-shan hsüeh-an*[38]

Chi-shan is a place near Shan-yin (Chekiang), where Liu taught his disciples. I single out the Record of the Chi-shan school because it offers confirmation of certain assertions made earlier: especially that Huang Tsung-hsi considers Liu's philosophy to be a synthesis of the whole of Ming thought.

In the preface to the Chi-shan school, Huang sets a somewhat polemical tone. Comparing Liu to Kao P'an-lung, he claims that Kao had been unable to free himself of Buddhist influences, while Liu was "the purest of the pure." He also repeated his earlier reference (in his own introduction to the whole work) to Liu's other disciple, Yün Jih-ch'u, as someone who did not understand Liu's thought and attempted to gloss over his teaching on intention[39]—an important point in a philosophy centered upon an inner doctrine of vigilance in solitude, that which assures a sincere intention, as recommended by the *Great Learning.*

For a further clarification of Huang's interpretation of Liu's thought, we may also turn to his other preface, that written for the so-called *Complete Works of Liu Tsung-chou.* Here Huang presents an even more complete statement of Liu's philosophy. He asserts that Liu alone has understood the meaning of vigilance in solitude:

Many people have taken vigilance in solitude as their central teaching. They either attend to "original being" *(pen-t'i)* and fall into vagaries, or rely upon independent knowledge *(tu-chih),* and concentrate effort upon the movement of thought *(tung-nien).* Only my deceased master understood that . . . the power of harmony and equilibrium . . . is naturally present in our daily activities and passivities. This is the solitary being *(tu-t'i).* . . . To be vigilant, is to be vigilant over this. . . . Former scholars regarded the intention to be a movement of the mind *(hsin).* My deceased master regarded intention as that which the mind contains [and cultivates]. . . .[40]

Huang Tsung-hsi reiterates elsewhere that Liu Tsung-chou's doctrine of vigilance in solitude can be understood in terms of Wang Yang-ming's doctrine of sincerity of intention.[41] He gives metaphysical status to intention, identifying it with solitary being as that which is present in the mind and yet transcends the mind. To cultivate such sincerity of intention is to cultivate Wang Yang-ming's *liang-chih,* the "true self" or, if we prefer, the "transcendental ego." It brings us into communion with the entire cosmic process, which is, after all, a macrocosmic image of the process of self-cultivation. It is in this same spirit that Huang Tsung-hsi has compiled *The Records of Ming Scholars,* leading us into the inner recesses of the minds and intentions of the great Ming thinkers and scholars by an examination of their philosophical discussions as well as the manner in which their lives gave witness to their moral convictions. For him, as for Liu Tsung-chou and Wang Yang-ming, solitude is never solitariness.[42] It is rather a state of inner consciousness that brings us out of ourselves into communion with the universe. The *Chi-shan hsüeh-an* serves as witness to the climax and summation of Ming thought and scholarship, since it gives the record of that thinker who had succeeded so well in uniting his knowledge with his action, his wisdom with his virtue.

Wang Yang-ming in the *Ming-ju hsüeh-an*

On the one hand, the *Ming-ju hsüeh-an* is structured around a clear focus of interest: the philosophical discoveries of Wang Yang-ming. On the other hand, Huang Tsung-hsi carefully unfolds for us a panorama rich in diversity—the diversity manifest in the later interpretations of these discoveries. This is shown by the many branches—schools of thought—spreading out from the same tree. Huang describes it in terms of "one root and myriad variations" *(yi-pen wan-shu).* In recording this diversity of opinion, he concentrates upon the central doctrines *(tsung-chih)* of each of these schools. Frequently, he recapitulates these doctrines in brief formulas. For Wang Yang-ming himself, this is "extending *liang-chih*"; for Chan Jo-shui, it is "realizing everywhere the principle of Heaven"; for Liu Tsung-chou, it is "vigilance in solitude." In this way,

Huang Tsung-hsi offers a key to understanding the nuanced development of Ming thought and enables his readers to find for themselves the richness and vitality of the philosophical discussions that took place during Ming times. In this way also, he leaves behind a refined and definitive genre for the recording of Chinese intellectual history: the *hsüeh-an* or "records of learning."

Given the close association between Huang Tsung-hsi and Liu Tsung-chou, has Huang diverged at all from Liu himself? How sound are his own philosophical positions? And what have Chinese and Japanese scholars today to say about his interpretations? These questions are asked now, but attempts at answering them will be postponed till the end of this book—in the Epilogue.

It is useful here to call attention to Huang Tsung-hsi's classification of Ming scholars according to their ardor or caution in their quest for sagehood.[43] Here he makes use of Confucius' characterization of disciples as being either "madly ardent" *(k'uang)* for the truth, or "extremely cautious" *(chüan)* and therefore reacting slowly. The perfect man is the man of the Mean *(chung-hsing),* whose behavior is not inclined to these extremes. But such is seldom to be found, and the sage himself states his satisfaction with men of "mad ardor" or of "extreme caution" *(Analects* 13: 21). The Sung and Ming philosophers themselves have frequently made reference to these characterizations. In *The Records of Ming Scholars,* Huang Tsung-hsi speaks of Ch'en Hsien-chang as exemplifying the quality of mad ardor or eccentricity and Hu Chü-jen as representing the more cautious seeker of sagehood. He also relates Wang Yang-ming's self-characterization as representing a man who was madly ardent about achieving sagehood. Although he did not say so explicitly, later scholars referred to Huang's own master, Liu Tsung-chou, whose philosophy of *shen-tu* emphasized the cultivation of a sense of moral and religious self-consciousness, as representing a man of extreme caution. In grounding his history of Ming thought on the two principal representatives, Wang Yang-ming and Liu Tsung-chou, Huang Tsung-hsi might therefore be said to have presented a certain dialectical profile of Ming thought, with the pendulum swinging between *k'uang* and *chüan.* Since his own position remains somewhere in between that of Wang Yang-ming and Liu Tsung-chou, it may also be said to point toward the transcending of these dialectical differences in the direction of increasing harmonization.

The *k'uang-chüan* characterization in the book can be said to represent the thinkers' positions regarding doctrinal orthodoxy. The "madly ardent" persons tend to be more sympathetic to Buddhism and Taoism, with the extremists among them becoming known as *k'uang-Ch'an*—mad Ch'an Buddhists. Such are the followers of the T'ai-chou branch of the Yang-ming school. Indeed, those whom Huang Tsung-hsi appar-

ently considers to be "too extreme"—such as Ho Hsin-yin and Li Chih
—are not even given biographies in his book. Similarly, the cautious
thinkers tend to be very conservative, adhering to more rigidly orthodox positions and are usually less tolerant of Buddhist or Taoist influences. For example, whereas Hu Chü-jen is critical of Buddhism, Ts'ao
Tuan shows himself especially disdainful of certain Taoistic practices.

The *k'uang-chüan* characterization is also related to the polarity of sudden enlightenment and gradual cultivation. While the two terms *wu* and
hsiu are not necessarily opposed to each other—enlightenment is usually
achieved, if at all, after a process of gradual cultivation—they designate
two kinds of spirits. Huang Tsung-hsi apparently respects mystical
enlightenment, while placing more importance on moral and spiritual
cultivation. He compares Liu Tsung-chou, a man of cultivation, favorably to Kao P'an-lung, who eagerly sought after enlightenment and
enthusiastically recorded it. After all, if the goal is moral perfection
rather than mystical enlightenment, the experience itself is relativized,
especially when desired for its own sake.

The persistent concern with cultivation or spiritual ascesis reveals a
dimension of spirituality as a principal preoccupation of the Ming
thinkers and scholars. Such technical terms as *shou-lien* (to gather oneself together in tranquility of mind), *hsing-ch'a* (to watch over oneself
and examine one's own words, thoughts, and behavior), and *shen-tu*
(vigilance in solitude) can be fully appreciated only in this context. Certainly the spiritual dimension is an important contribution of the Neo-
Confucian movement. In the Western scholarly world, spirituality is a
much neglected area of reflection and consideration, and Western spirituality remains a hidden dimension of the culture—hidden in ascetic
and mystical theology, with no place in Western philosophy. It is perhaps significant that most Western moralists—except for Socrates and
the Stoics and the medieval philosophers who were also theologians—
have usually shown more interest in the problem of evil than in that of
achieving sageliness.

III. Regional Variations

THE geographical factor has always had a certain importance in the development of philosophical ideas in China. Both Buddhism and Taoism are known to have developed northern and southern schools. In the case of Neo-Confucianism, the inspiration had originally come from the north, from the region near Loyang and K'ai-feng—in Sung times[44] a region that produced Chou Tun-yi, Chang Tsai (1020–77), Ch'eng Hao (1032–85), and Ch'eng Yi (1033–1107). But the war with the Jurchens and the division of China into two parts changed the situation. The great philosophers of the southern Sung, Chu Hsi and Lu Chiu-yüan, came from Fukien and Kiangsi respectively, although their ancestors were originally northerners. The flowering of Confucianism in southern China was not accompanied by any parallel development in the Jurchen north, where the philosophies of Chou Tun-yi and the Ch'eng brothers were also neglected until after the reunification of the country under the Mongols (1279). Northern China gained a reputation for being less concerned with philosophical questions and more interested in classical scholarship, whereas the south continued to produce the speculative thinkers, especially during Ming times.[45] Interestingly enough, Wang Yang-ming, a man of Yüyao, Chekiang, would become especially associated with the area of Kiangsi, the home province of Lu Chiu-yüan, his predecessor in philosophy.

The geographical distribution of the many branches of the Yang-ming school becomes in itself an interesting question. Huang Tsung-hsi paid special attention to this question, making note of the origins of these branches and their interrelationships. This does not necessarily mean that all the followers of a certain school of thought must be natives of a certain region. Rather the geographical region usually represents the place of origin of their principal representatives, as well as the area where their philosophies were best known.

It is important to remark here that the school of Wu Yü-pi, with which the book begins (ch. 1–4), is also based in Kiangsi, the province where Wang Yang-ming spent much time as an administrator and teacher of philosophy. Wu Yü-pi, of course, was the teacher of Lou Liang (1422–91),

who is sometimes regarded as having transmitted Wu's teaching to Wang
—although this appears more conjecture than fact, even if their brief meeting had exerted its influence upon Wang's development. Ch'en Hsien-
chang, another student of Wu Yü-pi, merits more attention (ch. 5–6). He
was the best known of all Wu's disciples and was a southerner from
Kwangtung, the home province also of Chan Jo-shui, his own best-known
disciple. Ch'en's philosophy, with its inner-oriented focus, was a clear
development of Wu Yü-pi's concerns, which foreshadowed the emergence
of Wang Yang-ming's philosophy. Indeed, some people have asserted that
Wang had been strongly influenced by Ch'en. But Wang was, of course, a
close friend of Ch'en's disciple Chan Jo-shui, the founder of the Kan-
ch'üan school, based also in Kwangtung.

The Northern Schools

The northern schools are presented in ch. 7–9. These include the school of
Hsüeh Hsüan, of the Ho-tung school, based in Shansi, Shensi, and
Honan, east of the Yellow River, the region that had produced the great
Sung philosophers Shao Yung (1011–77), Chang Tsai, Ch'eng Hao, and
Ch'eng Yi; and the San-yüan school of Wang Shu, also of Shensi. As mentioned earlier, northern China had witnessed the flowering of Confucian
philosophy during the northern Sung period but fell afterwards into the
hands of the Jurchens, who established the Chin dynasty. By Ming times it
was evident that the focus of philosophical concern and interest would
remain in the south, especially in the Yangtze area, but also further down
—extending to Kwangtung. The north would be, even more than before,
identified with conservative influences and a kind of stagnation in letters as
well as in philosophy. In *The Records of Ming Scholars* Huang Tsung-hsi displays some sympathy for Hsüeh Hsüan, the diligent student whose shoes
dug holes in the stone floor under his desk and who would be regarded by
others—Wang Yang-ming for one—as a man who carried to excess his fer-
vor for book learning. He hints at the possibility that Hsüeh might finally
have achieved interior enlightenment. He also has some kind words for Lü
Nan, Hsüeh's disciple. He considers the San-yüan school to be derived
from Hsüeh's giving of special mention to the high moral principles
evinced by scholars from that part of Shensi, the home province of Chang
Tsai. Such were the orthodox Confucian thinkers of early Ming: virtuous
men but without much originality.

The Yang-ming Schools of Chekiang and Kiangsi

Geographical distribution stands out once more in Huang Tsung-hsi's
description of the schools of Wang Yang-ming and his many disciples
(ch. 10–31). Huang Tsung-hsi says:

The path of Ming learning was opened by Ch'en Hsien-chang but became brilliant only with Wang Yang-ming.[46] The earlier custom was to memorize the known sayings of the former scholars, without reflecting carefully in oneself or seeking to develop their hidden points. This is the meaning of the statement that each man is only repeating Chu Hsi. Kao P'an-lung said: "The recorded dialogues of Hsüeh Hsüan and Lü Nan are without evidence of much real enlightenment." This is what he means also.[47]

Wang Yang-ming was a native of Yüyao, in Chekiang, a fellow countryman of Huang Tsung-hsi himself. Huang gives some importance to Wang's influence in his home province:

> The teaching of the Yang-ming school spread from near to far. Its first adherents were all from the same prefecture (Shao-hsing). After his experience at Lung-ch'ang (Kweichow) Yang-ming started to accept disciples from all over.[48]

Of Wang's disciples from Chekiang, Huang Tsung-hsi devotes some attention to Hsü Ai, Wang's brother-in-law and best friend, whose life was cut short at the age of thirty, and Ch'ien Te-hung, an early disciple and probably the most faithful. But he gives special importance to Wang Chi (to whom is devoted one entire *chüan*), the most metaphysically inclined as well as the most controversial. He mentions Chi Pen, an independent and balanced thinker, and Huang Wan (1477–1551), protector and father-in-law to Wang's son, who later developed his own philosophy in conscious opposition to Wang as well as to Chu Hsi.[49] Besides this, Huang Tsung-hsi also gives attention to a group of Wang's fellow countrymen that included the older scholar Tung Yün, a commoner; Lu Ch'eng, several of whose letters to Wang Yang-ming have been included in the *Ch'uan-hsi Lu,* part 2 (ch. 14); Wan Piao, and several others (ch. 15). He then moves on to Kiangsi, asserting that scholars of that region alone have transmitted the correct teaching of the master. The most important figure of this group is Tsou Shou-yi (ch. 16); the next, Ou-yang Te and Nieh Pao (ch. 17). All three were direct disciples of Wang Yang-ming. After these came a man who knew Yang-ming but was only recognized as his disciple after his death: Lo Hung-hsien (ch. 18). Then follow the many Lius of An-fu, especially Liu Wen-ming, Liu Pang-ts'ai, and Liu Yang (ch. 19). Coming after them are the representatives of the following generation, disciples of Tsou and the Lius, especially Wang Shih-huai (ch. 20), Teng Yi-tsan (ch. 21), Hu Chih (ch. 22), Tsou Yüan-piao (ch. 23), and others (ch. 24).

The Central Provinces and the South

From Kiangsi, Huang goes on to Nan Chihli (Anhwei) and Kiangsu, dealing first with those Yang-ming disciples who came from the areas outside of T'ai-chou. He speaks especially of Huang Hsing-tseng (ch. 25), T'ang Shun-chih (ch. 26), and Hsü Chieh (ch. 27). These were all Wang Yang-ming's own disciples. He then deals with the scholars of Hukuang, remarking here that Keng Ting-hsiang, a native of that province, was more accurately classified as a disciple of the T'ai-chou school. Wang had few disciples from Hukuang. Chiang Hsin (ch. 28) was equally influenced by Chan Jo-shui, perhaps even more than by Wang. Moving northward, Huang then points out the small number of Wang's followers (ch. 29). In the south, Kwangtung and Fukien, there were Hsüeh K'an and Chou T'an (ch. 30).

The T'ai-chou Branch of the Yang-ming School

After a chapter on Li Ts'ai (ch. 31), a soldier as well as a teacher of philosophy and a disciple of Tsou Shou-yi of the Kiangsi school, who set up his own teaching with a formula of *chih-hsiu* (rest and cultivation), Huang Tsung-hsi moves on to the school of T'ai-chou (ch. 32–36) in northern Kiangsu. This branch of the Yang-ming school exerted great popular influence while arousing much controversy.[50] The group of thinkers included cuts across traditional class lines as well as educational backgrounds. Its principal leader, Wang Ken, a disciple of Wang Yang-ming, was a man of little formal education and was a salt merchant by profession. His own disciples included a woodcutter, a potter, and a farm-worker, who were all barely literate. Other followers of T'ai-chou were Chao Chen-chi of Szechuan, a scholar of Taoist propensities; Lo Ju-fang, also a *chin-shih* and more influenced by Buddhist ideas of meditation; Keng Ting-hsiang, a *chin-shih* and a censor; as well as Chiao Hung, the *optimus* of the 1589 examination, a man much influenced by Buddhism and a precursor of the later philological revival. They shared a certain enthusiasm about Wang Yang-ming's teaching of sagehood and its universal accessibility, making of it a doctrine of the common man as a "ready-made sage."

The T'ai-chou school has been subject to much criticism for promoting ideas of social protest and nonconformist individual behavior, ideas that grew out of its exaltation of the common man. For the same reason, it has been praised by modern scholars in the People's Republic of China. Possibly Huang Tsung-hsi places it at the end of his treatment of the Yang-ming school and its offshoots because of the known controversies. Following upon this school comes the school of Chan Jo-shui and his disciples: the Kan-ch'üan school (ch. 37–42), an offshoot of Ch'en Hsien-chang, many—although not all—of whose disciples are from the southern province of Kwangtung. It occupies six solid chapters, a testimony to the importance of its teachings.

Kwangtung: The School of Kan-ch'üan[51]

The southern province of Kwangtung did not produce many Yang-ming followers but was the base and center for the Kan-ch'üan school, named after Chan Jo-shui (ch. 37–42), the disciple of Ch'en Hsien-chang and friend of Wang Yang-ming. While Yang-ming taught the "extension of *liang-chih*," Chan Jo-chui emphasized the "realization everywhere of the heavenly principle *(t'ien-li)*." They differed over the interpretation of the doctrine of "investigation of things *(ko-wu)*." For Wang, this phrase refers to the moral rectification of the mind; for Chan, it includes intellectual inquiry. In this way, Chan remained closer than Wang to the teachings of Chu Hsi. Huang Tsung-hsi has compared the interaction between the schools of Wang Yang-ming and Chan Jo-shui to that between the Chu Hsi and Lu Chiu-yüan schools:

> The schools of Wang Yang-ming and Chan Jo-shui each had its main doctrines. While Chan's disciples did not equal Wang's in number, many persons first studied under Chan and then finished under Wang, or studied first under Wang and then went to Chan, just as did the disciples of Chu Hsi and Lu Chiu-yüan.[52]

In the later Ming times, the followers of the Kan-ch'üan school attempted to remedy the effects of the extremist tendencies of the T'ai-chou school, which proclaimed that everyone was already a sage and did not require any discipline, intellectual or moral, to help him awaken to this reality present in himself. Among other things, the Kan-ch'üan school encouraged the practice of quiet meditation as a method for the discovery of the "heavenly principle." Its greatest representatives are: Lü Huai (ch. 38), Hung Yüan (ch. 39), T'ang Shu (ch. 40), Hsü Fu-yüan and Feng Ts'ung-wu (ch. 41), and Wang Tao (ch. 42).

The Tung-lin School[53]

The Tung-lin school derives its name from the Tung-lin Academy in Wusih (Wu-hsi), Kiangsu, founded by Yang Shih in Sung times and revived in the Ming by Ku Hsien-ch'eng and Kao P'an-lung (ch. 58). In *The Records of Ming Scholars,* it takes up four *chüan* (ch. 58–61). In philosophical questions, the Tung-lin school shared the concern of the Kan-ch'üan school and strove to bring about a certain reconciliation between the tendencies represented by the Yang-ming school and those of the orthodox philosophy of Ch'eng Yi and Chu Hsi. In political matters, it stood for independent discussions and a government free from corruption in high places. It took certain positions on issues surrounding the question of Emperor Shen-tsung's succession and on the events

following upon his death and the death of his successor, Emperor
Kuang-tsung (1620). For these reasons, it was hated by the dominant
eunuch party, especially their chief, Wei Chung-hsien. Many adherents
of the Tung-lin "party"—for that it became—found themselves accused
of alleged political crimes, taken to prison and even put to death. The
political martyrs included Huang Tsung-hsi's father, Huang Tsun-su
(ch. 61). As already mentioned, Huang himself associated with many
Tung-lin scholars, especially with those of them who were engaged in
the struggle against the Manchus. His teacher, Liu Tsung-chou, also
had close relations with the Tung-lin school.

Miscellaneous Scholars[54]

These make up a group of forty-three persons (ch. 43–57) who possess
no common philosophical bond. They have been placed together for a
negative reason: they lack direct or indirect connections with any of the
principal schools of Ming thought; they are without geographical areas
of influence or transmission lineages. This is not to say that they have
little philosophical influence. Many of them are quite important. We
have, for example, Fang Hsiao-ju, the early Ming scholar and follower
of the Ch'eng-Chu school, whose martyrdom in the cause of political
loyalty to a usurped sovereign hampered the development of Ch'eng-
Chu philosophy itself. We also have other thinkers such as the ortho-
doxy-conscious Ts'ao Tuan and Lo Ch'in-shun, who argued with Wang
Yang-ming over questions of investigation of things *(ko-wu)* as well as
over Yang-ming's views on Chu Hsi and his philosophy. There are,
besides, Wang T'ing-hsiang (1474–1544), an explicit follower of Chang
Tsai's philosophy of *ch'i,* Lü K'un, and Huang Tao-chou, who argued
for the philosophy of *li* and of *hsing* (nature).

That there should be so many thinkers who could be grouped
together in this way shows the vitality of Ming thought and the independence of mind of many of the philosophers and scholars. The chapters
on these miscellaneous scholars make up, in fact, one-fifth or more of
the whole *Records of Ming Scholars* with its two hundred entries. Huang
Tsung-hsi has made such arrangements clearly in order to highlight the
central importance of the Yang-ming school and its many branches. It is
interesting to note also that he has chosen to place these miscellaneous
scholars before the Tung-lin school, with its conscious effort to reconcile
the Yang-ming philosophy with that of Chu Hsi, in order to show the
intellectual association of Liu Tsung-chou with the Tung-lin school.
The chapter on Liu Tsung-chou is, of course, the final one of the book.
Here it should be remembered that the book also begins with Liu
Tsung-chou—with his diverse comments on various Ming thinkers
entitled *Shih-shuo* by his disciple Huang Tsung-hsi.

IV.   The Text and the Editions

THE Japanese scholar Yamanoi Yū reports that there are eight known editions of *The Records of Ming Scholars,* although only three of them are of importance: the Chia edition (1693), the Cheng edition (1739), and the Mo edition (1821).[55] Before evaluating these editions, we should first like to give an account of the process of development that led to their emergence, and also will explain their quality and worth.

Huang Tsung-hsi reports that he finished *The Records of Ming Scholars* in 1676, more than three decades after the establishment of Manchu power in China, much of that time presumably spent in collecting material for this work. According to his own account, various hand-written copies then began to circulate—before parts of the book were put to print, first by Hsü San-li of An-yang and then by a Fan family of Yin-hsien, Chekiang. In 1691, Wan Yen, son of Wan Ssu-nien, Huang's disciple and a noted historian in his own right, published about one-third of the entire work. This would become the basis of the later Cheng edition.[56] Huang was then in his eighty-second year.

The Chia Edition

This earliest complete edition of *The Records of Ming Scholars* was published by Chia Jen and his son Chia P'u. The younger man was Huang Tsung-hsi's disciple's disciple and had received from his teacher, so it seems, a hand-copied version of the work. He showed this to his father, who, upon reading it, decided to put it to print. This task was begun in 1691 but the father died before finishing it. Chia P'u finally did so in 1693. It is not known whether Huang Tsung-hsi himself was consulted at all or whether his approval was sought. But this is the edition described in *The Catalogue of the Four Libraries.* It includes a preface by Ch'ou Chao-ao and comments by Chia Jen.[57] The ordering of the contents of this edition is different from that of the later ones.

The Cheng Edition

After Huang's death in 1695, the original manuscript was kept in the Chen family of Tz'u-hsi (Chekiang). Cheng Chen was a close friend of

Huang Tsung-hsi, and his son, Cheng Liang, was Huang's disciple. Cheng Liang's son, Cheng Hsing, built a special library for the keeping of Huang's works, which included, so it seems, other manuscripts besides *The Records of Ming Scholars*.

In 1739, Cheng Hsing planned with Huang's grandson, Huang Ch'ien-ch'iu, to print the portion of *The Records of Ming Scholars* that had not been included by Wan Yen earlier. They began the work in 1735, completing it four years later. Cheng Hsing wrote a preface to this edition, to which Huang Ch'ien-ch'iu added a foreword. This complete edition included Wan Yen's earlier portion (ch. 1–18, 20, 21), as well as the part edited by Cheng Hsing (ch. 19, 22–61), and the final chapter (ch. 62), which was simply ascribed to Huang Tsung-hsi, presumably without any editing. Cheng declared in his preface that Chia P'u's edition had included miscellaneous comments not found in the original manuscript. His own publication was directed at making known Huang Tsung-hsi's authentic and integral work.

The Mo Edition

A very important edition appearing much later is that of 1821, published in Kiangsi jointly by Mo Chin and Mo Hsieh. They had reportedly worked on a hand-copied version, checking it against the Cheng edition. It carried Huang's original preface and Mo Chin's preface of 1821, which explains that the earlier Chia edition had tampered with the book's original structure, putting the Ho-tung school of Hsüeh Hsüan before the Ch'ung-jen school of Wu Yü-pi, which Huang had placed at the head of his book, and changing the title of the "schools of Wang Yang-ming" to that of "schools of transmission."[58] The Mo edition has become the one most accessible to scholars, through the SPPY and other collections.

An Evaluation

Why did the Chia edition not remain faithful to Huang's own work? It appears that Chia Jen was not entirely happy with the original version as it came from the author and compiler. In his own essay, reviewing the book, he stated that the early Ming thinkers, including Fang Hsiao-ju, Hsüeh Hsüan, and Wu Yü-pi, had largely remained faithful to the Sung philosophy; the late-comers, however, especially Ch'en Hsien-chang and Wang Yang-ming, had sought particularly the learning of the mind and might be held responsible for the revival of Ch'an Buddhism that took place in the later years of the reign of Emperor Shen-tsung (r. 1572–1619). Chia criticized Huang's book for giving central importance to the school of Wang Yang-ming without clearly discerning between its merits and its defects. He proposed that it would be better to expand upon the materials concerning the early Ming schools and to diminish those relating to the later ones. This, however, he regretted that he was unable to undertake personally, on account of his poor health. It would therefore appear probable that he did make certain adjustments in editing Huang Tsung-hsi's work.

What about the Cheng edition, which is based essentially on the original family manuscript handed down by Huang himself? Has it been entirely faithful to this manuscript, or has it not?

The problem with the Cheng edition emerges when it is compared with both the Chia edition and the later Mo edition. It appears that several of the figures included in the Chia edition are absent in the Cheng edition. It appears also that the Cheng edition contains something unique: certain supplements not found anywhere else. The editor, Cheng Hsing, claims that he had used a copy written in Huang Tsung-hsi's hand and transmitted by a Yen family. Owing to the close relations between Huang's family and Cheng's, his statements can hardly be subject to doubt. What one may question is whether these supplements were intended by Huang Tsung-hsi to form an integral part of the definitive *Records of Ming Scholars*.[59]

The Mo edition has become the best known and standard edition. It gives the order of the schools of thought set down by Huang Tsung-hsi himself and followed by the Cheng edition. It does not include the Cheng supplements. The figures it includes are exactly the same as those found in the Chia edition. It became standard, however, in the later part of the Ch'ing period, especially because of the favorable judgment of Fan Hsi-tseng,[60] the noted bibliographer.

Which is the superior edition, Cheng's or Mo's? This problem has not yet been resolved. Where philosophical content is concerned, the differences appear to be minor and cannot affect the work as a whole in either case. Possibly the Cheng version might have served better as a standard text than Mo's.

What has the Imperial Catalogue *(Ssu-ku t'i-yao)* to say about *The Records of Ming Scholars?* Here we encounter an instance of prejudiced judgment, an unfortunate occurrence but one characteristic of the narrow philosophical outlook that underlies this great source of bibliographical information. The description of the book given is that of the Chia edition, which places the Ho-tung school before the Ch'ung-jen school. The writer says in his comments:

> Huang Tsung-hsi was born in Yao-chiang. He was reluctant to discredit Wang Yang-ming and honor Hsüeh Hsüan; yet he did not dare to discredit Hsüeh Hsüan and honor Wang Yang-ming. So he gives importance outwardly to Hsüeh's disciples, but criticizes them in his text. He also gives an impression of attacking Wang's disciples outwardly, while defending them in his text. Now the teachings of both schools have their merits and limitations. The defects of their latter day disciples would be such that these aroused

much polemical discussion, which in turn led to partisanship, love-hate relationships and mutual recriminations. From the time of Cheng-te and Chia-
ching (1506–66) on, even worthy men were not free of such [partisan spirit].
Huang Tsung-hsi's book is another example of Ming factionalism. It is not
just written for the sake of *chiang-hsüeh* (philosophical teaching).[61]

It appears that Chia's rearrangement of Huang's original text has
been to a great extent responsible for this biased attack on Huang's
work. The commentator, however, has a few words of positive appraisal
as well:

In relating the unity and diversity of the Confucian schools, [Huang
Tsung-hsi] has presented a rather detailed account, which yet allows the
readers to discern their merits and limitations, and learn the causes of the
calamities of the late Ming factional politics. It gives, therefore, a good mirror of history.[62]

V. The *Ming-ju hsüeh-an* and the *Sung-Yüan hsüeh-an*[63]

BESIDES the *Ming-ju hsüeh-an,* Huang Tsung-hsi is known for compiling also the *Sung-Yüan hsüeh-an* (Records of the Sung and Yüan Scholars). Most probably, he began the latter work right after the completion of the former (1676). He was then in his sixty-sixth year and would live on for another two decades. But such a work could not be done by one man alone in this much time. Huang Tsung-hsi's drafts were taken over by his son, Huang Po-chia, who did some editing but died himself without finishing. It took a third man, Ch'üan Tsu-wang (1705–75), also a native of Chekiang, at least ten years to finish the *Sung-Yüan hsüeh-an.* As the work stands, the greater part has been edited and expanded by Ch'üan Tsu-wang, who also added much to the original draft. Still, Ch'üan was unable to put it to print. This could take place only after his death, with the help of his own family and disciples, as well as Huang Tsung-hsi's descendants, in whose hands the work was once more copied and edited. A final scholarly contribution was made by Wang Tzu-ts'ai, who checked and amended the text, arranging it in one hundred *chüan* according to Ch'üan Tsu-wang's earlier wish. It appeared in print for the first time in 1838, the result of scholarly collaboration lasting for several generations and for over a century.[64]

Even more than Huang Tsung-hsi, Ch'üan Tsu-wang was responsible for the completion of the *Sung-Yüan hsüeh-an.* However, the relationship between Sung thought and Ming thought is such that one could hardly speak of the *Ming-ju hsüeh-an* without speaking of the *Sung-Yüan hsüeh-an.* Certainly the second work represented a more difficult task, on account of its wider scope and the greater length of time between its compilers and the Sung and Yüan periods. But the *Ming-ju hsüeh-an* would serve as a model for the completion of the *Sung-Yüan hsüeh-an.* Besides, Ch'üan Tsu-wang was also Huang's fellow countryman and a follower, like Huang, of the Wang Yang-ming school. The work would therefore maintain a consistency of perspective with the *Ming-ju hsüeh-an.* It may come as no surprise that the section on the school of Hsiang-shan (Lu Chiu-yüan) has been described as the best in the book, with those of Chang Tsai, Ch'eng Hao and Ch'eng Yi, Lü Tsu-ch'ien, Ch'en Liang, and Yeh Shih, coming next. The section on Chu Hsi is reportedly mediocre, while that on Wang An-shih is considered even more so.[65]

VI. Conclusion

HUANG TSUNG-HSI has described for us the methods of research according to which he compiled his famous work. He went to the original sources rather than merely using secondary references or copying from these. He was careful in distinguishing between the main doctrines of each of the schools of thought represented in his work, taking note especially of their differences.[66] He produced a classic, which is at the same time comprehensive in its inclusion of two hundred thinkers and scholars and in the wide scope of philosophical ideas and movements represented by these men. In a well-known work, Liang Ch'i-ch'ao states four conditions for the writing of any history of thought and scholarship. I shall give them in summary form:

1. All the important schools of that epoch should be included according to impartial norms of selection.
2. The essential characteristics of each school should be reported so that readers may acquire a clear notion of what each represents.
3. The true features of all the schools should be given according to objective evaluations.
4. The lives and times of all the figures concerned should be narrated so that the personalities of each may be known.[67]

According to Liang Ch'i-ch'ao, Huang Tsung-hsi's work has fulfilled all these conditions and remains a useful model for all who wish to write histories of philosophy, even if, "in matters of organization, there are places which can be improved."[68]

The Records of Ming Scholars is an integration of philosophical judgment and historical scholarship. In judgment, Huang Tsung-hsi shows himself a true heir to Ming thought. In scholarship, he is a predecessor to the Ch'ing emphasis on documentary evidence and objective scholarship. He has done well. For he has left us not only with a history of philosophy but also with a work that is in itself a classic—of both history and philosophy. Modern readers may wish that the work were otherwise, that it were a directly personal production written in a narrative style and following a stricter philosophical method. But they cannot deny that Huang Tsung-hsi's work has already become a classic of its own genre. It remains a selected anthology from various (two hundred) thinkers and scholars with their biographies and with the compiler's comments. But it has preserved for us certain materials that are no longer extant. It allows us not only to have direct experience of the philosophers through their collected sayings but gives us also Huang Tsung-hsi's evaluations—the evaluation of a great philosopher-scholar.

Many difficulties remain in the study of *The Records of Ming Scholars*. One discovers Huang Tsung-hsi's inconsistencies, his moving from philosophical statements to classical allusions to polemical discussions, usually without any warning to the reader. One discovers also Huang's numerous mistakes, the misplaced quotations as well as the misquoted statements. One wonders whether this was the result of circumstances —the absence of available references—or his excessive reliance on memory, or perhaps both. One may not even agree with Huang's evaluations, whether of Wang Chi or of Lo Ch'in-shun. And yet, these defects only serve to underline the vastness of his erudition and the keenness of his judgments, as shadows serve to point to light. Huang Tsung-hsi has succeeded in giving to posterity a classic of its genre, a colorful rendering of the story of Ming thought and scholarship, which was written and compiled with real passion and continues to communicate to the modern reader some of the passion that went into the making of the story itself.

NOTES

This Introduction was first published in a somewhat different form. See Julia Ching, "The Records of the Ming Philosophers: An Introduction," in *Oriens Extremus* 23 (1976), 191–211. It has since been expanded and improved. We have explained the reason for entitling the book *The Records of Ming Scholars* in the Editor's Note.

1. I have consulted the *Sheng-hsüeh tsung-chuan* (1606) and the *Li-hsüeh tsung-chuan* (1666). The latter is a reprint (Taipei, 1969). See also Huang Tsung-hsi's own Introduction *(Fa-fan)* to the *Ming-ju hsüeh-an*. See Liang Ch'i-ch'ao, *Chung-kuo chin-san-pai-nien hsüeh-shu shih* (Shanghai, 1941), 40–46 and Wing-tsit Chan, trans., *Instructions for Practical Living* (New York, 1963), 312.

2. For Ku Yen-wu, see Liang Ch'i-ch'ao, ibid., 60–63.

3. For Ku's work, see *Jih-chih lu chi-shih*, SPPY ed.

4. See the Author's Introduction.

5. See Huang Tsung-hsi's biography by Tu Lien-che, in Arthur W. Hummel, ed., *Eminent Chinese of the Ch'ing Period (1644–1912)* (hereafter *ECCP*) (Washington, 1943), v. 1, 350–52. See also Étienne Balazs, *Political Theory and Administrative Reality in Traditional China* (London, 1965), 17–29.

6. See his biography in this volume.

7. Huang Tsung-hsi had two brothers: Huang Tsung-yen (1616–86) and Huang Tsung-hui (1618–63). All studied under Liu Tsung-chou and were ardent patriots as well as gifted scholars. Huang Tsung-yen was a noted classi-

cist and a painter; Huang Tsung-hui, the youngest and the first to die, was most affected by the change of dynasties. See *ECCP,* v. 1, 355.

8. English translation adapted from J. Legge, trans., *The Chinese Classics* (Oxford, 1892), v. 1, 367.

9. Ibid., 384.

10. *Liu-tzu ch'üan-shu* (1822 ed., Taipei reprint, n.d.; hereafter *LTCS*), 40:29a–b. See also Liu's comments on Wang Chi *(Shih-shuo),* given in the section, "Quotations from Liu Tsung-chou."

11. See Huang Tsung-hsi's biography of Liu, *LTCS* 39:3b–4a, and Liu's Chronological Biography *(Nien-p'u),* *LTCS* 40:29a, 41:24b.

12. See Ch'üan Tsu-wang's belated epitaph in honor of Huang in Ch'üan's Collected Writings, *Chieh-ch'i-t'ing chi,* 1872 ed., 11:2–3.

13. For the Fu-she see William S. Atwell, "From Education to Politics: The Fu-she," in W. T. de Bary, ed., *The Unfolding of Neo-Confucianism* (New York, 1975), 333–68.

14. See Huang's biography in *ECCP,* v. 1, 351. See also Julia Ching, "Chu Shun-shui, 1600–82, A Chinese Confucian Scholar in Tokugawa Japan," *Monumenta Nipponica* 30 (1975), 181, n. 26.

15. See Chi Yün, *Ssu-k'u ch'üan-shu chung-mu t'i-yao* (abbrev. as *SK*), (Shanghai, 1933), 87, 422, 747, 1285–86, 1599, 1624, 1865, 2007, 3764, 3994, 4226, 4384, 4333–34.

16. For Huang's writings, see Hsieh Kuo-chen, *Huang Li-chou hsüeh-p'u* (Shanghai, 1932), 13–16. See also Liang Ch'i-ch'ao, *Chung-kuo chin-san-pai nien,* 45–50.

17. For the *Ming-yi tai-fang lu,* see W. T. de Bary, "Chinese Despotism and the Confucian Ideal: A Seventeenth Century View," in John K. Fairbank, ed., *Chinese Thought and Institutions* (Chicago, 1957), 163–203.

18. Liang Ch'i-ch'ao, *Chung-kuo chin-san-pai nien,* 46–48 (especially n. 1).

19. See Juan Yüan's biography of Huang Tsung-hsi included in *Li-chou yi-chu hui-k'an (Collected Writings of Huang Tsung-hsi)* and given in *Ming-Ch'ing shih-liao hui-pien,* ed. by Hsüeh Feng-ch'ang, 6th collection, 7a–8b. In this regard, Huang Tsung-hsi opened the way for Mei Wen-ting (d. 1721), the noted scientist and mathematician. See Liang Ch'i-ch'ao, *Chung-kuo chin-san-pai nien,* 50, 147–49.

20. See Huang Tsung-hsi's biography by Ch'ien Lin and Wang Chao in *Li-chou yi-chu hui-k'an,* 13a. It is also stated in Chiang Fan's biography given in the same collection (11a).

21. It was due to Huang's advice that the *Ming-shih* did not have a special category for *Tao-hsüeh.* See Huang Tsung-hsi, *Nan-lei wen-ting* (1910 ed.), 4:5–7. See also Huang K'ai-hua, *Ming-shih lun-chi* (Essays on Ming History) (Taipei, 1972), 674.

22. Fung Yu-lan, *Chung-kuo che-hsüeh-shih* (Shanghai, 1935), 22.

23. The plan given here is that of the SPPY ed. In this English translation, the Author's Introduction *(Fa-fan)* is being placed right after the Author's Preface rather than after the Quotations from Liu Tsung-chou *(Shih-shuo,* i.e., Teacher's Sayings), to avoid confusion. This happens to be the plan of certain other editions, such as that of the World Press *(Shih-chieh shu-chü)* (Taipei, 1965).

24. See Huang Tsung-hsi's Preface (i.e., Author's Preface).

25. Ku Yen-wu, *T'ing-lin wen-chi,* SPPY ed., 3:2a; see also W. T. de Bary, ed., *Self and Society in Ming Thought* (New York, 1970), Introduction, 28.

26. See Huang Tsung-hsi's Author's Introduction.

27. "Introvertive" suggests looking into one's inner self, just as "extrover-

tive" suggests going out of oneself, relating to God or to nature. See W. T. Stace, *Mysticism and Philosophy* (London, 1960), ch. 5–7.

28. For the philosophy of mind, see Fung Yu-lan, *Chung-kuo che-hsüeh shih,* ch. 14, Eng. trans., *A History of Chinese Philosophy* (Princeton, 1953), v. 2, ch. 14. Let it be noted that the Chinese "philosophy of mind" is quite different from the Western equivalent, especially as this is known in analytical circles, where the focus is on problems of knowledge and certainty, of mind-body dualism and mind-brain identity, of minds, machines, and computers.

29. Julia Ching, *To Acquire Wisdom: The Way of Wang Yang-ming* (New York, 1976), Preface and Conclusion.

30. Ibid., Conclusion.

31. Ibid., Introduction.

32. See Julia Ching's biography of Wang Chi, *DMB*, v. 2, 1351–55.

33. *LTCS,* 40:28b–29a. English translation by Julia Ching.

34. This is a quotation of a line from Wang Yang-ming's poem, to be found in *Wang Wen-ch'eng kung ch'üan-shu* (Complete Writings), SPTK ed., 1st series, 20:629b. See J. Ching, *To Acquire Wisdom,* 243. See also "Yang-ming ch'uan-hsin lu," in *Liu-tzu ch'uan-shu yi-p'ien* (1850 ed., 1895 reprint), 11:10a.

35. *MJHA, Shih-shuo,* 4a.

36. Ibid., 4b.

37. Ibid.

38. *MJHA,* ch. 62.

39. *MJHA,* 1a.

40. *LTCS,* Preface, 1a–2a. English translation by Julia Ching.

41. *LTCS,* 39:41a–b.

42. Ibid.

43. See Julia Ching, *To Acquire Wisdom,* ch. 1.

44. See *Sung-Yüan hsüeh-an* for biographies of thinkers concerned.

45. See Liu Shih-p'ei, "Nan-pei li-hsüeh pu-t'ung lun," *Liu Sheng-shu hsien-sheng yi-shu* (1936), v. 15, 4a–6a.

46. Literally, Yao-chiang, another name for Yüyao, Wang Yang-ming's native place. It comes from the name of a river that is also called Shun-shui.

47. See Huang Tsung-hsi's preface to the section on the Wang Yang-ming school (*MJHA,* ch. 10).

48. *MJHA,* ch. 11 (Preface to the section on the central Chekiang branch of the Yang-ming school).

49. For Huang Wan's ideas, see his work, *Ming-tao p'ien* (Peking reprint, 1959). See also J. Ching, *To Acquire Wisdom,* Epilogue.

50. See W. T. de Bary, "Individualism and Humanitarianism in Late Ming Thought," *Self and Society in Ming Thought,* 157–225.

51. Kan-ch'üan was another name for Chan Jo-shui.

52. *MJHA,* ch. 37 (Preface to the Kan-ch'üan school).

53. For the Tung-lin school, see Heinrich Busch, "The Tung-lin Academy and Its Political and Philosophical Significance," *Monumenta Serica* 14 (1949–55), 1–163.

54. The "Miscellaneous Scholars" *(Chu-ju)* include mostly scholars with some philosophical interests but who did not establish their own schools of thought.

55. Yamanoi Yū, "Minju-gakuan no shikōteiyō ni kansuru nisan no mondai," *Tōkyō Shinagakuho* 12 (1966), 75–95. He gives a list of eight editions on pp. 77–78. See also Ch'en T'ieh-fan, *Sung Yüan Ming-Ch'ing ssu-ch'ao hsüeh-an so-yin* (Taipei, 1974), Introduction.

56. Yamanoi Yū, op. cit., 80–86. See also Hsieh Kuo-cheng, *Huang Li-chou hsüeh-p'u,* 9–16, 120.

57. Ibid., 82. A chart giving a comparison of contents and organization of the three editions (Chia, Mo, Cheng) is given on p. 79. Consult also the Author's Preface to the *MJHA,* where Huang Tsung-hsi mentions Chia's edition.

58. Yamanoi Yū, op. cit., 82.

59. Ibid., 83–85. (Yamanoi doubts that the Mo edition was based on an original manuscript, considering it rather a harmonization of the Chia and Cheng editions. His preference is for the Cheng edition.)

60. See *Shu-mu ta-wen pu-cheng* (Peking reprint, 1963), 128. For Yamanoi's objection, see above, n. 55.

61. *SK,* 1285–86. English translation by Julia Ching.

62. Ibid., 1286.

63. Since this is an introduction to the *MJHA* in translation, we confine ourselves to a descriptive comparison here.

64. Liang Ch'i-ch'ao, *Chung-kuo chin san-pai nien hsüeh-shu shih,* 91–93.

65. Ibid.

66. See the Author's Introduction (i.e., Huang Tsung-hsi's) to the *MJHA.*

67. Liang Ch'i-ch'ao, *Chung-kuo chin san-pai nien,* 48–49.

68. Ibid.

Part Two
The Records of Ming Scholars

Translation

I.   Author's Preface

THAT which fills Heaven and Earth is Mind. Its transformations are unfathomable and cannot but assume myriad forms. The Mind has no original substance *(pen-t'i)* except what is achieved by its activity *(kung-fu)*. To exhaust and comprehend principles *(li)* is to exhaust and comprehend Mind's myriad manifestations rather than the myriad manifestations of all things. That was why the gentlemen of old preferred to dig out a mountain road themselves, as did the five laborers [of Ch'in],[1] rather than rely on the wild horses of Han-tan,[2] and the paths they took all had to be different. Unfortunately, the gentlemen of today insist upon everyone taking the same path, obliging those with excellent endowments to become dried up like scorched shoots or abandoned harbors.[3] But the recorded dialogs of the former scholars show that each of them was different, although they all reflected the mind-in-itself *(hsin-t'i)*, which is always changing and quite without rest. One's insistence upon fixing the situation will turn out to be quite futile and useless. There is no other reason for this. Only after cultivating virtue could learning be discussed. Today, learning is being discussed *(chiang-hsüeh)*[4] without virtue being cultivated. No wonder people point only to one thing while neglecting one hundred. The times are getting worse. Even those who learn by rote[5] presume to call themselves scholars, when they are only mouthing clichés. And booksellers too have their tricks. They appeal to [the story of the son] addressing his mother by name to publish their books.[6] Who can stand at court as the selected candidate, when the nine grades are all confused?[7] The situation resembles more the inner divisions of Buddhism, with the five schools fighting one another.[8] So this small Almond Terrace[9] has been made into a noisy marketplace. How tragic!

As a youth, I, Huang Tsung-hsi, suffered a family tragedy.[10] Fortunately my deceased master Liu Tsung-chou regarded me as a son. He supported my weakness and balanced my unsteadiness, while I had the opportunity to hear words of inspiration every day. But I was then too young and in shock. Only after his death did I begin to learn about his main doctrines from his surviving writings, while many of my fellow disciples had already sacrificed their lives through loyalty [to the Ming house]. In the year 1669, Yün Jih-ch'u of Pi-ling[11] came to Shao-hsing (Chekiang) to work on the *Liu-tzu chieh-yao* (Essential Teachings of Liu Tsung-chou). Yün was a respected disciple of our deceased master. When he had completed the book, I saw him off to the river bank. He held my hand and urged me, saying, "Today, there are only the two of us, you and I, who know our deceased master's teachings. But discussions of these teachings should not be allowed to grow in more than one direction. Where it concerns his teachings on 'intention,' let us harmonize more." I replied, "It is precisely on this issue of 'intention' that our deceased master differs in his teaching from other scholars. How can we not allow this to become known?"[12] Yün had wanted me to write the preface to his book; I never dared to accept. With regard to a teaching that allows different pathways to truth and a hundred ideas, Yün showed that he still held a rigid position and could not change.

In compiling these *Records of Ming Scholars,* I have made manifest the profundity and shallowness, the perfections and faults of the various gentlemen included. Only where they have given the best of their efforts and exhausted the myriad dimensions of their minds, without working fuzzily or falsely appropriating the chaff of others' learning, have they established schools of thought. I have distinguished between the sources and tributaries, as of the rivers, in order to make clear their essential doctrines and to show how these should be followed as if they were the ears and eyes of the sages. At times, I have made a special effort to discover where the foundations of learning are to be found but without daring to add to or subtract from what I find. This can be likened to a water pot placed at the main thoroughfare.[13] Later people need only use a bowl or a wooden ladle and take from it all the water they wish. None of them should go away unsatiated.

I finished the book some time after 1676. Hsü San-li of Honan and Wan Yen[14] each printed several *chüan* without finishing the whole task. But many hand-copied versions are now circulating and have received the approval of serious scholars. In the past T'ang Pin[15] once said, "The records of the various schools of thought are very complex, but if you know how to read them, you will find that they are not without some unifying thread." This was also the report passed down by Ch'en Hsi-ku.[16] In August, 1692, I was sick to the point of dying and had to give up all writing and related work. I received a letter from Ch'ou Chao-ao[17] written from the capital, telling me that a hermit in the north named Chia Jen had copied the whole book by hand and had said with a sigh, "This book gives us the development of learning of the several centuries that made up the Ming dynasty. How can we allow it to become lost and buried?" Shortly afterwards, Chia Jen died, but his son Chia P'u followed his wishes and had the book printed.[18]

Alas, when Ssu-ma Kuang finished his *Tzu-chih t'ung-chien* (Comprehensive Mirror for the Guidance of Government),[19] he lamented the fact that so few people would ever read through his whole book. What good fortune is mine, that my book should not be forgotten by our gentlemen? With my dying breath, I personally dictate this to my son, Huang Po-chia, and have him record this preface.

Preface by Huang Tsung-hsi, written in 1693.

NOTES

There are actually three extant versions of this preface. Two are included in *Huang Li-chou wen-chi* (Collected Works) (Peking, 1959), one of which is probably the earliest version because it is lengthier and less polished. The second one was entirely rewritten and included in the *Nan-lei wen-ting wu-chi, Huang Li-chou wen-chi,* pp. 380–81, and the last one was printed with the *Ming-ju hsüeh-an* when Huang was still alive.

1. Literally, "dig out mountain roads as did the five laborers [of Ch'in]," reference to a story in the *Shui-ching chu* (Commentaries on the Water Classic); see the version compiled by Li Tao-yüan (Shanghai, 1958 reprint), p. 27.

2. It is not known what story he is referring to here, but it is given in contrast to the story of note 1 and represents something easy to do.

3. Huang Tsung-shi is using Buddhist language. Obviously he is voicing his predilection for philosophical pluralism, rather than for rigid conformity to any one orthodox system.

4. The term refers particularly to philosophical teaching.

5. Literally, "[teachers of the] T'u-yüan-ts'e" or digests designed to help in cramming.

6. Reference to a story recorded in the *Chan-kuo ts'e* (Intrigues of the Warring States). It recounts that a young man left home to study for three years and, on returning, addressed his mother by name. When reproved for rudeness, he answered that since one is allowed to call such sages as Yao and Shun by name, there is no reason one should not call one's mother by name also. The story is alluded to here, to represent those booksellers of the market place who were publishing mediocre things and making false classical allusions. See *Chan-kuo-ts'e,* ch. 4 (Intrigues of Wei, part 3).

7. Reference to the selection system for recruitment to government service, set up by Emperor Wen of Wei (r. 220–26), according to which prefectures and provinces grade their recruits into nine classes. It was a system partial to aristocrats. But Huang refers to it merely to indicate the confused state of learning.

8. See note 8 to the Author's Introduction.

9. The Almond Terrace refers to the temple of Confucius at his native place, Ch'ü-fu (Shantung), the site where he reportedly held lectures. Huang is here lamenting the internecine conflicts within the Confucian school.

10. References to his father's death at the hands of powerful eunuchs.

11. Yün Jih-ch'u, *tzu* Chung-sheng, *hao* Hsün-an, a native of Wu-chin (Nan Chihli), compiled the *Liu-tzu chieh-yao* in 14 *chüan,* modeling his work structurally upon Chu Hsi's *Chin-ssu lu,* devoting each *chüan* to a specific topic.

12. Huang claims that Liu's special doctrine of vigilance in solitude *(shen-tu)* is based upon the sentence "Intention is master of the mind." But Yün finds this embarrassing because the word *yi* (intention) can also refer to stubbornness, as

for example in *Analects* 9:4, "Confucius . . . was free of . . . foregone conclusions [i.e., stubbornness] *(yi)*," where the word *yi* has a different meaning from
that of "intention." So he did not think it proper to make "intention" one's
main teaching and attempted to cover up for Liu by summarizing all those passages in his writings that speak of *yi*. Huang disagrees with this position. See
Huang's *Chronological Biography,* compiled by Huang Hou-ping and given in *Li-
chou yi-chu hui-k'an* (Surviving Writings) (Taipei, 1969), 34.

13. Allusion to *Huai-nan-tzu,* ch. 10. The water pot or earthen vessel represents the way of the sages.

14. For Hsü San-li, *hao* Yü-shan, see his epitaph, written by Huang in *Nan-lei
wen-yüeh,* ch. 2:14–15. Wan Yen, *hao* Chen-yi, was Huang's disciple and a historian in his own right. He came from Ningpo, thirty miles east of where Huang
lived. See *ECCP,* 805.

15. T'ang Pin, *hao* Ch'ien-an. See *Ch'ing hsüeh-an hsiao-shih* (Notes on Ch'ing
Scholars), by T'ang Ch'ien (1845 ed.), ch. 3. See also *ECCP,* 709.

16. Ch'en Wen-huan, *hao* Chieh-mei. See Huang's letter to Ch'en in *Nan-lei
wen-an,* ch. 2, 11–12, given in *Ming-Ch'ing shih-liao hui-pien,* compiled by Shen
Yün-lung, part 6.

17. See Yamanoi Yū's contribution in *Yōmei monka* (Yang-ming's Disciples) in
Yōmeigaku taikei (A Compendium of the School of Wang Yang-ming), compiled
and edited by Goto Motomi and others, v. 7 (Tokyo, 1974), 297, note.

18. See Part One: Introduction.

19. This refers to Ssu-ma Kuang's famous general history.

II. Author's Introduction

1. Where books on (Neo-Confucian) philosophy[1] are concerned, we have Chou Ju-teng's earlier *Sheng-hsüeh tsung-chuan*[2] and Sun Ch'i-feng's later *Li-hsüeh tsung-chuan*.[3] These contain quite complete accounts of the teachings of many scholars. Yet T'ao Wang-ling said in a letter to Chiao Hung: "Chou regarded himself as being confined to the rustic mountains and rivers, with a narrow scope of information. He desired to collect records from everywhere, for the sake of rounding out his own knowledge. He did not dare call his book a definitive text. Besides, while every school of thought has its own principal doctrines, Chou preferred Ch'an Buddhist teachings, melting gold, silver, copper, and iron into one vessel. This was his own idea, not that of all the schools. As to Sun, he collected information indiscriminately without careful discernment and classification. His own comments are not necessarily to the point. His information is like Chou's."[4] Scholars only have to read my book to recognize the coarseness and negligence of the other two works.

2. Every teaching usually has its main doctrine. This is where the thinker in question applied his most effective effort. It is also the student's starting point. The moral principles of the things in the universe are inexhaustible. Unless one is able to define them in a few words, how can they be summarized and identified as one's own? Thus, he who teaches without any main doctrine, even if he has some fine words to say, gives what resembles entangled silk having no beginning. The student who reads his books and does not understand the thinker's main doctrine resembles Chang Ch'ien[5] when he first went to Ta-hsia and could not understand anything important about Yüeh-chih. For this reason, this book discerns between the thinkers' main doctrines and acts as a lamp in the shadow. Tu Mu[6] once said: "A ball may roll around on a game-table: horizontally, diagonally, circularly, or vertically. One does not really know all the directions it may take. All one could know for sure is that it will not leave the table." This can be applied to the thinkers' doctrines too.

3. I used to say: "In letters as well as in exterior accomplishments, the Ming dynasty was inferior to the earlier ones. Only in philosophy is

it superior. Every nuance, be it fine as the ox's hair and the cocoon's silk, has been carefully discerned and analyzed. What former scholars did not develop has been done for them. For if Ch'eng Yi and Chu Hsi had criticized Buddhism in many and complex words, they dwelt only on the exterior signs, without being able to distinguish what in Buddhism is close to principle *(li)* and yet wrong. The Ming scholars were able to bring to light the smallest differences and nuances." T'ao Wangling also said: "Judging from their understanding, many of our contemporary thinkers are superior to earlier ones."[7] This happens to coincide with what I have to say.

4. Frequently I find that compilers of the former scholars' recorded dialogs tend to select at random some sayings without knowing why they have made such selections. And yet, if the spirit of a man's entire life has not been revealed, how can his learning be made visible? My own work is compiled from the scholars' collected writings and not copied from the earlier anthologies.

5. Confucian learning—unlike the five schools of Buddhism[8]—need not be traced back to Ch'ing-yüan and Nan-yüeh. Confucius himself did not receive his learning from any particular teacher. Chou Tun-yi arose without any predecessor. What Lu Chiu-yüan taught was not what he had learned from anyone else. And yet, from the times of Ch'eng Yi and Chu Hsi to those of Ho [Chi], Wang [Po], Chin [Li-hsiang], and Hsü [Ch'ien][9]—that is, over an interval of several centuries—the norms of the ancestors' rules were still observed. This kind of transmission differs from the Buddhist custom of making only a tenuous association of intellectual lineages. In this book, therefore, the schools of thought are divided first according to their transmissions. Those which arose in isolation and from the later, less-known scholars are all collected in the "Record of the Miscellaneous Scholars."

6. In learning, we regard as truth what each person has discovered himself and made prominent. Those who depend upon other schools and copy from other people are either vulgar scholars or professional students. Included in this book are partial opinions as well as their opposite views. Students should pay attention to the differences. This is the meaning of the same root dividing into myriad branches. To simply add water to water cannot be called learning.

7. Hu Ta-shih[10] had studied under Chu Hsi, who had made him read Mencius. One day Chu asked him, "Do minds alone have nothing in common?"[11] Hu offered his own understanding of the subject which Chu regarded as incorrect, even saying that he was studying carelessly and without reflection. Hu thought so hard about this that he became sick. Only then did Chu explain to him the meaning of the passage. This shows that the ancients did not lightly transmit their teachings, as they wanted students to make their own discoveries. Even the Buddhists

fear that when [the riddle of truth] has been given out, people will play with its externals. This book cannot avoid giving many easy generalizations. If students gather information from it without making genuine effort, I would have done injury to the world for having written it.

8. The book contains quite an extensive collection. But one man's information is limited; there is need yet for more findings. For example, I have not included certain writings that I once saw and then lost, such as the recorded dialogs of the commoner Chu [Shu], as well as the collected writings of Han Pang-ch'i, Nan Ta-chi, Mu K'ung-shui, and Fan Huan.[12] I request that everyone in the world who feels responsible for our learning instruct me generously. This is not a task for just one single person.

NOTES

The translator has numbered the points included in the Remarks.

1. Literally, *Li-hsüeh* or the study of "principle." It can be broadly translated as philosophy, or philosophy of "principle."

2. This book was finished in 1606.

3. This book was finished in 1666.

4. T'ao Wang-ling was a disciple of Chou Ju-teng. See *MJHA*, ch. 36. The quote comes from T'ao's *Collected Writings, Hsieh-an chi,* Taipei reprint, 1976, 16:60a.

5. Chang Ch'ien (fl. 126 B.C.) was sent as envoy to Yüeh-ti in Central Asia but was detained by the Hsiung-nu people for over ten years. He was eventually successful in establishing contact with many countries in Central Asia. See his biography in *Han-shu,* ch. 61.

6. Tu Mu (803–53), *tzu* Mu-chih, was a poet, scholar, and official known for his outspokenness. Huang Tsung-hsi's paraphrased quotation is from *Fan-ch'uan wen-chi* (Collected Writings of Tu Mu), SPTK ed., ch. 10, 89.

7. For this quotation from T'ao Wang-ling, see *MJHA* 36:8b.

8. The five schools of Buddhism refer to five lineages which go back to Hui-neng (638–713), the sixth patriarch of Ch'an Buddhism, who was responsible for the spread of Ch'an into southern China. They include the Ts'ao-tung, Yün-men, and Fa-yen schools, which developed originally out of Ch'ing-yüan (Kiangsi), and the Lin-chi and Kuei-yang schools, which developed originally out of Nan-yüeh (Hunan). See the eleventh-century work by Ch'i-sung, *Ch'uan-fa cheng-tsung chi, TSD,* no. 2078, ch.7–8, especially p. 763. Consult also Huang Kung-wei, *Chung-kuo Fo-chiao ssu-hsiang ch'uan-t'ung shih* (The History of the Transmission of Buddhist Thought in China) (Taipei, 1972), 185–93.

9. The dates of these men are Ho (1188–1268), Wang (1197–1274), Chin (1232–1303), and Hsü (1270–1337). See *SYHA,* ch. 75. Ho Chi was a disciple of Chu Hsi's disciple Huang Kan (1152–1221). His own disciple, Wang Po, was in turn the teacher of Chin Li-hsiang, who had as a disciple Hsü Ch'ien. In referring to these four men, Huang Tsung-hsi is pointing out the fidelity of each to a doctrine transmitted from generation to generation. In the *SYHA,* Huang Po-chia, Tsung-hsi's son, also adds the note that Ho Chi, Wang Po, Chin Li-hsiang, and Hsü Ch'ien represent the legitimate lineal descendants of the master Chu Hsi himself. (Huang Kan was also Chu's son-in-law.)

10. For Hu Ta-shih, *tzu* Chi-sui, see *SYHA,* ch. 64. He was Hu Hung's son and Chang Shih's disciple and son-in-law. After Chang Shih's death, he studied with Ch'en Fu-liang, a member of the school of Lü Tsu-ch'ien, who was a friend of Chu Hsi. At the same time, Hu frequently asked questions of Chu Hsi himself. Later, Hu became a disciple of Lu Chiu-yüan. In the *SYHA,* he is still classified as Chang Shih's disciple.

11. Allusion is to *Mencius* 6A:7.

12. Han Pang-ch'i, *hao* Yüan-lo, Nan Ta-chi, *hao* Jui-ch'uan, Mu K'ung-hui, *hao* Yüan-an, Fan Huan, *hao* Li-chai. For Han, see *MJHA* 9:6b; for Mu and Nan, see *MJHA* 29:1a–b and 11a–b.

III. Quotations from Liu Tsung-chou

On Fang Hsiao-ju[1]

The age of the holy sages being long past, calamities and disorders have followed upon each other. Rare are the scholars and officials who regard living people as their responsibility and the way of the prince as their concern. After the fall of the Sung, such have become even rarer. Fang Hsiao-ju was endowed with a unique native talent and took upon himself generously the mission of reviving this culture. It happened that the culture and brilliance [of Chu Yüan-chang, founder of the Ming dynasty] started a new age,[2] a unique moment in a thousand years. Fang was deeply conscious both of the intention of Heaven above in giving him life and of that which the ancient sages and worthies strove for. He wanted truly to rid the world of floods and droughts and to begin an era like that of the two [sage] Emperors, to repel the Hegemons and make manifest [the way] of the Three Kings[3] and further promote their virtuous influence in order to contribute to future generations. [He was the] one person in whom was united the figures of Yi Yin, the Duke of Chou, Confucius, and Mencius. If his learning had not reached the stage of perceiving the whole profile of his own nature and endowment, this would have been impossible.

But time and destiny were not opportune, and with nine deaths Fang was to accomplish the one right,[4] achieving in this way his universal and historical mission. The support he gave to the moral teaching of the world is evidently that of a true and correct scholar who will not be dishonored in a thousand years.

In his lifetime, Fang was called a reincarnation of Ch'eng Yi and Chu Hsi. Yet later men pointed to his death as that which erases the serious efforts of a whole life, saying that heroic virtue and the study of philosophy are two different things, that he may have one and not the other. And so in their minds, Fang could not even be ranked with Yang Hsiung and Wu Ch'eng.[5] Thus the teaching of martyrdom (literally: completion of humanity and choice of righteousness)[6] becomes a subject forbidden to the world, while treasonous ministers and rebellious sons would multiply everywhere under Heaven. How sad!

Some praise Fang's loyalty as perfect but regard as extreme the sacrifice of his ten relations. I reply: Fang only prepared to die once. That his action should force the killing of ten clans of relations meant that each member of these clans had to die once also. There is no place under Heaven that does not belong to the prince. Are ten clans too many to lose?

In his daily learning, Fang earnestly taught that a minister should be perfectly loyal and a son perfectly filial, basing all on what the conscience already possesses. He led the entire world in this direction for the length of several decades until he almost changed the world's morals. Hence when the day came, and he was able to radiate his special brightness, it became impossible to cover its light. This is fitting, since perfect sincerity manifests itself in all our movements. It is not what human strength can reach by itself. If one should say that Fang's was the way of the Mean,[7] it would be quite correct.

NOTES

These sayings *(Shih-shuo)* probably derive from Liu's *Huang-Ming Tao-t'ung lu* (compiled in 1627), which is no longer extant. See its description given in Liu's *Chronological Biography, Liu-tzu ch'üan-shu,* 39:41b–42a. I raised this point at an Association for Asian Studies panel (March, 1977). Subsequently Wing-tsit Chan published an article in Chinese, in which, among other things, he develops this point at some length. See *"Lun Ming-ju hsüeh-an chih Shih-shuo"* (On the "Teacher's Sayings" in *The Records of Ming Scholars*), *You-shih* Monthly, 48 (1978), 6–7.

1. For Fang Hsiao-ju (1357–1402), see also his biography in this volume.

2. Allusion to the commentary on the text of the First Hexagram of the *Book of Changes, Ch'ien.* According to the Wilhelm/Baynes translation, the line reads: "The Dragon appearing in the field, through him the whole world attains beauty and clarity" (p. 380). The meaning suggested is that Fang looked forward to serving a great prince at the beginning of a new dynasty.

3. The extravagant language strengthens the suggestion offered above in n. 2. The Three Kings refer to the sage kings of legendary antiquity.

4. Allusion to Fang's tragic death for refusing to serve under a usurper, the Emperor Ch'eng-tsu (r. 1402–24), who commanded that Fang be executed together with all those related to him within the nine degrees of kinship.

5. Yang Hsiung (53 B.C.–18 A.D.) was a philosopher of the Han dynasty. Wu Ch'eng (1249–1333) was a philosopher of the Yüan dynasty.

6. Allusion to the teachings of Confucius and Mencius on the kind of martyrdom that may be required by perfect virtue.

7. The Mean *(Chung-yung)* refers to perfect virtue, that manifested by a sage. Liu's high praise of Fang Hsiao-ju is significant on account of Liu's own martyrdom afterwards, during the Manchu invasion of China. Huang Tsung-hsi subtly reveals that according to Liu a true Confucian scholar should remain loyal to his prince and refuse to serve under a usurper. In this spirit he placed Wu Yü-pi first among Ming scholars for doing so and for teaching his students to do the same.

On Ts'ao Tuan[1]

Ts'ao's learning was not received from teachers. Rather, he searched the old texts for records of the ancients and had profound insights into the meaning of creativity *(tsao-hua)*. So he assumed the name Yüeh-ch'uan (Moon-river)[2] to express what he had learned. He then turned inward and sought it in his own mind. For him, mind is the Ultimate.[3] The mind's movement and quiescence are *yin* and *yang*. The mind's daily responses [to events] are the changes and minglings of the Five Agents. His idea was to regard attention to the mind as the entrance to the Way. His perceptions are penetrating but not mysterious; his learning is precise but not complex. We may call him the Chou Tun-yi of today.

According to Ts'ao's own account, until age forty he still found the Way painfully difficult and incomprehensible. After another ten years he had a sudden enlightenment and understood then that there is nothing in the world outside nature *(hsing)* and that nature is everywhere. What is called principle *(li)* of the Great Ultimate is nothing else but this. For the Tao is so difficult to find that scholars should practice caution and not speak lightly of enlightenment.

Ts'ao's disciple, the minister of war, P'eng Tse, once remarked that for this (Ming) dynasty, the height of culture and the art of managing the world's affairs are best reflected in Liu Chi and Sung Lien.[4] But the transmission of the Way began definitely with Ts'ao Tuan of Mien-ch'ih (Honan). P'eng memorialized the throne to request that Ts'ao be celebrated in the Confucian temple.[5] In my humble opinion, the transmission of the Way was interrupted after the death of Fang Hsiao-ju. It was later resumed by Ts'ao Tuan. Hsüeh Hsüan also arose after hearing of Ts'ao's example.

NOTES

1. See Ts'ao Tuan's (1376–1434) biography in this volume.
2. "The moon in the river" suggests the reflection of truth.
3. According to the editors of the Imperial Catalogue, Ts'ao's opinions on the Great Ultimate were given in his short treatise of explanation of Chou Tun-yi's Diagram, a work that is no longer extant. See *SK* (1930); see ibid.
4. For Liu Chi and Sung Lien, two statesmen of early Ming, see their biographies by Hok-lam Chan and F. W. Mote in *DMB*, v. 1, 932–38, v. 2, 1225–31.
5. P'eng's request was rejected by the the ministry of rites. It was not until 1860 that Ts'ao Tuan's name was included in the Confucian temple. See T. Watters, *A Guide to the Tablets in the Temple of Confucius* (n.p., 1879), 196.

On Hsüeh Hsüan[1]

As I understand it, in the discussions of Confucian thinkers of this dynasty, Hsüeh Hsüan was the only one who escaped criticism by earlier scholars. Is that not on account of his being a scholar who personally practiced what he knew? But Hsüeh was a censor during the two periods of Hsüan-te (1426–34) and Cheng-t'ung (1435–49) and never criticized any government policy. When Emperor Ching-ti changed his heir,[2] Hsüeh was director of the court of judicature and said nothing. Some people make excuses for him, saying that he was then occupied in Kweichow in charge of the transfer of military supplies. But in the trial and execution of Yü Ch'ien[3]—which at that time was the case of utmost consequence where merit and crime, right and wrong were concerned —Hsüeh only asked that Yü's punishment be diminished. He watched the execution of a good and loyal man without attempting rescue. Of what use is a minister like that?

Regarding these affairs, if he had been right in remaining silent in the earlier case, then he made a mistake in speaking out in the latter case. Of the two, he could only choose one course.[4] He was already ashamed and could not contain himself and so begged for leave. But where the Way is concerned, he lacked much of what the ancients had, of the knowledge of the whole truth and its great application. But in his behavior, from beginning to end—including his advancement and retirement —there is much to be commended. This earned him the title Wench'ing. When we read his *Tu-shu lu* we find statements regarding self-examination of words and conduct. I suppose this is why personal practice is considered the chief substance of his message. Some people refer to [the poem], "After seventy-six years with nothing to show, this mind senses only the unity of nature and Heaven,"[5] to say that he found the Tao in his old age. This was certainly possible.

NOTES

1. See his biography in this volume.

2. Reference to Emperor Ching-ti's effort to reserve the throne for his own son rather than return it to his elder brother and nephew, to which it rightfully belonged. *MS,* ch. 11.

3. Yü Ch'ien had served the country well during the Oirat invasions but was executed by Emperor Ying-tsung after his restoration to the throne occupied during an interval by his younger brother Ching-ti. See *MS,* ch. 12.

4. Liu Tsung-chou's judgment of Hsüeh Hsüan is all the harsher when compared to what he has to say about Wu Yü-pi.

5. Reference to this poem is made in the selections given in *MJHA,* ch. 7.

On Wu Yü-pi[1]

Wu Yü-pi was criticized by his contemporaries especially for having
sued his younger brother[2] and for calling himself a retainer of Shih
Heng[3] in his epilogue to Shih's clan genealogy. Chang Yüan-chen[4]
heard of it and said, "This ought to be reported to the uncrowned king
above (i.e., Confucius), so that names may be rectified and crimes
punished and that Wu might not long usurp an undeserved reputation."
For a time, many important people were in an uproar, which, I fear,
was instigated by some to show which side they were on. In my opinion,
Wu's fault was not just in suing his brother but rather in not having persuaded his brother to follow the Way. It was because he was unable to
convert his brother to the Way that he was obliged to bring him to court,
having to appear before the authorities in prisoner's clothes with no
attempt to cover up. His fault resembled unveiling the sun and the
moon that were seen by all. As to the epilogue in the clan genealogy, I
think that it might have been fitting for him to sign his name as a
retainer. Remember, Hsü Hsi,[5] when recommended to office by others,
did not always respond to the call, but whenever the men who recommended him died, he always traveled long distances to give his condolences. Was Wu's intention also to practice the Way of the ancients?
Later men judged others with norms of success and failure. As Shih
Heng was to suffer execution, they said that Wu should not have associated with him, without realizing that Wu had already disassociated
from Shih and had resigned from office at the time he replied to the
imperial summons. To seek for his behavior somewhere else rather than
here, to pay minute attention to addresses and words and language,
such is the excessive criticism applied by others.

Wu's learning was acquired through hard work, frequently coming
from the sweat and tears that he shed on his pillow at early dawn. But
he could take pleasure in his insights and discoveries and did not know
how to prevent himself from dancing with his hands and feet. For him,
seventy years were like one single day, and anger and joy gave birth to
each other. Thus he may be said to have alone acquired the subtleties of
the mind of the sages and worthies. As to the path of his learning, it lies
essentially in the cultivation of nature and emotions, with the conquest
of self and contentment in poverty as his real foundation. This is what
Confucius and Yen-tzu looked for in their own exercises and efforts at
improvement. He did not give himself to writing and publishing but
understood the truth of the Way. His words and actions were all peaceful and serene. In what concerns his action in later life, he set a sublime
example to the world while remaining content, without any undue display for publicity's sake. Unless he had acquired the Way, how could he

have acted so? The verse: "Serene as the taste of autumn water in pov-
erty/Peaceful as the work done in silence by the spring breezes,"[6] may
be called his self-portrait. What he achieved was almost the state of consciousness described in the *Doctrine of the Mean* as "though he may be all
unknown, unregarded by the world, he feels no regret."[7] I once tried to
assess the men of those days. I find that Hsüeh Hsüan's problem was in
remaining ordinary and not outstanding; Ch'en Hsien-chang's difficulty was in his attachment to his reputation. Only Wu Yü-pi could be
called the purest of the pure.

NOTES

1. The *MJHA* biographies begin with Wu Yü-pi (1392–1469), ch. 1.
2. The story of Wu suing his own half-brother is included in *MS,* ch. 282.
Chaoying Fang doubts its authenticity. See *DMB,* v. 2, 1500.
3. Shih Heng (d. 1460) was a soldier and military leader who plotted successfully to restore Emperor Ying-tsung to the throne and to put Yü Ch'ien to
death, out of motives of personal hatred. See his biography by Wolfgang
Franke, *DMB,* v. 2, 1202–4. The preface to Shih Heng's genealogy was written
in 1458 and later included in Wu's *Collected Writings* even after Shih's fall from
favor.
4. For Chang Yüan-chen (*tzu* T'ing-hsiang, *hao* Tung-po), see *MJHA,* ch. 45.
5. Hsü Hsi (*tzu* Ju-tzu) was a virtuous scholar of the Han dynasty.
6. The quotation is from Wu's own writings. See *K'ang-chai chi* (Collected
Writings of Wu Yü-pi), The Imperial Catalogue Rare Books Collection, Part 4
(No. 335–36), 11:5b.
7. *Doctrine of the Mean,* ch. 11. The text goes on to describe such a person as a
sage.

On Ch'en Chen-sheng[1]

Ch'en's learning was modeled upon that of Hu Chü-jen, but his cultivation did not reach Hu's level since he allowed his physical nature to
govern his [management of] affairs. His practice of quiet-sitting in later
life suggests more improvement, but, unfortunately, I have not seen his
Complete Works.

NOTE

1. For Ch'en Chen-sheng (*tzu* Shen-fu), see *MJHA,* ch. 46.

On Chou Hui[1]

I find that the two sentences, "Unless it is about sagehood, do not learn;
only when it is about sagehood should one learn," really point directly
to the source of the mind. (This is taken from Tuan Chien's instruction
to Chou Hui.)[2] Besides, these two men were also able to transcend the

art of conversation and dialog. That their learning reached that of the sage, making a thousand *li* of progress in a single day, is without doubt. For the way of sagehood is adequately found within oneself when one turns inward. There is no need to seek it outside. One only has to learn what one already possesses. Therefore Chou only spoke of the learning of sagehood. Tuan also said, "Why should there be such vastness as Heaven and Earth? Believe that the Infinite is itself the past and present." I think that Chou Hui already believed this; he was not one who would flatter others. At that time, the learning of Kuan-chung (Shensi) came to it from the Ho-tung school but became transformed as the Way.

NOTES

1. For Chou Hui (*tzu* Hsiao-ch'uan), see *MJHA*, ch. 7.

2. A parenthesis in the text indicates: "This is taken from Tuan Jung-ssu's instruction to Chou Hui." Tuan Jung-ssu is the other name of Tuan Chien (see *MJHA,* ch. 7). The instruction itself is also given in the biographical account of Chou Hui in *MJHA*. Chou studied for a time under Tuan in Lan-chou (Kansu).

On Ch'en Hsien-chang[1]

I think earlier generations have adequately discussed Ch'en Hsien-chang. Now let me discuss him once more, particularly with regard to what his learning appears to resemble.

Ch'en's philosophy is based on the natural *(tzu-jan);* its essentials consist in acquiring insights for oneself *(tzu-te).* Because he emphasizes acquiring insights for himself, he can draw deeply upon this and find its source wherever he turns, being as lively as the hawk and the fish and returning to himself by grasping hold of the pivot that controls the creative processes. He may be said to have started a new school of thought by himself, standing out among his fellows. And when asked what is meant by the word *te* (acquire), he replied that it referred to the "starting point" *(tuan-ni)* that issues out of the cultivation of stillness. He had earlier sought this in classical texts for years without acquiring anything, but acquired it one day in quiet-sitting. This seems to differ from what the ancients said about *tzu-te*. Mencius has said: "The gentleman steeps himself in the Way because he wishes to acquire it in himself."[2] We have not heard Mencius say that he acquired it by the natural. Is the subtle technique of quiet-sitting not perhaps a superficial method and a shortcut? To acquire by the natural is to acquire without exercising thought, to hit the mark without an effort, embodying the Way naturally and with ease—[a portrait of] the sage. We have not heard that this is acquired by quiet-sitting. After all, Ch'en has acquired what he has acquired. That is all. The Way is rooted in the natural; no one can acquire it with the effort of his intelligence. The moment one desires to be natural, one has become unnatural. Hence it is said: "If you know how to acquire it, you can do so in an active manner; if you do not know how to acquire it, you will only play with your own consciousness."[3] As to the starting point that issues out of the cultivation of stillness, I do not know what it really is. This starting point is what the mind is able to acquire for its articulation. It is after all not so different from playing with one's own consciousness. Now when we investigate what Ch'en has said about the verification of his learning, we find that he has spoken mostly of the effort of the natural. In subtler matters, it is beyond our description; [once more], after all, it is a matter of playing with one's own consciousness.

For Ch'en's interests are close to Chou Tun-yi's, although he is behind Chou in his investigation of principles *(li)*. Ch'en's scholarship is akin to Shao Yung's,[4] although he has articulated it too early. When tested against the school of the sages, he cannot avoid the defects of being desirous of quick results and of looking for small advantages. He appears to be a Ch'an Buddhist but is not a Ch'an Buddhist; that is all.

NOTES

1. For Ch'en Hsien-chang (1428–1500), see his biography in this volume.
2. *Mencius* 4B:14. Eng. translation adapted from J. Legge, *The Chinese Classics,* v. 2, 322–23.
3. *Doctrine of the Mean* 20. See Legge, *The Chinese Classics,* v. 1, 413.
4. For Shao Yung, a Sung thinker, see *SYHA,* ch. 9.

On Ch'en Hsüan[1]

I find that Ch'en Hsüan lived purely according to his principles and was undoubtedly an exemplary disciple of the sages. The learning and efforts of his whole life are entirely manifest in the memorial regarding Chang Ken.[2] Such perfect sincerity has never failed to move others.[3]

In [the book] *T'ung-chi,* his philosophy is criticized as not being perhaps completely correct, but his [character] is much praised. Hsieh To[4] loved the past and believed in the Way. He was a true friend of Ch'en Hsüan's.

NOTES

1. Ch'en Hsüan *(hao* Ko-an), see *MJHA,* ch. 46; *MS,* ch. 161.
2. Chang Ken served as a minor official under Ch'en and was dismissed by him. Ch'en's enemies sought to use Chang to accuse Ch'en falsely, but even after torture, Chang refused. After Ch'en died, Chang submitted a memorial testifying to Ch'en's righteousness in office *(MJHA,* ch. 45).
3. Allusion to the *Doctrine of the Mean,* ch. 22–23.
4. Hsieh To *(tzu* Min-chuan)—see biography in *MS,* ch. 163.

On Lo Lun[1]

I remember Lo Lun once saying: "I have a strong character; when I meet strong personalities, I take to them as the hungry or thirsty person takes to food and drink and can hardly restrain my mouth. When I seek for such and find none, I look one up from the past and speak with him about his own generation, as though I were waiting upon him at his side and listening to his soft and strong cadences. I sigh and lament, I admire and envy to the point of shedding tears. My fondness for strong personalities comes to me from my natural endowment. Confucius once said: 'I have not yet seen a strong personality.' And Mencius said: 'I am good at cultivating my flood-like *ch'i*. This is very great and strong. It fills the space between Heaven and Earth.'[2] And also: 'Riches and nobility cannot contaminate, poverty and lowliness cannot change, and might and awe cannot subdue.'[3] This is really the strongest of the strong. What Confucius and Mencius regard as strength is what I admire."

This may be regarded as coming from Lo Lun's *True Records*. Lo's learning is strong and correct. It has been incorrectly compared to K'ung Jung's.[4] It has also been reported that when Lo was degraded and passed Ch'ung-jen (Kiangsi), he went to visit Wu Yü-pi but Wu did not receive him at once, wanting him to wait and express his desire several times before finally seeing him. Lo Lun got angry, left a poem and departed. Wu Yü-pi declined to see him out of a deep desire to improve him. Unfortunately, Lo Lun did not awaken to this. Also, at the time, Chang Yüan-chen particularly disliked Wu Yü-pi and therefore Lo Lun also disliked him. But after all Wu Yü-pi was someone far superior.

NOTES

1. For Lo Lun, *hao* Yi-feng (1431–78), see *MJHA*, ch. 45. See also his biography by Julia Ching and Huang P'ei in *DMB*, v. 1, 984–85.
2. *Mencius* 2A:2, J. Legge, *The Chinese Classics*, v. 1, 189–90.
3. *Mencius* 3B:2, Legge, *The Chinese Classics*, v. 1, 265.
4. K'ung Jung, a direct descendant of Confucius, was known for his precocity. He was killed by Ts'ao Ts'ao. See K'ung's biography in *Hou-Han shu* (History of the Latter Han Dynasty), ch. 90A, 188–90.

On Ts'ai Ch'ing[1]

Ts'ai Ch'ing cultivated himself in private, practicing virtue with earnestness, without gathering disciples and without teaching philosophy. His learning did not come to him from teachers. He arose suddenly after a long period of time [which witnessed few talents]. He always regarded the Six Classics as the gateway to truth and the Four Books as presenting the norm. He reflected upon himself, making hard efforts and founding all on stillness and emptiness. This may be called real virtue and real destiny and can be acquired in the Mean *(chung)*. After a long time, his cultivation reached such a level of profundity, with daily changes and monthly transformations, that he attained the state of an authentic gentleman. Earlier scholars have praised Yang Lien[2] above Ts'ai Ch'ing. This was not right. Yang was to Ts'ai Ch'ing somewhat as Tzu-hsia was to Tseng-tzu.[3] As to Ting Chi, he cultivated himself assiduously and could almost be regarded as Ts'ai's equal. Unfortunately, he was unable to persevere to the end. Moreover, Ts'ai was a friend of Lin Chün.[4] Lin served at court and had a high reputation for virtue. He frequently recommended [to the attention of the court] such men as Lo Ch'in-shun, Wang Yang-ming, Lü Nan, and Ch'en Hsien-chang. This shows that his example and reputation could have influenced others. I shall await further research to say more.

NOTES

1. See *MJHA*, ch. 46 for Ts'ai Ch'ing, *hao* Hsü-chai.
2. For Yang Lien, see *MS*, ch. 283.
3. Tzu-hsia and Tseng-tzu were both Confucius' disciples.
4. Lin Chün (*tzu* Tai-yung, *hao* Chien-su) was a minister of justice.

On Wang Yang-ming[1]

Wang Yang-ming inherited a learning that had become extinct after the [period of domination exercised by] the pursuit of literary styles [required by examinations] and philology [as demanded by Sung scholars]. He turned inward to find the truth of mind and acquired that to which his nature had awakened, which is called *liang-chih*. So he instructed others in the essentials of finding the beginnings of virtue and applying effort, which is called extending *liang-chih*. *Liang-chih* is knowledge; it is the knowledge of realization that is not limited to seeing and hearing. Extending *liang-chih* is action; it is the action of realization that is not confined to one corner. Knowledge is action, mind is object, activity is stillness, reality is also its manifestation, effort is also original substance, the lower is also the upper. There is nothing that cannot be returned to unity. In this way, he sought to rescue scholars from the defects of a learning that was fragmented, distracting, and superficial. He may be likened to the thunderbolt that awakens people from sleep, the blazing sun that pierces through obscurity. From the time of Confucius and Mencius, there has not been such profound and clear teaching. But when his philosophy is compared to that of Chu Hsi, contradictions are not lacking. And the philosopher he sought with all his might to make known was really Lu Chiu-yüan.[2] For this reason, people have suspected him of being a Ch'an Buddhist. Actually he had been for a time associated with Ch'an Buddhist circles, but later, discovering the mistakes of Ch'an Buddhism, he abandoned it.

Now the one truth is sincerity, the way of Heaven. That which makes [us] sincere is intelligence, the way of man, the extension of *liang-chih*. To attain sincerity through intelligence, to unite man with Heaven, is called sagehood. What is Ch'an Buddhist about this? As to what Lu Chiu-yüan said about the original mind, I suspect it is the teaching from which *liang-chih* had been derived. But to seek the original mind in *liang-chih* makes the instruction more personally relevant. To join the extension of knowledge to the investigation of things makes the exertion more balanced and reliable. When compared to Lu Chiu-yüan, who tried to merge man and the Tao in the one Mind and sought enlightenment in the original Mind, is there not yet an infinitesimal difference? Wang Yang-ming has said, "The knowledge of the good *(liang-chih)* is the knowledge of self in solitude."[3] This was not originally meant to be mysterious. Later scholars arbitrarily regarded it as mysterious and close to Ch'an Buddhism. This was definitely not Yang-ming's original intention.

As to Yang-ming's differences with Chu Hsi, these refer to their interpretations of the *Great Learning*. In explaining the *Great Learning,* Chu Hsi first talked of the investigation of things and the extension of knowledge, and only afterwards taught the sincerity of intention. Yang-ming, in explaining the *Great Learning,* identified investigating things and extending knowledge with the sincerity of intention. In their efforts at self-cultivation, the two men seem to differ by separating [the steps] or by uniting them. But when one examines in detail the points that they most emphasize, one finds that these do not go beyond the meaning of vigilance in solitude *(shen-tu)*. This means that they are one in teaching that perfect sincerity is reached through intelligence and can lead to the way of sagehood. This is why Yang-ming has also expounded upon Chu Hsi's mature views. For the *Great Learning* gives a teaching in sequential terms, as though moving from step to step. In reality there is no such difference in the order of sequence, so that the Eight Items[4] listed are all about one thing.

Wang Yang-ming was a hero among men in an extraordinary epoch. His experience of enlightenment at Lung-ch'ang came to him from heavenly revelation. He also spoke of it as something that has been verified by the Five Classics. There is no doubt that he represents the open path to sagehood. But he was impatient in desiring to make manifest the Way, often instructing others lightly in the subtle doctrines that concern the higher level of truth. This has opened the floodgates for later scholars to attempt [to attain the goal by] missing intervening steps. Had

Heaven given him longer years, permitting him to develop to maturity his exalted and superior ideas, while grounding them on a solid foundation, how could we not also have heard his own mature views? And then, it should go without saying that he would have penetrated into the realm of sagehood, being able to integrate the teachings of Chu Hsi and Lu Chiu-yüan as well as to mediate between them. While near the point of dying, Yang-ming said, "My lifelong learning has only yielded a partial result. I regret not being able to complete it with the help of my friends." This partial result he referred to already made him a man above those who were good and true.[5] There has been no one like him since the time of Ch'eng Hao. Yang-ming's disciples have spread everywhere under Heaven. From Tsou Shou-yi down, the gentlemen [of Kiangsi] appear to be the best known. Moreover, the sources and tributaries, the separation and merging [of the various schools of thought associated with Yang-ming] might also be seen from this.

NOTES

1. See his biography in this volume.
2. For Lu Chiu-yüan, see *SYHA*, ch. 58.
3. For this sentence, see Yang-ming's poem translated into English, in Julia Ching, *To Acquire Wisdom*, 243.
4. The Eight Items refer to the investigation of things, extension of knowledge, sincerity of intention, rectitude of mind, cultivation of self, ordering of family, governing of state, and manifesting of virtue in the world.
5. Allusion to *Mencius* 7B:25.

On Tsou Shou-yi[1]

According to Teng Yi-tsan,[2] Wang Yang-ming's philosophy was without doubt the teaching of the sages, although his own disciples frequently contradicted what he said. Teng also preferred especially Lo Hung-hsien.[3] But why did he overlook Tsou Shou-yi? Tsou considered the knowledge of oneself in solitude to be *liang-chih,* and the practice of caution and apprehension, of vigilance in solitude as the work of extending *liang-chih.* This was the original teaching of the master himself but was later forgotten by scholars who slipped into the path of the cautious *(chüan)* and the madly ardent *(k'uang).* Only Tsou Shou-yi personally practiced what he learned, making of this intention a concrete effort, carefully following the regulations of the sages. His discussions are entirely free of the ensnarements of those others who do philological studies on *liang-chih.* Owing to his efforts, the master's teachings remained undistorted. He can be said to have contributed much to the school of the master. The later theory of Lo Hung-hsien concerning gathering oneself together, keeping inner composure, actually came from this.[4]

NOTES

1. See also his biography in this volume.
2. Têng Yi-tsan (*tzu* Ju-te, posthumous honorific Wen-chieh) was a disciple of Wang Chi (1542–1599). See *MJHA*, ch. 21.
3. See his biography in this volume.
4. See *MJHA*, ch. 17, 6a–9a. Lo Hung-hsien interprets extending *liang-chih* especially in terms of cultivating the harmony of the emotions.

On Wang Chi[1]

According to my research, the teaching of the Four Sentences[2] is not found in the writings of Yang-ming. Its articulation really came from Wang Chi. The Four Sentences might have represented Yang-ming's inconclusive opinions, something he discussed at some time but did not dare to put in writing for fear of confusing the scholars. Only with Wang Chi was it said, "The teaching of the Four Positives (*ssu-yu*) is a complex and fragmented one."[3] He had to transform the [Four Sentences] into the Four Negatives (*ssu-wu*) before he could become content. But if there was no distinction between good and evil, how could there be mind, intention, knowledge, and things? So he had also to move to the denial of mind, intention, knowledge, and things before he could consider this a profound teaching. But then, where are the three words *chih liang-chih* (extending *liang-chih*) made manifest? Wang Chi alone awakened to the fact that nothingness (*wu*) referred to a separate transmission outside the original teaching. Actually even this nothingness was nothing (*wu*). And, without establishing being and nothingness, good and evil also disappeared. All that remained was the *ch'i* of an empty spiritual consciousness, which moves without being attached or detached to any one place. How could this not make him fall into the pitfall of Buddhism? For the Buddhists have abandoned worldly cares to concentrate only on *saṃsāra*. [For them,] there is no evil to avoid and no good to perform. All that remains is the really empty ground of nature where real consciousness may become manifest. To gain enlightenment from this point of entry is the teaching of Ch'an Buddhism. As for us Confucians who daily seek to understand nature and destiny in the dharmas of this world, we are full of desires that appear and disappear. In such a situation, if we speak of the absence of good and evil, we are only making it easier for evil to become dominant.

Wang Chi earnestly studied the Way for eighty years and yet without finding his real abode. He was unable to avoid moving from door to

door, asking for alms, exercising his mind, experimenting with his consciousness, and secretly attempting to control his own destiny. As to
what is good and evil, these are only words that he muttered with his
mouth as an itinerant ascetic, without escaping his status of lay Buddhist. Alas, that he should so waste his life, which is rooted in nothingness!

In Yang-ming's school, both Wang Ken and Wang Chi preferred
enlightenment in their teachings and were called the Two Wangs.
Although Wang Ken spoke of enlightenment in an exalted and transcendent language, he did not depart from the master's essential teachings. But Wang Chi regarded *liang-chih* virtually as the Buddha-nature,
desiring enlightenment in a vacuum, and ended up playing with his
own consciousness. It is possible to describe him as a man who carries
the spear into his own house.[4]

NOTES

1. See also his biography in this volume.
2. For the Four Sentences, see *Ch'uan-hsi lu,* pt. 3.
3. See Wang Chi's *Complete Works, Wang Lung-hsi hsien-sheng ch'üan-chi
(WLCC)* 1822 ed., ch. 1.
4. I.e., he was to destroy his own house—the school of Wang Yang-ming. Liu
Tsung-chou is unusually harsh in his judgment of Wang Chi.

On Lo Ch'in-shun[1]

I consider Lo's learning to have been acquired through Ch'an Buddhism. He attained enlightenment from the *kung-an (koan)* concerning
the pine tree in the courtyard.[2] This happened one evening when he had
his cloak on, felt perspiration over his whole body, and wondered why
all had come to him with such ease. Reflecting upon this experience, he
sought for [confirmation of his insights] in the Confucian teachings and
found that the two did not harmonize. Only then did he know that Buddhists regarded consciousness as nature, the mind as root, and differed
from our Confucian teaching of fully investigating principles, fulfilling
nature, and attaining destiny. So he sought for truth on the basis of the
doctrine of the investigation of things and extension of knowledge
according to Ch'eng Yi and Chu Hsi. After twenty long years, he began
to perceive what is called the beginnings *(tuan)* of nature and of the way
of Heaven. To put all this together, one may say that the wonder of
nature and destiny lies in the unity of principles *(li)* and their manifold
manifestations. To expound upon this, one might say that these principles are between the mind and the eyes, and that proceeding from the
roots to the branches, the myriad phenomena are manifold but not disorderly, while proceeding from branches back to the root, the one reality

is clear, still and without residue.[3] In this way, he sought to attach himself to the sublime insights of [Chu Hsi], in an effort that may be called painful and difficult.

As I think over what Lo referred to as "between the mind and the eyes," I do not know where it really is, and I wonder about the statement regarding proceeding from the root to the branches and returning to the root from the branches, being puzzled as to where the starting point is, and where the final point of return is. That principles are one and their manifestations many[4] is nothing other than the all-pervasive teaching of Confucius. Its essential doctrine is not outside of loyalty and reciprocity. In this case, that the Tao is not far from the mind of man may also be decided. But Lo insisted upon discerning Confucianism and Buddhism by referring to teachings on mind and nature, asserting that Buddhism is concerned with the discovery of mind. So he preferred to set aside mind to talk of nature, separating them (mind and nature) into two. Hence he situates principles *(li)* between that which is neither outer nor inner, while pointing to another realm of the mind and eyes and, in so doing, continuing to contemplate the principles of things in the abstract. Therefore, what he said about proceeding from root to branches and returning from branches to root refers yet to things proceeding naturally and returning naturally and has nothing to do with the self. In this way, he was not himself conscious of having fallen into vagaries.

I find that Lo's strength is especially in taking the moral mind *(Tao-hsin)* as nature, identifying this with [the state of mind] before the stirring of emotions, and in taking the human mind *(jen-hsin)* as emotions, identifying this with [the state of mind] after the stirring of emotions.[5] He claims that [his philosophy] is therefore different from that of the Sung scholars, and that when one sees things clearly on this point, one can proceed everywhere and never be incoherent. Now if we reflect upon his words, we find that mind, nature, and emotions refer actually to the one same person. Therefore the distinction should not be made between that which is prone to error being the mind and that which is subtle not being the mind. The problem is that Lo firmly believed that to hold consciousness to be nature is Buddhistic, since, for him, consciousness belongs to [the state of mind] after emotions are stirred and hence refers to emotions and not to nature; indeed, the mind that concerns the root of all things is only the mind that is prone to error, while there is no [such thing as the] mind that is subtle. In this way, what is subtle is pushed outside the mind and sought for in the appearances of Heaven and Earth and all things. Thus he said that there is nothing in the world outside of nature, that the investigation of things and the extension of knowledge is that which pervades roots and branches. This ought to be accomplished before passing on to sincerity of intention and rectitude of mind, in order to establish the great root of all under Heaven. Hence he almost regarded nature itself as something that belongs to the outer realm. For this reason I say that Lo Ch'in-shun did not really perceive nature, since he makes it something external.

Is nature really external and is the mind material? Terms such as mind and nature are not to be confused; neither are such terms as *li* and *ch'i*. Yet they cannot be found in separation, nor can *li* and *ch'i*. Since Lo does not agree with the Sung scholars in their teachings concerning the heavenly destiny and the physical endowment *(ch'i-chih)*, while covering all with the statement that principles are one but their manifestations are many, [it was correct of him] to say that principles are the principles of *ch'i;* he did not say that nature is also the nature of mind. For the mind represents the concentration of *ch'i* in man, while nature represents the concentration of *li* in man. As *li* and *ch'i* are one, mind and nature cannot be two, and as mind and nature are one, nature and emotions also cannot be two. Should these three be ultimately separated from one another, then what do *li* and *ch'i* refer to, and what do mind, nature, and emotions refer to? If there is a *li* between Heaven and Earth that is one with *ch'i* and also a *li* separate from *ch'i*, if there is a nature that is separate from mind and also emotions separate from nature, then how can we speak of them as being basically one? We Confucians base our teachings on Heaven while Buddhists base their teachings on the mind; this has been the firm judgment of the ancients. Lo Ch'in-shun discusses this with eloquence and may be said to have been a meritorious servant of the school of sages. What is important is that those who discourse well on Heaven do not fear harmonizing Heaven with man, while those who discourse well on the mind do not go off into Buddhist teachings. Lo Ch'in-shun could not avoid the temptation of abandoning food for fear of choking himself, thus clearly drawing boundaries [between mind and nature]. In so doing, he sufficiently exposed the faults of others but could not prevent the relinquishing of his own base. We reflect that he spent between twenty and thirty years' effort upon the one instruction of investigation of things, and only afterwards did he speak of mind, nature, *li*, and *ch'i*. If he had not uttered one word wrong, he would have given only a correct and proper description but without having made any gains in the task of cultivation.[6]

Lo was serene, concentrated, tranquil, and correct; his virtuous behavior can be compared to pure gold and precious jade. He was without doubt a disciple of the sages. This was his natural endowment and had nothing to do with his effort at learning. In a letter he once wrote to Wang Yang-ming, he said:[7] "If one wanted to regard learning as a task that does not depend on searching outside of oneself, that requires only the effort of self-reflection and inner examination, then the words 'sincerity of intention' and 'rectitude of mind' should contain everything, and there would be no more need of burdening [the student] with the effort of investigation of things at the beginning of his quest." Alas, a man like Lo was really hampered by the effort concerning investigation of things, not only at the beginning of his career but all during his life! Had that not been so, given his endowment, had he early sought to improve himself by aiming higher, he should have entered the realm of sagehood with ease. Unfortunately, he only stopped where he did. Although he began by acquiring enlightenment with relative ease, he could not avoid making a mistake of infinitesimal proportions that eventually troubled him all his life, annoying him till the very end, almost misleading him a thousand *li* away. Moreover, by that time, the learning of Ch'eng Yi and Chu Hsi was already showing its own defects. If one should follow what he had to say, [shackle] the student, and prevent him from ever entering the Way all his life until after twenty or thirty years of laborious effort but before getting anywhere—and then getting very little—the student would have cause to regard the learning of the sages as an almost impossible virtue. For this reason, Wang Yang-ming was to arise [and remedy the situation of learning].

NOTES

1. For Lo Ch'in-shun, see his biography in this volume.

2. See *K'un-chih chi* (Painful Learning) by Lo Ch'in-shun in CYTC ed., 2:3a–b, in which he gave his own account of this experience. According to him, an old monk he met casually at the capital answered the question as to why he became a monk by saying that the Buddha was present in the pine tree. Lo thought over it all night and attained an experience of enlightenment at dawn.

3. See *K'un-chih chi*, 3:9a.

4. *K'un-chih chi*, 2:10a.

5. See *K'un-chih chi*, 3:1a–4b.

6. Literally, "having made any gains for sitting down" *(tso-hsia)*. Judging from another context where this expression also occurs, with reference to Li Ts'ai, it has less to do with quiet-sitting than with the task of cultivation or the quest of sagehood. "Sitting down" can refer also to taking an inferior seat, as a gentleman is supposed to do out of modesty. See *Li-chi* (Book of Rites), ch. 50. English translation by James Legge, *Li Ki, SBE,* v. 27, pt. 2, 287.

7. See *Lo Cheng-an hsien-sheng ts'un kao* (Surviving Writings), CYTC ed., 1: 7b–8b.

On Lü Nan[1]

The teachings of Kuan-chung[2] have had their special lineage for generations, being always based on personal behavior and the teaching of propriety. Lü Nan was especially its great synthesizer. If we observe his words and actions, we can see that none of these failed to conform to the Way. One can have no doubt of this, even in any infinitesimal proportion and also with regard to the hidden and subtle points of his mind.

Undoubtedly he was a sublime disciple of Min Tzu-ch'ien and Jan Po-niu.[3]

At that time, Wang Yang-ming was teaching the doctrine of *liang-chih*, originally placing emphasis upon personal behavior. But he was misunderstood by other scholars, who abandoned action to speak of knowledge. Fortunately Lü's teaching on the importance of action could rescue [the fate of Yang-ming's teachings], and that at a time of great danger. For a time, Lü's lectures were almost as popular as Yang-ming's. Many of those who were earnest in action and had proper self-respect came from his school.

NOTES

1. For Lü Nan (1479–1542), see his biography by Julia Ching in *DMB*, v. 1, 1010–12.

2. The teachings of Kuan-chung refer to those of Shansi and Shensi (Hotung), which may be said to go back to Chang Tsai.

3. Two disciples of Confucius known for their virtues. See *Analects* 3:6.

On Meng Hua-li, Meng Ch'iu, and Chang Yüan-pien[1]

I find that the two Mengs are [bright and clear] like a jug of ice and the autumn waters,[2] each reflecting upon the other, upholding their family teachings from a possible decline. They may be called the sun and moon of the northern regions. My fellow countryman Chang Yüan-pien, on the other hand, may be described as having gained a greater reputation for his attachment [to the two Mengs]. One only has to read his poem, *Erh-Meng hsing*, to believe this. Chang also wrote the poem *Chuang-tsai hsing* to present to Tsou Shou-yi, when the latter was exiled to Kweiyang. His preference for our people shows itself in such ways. What a gentleman he was! Today we can no longer see his like. Chang was also a literary friend of his fellow countryman Lo Lun. When Lo became later the examiner at the metropolitan examinations, Chang remembered their old friendship and did not sign himself as Lo's disciple. Although Lo was annoyed with this, Chang paid no attention. In his palace examination, the reader of his essay was Kao Kung.[3] But later, when Chang met him, he did not sign himself as his disciple either. Such was his independence of spirit. Chang was also a great friend of Teng Yi-tsan. On Chang's death, Teng wrote a sacrificial essay, praising him for his love of virtue and for his sense of responsibility regarding the world.

NOTES

1. For the Two Mengs (Meng Hua-li, *hao* Yün-p'u, and Meng Ch'iu, *hao* Wo-chiang), see *MJHA*, ch. 29. For Chang Yüan-pien (*hao*), see *MJHA*, ch. 15.

2. Both images represent a pure mind, that is, one without official ambition. See especially the poem by Wang Ch'ang-ling (698–757) in the collection, *Wang Ch'ang-ling shih chiao-chu,* comp. by Li Kuo-sheng (Taipei, 1973), 176.

3. Kao Kung (*tzu* Chung-yüan). See *MS,* ch. 213.

On Lo Hung-hsien,[1] Chao Chen-chi,[2] Wang Shih-huai,[3] Teng Yi-tsan[4]

Of the disciples of the school of Wang Yang-ming, Wang Ken in particular propagated his teachings far and wide. Starting from the teaching of "without learning, without reflection,"[5] he moved to the label of the natural *(tzu-jan)* and then of the joy of learning. The latter-day followers of his school included numerous degenerates, who were mediocre men having no inhibitions. Lo Hung-hsien emerged later and was much concerned. He pointed out especially the words "recollection and concentration" as the formula for extending *liang-chih.* Hence his teaching focused on the moment before the emotions arose and regarded stillness and desirelessness as highly important. All this showed his solicitude for the defense of the Way.

Some people have said: "In emphasizing stillness, is Lo not a Ch'an Buddhist?" I answer: "The ancients have always taught 'contingent doctrines' *(upāya).* After someone like Wang Yang-ming, Lo Hung-hsien is absolutely necessary. I prefer his having been able to sustain this Way from further falls." Moreover, Lo recognized where Buddhist teachings appeared to be correct and was able to utilize them. In abandoning Yang Chu[6] and returning to Confucianism was he not closer to us than those who had no inhibitions? As to Chao Chen-chi, Wang Shih-huai, and Teng Yi-tsan, did they also continue his intentions? Teng was particularly subtle; his character could be compared to Lo's.

NOTES

1. See Lo Hung-hsien's biography in this volume.

2. See Chao Chen-chi in *MJHA,* ch. 33.

3. See Wang Shih-huai (*tzu* T'ang-nan) in *MJHA,* ch. 20.

4. See Teng Yi-tsan (*tzu* Ting-yü) in *MJHA,* ch. 21.

5. Allusion to *Mencius* 7A:15, which originally referred to an innate moral intuition *(liang-chih)* and an innate moral ability *(liang-neng).* But Wang Ken interpreted this to mean that learning and reflection are superfluous in self-cultivation.

6. Yang Chu was an early Taoist described as a heretic by Mencius for proposing an extreme form of individualism. See *Mencius* 3B:9; 7A:1–2.

On Lo Ju-fang[1]

At a time when the Six Classics were regarded as mud and hemp,[2] Teng [Yi-tsan] alone manifested a special concern for antiquity, investigating into the extant classics of the former sages, slightly amending them, giving them an orderly appearance, and so rescued scholarship from subjective biases of the mind and unjust accusations against the teachings of the past. His accomplishments may be described as great. But his learning was really based on Tsou Shou-yi's; he alone heard the teaching of caution and apprehension, of vigilance in solitude, so it is possible to call him the lineal descendant of Wang Yang-ming's school. I once heard the famous scholars of Kiangsi say that Teng's learning was based on cultivation, while Lo Ju-fang's learning was based on enlightenment and that the two men disputed much upon these points. However, in later life, Teng became a great admirer of Lo Ju-fang and was fully convinced by Lo.[3] From his sacrificial essay in Lo's honor, we can see something of this development. In that case Lo's cultivation must have surpassed that of others in many ways. I have therefore chosen certain passages that are relevant and to the point to record in writing, and so remove from those rash scholars the excuse of appealing to Lo Ju-fang.

NOTES

1. See Lo's biography in this volume. Liu Tsung-chou's comments here regard Lo only indirectly and deal more with Teng Yi-tsan.

2. I.e., despised by scholars. Reference is actually to the T'ai-chou branch of the Yang-ming school.

3. Literally, he "unconsciously moved his seat [mat] toward the speaker [i.e., Lo]," signifying a process of conversion.

On Li Ts'ai[1]

After the appearance of Wang Yang-ming, Li Ts'ai then emerged, with his own special teaching, using earnestly the two words *chih-hsiu* (rest and cultivation) to overcome *liang-chih*. He also [compared his action] to that of Confucius and Tseng-tzu who awaited the coming of the later sages. In this way, he established himself as a rival for the position of teacher and was able to lead the whole world in his train, as did Wang Yang-ming himself. Formerly, people said that *liang-chih* referred to something bright and vast and was not as solidly based as the words *chih-hsiu*. But they appeared to be only searching for an attractive topic to write an essay about, having nothing to do with the quest for sagehood. Were we conscious of the difference between *liang-chih* and *chih-hsiu?* Li Ts'ai had great ambitions, considering the management of the world as his learning and modeling himself carefully upon Wang Yang-ming. And so everywhere he manifested a fondness for external accomplishments. If one were to ask him his final goal, it would usually be the seeking of what is possible, what is achievable. How could he dare even to look at the dust behind Wang Yang-ming's carriage? In interpreting the *Great Learning,* Ch'eng Yi and Chu Hsi spoke of sincerity of intentions and correctness of mind, Yang-ming spoke of extending knowledge, Wang Ken spoke of investigation of things, Lo Ju-fang spoke of making manifest clear virtue, and Li Ts'ai spoke of self-cultivation. Is there yet anything left untouched?

NOTE

1. See his biography in this volume.

On Hsü Fu-yüan[1]

I have studied personally under Hsü Fu-yüan and found him sober, concentrated, open and broad, his actions and words serious and quite in accord with Confucian norms. He carefully cultivated his mind and body without ignoring the least detail. He paid threefold attention to the distinction between heavenly principle and human desires. He once gathered in the depths of night with his disciples, in profound and quiet meditation, recounting the diminution and growth of the indulgence of wine, sex, wealth, and temper in his own life, in order to attest to his own [cultivation]. So solid and true was his learning.

NOTE

1. See his biography in this volume.

IV. The Records

1. The Ch'ung-jen[1] School

Wu Yü-pi promoted the Way at Hsiao-p'o,[2] following faithfully the established teachings on the Sung people. Speaking of mind *(hsin),*[3] he regards consciousness *(chih-chueh)* and principle *(li)* as two things. Speaking of the method [of spiritual cultivation] *(kung-fu),* he counsels preserving [mind] and nurturing [nature] in tranquility and watching over oneself in activity. Hence, only when reverence and righteousness serve as mainstays [for action],[4] when understanding and sincerity advance together [in the mind],[5] could the effort of learning become complete.

As followers of the school that Wu transmitted, Lou Liang and Wei Chiao[6] showed slight differences from the master, but they never dared to leave Wu's established norms. Ch'en Hsien-chang was his disciple but said that his own learning did not come from Wu. He should thus be considered as of another school. But lo! a wheel without spokes is the mother of the carriage, while deep ice is formed from accumulated water. Without Wu Yü-pi, how could later [Ming] learning have flourished?

NOTES

The remainder of this translation consists of selected biographies from the *MJHA*. For each individual's biography, the page reference to the Chinese text is given at the end of the selection. Page references for the prefaces discussing the schools are not given in this translation, however, as the prefaces are readily found at the beginnings of sections in the Chinese text.

1. Ch'ung-jen is the name of the place (Kiangsi) from which Wu came.

2. Hsiao-p'o is the name of the village where the Wu family's farm was situated.

3. For a summary account of Wu Yü-pi's life and thought, see his biography in this volume.

4. Allusion to the philosophy of Ch'eng Yi. See especially his treatise, "What Yen-tzu loved to learn," in the *Erh-Ch'eng ch'üan-shu* (*Yi-ch'uan wen-chi,* 4:1a–2a). English tr. in Wing-tsit Chan, *A Source Book of Chinese Philosophy* (Princeton, 1963), 547.

5. Allusion to the *Doctrine of the Mean,* ch. 21–22. In Ch'eng Yi's treatise (see above, n.4), he is commenting also on these chapters.

6. Lou Liang and Wei Chiao are both listed under *MJHA,* ch. 1.

Wu Yü-pi

Wu Yü-pi, *tzu* Tzu-fu, *hao* K'ang-chai (1397–1469),[1] was a native of Ch'ung-jen County in Fu-chou Prefecture (Kiangsi). His father, Wu P'u,[2] served as dean of the National University. When Wu Yü-pi was born, his grandfather had a dream in which he saw their ancestor's tomb encircled by a thick vine. An old man in the dream pointed that out as "the vine that grasps on to the official carriage's shaft." So the child was first called Meng-hsiang (Auspicious Dream). At eight or so he already assumed a distinctive demeanor. At [fourteen] (1409) he visited his father at the capital (Nanking) and studied under the instructor to the heir-apparent, Yang P'u.[3] While reading the *Yi-lo yüan-yüan lu,*[4] Wu set his mind wistfully on the pursuit of the Way. He observed that if the elder Ch'eng[5] could take pleasure in watching hunting, by inference sages and worthies were also human; who could then say that sagehood could not be acquired by learning? So he gave up his preparations for civil examinations, kept away from social company, and lived alone in a small room upstairs, pondering over the Four Books and the Five Classics and the recorded sayings of the many scholars. He kept their teachings close to his mind and body, savoring them by experience, without going downstairs for two years. He became aware at this time of his choleric temperament, and made an effort to overcome its excesses.

In 1411 his father ordered him to return to his native place and get married. On his way, a storm arose on the Yangtse River and his boat was on the verge of capsizing, but he remained seated and fully dressed, with calm and serious composure. When it was over, someone asked him how he could remain so calm, and he answered, "I keep doing what is right, to prepare for whatever may happen." After the wedding, he did not enter the bedchamber until he had returned from Nanking, where he went to report everything to his parents. In his travels, he wore coarse clothes and old shoes. People could not discern that he was the son of the dean of the National University. He personally ploughed the fields at home and lived on the fruits of his labors. Many students came to study with him. Among them he singled out Lou Liang[6] as a reliable and solid man, Yang Chieh as a sincere and refined man, Chou Wen as a brave and straightforward man. On rainy days, he would wear his bamboo coat and hat, carry a plow and a spade over his shoulder, and go to till the land with his students. He told them that the principles of the eight trigrams, Ch'ien, K'un, K'an, Li, Keng, Chen, Tui, and Hs'ün, in the *Book of Changes,* could be understood by contemplating the hoe and the plow.[7] After work, he would put away the tools and join his students in a meal of unpolished rice with vegetables and beans.

Ch'en Hsien-chang came from Kwangtung to study with Wu. At daybreak Wu was already winnowing grain while Ch'en was still in bed. Wu said aloud: "If a young student should be so lazy, how could he ever reach the threshold of Ch'eng Yi, or even of Mencius?" Another day while mowing grain with a sickle, he hurt his finger but bore the pain quietly and went on mowing. He said, "How can I let myself be dominated by matter?" He lamented that there should be so many and such complex commentaries and annotations, which were more harmful than beneficial. For this reason, he did not lightly engage in writing. The administrative authorities of both his prefecture and his province recommended that he go to the imperial court (to be graded for an official appointment), but he did not go. Heaving a long sigh, he said, "Unless we get rid of the eunuchs and the Buddhists, it is too difficult to get good government. For what should I go?" Early in the T'ien-shun period (1457), Duke Chung-kuo, Shih Heng,[8] was acting very ostentatiously and knew that the emperor[9] was suspicious of him. His follower Hsieh Chao, repeating what Chang Hsüeh[10] had told Ts'ai Ching, proposed that Wu be recommended for office in order that the government might gain more respect among the people. Shih Heng discussed this with the grand secretary, Li Hsien, who wrote for Shih the memorial recommending Wu to the emperor. The emperor asked Li what kind of man Wu was. Li reported that he was a Confucian scholar who shunned fame and fortune, and that since the enlightened kings of the past all patronized worthy men and good scholars, the emperor would do great credit to the dynasty by inviting Wu to the government. So the emperor sent a messenger, Ts'ao Lung, to Ch'ung-jen to invite Wu. Wu accepted the invitation and was on his way. The emperor was very pleased and asked Li Hsien what rank and office Wu should be offered. Li answered that since the heir-apparent was receiving lectures, a mature scholar was needed to take charge of his instruction and that this was a position most suited to Wu himself. The emperor agreed to make Wu a moral instructor to the prince. Wu was summoned to present himself at the Wen-hua palace. The emperor said, "We have long been apprised of your high virtues and invite you especially to come and advise the crown prince." Wu replied, "Your servant is a lowly man and has since childhood been afflicted with many maladies, living a secluded life without accomplishing anything special. It is only because of an undeserved reputation that I have been recommended to your attention. Your Majesty has believed in these reports and sent out an invitation to me on my farm. Your servant is ashamed with all this attention and has come here in spite of illness to beg to be excused from holding any office."[11] The emperor said, "The position of serving the crown prince permits much leisure with honor. You need not decline such an offer." Then he favored Wu with gifts of silk, wine, and lamb and ordered the eunuch Niu Yü to accompany him to his residence. The emperor then turned to Li Hsien and said, "People call this old man a stubborn fool. That is not true."

At that time, Li Hsien took the initiative in treating Wu as an honored teacher. Nobles and officials, high and low, respecting his reputation, waited at Wu's gate for an audience. But the general public considered this strange, and slanders arose. The eunuchs, who observed Wu acting and speaking at court in accordance with ancient rituals, gathered together to laugh at him. Someone told Li Hsien about it. Li explained that Wu was behaving as he did in order to encourage better manners and to shame those who competed merely for favors. Wu begged three times to be excused from office. After that he said he was too ill to leave his bed. The emperor asked Li Hsien why Wu did not wish to take office, commenting that if Wu indeed preferred to return home, he could do so in autumn when the weather was milder, and then with a lifelong stipend. Li passed the word to Wu, who only declined more vigorously. The emperor said, "In that case, it is impossible to keep him." And so his wish was granted. Wu then submitted a memorial on ten points.[12] He was summoned to another audience, given a travel order with the imperial seal and presents of silver and silk. The emperor sent the imperial messenger, Wang Wei-shan, to accompany him home. Local officials were instructed to give him a monthly rice ration.

It seems that Wu foresaw Shih Heng's eventual downfall and kept his own purity by leaving the court. After he returned south he was asked why he did so, and he merely answered that it was in order to keep his own life intact. In the ninth month of 1459, he sent a student to the emperor with a memorial, in which he expressed gratitude. Two years later, he went to Hukuang to pay homage to the tomb of Yang P'u. In spring of 1462, he traveled to Fukien to visit Chu Hsi's former residence and shrine[13] and pledged there to be his follower. He died at age seventy-seven on November 20, 1469.

Wu Yü-pi's learning is not derived from any known master, although he was the first person in Ming times to seek the Way. He practiced assiduously all that he learned personally, while doing small errands and in both speech and silence. Whether working outside or resting at home, he never forgot what he learned. After some time, this developed naturally into a habitual rule of life. It is what one describes by saying, "Reverence and righteousness serve as mainstays; understanding and sincerity advance together."[14] He refrained from mentioning all that is mysterious and preternatural. Students who follow him have a clear path marked out for them. Chang Kun of Lin-ch'uan (Kiangsi) said that Wu wrote his *Diary (Jih-lu)*[15] as his personal history, recounting everything about himself; this is different from having someone else write up a diffuse account discussing a wide spectrum of different subjects, mixing up personal opinions with known teachings, or attaching known teachings to personal opinions. Ku Hsien-ch'eng[16] said that Wu represented an atmosphere of pristine *ch'i,* with a simplicity reminiscent of that of early antiquity.

Those in the world who criticized Wu Yü-pi voiced many attacks. They said, among other things, that Wu declined office because the position of instructor to the heir-apparent disappointed his high expectations, aroused by the emperor's solemn invitation, of the kind addressed to the ancient sage ministers Yi Yin and Fu Yüeh.[17] But even the sage Shun had to go through many tests before he was trusted with all affairs of the country, nor was Yi Yin or Fu Yüeh named prime minister on the first appointment. No common fool would compare official appointments in this crude way, let alone Master Wu! Ch'en Chien's[18] *T'ung-chi* had merely picked up and repeated a groundless slander such as this, which is not worth considering. But Hsüeh Ying-ch'i,[19] himself a Confucian scholar, made the same mistake in his *Hsien-chang lu.* It also gave the story of Wu Yü-pi's litigation with his younger half-brother over some farm land, describing him as having to appear in court, hatless, unkempt and on his knees, wearing a short dress and an apron. Chang Yüan-chen[20] even addressed a public letter to Confucius, urging that "names may be rectified and crimes punished, that Wu might not long usurp an undeserved reputation."

But Master Liu Tsung-chou[21] said, "Of the men of our [Ming] dynasty, I admire Wu Yü-pi most. When his brother was indiscreet enough to sell out some sacrificial farmland [belonging to the whole family], Wu Yü-pi took the matter to court, giving testimony in plebeian litigant's dress, with no pretence or affectation. Unless his desire for fame had been completely cleansed, he could not have acted this way." However, according to Yang Shih-ch'iao's[22] *Ch'uan-yi-k'ao,* "Wu Yü-pi never once referred to the subject of his official rank after he began working on the farm in commoner's garb. Rather, Chang Kuei (a native of P'an-yü), the prefect of Fu-chou where Wu lived, angered by Wu's refusal to receive him and knowing that influential persons in Peking (like Yin Chih)[23] disliked Wu and wanted to spoil his reputation, tried for a long time to find someone who would sue Wu, but without success. So he pressured someone to use the name of Wu's younger brother to bring suit against Wu. As soon as the complaint was presented, Chang immediately sent men with a summons to arrest Wu. Wu's disciples, Hu Chü-jen[24] and others, advised him to present himself in official dress. But Wu went instead in commoner's garb. Chang treated him rudely at first but then dismissed him with courtesy. Wu took the whole thing with composure, understanding that the case was not intended by his brother, with whom he remained on good terms as always. But Chang won the favors of some eunuchs for having brought this dishonor on Wu. Chang Yüan-chen had at first believed Wu to have been at fault and only later realized his misunderstanding." This is what really happened.

Another story had it that Master Wu wrote a postscript to [General] Shih Heng's clan genealogy, calling himself Shih's protégé. Ku Yün-ch'eng[25] had this to say about it: "This is a busybody's tale. Wu Yü-pi loved the Way, was content in poverty, serene, and happy with himself. He was like a phoenix soaring ten thousand feet up, who looked down at this world below as unworthy even of a passing glance. How could such a small thing as a general's recommendation make any big difference to him? Would he really have reacted with such gratitude as befitted a protégé of a powerful house and regarded his protector the way a worldly man would look up to his patron or sponsor? This is my first reason for not believing in such a story. Besides, the general had long been arrogant, and even the man in the street could foretell his eventual fall from power. How much more would Wu have known this, he who, by firmly declining the instructor's offer, showed that he did not wish to become involved with Shih and tried his best to hurry away! How would he then make up to him later and make himself willingly a retainer of Shih, who was an unjust man? This is my second reason for not believing in this story."

As I, Huang Tsung-hsi,[26] see it: Shih Heng's power was very great indeed. He had recommended Wu to office in order to show himself off to the world and acquire thereby the reputation of being a scholar's patron. Had Wu refused to call himself a protégé, he would have given grave offense to Shih and might not even have been able to return home safely. Wu had said that he wanted to keep his own life intact, giving this as a reason for declining office. Could he not have acted under pressure in certain circumstances?

(*MJHA* 1:1a–2b)

NOTES

1. See Wu Yü-pi's biography by Chaoying Fang and others, *DMB*, v. 2, 1497–1501.

2. Wu lived for forty-seven years as a peasant and teacher, before he was summoned to court in 1458. Chaoying Fang cites his difficulties with his father over the latter's service to Emperor Ch'eng-tsu (Chu Ti, r. 1402–24), a usurper of the Ming throne who had killed many scholars, including Fang Hsiao-ju. See also Chu Ti's life by F. W. Mote and L. C. Goodrich, *DMB*, v. 1, 355–65.

3. Yang P'u, posthumous honorific Wen-ting, 1372–1446, was instructor to the heir-apparent before becoming grand secretary from 1436 to 1446. See

DMB, v. 2, 1537–38. The text of the *Ming-ju hsüeh-an* gives Wu's age then as seventeen, which is impossible.

4. This book, compiled by Chu Hsi, gives the account of the beginning of Sung Neo-Confucianism.

5. Ch'eng Hao, *tzu* Po-ch'un.

6. Huang Tsung-hsi is to assign an entire biography to Lou Liang but nothing more to Yang Chieh and Chou Wen. Lou supposedly gave some instruction to Wang Yang-ming and serves therefore as a link between Wang and Wu, a reason sometimes given for Huang's selection of Wu as the first thinker in this book. Chaoying Fang believes that Wu's moral independence and refusal to serve the government of Chu Ti, which he believed to be illegitimate, was also an important factor in Huang's consideration. This can be better appreciated when we remember that Huang himself never served the Manchus, and that his teacher, Liu Tsung-chou, preferred death to submission to the Ch'ing dynasty.

7. The eight trigrams, standing for the great symbols of nature, have special meaning in agriculture.

8. Shih Heng was to fall from power and die (1460) shortly after recommending Wu. See also "Quotations from Liu Tsung-chou," on Wu Yü-pi, note 3.

9. This was Emperor Ying-tsung, who reigned 1436–49 and again, 1457–64. See his biography by Chaoying Fang and Lien-che Tu Fang, *DMB,* v. 1, 289–94.

10. Chang Hsüeh, tutor to Ts'ai Ching's children, warned them of the dire consequences their father's misuse of power as prime minister (1103–6, 1107–9) would bring about. He also recommended to Ts'ai Ching the recruitment of righteous scholars, proposing especially Yang Shih (1053–1135). See Sun Ch'i-feng, *Li-hsüeh tsung-chuan,* op. cit., 15:1b–2a.

11. See Wu's memorial declining the offer, in his *Collected Writings, K'ang-chai chi,* Imperial Collection Rare Books series, 8:1a–4a.

12. Ibid., 8:4a–12b.

13. Chu Hsi, *hao* K'ao-t'ing.

14. See Preface to "The Ch'ung-jen School," notes 4 and 5.

15. *K'an-chai chi,* ch. 11.

16. Ku Hsien-ch'eng, *hao* Chin-yang. See his biography. This description of Wu may be translated as saying, "Wu is endowed with a transparent nature." The reference to *ch'i* alludes to the philosophy of *ch'i* as well as to the theory concerning physical endowment (*ch'i-chih*) that was developed by the Sung thinkers. See the Glossary of Technical Terms.

17. Reference to the sage ministers of antiquity.

18. See Ch'en Ch'ien (1497–1567) biography by Lien-chi Tu Fang, *DMB,* v. 1, 148–50. His *Huang Ming t'ung-chi* (1555), 27 ch., is an annal of the Ming dynasty from its beginning to the end of the Cheng-te period (1521).

19. Hsüeh Ying-ch'i, *hao* Fang-shan (1500–73), is included in *MJHA,* ch. 25. See his biography by Mou Jun-sun and L. C. Goodrich, *DMB,* v. 1, 619–22. His *Hsien-chang lu* gives the yearly account of government from 1368 to 1521.

20. For Chang Yüan-chen, see *MJHA,* ch. 45.

21. See also the "Quotations from Liu" *(Shih-shuo).*

22. Yang Shih-ch'iao, posthumous honorific Tuan-chieh. *MJHA,* ch. 42.

23. Yin Chih, 1427–1511, was a Hanlin compiler. See Yang Ming's biography by Hok-lam Chan, *DMB,* v. 2, 1523–25. Yin's *Chien-chai so-chui lu* collects gossip about Wu.

24. See Hu Chü-jen's biography in this volume.

25. Ku Yün-ch'eng, *hao* Chin-jan, was Ku Hsien-ch'eng's younger brother

(*MJHA*, ch. 62). He and others do not appear to have seen this clan genealogy, which Wu included in his *Collected Writings*. See also Heinrich Busch, "The Tung-lin Academy," 145.

26. Huang Tsung-hsi appears to believe in the existence of Wu's postscript to Shih's genealogy, although he condones Wu's action here.

Hu Chü-jen

Hu Chü-jen, *tzu* Shu-hsin (1434–84),[1] was a native of Yü-kan, Jao-chou (Kiangsi). Scholars called him Master Ching-chai. Soon after he was capped [when barely twenty], he enthusiastically set his mind to the learning of sages and worthies. He went to study at the school of Master Wu Yü-pi and subsequently gave up his intention of taking civil service examinations. Instead, he built a house in the Mei-hsi Mountain[2] and, aside from serving his parents and the work of teaching, did not involve himself in worldly affairs. Later, desiring to broaden his experience, he traveled to Fukien, passed through Chekiang, arrived at Nanking, and returned home by route of the Po-yang Lake. Wherever he went, he searched out and visited scholars who pursued true learning. On his return, together with his fellow provincials Lou Liang, Lo Lun, and Chang Yüan-chen, he formed associations at Kuei-feng in Yi-yang (Kiangsi) and at Ying-t'ien temple in Yü-kan. The education intendants, Li Ling[3] and Chung Ch'eng, successively requested him to take charge of the White Deer Academy.[4] A group of students later also invited him to teach at the Tung-yüan Academy in Kuei-hsi (Kiangsi). The prince of Huai,[5] who had heard of Hu's reputation, invited him to lecture on the *Book of Changes* at the princely residence. Indeed, the prince desired to publish Hu's poems and essays, but Hu declined the offer, saying, "I need yet to improve them."

Hu was firm and severe toward himself, lived in poverty, and disciplined himself rigidly. He set up for himself a daily order and recorded in detail his good deeds and his mistakes, all for his self-examination. He carefully marked every small thing and article, keeping each in perfect order. When his father was sick, he even tasted the stool to test the severity of the illness.[6] Whenever his elder brother returned home from travel, he went out to the gate to greet him; every time the brother was ill, he personally mixed the medicine for him. In observing mourning for his parents, he refrained even from broth until his bones stood out like withered branches, and he was unable to rise without a staff. He did not enter his own bedroom for those three years [but slept by the site of the graves]. In every one of his actions, he followed ancient rituals rather than prevalent customs. While seeking a propitious grave for his father by divination, he was harassed by a fellow villager and, reluctantly, had to bring the case to court. So he went to the magistrate's office dressed in a heavy mourning garment, and many people laughed at him.[7]

The Hu family had been farmers for generations. By Hu's time, they were quite poor. Yet in spite of shabby clothing and coarse food, Hu Chü-jen was a picture of contentment and said of his life: "To nurture the body with humility and righteousness and the house with some books [literally, "with book labels"] is quite enough for me."[8]

Hu died on April 7, 1484, at age fifty. He was enshrined in the Confucian temple in 1585. His whole life was spent in practicing reverence, and his achievements are noteworthy. Chou Ying[9] said of him:

> The reaches of your learning have depths I cannot fathom;
> Its direction is correct—of that I have no doubt.
> Had your years and months been longer, each day could bring more gains.
> Alas that life is not forever: your progress has been cut short by time.

This is the established judgment.

Hu's description of self-cultivation in tranquility is in the words: having a master (*yu-chu*).[10] This has served scholars especially well. And this is precisely what Ch'en Hsien-chang[11] called "the beginnings (*tuan-ni*) [of wisdom] nurtured in tranquility, in possession of which I can do what I wish in daily responses and activities, since I am like a horse guided by bit and bridle."[12] How fitting that Hu and Ch'en, as disciples of the same master, should concur thus in silence. But Hu insisted on criticizing Ch'en for being a Ch'an Buddhist. He reiterated this opinion in his writings.[13] For Hu was an extremely cautious (*chüan*) Confucian while Ch'en was very audacious (*k'uang*) (i.e., less concerned with judgments of orthodoxy). But one need not doubt the correctness of one for the sake of the judgment of the other.

Hu was especially ardent in refuting Buddhists. He said, "They conjure up their Way and its principles. What they see is not true."[14] He also said, "They empty the mind, kill the mind, and manipulate the mind."[15] But all these criticisms cannot adequately convince the Buddhists of their errors. It is simply not true to say that Buddhists have no true insights. What happens is that their minds first die and then live again; they are first manipulated and then become luminous. What they call true emptiness is actually wondrous being. This is not where they are so close to principle as to be like truth.

In the flow of process, cosmic transformation makes no distinction between day and night and permits no pause. To view this [Great Transformation] under the form of change is to see *ch'i*. But it also waxes and wanes, fills up and empties out, as summer always follows spring, and autumn always turns to winter. Men cannot change into things, nor things into men. Grass does not turn into trees, nor trees into grass; it has been always like this since antiquity. To view the Great

Transformation under the form of constancy, one finds *li*. This is also the case with men. The things that change in man are pleasure, anger, sorrow, and joy, sometimes aroused, sometimes at peace. That which alternates between activity and tranquility, going from one to the other without end, is mind. The things that do not change are commiseration, shame, deference, and a sense of right and wrong. That which experiences many confusions and yet does not prevent the seeds of goodness from sprouting anew is nature. The Confucian Way is to acquire that which does not change in that which always changes. Only after this will mind and principle *(li)* become one. The Buddhists merely see the *t'i* (reality) in the flow process, with its unfathomable changes. So they consider the stream of consciousness itself to be nature. Taking the functioning *(tso-yung)* of consciousness to be that which reveals nature, they identify the unborn and undying *(nirvāṇa)* with that which is constantly changing. After peeling off layers of reality, they leave no single *dharma* behind. According to them, the transformations of Heaven and Earth and the myriad things are also our transformations, while that which remains unchanging in the midst of change itself no longer has any place. But if *li* is completely good, *ch'i* is mixed, complex and uneven in its interaction, giving rise to such variations as the clear, the muddled, the partial, and the straight. And although nature is completely good, mind has its modes of activity and tranquility, of response and passivity, which may be either genuine or not genuine. In taking constant change as reality *(t'i)*, the Buddhists have no choice but to follow its constant flow, so that reckless and wild effects become principles of nature. Even when they practice quiet-sitting and allow their minds to wither away, their aim is not to preserve mind and nurture nature but to see this *t'i* in its flow of consciousness. They really see what they claim to see, even if Confucians (like Hu Chü-jen) say that what they see is not real, but only a semblance of the real. That is why the more the Confucians [like Hu] seek to curb them, the more their influence actually grows.

In discussing methods of government, Hu maintained that as long as the ancient custom of farmer-soldiers *(yü-ping)*[16] remained defunct, the practice of military colonization *(tun-t'ien)*[17] ought to be followed, and as long as the practice of regional recommendation of worthy men *(pin-hsing)* remained defunct, a method of simple recommendation might be followed.[18] On the well-field system, Hu suggested that one take the field to be "mother," dividing it into plots of fixed size, and the people as "sons" who, in groups of larger or smaller size (depending on population fluctuations), should be given plots of fixed size.[19] On the appointment of officials, Hu proposed that, although major officials should be appointed by the court, and their higher staff should be reported to the court for approval, the other subordinate positions should be filled by the officials themselves.[20] Such are not the words of a regressive scholar. Should a true king arise, he ought to heed this advice.

(*MJHA* 2:1a–2a)

NOTES

1. See Hu's biography by Julia Ching, *DMB*, v. 1, 625–27.

2. For an account of the house in the Mei-hsi Mountain see his *Collected Writings, Hu Ching-chai chi,* CYTC ed., 2:5b–6b. It was built in 1465 after a move from Ta-yüan in An-jen Prefecture back to Yü-kan. Hu describes his property as being on the crest of a hill surrounded by fields, woods, pastures, streams, and mountains. The house itself had mud plaster walls, a thatched roof, and was surrounded by a windbreak of bamboos.

3. For Li Ling, see Mao Te-ch'i, *Po-lu shu-yüan chih* (On the White Deer Academy) (1795 ed.), 3:2b–3a. As an education intendant Li became involved with the White Deer Academy in 1467. He expanded the number of buildings, acquired support fields for it, and replaced its sacrificial vessels, besides expanding its library and inviting Hu to become its master.

4. The White Deer Academy, one of the oldest and most famous of Chinese academies *(shu-yüan)*, was located on Mount Lu north of Po-yang Lake in northern Kiangsi. See Mao Te-ch'i, op. cit., and Lu Kuang-huan, "The *Shu-yüan* Institution Developed by Sung-Ming Neo-Confucian Philosophers," *Chinese Culture* 9 (September, 1968), 98–122. It was particularly important after its revival by Chu Hsi around the year 1180. Hu Chü-jen served as its headmaster on two occasions: the first time, summoned by Li Ling, from late 1467 to 1468; the second time, invited by Chung Ch'eng, around 1480. Between 1468 and the later date, he mourned the deaths of his mother (1468) and his wife (1478) and endured a period of illness. See his *Chronological Biography (Nien-p'u)*, 18a.

5. The prince of Huai was Chu Ch'i-chüan (d. 1502). Hu delivered his lecture in 1483. See *DMB*, p. 627.

6. See the epitaph, by Kao Ming, in Yang Lien et al., *Huang-Ming ming-ch'en yen-hsing lu* (On Famous Ming Officials), 4:104b.

7. The sources for this incident and the subsequent court case are vague and conflicting. The *Jao-chou fu-chih*, 18:10b, contains the most complete account and says that after a grave site had been selected by divination, a local scoundrel dug it up—or in some way violated it. Hu replied by saying: "While I dare not offend the officials with a litigation case lacking substance, the outrage to my father is such that I have sworn not to live under the same heaven with that rogue." But, as it turned out, the rogue managed to turn the case around and have Hu thrown into jail. Ch'en Hsien-chang then wrote a letter on Hu's behalf to a local official who finally rescued him from jail and obtained justice for him. A different account appears in Chang Chi's preface to Hu's *Chü-yeh lu*. He notes that Hu had been very exacting about selecting a proper site for his father's grave and had been troubled so much by a local scoundrel that he had no choice but to sue the man. Wearing the heavy mourning robes prescribed by ancient rituals, he went to the local magistracy to press his case. But since the ancient burial and mourning rites in question had long become obsolete, his strange behavior was judged sympathetically by those who regarded him as an upright scholar and ridiculed by others who could not understand.

8. Literally, *ya-ch'ien,* or ivory labels. Chinese books used to be mounted on scrolls, laid on shelves, each scroll with a label hanging from the end of the roller for quick identification.

9. Chou Ying, *hao* Ts'ui-ch'ü, *chin-shih* of 1469. See *MJHA,* ch. 46. He was a friend of both Hu and Ch'en Hsien-chang, although he disagreed with Ch'en on a number of issues and agreed with Hu on the importance of practicing reverence.

10. See, for example, Hu's *Chü-yeh lu,* CYTC ed., 1:4b, 2:2b–3b.

11. Ch'en Hsien-chang, *hao* Po-sha. See his biography in this volume.

12. See Ch'en Hsien-chang, *Po-sha-tzu ch'üan-chi* (Complete Works), 1771 ed., bk. 3, ch. 3, 22b–23a.

13. For Hu's criticisms of Ch'en, see *Chü-yeh lu,* 1:5a–12a–b.

14. For similar comments, see *Chü-yeh lu,* 7:5a–b, 6b, 7b.

15. An exact quotation from *Chü-yeh lu,* 7:7b.

16. For the farmer-soldiers *(yü-ping),* see *Chü-yeh lu,* 5:12b–13a.

17. *Tun-t'ien* refers to a system of self-supporting military colonies that engaged in both fighting and agriculture. It had been in use from the Han dynasty on. Hu's comments are in *Chü-yeh lu,* 5:13a, 15a–b. Huang Tsung-hsi himself has discussed such questions in his *Ming-yi tai-fang lu* (Taipei, Kuang-wen, 1965), 72–78.

18. *Pin-hsing* was a system of recommendation described in the *Institutes of Chou,* whereby village officials feasted local worthies and men of talent and recommended them to the lord. It developed into the recommendation of worthy candidates to the National University. Hu comments on *pin-hsing* and *chien-chü* systems in *Chü-yeh lu,* 5:6a–8b.

19. *Chü-yeh lu,* 5:10b–11a.

20. *Chü-yeh lu,* 5:5a–b.

Lou Liang

Lou Liang, *tzu* K'o-chen, *hao* Yi-chai (1422–91),[1] a native of Shang-jao, Kuang-hsin Prefecture (Kiangsi), resolved early to devote himself to the learning of the sages. He sought everywhere for a teacher without finding one, looking down on those [who aimed only at passing examinations], saying, "Preparing students for civil examinations has nothing to do with personal cultivation and the learning of the mind." He heard that Wu Yü-pi was at Lin-ch'uan and went to follow him. Wu was pleased to see him, saying, "I am perceptive and sharp-witted. You are the same." One day, Wu was cleaning the floor and summoned Lou to observe him, saying that the scholar should personally attend to small matters. Lou had been rather unrestrained; from that he learned to be humble and to attend personally to such matters as sweeping and cleaning, without leaving them to servants. In this way, he became a formal disciple of Wu's. Anything that Wu did not tell other disciples, he shared with Lou. Wu had a rule: he would only see those who came to study with him, but not others. Lo Lun[2] sought a visit with Wu before he had passed his examinations, but Wu would not receive him. Lou said to Wu, "This is a scholar known for his good resolutions. Why do you not receive him?" Wu replied, "Where can I find time to see this young man?" Lo Lun was displeased and wrote everywhere saying that Wu Yü-pi was doing strange things in the name of Confucianism. Chang Yüan-chen agreed and echoed all Lo said. Wu behaved as though he had heard nothing. Lou told these two men: "Gentlemen and small men cannot coexist. Should later generations consider Wu Yü-pi to be a small man, you will without doubt be considered gentlemen. But if later generations should judge Wu to be a gentleman, what would become of you two?" In this way he stopped them from further slandering.

In 1453 Lou Liang passed the provincial examinations. He went home and studied for another ten or more years, before setting out for the capital to take further examinations. However, after reaching Hangchow, he turned back home.[3] The following year, 1464, he went once more and failed, although his name appeared on the secondary list. He was appointed to a teaching position in Ch'eng-tu (Szechuan). Soon he was permitted to return home, where he devoted himself to writing books and educating the young. He wrote a daily record, *Jih-lu,* of 40 *chüan,* giving a pure teaching in an unadorned prose with no effort to please. He also compiled a critical study of the three classical ritual texts, *San-li ting-ô,* of 40 *chüan.* He considered *Chou-li,* which consists of rituals for the emperor, as a book laying down institutions for the state. He regarded *Yi-li,* which consists of the rituals for the nobility, for higher and lower officials, and for common people, as a book determining family regulations. Taking the *Book of Rites,* or *Li-chi,* to be entirely a group of commentaries on the other two Classics, he distributed its passages, attaching each to its related chapter, just as the essay "Definitions of Capping" *(kuan-yi)* is placed at the end of the chapter on capping ceremonies [in the *Yi-li*] *(kuan-li).* Passages from the *Book of Rites* that could not be attached to any chapter were grouped as appendices to either one Classic or to both, following the example by which the "Great Treatise" *(Hsi-tz'u chuan)* has been appended to the *Book of Changes.* Besides, thirteen passages, added improperly to the *Book of Rites* by various scholars, were eliminated after consultation of the studies by Ch'eng Yi and Chu Hsi. He also compiled the *Ch'un-ch'iu pen-yi,* 12 *p'ien,* using only explications of the text of the *Spring-Autumn Annals* to allow the meaning of the classic to become clear, with no reference to its three commentaries.[4] He said, "If the *Spring-Autumn Annals* had to await its three commentaries to be made clear, then the *Spring-Autumn Annals* would be itself a useless book."

Lou regarded the doctrine of recovery of the lost mind (*Mencius* 6A: 11) as the starting point for "abiding in reverence"; "what thought and deliberation"[5] and "neither forgetting nor helping" (*Mencius* 2A: 2) as the essential doctrine of this abiding in reverence. He, Ch'en Hsien-chang, and Hu Chü-jen[6] were the most famous disciples of the school of Wu Yü-pi. Lou and Ch'en were also the two whom Hu criticized the most. Hu said that both were Confucians who had drifted into hetero-dox teachings, but that Lou was ready to investigate principles where Lu Chiu-yüan[7] was not, and to study books where Ch'en Hsien-chang was not; however, in Lou's case, investigation of principles and the study of books only served to have sages' and worthies' sayings support his own opinions. Lou's books are lost and cannot be seen,[8] but these words of Hu's show that he did not just copy his teacher. Hu also said, "When Lou saw a man carrying wood in a proper way, he would say that this man had the Tao. It is like [the story of Hui-neng][9] carrying water and moving firewood. He regarded consciousness and its opera-tions as nature and so spoke that way." Although it is true that there is no place where the Tao is not found, only what is in accord with ethical teachings and without selfishness should be regarded as Tao. How could the wood carrier be said to possess it? For although the wood carrier need not know the Tao, to carry wood in a proper manner is to be in accord with ethical teachings and should not be said to be contrary to the Tao. It is only that his action is not manifest, and his practice is not noticed. Lou's words are not therefore incorrect.

Lou practiced tranquility long and achieved special understanding. When he traveled to Hangchow and then turned back, people asked for his reasons. Lou answered, "Going to Peking at this time would not only yield no success, but would even bring about a disaster." That year the examination hall caught fire, and many candidates died. When Mount Lin collapsed, Lou said, "This means my turn has come." So he quickly summoned his children for the final farewell and instructed his disciple Ts'ai Teng to check the dates of death of Chou Tun-yi and the Ch'engs. Then he said, "Both Master Chou and Master Ch'eng died in the summer months. What regret then have I? It was July 3, 1491, and he was sixty-nine years old. His disciples gave him the private honorific of Wen-su. Lou's son Lou Hsing was a bureau director in the ministry of war. Lou Hsing's daughter married the prince of Ning (Chu Ch'en-hao). When the latter rebelled, Lou's descendants were all imprisoned and his writings were allowed to be lost, so that his students became inferior to the students of Ch'en Hsien-chang and Hu Chü-jen. But when Wang Yang-ming was sixteen years old and on his way to meet his bride, he passed Kuang-hsin, visited Lou,[10] asked him about his teach-ings, and was happy with his answers. So the learning of Wang Yang-ming might be said to have as its source the teaching of Lou Liang. Lou's son Lou Ch'en, *tzu* Ch'eng-shan, *hao* Ping-hsi, remained in retirement and did not come down from upstairs for ten years. So many people came to listen to him that a monastery was not big enough to hold them all. One of his disciples even built a tree house with wood in order to study in it.

(*MJHA* 2:8a–9a)

NOTES

1. For Lou Liang, see the biography by Julia Ching and Huang P'ei, *DMB*, v. 1, 989–90. (Note that there are a few errors concerning Lou's writings that have been set straight here, thanks to Chaoying Fang).

2. For Lo Lun, *hao* Yi-feng, see *MJHA*, ch. 45.

3. The reason for such strange behavior will be explained later in this biography.

4. The three commentaries refer to the three forms under which the *Spring-Autumn Annals* were allegedly transmitted: the *Annals of Tso*, the *Kung-yang*, and *Ku-liang*.

5. Allusion to the *Book of Changes*, "Appended Remarks," pt. 2, ch. 5. See J. Legge, trans., *Yi King*, 389.

6. See their respective biographies in this volume.

7. Reference to the Sung philosopher.

8. Lou's books were lost after the unsuccessful rebellion of the prince of Ning, Chu Ch'en-hao, who was married to Lou's granddaughter.

9. Reference to the Ch'an Buddhist patriarch, an illiterate made to do hard work at the monastery of his master, Hung-jen. See *The Platform Sutra of the Sixth Patriarch*, trans. by Philip Yampolsky (New York, 1967), 127–28.

10. Huang Tsung-hsi takes this episode in Wang Yang-ming's life seriously enough to have arranged his book so that the school of Wu Yü-pi, Lou's teacher, heads the book, preparing the way for the appearance of Wang Yang-ming himself, considered, through his brief association with Lou, an heir to Wu's teachings.

2.   The Po-sha[1] School

With Ch'en Hsien-chang, Ming learning started to become precise and subtle. The effort he emphasized is entirely that of interior cultivation: of a state that is prior to joy and anger and yet not empty, and of a state that is amid ten thousand entangled emotions and yet unmoved.[2]

This teaching gained importance with the rise of Wang Yang-ming. The teachings of the two masters (Ch'en and Wang) are extremely close. I do not know why Yang-ming never mentioned Ch'en. But his close disciple, Hsüeh K'an, was responsible for submitting a memorial in 1509 [*sic*] requesting for Ch'en a place in the temple of Confucius. He must have recognized the similarities between his master's and Ch'en's teachings.[3]

Lo Lun once said: "Ch'en Hsien-chang contemplated the subtle relationship between Heaven and man and probed deeply into the collected wisdom of sages and worthies. For him, fulfilling the Way is wealth, esteeming virtue is honor. While the world held many lovely and desirable things, he remained utterly unmoved in their midst."

How true is this statement! For this reason, many of his followers embraced a life of honorable poverty and independence with no regard for wealth and honors. Ch'en's moral influence was far-reaching indeed.

NOTES

1. Po-sha is the other name of Ch'en Hsien-chang. See Ch'en's biography by Julia Ching and Huang P'ei, in *DMB*, v. 1, 153–56.

2. Reference is to the *Doctrine of the Mean*, ch. 1.

3. See Hsüeh's biography. See also W. T. Chan, trans., *Instructions*, p. 53, n. 85. Huang Tsung-hsi gives a wrong date (1509). It should have been 1530, although the request then was denied, and Ch'en was admitted to the temple much later.

Ch'en Hsien-chang

Ch'en Hsien-chang, *tzu* Kung-fu (1428–1500),[1] was a native of Po-sha village in Hsin-hui (Kwangtung). Ch'en was eight (Chinese) feet tall with eyes that shone like stars. He had seven black spots on his right cheek, in the shape of the Great Dipper. From youth on, he surpassed others in intelligence, being able to memorize books after a single reading. Once, after reading what Mencius said about "the subjects of Heaven" *(T'ien-min)*,[2] he sighed and said, "Such is the kind of man one ought to become." He dreamed that he was plucking a stone lute and making a deep, resonant sound. Someone said to him, "Of the eight sounds,[3] that produced by stone is hardest to harmonize, and yet you are able to do so. You should some day acquire the Tao." As a result of this dream, Ch'en took the additional name Shih-chai or "Stone Studio."

In 1447, Ch'en passed the provincial examination in Kwangtung. The following year he took the metropolitan examination and was placed on the secondary list. So he went to study at the National University. Later he went to Ch'ung-jen (Kiangsi) to study under Wu Yü-pi.[4] On returning home, he gave up his earlier intention to take civil service examinations and built instead a dwelling called the "Sunny Spring Terrace," where he practiced quiet-sitting, without ever leaving its doors for several years. Shortly afterwards, he suffered a family disaster.[5] In 1446, he re-entered the National University. The chancellor, Hsing Jang, tested him by requesting him to match a certain poem by Yang Shih, "This Day Cannot Come Back."[6] His composition caused Hsing to exclaim with astonishment, "Even Yang Shih cannot compare with this man." Hsing spread word at court that a true Confucian had once more appeared in the world. As a result, Ch'en's fame shook the imperial capital. Lo Lun,[7] Chang Mao,[8] Chuang Ch'ang,[9] and Ho Ch'in[10] all regretted not having met him earlier, and Ho even studied under him.

On his return home from the capital, Ch'en received even more disciples. In 1482 he was recommended to the government by both P'eng Shao, the administration commissioner, and Chu Ying, the censor-in-chief. P'eng[11] memorialized the emperor, saying, "This country regards humane and worthy men as treasures. I, your minister, consider myself far behind Ch'en Hsien-chang in talent and virtue and yet enjoy an undeserved high position, while Ch'en is allowed to grow old in obscurity. I am afraid we are losing the services of a state treasure."[12] Ch'en was then summoned to the imperial capital (1483). But the ranking ministers of the secretariat tried to make things hard for him, ordering him to take a test at the ministry of personnel. Pleading illness, he declined and submitted a memorial requesting permission to go home and care for his mother. The emperor granted him the position of Hanlin corrector and let him go home. When someone pointed out to Ch'en that he had acted differently from Wu Yü-pi,[13] Ch'en replied, "My late teacher was recommended by Shih Heng and would not therefore accept a position. As a student of the National University awaiting selection to office, I have always been willing to serve in government, and I dare not fish for an empty reputation by means of false pretenses. My accepting a position and my teacher's not accepting one were both correct." However, in spite of repeated recommendations, he never again emerged from his life in retirement. He died at age seventy-two on March 10, 1500. When he was seriously ill, the county magistrate, a certain Tso, came to him with a doctor. A disciple went in to Ch'en and said, "Nothing can be done for the illness." Yet Ch'en said, "We should give satisfaction to the feelings of a friend." So he drank a spoonful of the medicine before sending the magistrate away.

In his [philosophical] teaching, Ch'en regarded emptiness as the foundation and tranquility as the entry point. He took the meeting and convergence of the four directions, the high and low of space, the past and present of time, to be the context, the differentiations of daily actions and common practices to be efforts and functions. He further considered "neither neglecting nor assisting [the work of cultivation]"[14] as a rule for personal realization and functioning well without exerting effort as real progress. No doubt he would have been a Tseng Tien[15] in ancient times or a Shao Yung in more modern times. On account of his teaching, many Confucians of the Ming period did not lose their standards for the good life. Only with him did the effort of acquiring sagehood become clear to be further developed by Wang Yang-ming. Had

Ch'en Hsien-chang and Wang Yang-ming not appeared in the world, those who agreed with Chou Tun-yi[16] and the Ch'eng brothers[17] would still have perceived and inferred from the hidden meaning of the subtle and profound teachings of Chou and the Ch'engs, while others who disagreed with them would have clarified their differences. But they would not have done as well as they are doing today.

It has been said that Ch'en's teachings were close to those of Ch'an Buddhism for two reasons. First, the learning of the sages has long been declining. Scholars have been pursuing nonessential things, knowing activity but not tranquility. As a result, anyone touching upon the subject of the "state of consciousness preceding that of tranquility in which man is born"[18] is said to border on heresy. Such opinions of foolish men are not worth refuting. Second, Lo Ch'in-shun[19] said, "Ch'en Hsien-chang has not been without merit in promoting the study of the Tao in recent times, but I fear that certain errors in scholarship also began with him. 'That which is utmost nothingness is yet active, that which is nearest at hand is yet spiritual.'[20] This statement describes Ch'en's marvellous insights. But he merely perceived what was 'most spiritual'[21] and regarded it to be where the Tao resides. He was unable to reach the depth or to examine the subtlety.[22] That is his shortcoming."[23] Throughout his life, Lo regarded mind and nature as two. So he criticized Ch'en for only understanding mind but not perceiving nature. This is actually Lo's error and no concern of Ch'en's.

In describing his own pursuit of learning, Ch'en said, "Only at the age of twenty-seven did I resolve to study with Wu Yü-pi. He taught me all the books that ancient sages and worthies handed down as instructions. But I still did not know the entrance into truth. After my return to Po-sha, I shut myself up at home without ever going out, devoting myself solely to the quest for a direction in applying my efforts. With no help from teachers or friends, I looked for this, relying daily on books and texts, forgetting to sleep and to eat, and continuing in this manner for many years without ultimately getting anywhere. What I mean by not having got anywhere refers to my mind and principle *(li)* not converging or tallying. So I forsook the complexities of book-learning and sought to find what was simple and essential within myself, and that, only by quiet-sitting. After a long time I saw my mind-in-itself emerging dimly, but as though it were a thing. In my daily life, I did all that I desired like a horse guided by bit and bridle. In realizing the meaning of things and in examining the teachings of sages, I found that each had its order and its origin, just as every stream has its source. So I became very self-confident and said, 'Could this not be the effort of becoming a sage?' "[24]

In describing Ch'en's pursuit of learning, Chang Hsü[25] said, "After

returning home from his visit with Wu Yü-pi, Ch'en practiced quiet-sitting in a room. Even his family rarely saw him. After a few years, he
still had not gotten anywhere. So he put aside these practices and went
singing loudly in the woods, whistling by himself on a solitary island,
boating and fishing in streams and estuaries. He forsook the knowledge
of his eyes and ears as well as that of his intellect. After a long while, he
finally acquired some insight. For by emphasizing tranquility, one
becomes able to perceive what is great. Having made efforts like this for
as long as twenty or more years, Ch'en came to the realization that all
that is broad and great, lofty and luminous, is not apart from daily life;
once the myriad affairs are seen in the light of one truth, they show their
own completeness without requiring human effort. So there is no opposition between the active and the tranquil, the inner and the outer, the
great and the small, the fine and the coarse."[26] Ch'en's learning proceeds from what is comprehensive to what is fine. So different is this
from the teaching of Ch'an Buddhism!

In *So-chui lu,* Yin Chih[27] said, "Soon after arriving in the imperial
capital, Ch'en secretly composed ten poems praising the eunuch Liang
Fang.[28] Fang spoke of him to the emperor, which led to his being
awarded a post. Later, when he requested permission to go home, he
left the imperial city, riding in a sedan chair with a canopy over his head
and armed guards clearing his way. He no longer behaved as in the
past. Ch'iu Chün[29] entered this story into the *Veritable Records of Emperor
Hsien-tsung.*[30] Ch'en can therefore be said to have left behind a tarnished
reputation in history."[31] On the other hand, [Hsüeh Ying-ch'i's] *Hsien-
chang lu*[32] maintained that the person who picked up this story and
recorded it was Chang Yüan-chen. Yet in his letter to Ch'en asking
about learning, Chang talked about the need for flexible moral principles and for spontaneous, free, and unrestrained demeanor.[33] He also
instructed disciples to present gifts to Ch'en, whom he deeply admired.
So, although he did send Ch'en poems, expressing his feeling that
Ch'en's learning resembled that of Ch'an Buddhism, it would be contrary to reason to suppose that he would have entered into historical
records such a fabrication [as mentioned above]. Ch'iu Chün, on the
other hand, was sharp and caustic, fond of advancing and loath to
retreat. This was first seen in the case of Chuang Ch'ang and again in
the case of Ch'en Hsien-chang. He was not so different from Yin
Chih.[34]

In 1585, an edict ordered Ch'en to be enshrined in the Confucian
temple, with the title of "the late [honored] Confucian scholar *(Hsien-ju)*
Master Ch'en." His posthumous honorific was Wen-kung.

(*MJHA* 5:1a–3b)

NOTES

1. See his biography by Julia Ching and Huang P'ei, *DMB*, v. 1, 153–56.

2. *Mencius* 7A:19.

3. Eight sounds produced from instruments of calabash, earthenware, stretched hides, wood, stone, metal, silk strings, and bamboo.

4. For Wu Yü-pi, see his biography. Ch'en went to study under Wu in 1454.

5. In 1454 after Ch'en failed the metropolitan examination, he went back home but on his way stopped at Ch'ung-jen to study under Wu Yü-pi. Thereafter he stayed home for ten years to study, which meant that he followed Wu's example and refused to take civil examinations. It seems that in 1464 he came out of retirement and collected some students to practice archery together. This apparently aroused the suspicion of local authorities, who probably investigated him and his family. Perhaps this is what Huang Tsung-hsi meant by the family disaster. It is recorded that a magistrate advised Ch'en to stop such military exercises and resume his career as a candidate for the civil service, in order not to cause his mother further worries. Following this advice, Ch'en re-entered the university in 1466.

6. This poem is included in Yang's *Kuei-shan chi*, Imperial Catalogue ed. (Taipei, 1973), 38:1a–2a. Yang Shih's dates were 1053–1135.

7. See *MJHA*, ch. 45.

8. Chang Mao, *hao* Feng-shan (1436–1521), *MJHA*, ch. 45.

9. Chuang Ch'ang, known as Master Ting-shan (1437–99), *MJHA*, ch. 45.

10. Ho Ch'in, *hao* Yi-lü (1437–1510). See his biography by Julia Ching and Huang P'ei, *DMB*, v. 1, 509–10.

11. Inserted according to Ch'en's biography, which identified the memorial as P'eng Shao's. See his *Collected Writings, Po-sha-tzu ch'üan-chi* (Taipei, 1973), Addend 5a.

12. I have not been able to locate the original memorial.

13. See Wu's biography in this volume.

14. *Mencius* 2A:2.

15. A disciple of Confucius. See *Analects* 2:25 and W. T. Chan's translation and comment, *A Source Book of Chinese Philosophy*, 37–38. Tseng was well known for his spirit of freedom.

16. Chou Tun-yi, *tzu* Mao-shu (1017–73). *SYHA*, ch. 11.

17. Ch'eng Hao, *hao* Ming-tao (1032–85), and Ch'eng Yi, *hao* Yi-ch'uan (1033–1107). *SYHA*, ch. 13.

18. From the *Book of Rites*. See James Legge, trans., *The Li Ki* (Oxford, 1885), v. 2 (SBE, v. 28), 96.

19. Lo Ch'in-shun, Wen-chuang being his posthumous honorific. See his biography in this volume.

20. A famous saying of Ch'en's. See his letter to Chang Yüan-chen, in *Po-sha-tzu ch'üan-chi*, 2:13a.

21. Ibid.

22. Ibid.

23. *K'un-chih chi* (1622 ed.), 2:24a. Huang gives here almost an exact quotation except for minor differences in wording.

24. *Po-sha-tzu ch'üan-chi* 2:27a–b.

25. Chang Hsü, *hao* Tung-so (1455–1514).

26. *Po-sha-tzu ch'üan-chi*, Supplements, 20a–b.

27. Yin Chih, *hao* Chien-chai (fl. 1454).

28. The eunuch Liang was a powerful figure between the years 1476 and 1487. See his biography by Chaoying Fang, *DMB,* v. 1, 896–98.

29. Ch'iu Chün's posthumous honorific was Wen-an. See his biography by Chi-hua Wu and Ray Huang, *DMB,* v. 1, 249–52. (The text here twice calls him Wen-chuang by mistake.)

30. Emperor Hsien-tsung reigned from 1465 to 1487. See his biography (Chu Chien-shen) by Liu Lin-sheng and Lienche Tu Fang, *DMB,* v. 1, 298–305.

31. Yin Chih, *Chien-chai so-chui lu* (Taipei, 1969), 184–85.

32. See Wu Yü-pi's biography, note 21.

33. Ch'en's reply to Chang's inquiry is in *Po-sha-tzu ch'üan-chi,* 2:13a–14b.

34. The reason Ch'iu Chün is identified here instead of Lo Ch'in-shun (Wen-chuang) is that Huang was discussing, who—Chang Yüan-chen or Ch'iu Chün—was responsible for recording in the *Veritable Records* the story of Ch'en's changed behavior. Ch'iu participated in the compilation of these records.

3.   The Ho-tung[1] School

The teachings of the Ho-tung school are solid and unadorned, in careful accord with the standards laid down by the Sung scholars. Even after several generations of transmission and without asking questions, one can still determine from discussions and deportment those who are followers of the Ho-tung school. To the contrary, among the followers of Wang Yang-ming, even his closest disciples frequently departed from the master's teachings, precisely because he said things that were too sublime.[2]

However, Hsüeh Hsüan has been derided for lacking insight into human nature. But he did say that "this mind now senses that nature and Heaven are one."[3] This was certainly not said in deception. It rather shows that he did not seek to display his own achievements.

NOTES

1. Literally, east of the Yellow River, Ho-tung refers to the region centering on Honan.

2. Reference to Wang Chi and Wang Ken. See their biographies in this volume.

3. See Hsüeh's biography in this volume.

Hsüeh Hsüan

Hsüeh Hsüan,[1] whose *tzu* was Te-wen and whose *hao* was Ching-hsüan (1389–1464), was a man of Ho-chin in Shansi. He was born after his mother dreamed of a visit from a man clothed in purple. At birth, the texture of his skin was like crystal and his five viscera were all visible, which astonished the members of his family. Upon hearing him cry, the grandfather exclaimed, "This is not an ordinary child." In his youth, he was able to recite books after only a single glance. His father, Hsüeh Chen, an instructor at Yung-yang, Honan, had heard that the two masters Wei and Fan were accomplished in the philosophy of *li*. (Master Wei, whose name was Ch'un and whose *tzu* was Hsi-wen, was a man of Kao-mi in Shantung. Master Fan's identity awaits inquiry.)[2] So he sent Hsüeh Hsüan to study with them and follow instructions in the various works of Chou Tun-yi and the Ch'eng brothers. [Greatly impressed], Hsüeh sighed, saying, "These works chart the correct course for learning." So he completely abandoned his previous studies.

When his father was transferred to teach at Yen-ling, Honan, Hsüeh Hsüan enrolled there as a student. He placed first in the Honan provincial examination in 1420 and achieved the *chin-shih* degree a year later. Early in the Hsüan-te period (1426–34), he was appointed as a censor. The three Yangs[3] desired to gain his acquaintance and sent someone to invite him. He declined, saying, "As someone in charge of censorial matters, how dare I have private visits with high officials?" The three Yangs sighed in admiration.

While on a mission as inspector of silver mines in Hukuang, Hsüeh copied the book *Hsing-li ta-ch'üan*[4] in his own hand, staying up all night without sleep. He also recorded his insights as they occurred to him. When Emperor Ying-tsung ascended the throne (1435), he was sent out to Shantung as assistant surveillance commissioner of education; in this capacity he emphasized the primacy of earnest personal practice over arts and letters and was popularly acclaimed "Master Hsüeh."

At that time, the eunuch Wang Chen was in power and asked the three Yangs, "Of my fellow provincials, who is worthy of high office?" They all suggested Hsüeh. So he was summoned to become vice minister[5] of the grand court of revision (1441). The three Yangs wanted him to go and thank Wang Chen. Hsüeh refused. Then they sent Li Hsien[6] to persuade him further. Hsüeh responded to Li by saying, "So you, too, say such things. But to serve as public official at court and yet thank a private person for it is something I cannot do." Later when Hsüeh met Wang Chen in the East Hall in the palace, he merely bowed, without prostrating himself, while other officials all knelt down. So Wang Chen grew to hate him.

It so happened that a jailor died of illness. His concubine wanted to remarry, but the principal wife would not hear of it. So the concubine charged the wife with contributing to the husband's death. Hsüeh exposed the falsity of the charge. Acting upon Wang Chen's wishes, the censor-in-chief Wang Wen impeached Hsüeh for this verdict. Hsüeh refuted Wang Wen in court. Nevertheless, Wang Wen had him imprisoned and condemned to death, claiming that the defendant was not satisfied with Hsüeh's handling of the trial. While in prison, Hsüeh read the *Book of Changes* without stopping. When he failed in his appeal and was about to be executed, an old servant of Wang Chen's, who was also a man of Shansi, wept by the kitchen stove. Surprised, Wang Chen asked the servant why and got the reply, "I weep because I heard that Master Hsüeh will soon be executed." Wang Chen asked him again, "How do you know that there is this Master Hsüeh?" He answered that Hsüeh was a fellow provincial, and then proceeded to tell Wang Chen about Hsüeh's life. Wang Chen was disconcerted and immediately ordered that Hsüeh be exiled to the frontier instead. Shortly thereafter, he was released and allowed to return home.

Early in the Ching-t'ai era (1449–56), Hsüeh was recalled to be chief minister of the grand court of revision in Nanking. During famine, the starving people of Soochow and Sung-chiang[7] were unable to borrow any grain. [In anger] they set fire to the houses of those who stored grain. Wang Wen accused them of plotting rebellion. Hsüeh defended them in a memorial of protest and provoked Wang Wen into saying, "This old man is as stubborn as ever." When the eunuch Chin Ying[8] was dispatched on a mission and passed through Nanking, the high officials there held a feast for him on the Yangtze River. Hsüeh was the only one who did not attend. On his return to the imperial capital, Ying said to a number of people, "Minister Hsüeh is the only good official in Nanking."

In autumn of 1452, Hsüeh was called back to the imperial capital to serve in his old capacity as chief minister of the grand court of revision. After Emperor Ying-tsung was restored to the throne (1457), he joined the grand secretariat with a new rank of right vice-minister of rites and, concurrently, as chancellor of the Hanlin academy. When Yü Ch'ien[9] and Wang [Wen], then junior guardians of the heir-apparent, were condemned to be executed, Hsüeh said to his colleagues, "This Yü-Wang incident is well known to all. But we all have children and grandchildren."[10] The remark enraged Shih Heng,[11] who said, "The matter has already been settled. There is no need for further talk." The emperor summoned the ministers of the grand secretariat for a meeting during which Hsüeh said, "That Your Majesty has once more ascended the throne is the will of Heaven. Nevertheless, it is now springtime and severe punishments may not be applied." His colleagues were all speechless. The emperor ordered that the sentence for Yü and Wang be reduced by one degree (1457).[12] Returning from this meeting, Hsüeh sighed, saying, "To consider killing as an accomplishment is something that a humane man would not do."

One day, Hsüeh was summoned by the emperor to an audience in an auxiliary palace. As the emperor did not have his cap and gown in proper order, Hsüeh stood still at the door and did not enter. The emperor understood his meaning and changed the cap and gown immediately. Only then did he enter.

The emperor hated Shih Heng's overbearing manners. Returning from a court meeting, Hsü Yu-chen, Li Hsien and Hsü Pin divulged that the censor-in-chief Keng [Chiu-ch'ou][13] had ordered the censors to impeach Shih Heng. Hsüeh said to these gentlemen, "The *Book of Changes* warns against the failure to maintain secrecy. The *Spring-Autumn Annals* criticize the leaking of information. Your misfortune will begin with this." Soon afterwards, these gentlemen were all ordered to be imprisoned.

The emperor valued Hsüeh highly, considering him as mature and accomplished in both learning and practice. However, one day, in addressing the emperor, Hsüeh inadvertently called himself a student. As a result, the emperor's fondness for him cooled.[14] On his part, he was also aware that since Ts'ao Chi-hsiang[15] and Shih Heng were in power, it was not a time to practice the Way. So he requested permission to resign. Just before his departure, Yüeh Cheng[16] asked him for instruction. Hsüeh said, "Excessive display of brilliance is most harmful." Later when Yüeh fell from power, he recalled these words and said, "I am guilty of what he talked about."

Hsüeh remained at home for eight years, and many flocked there to study with him. He died on July 15, 1464, at age seventy-five, and left behind a poem which said,

After seventy-six years, with nothing to show,
This mind of mine senses the unity of nature and heaven.[17]

Hsüeh took restoring nature as his purpose and the practice of the teachings of Chou Tun-yi and the Ch'eng brothers as his goal. He wrote the *Tu-shu lu,* which is largely a commentary on the diagram of the Great Ultimate, the "Western Inscription," and the "Correction of Youthful Ignorance."[18] The work is frequently repetitious and disorganized. It was never properly edited. This is because Hsüeh did not intend to write a book but merely recorded what he had experientially realized in body and mind. He maintained that *li* and *ch'i* were neither prior nor posterior to each other,[19] since "There is no *li* without *ch'i,* and no *ch'i* without *li.*[20] This cannot be changed." However, he also said, "*Ch'i* gathers and disperses whereas *li* does not gather or disperse."[21] He further compared *li* and *ch'i* to sunlight and a flying bird, saying, "*Li* is like sunlight, while *ch'i* is like a flying bird. *Li* moves by riding on *ch'i* just as sunlight rides on the back of a bird. When the bird is flying, the light of the sun, although not away from its back, does not actually fly away with it and so continues to exist without interruption. Likewise, when *ch'i* moves, *li,* though not separate from it for a moment, does not actually disappear with it and so is never extinguished."[22]

I, Huang Tsung-hsi, personally consider *li* to be the *li* of *ch'i.* There can be no *li* if there is no *ch'i*. And if there is sunlight when there is no bird flying, there can also be birds flying when there is no sunlight. So sunlight and flying birds cannot serve as analogies for *li* and *ch'i*. To borrow the expression, "Great virtue is capable of mighty transformation,"[23] *ch'i* is inexhaustible and *li* too is inexhaustible. *Li* does not gather or disperse, but *ch'i* also does not gather or disperse. To borrow the expression, "Small virtue flows like a river current,"[24] and there is daily renewal[25] without cease. Past *ch'i* is not to be taken as future *ch'i*. Nor is past *li* to be taken as future *li*. Not only does *ch'i* gather and disperse, but *li* also gathers and disperses.

[With regard to *li* and *hsin*] Hsüeh said, "Even a fine hair becomes visible when the water is clear, so too does the heavenly principle become visible when the mind is pure."[26] He also used an analogy, saying, "*Li* is like a thing, and *hsin* [mind] a mirror. Just as a thing is fully reflected without distortion when the mirror is clean, so too is *li* without a trace of obscurity when the mind is luminous."[27]

I, Huang Tsung-hsi, personally consider *jen* to be the mind of man. That the mind cannot be *li* is due to obscuration. However, if the mind returns to its pure and luminous essence, it becomes *li*. To say that *li* becomes visible when the mind is pure is to regard *li* and *hsin* as two. But the return of the mind to its pure and luminous essence is what Hsüeh spoke of as "original capacity" *(pen-ling)*.[28] How can that be questioned?

Ts'ui Hsien[29] said, "Hsüeh got to the grand court of revision because of Wang Chen's help. Had he declined the position at the time without going to the capital, would it not have been better than resisting Wang Chen later and suffering thereby dire consequences? Moreover, Yü Ch'ien had merited well of the state and society. When he was condemned, Hsüeh did fight for him. But it would have been more honorable and heroic if, having fought without success, Hsüeh had left the government on this account."

In 1439, Lin Kan, prefect of Nan-an (Kiangsi), said in a memorial to the emperor, "Recently, the educational intendant Hsüeh Hsüan has tried to retrieve the rice stipends from students who have been dismissed from school because of illness. As your minister, I am of the opinion that if a student unfortunately becomes ill, he may be dismissed, but the rice stipends have already been spent up over the years. It is certainly difficult to try to retrieve them in a day. Moreover, no fathers and elder brothers can guarantee that their sons and younger brothers will not become ill. If we should inflict upon them the misery of repaying the stipends, who would be willing to send sons and younger brothers to school?" The emperor agreed with Lin Kan.

Hsüeh's conduct and integrity are not matters that a later scholar like myself dares to discuss lightly. But it may be said that Hsüeh was most admirable but not always perfect. Early in the Ch'eng-hua era (1465–87), he was given the honorific Wen-ch'ing. In the fifth year of the Lung-ch'ing era (1571), Emperor Mu-tsung ordered that he be enshrined in the Confucian temple with the title "the late [honored] Confucian scholar Master Hsüeh."

(*MJHA* 7:1a–2b)

NOTES

1. For Hsüeh Hsüan, see the biography by Cze-tong Song and J. Ching, *DMB,* v. 1, 616–19.

2. This parenthesis comes from the text of the *MJHA* itself.

3. Yang Shih-ch'i, Yang Jung, and Yang P'u, two of whom have biographies in *DMB,* by T. Grimm (v. 2, 1535–38) and Charles Hucker (v. 2, 1519–22).

4. Reference to the compendium compiled by Hu Kuang (1415) according to imperial order.

5. Huang Tsung-hsi had by mistake given his rank as "chief minister," which he did not become till much later.

6. Li Hsien, *tzu* Te-yüan, Wen-ta being his *hao.* See T. Grimm's biography of Li in *DMB,* v. 1, 819–22.

7. Both in modern Kiangsu.

8. See *DMB,* v. 1, 246–47.

9. Yü Ch'ien, later honorific Chung-shu; see biography by Wolfgang Franke, *DMB,* v. 2, 1608–11.

10. Note Hsüeh's generosity toward Wang Wen, who had not been kind to him. But the statement itself is a cryptic way of condemning an injustice.

11. See his biography by W. Franke, *DMB,* v. 2, 1202–4.

12. The sentence of lingering death, a most cruel form of punishment, was commuted to that of beheading.

13. See *DMB,* v. 1, 711–13. (Hsü Yu-chen, *tzu* T'ien-ch'üan; Hsü Pin, *tzu* Tao-chung.)

14. It was considered courteous for the Hanlin scholar to call himself a student when speaking to subordinates or equals but not when speaking to the emperor.

15. See *DMB,* v. 2, 1298–99.

16. Yüeh Cheng, *tzu* Chi-fang (1418–72).

17. The last two lines of a four-line poem, from his *Collected Works, Hsüeh Ching-hsüan hsien-sheng chi* (Kuang-li-hsüeh pei-k'ao edition, Preface 1702), 100b. This is also quoted by Liu Tsung-chou in *Shih-shuo.*

18. Reference to writings by Chou and Chang Tsai.

19. A prominent theme in the *Tu-shu lu* (1827 ed.), 2:19b, 3:2a, 21b, 4:14a–b, and *Tu-shu hsü-lu* (1827 ed.), 3:3a, 6b.

20. A direct quotation from *Tu-shu hsü-lu,* 12:3b.

21. A direct quotation from *Tu-shu lu,* 4:15b, 5:7b, 6:3a.

22. A direct quotation from *Tu-shu lu,* 5:7a–b.

23. Reference to the *Doctrine of the Mean,* ch. 30. In this biography, Huang Tsung-hsi gives his opinion of Hsüeh's philosophy in a solemn fashion, unusual for the *MJHA.* He is most emphatic about the interpenetration of *li* and *ch'i,* refusing to subordinate it to *li.* See also his Author's Preface to the book.

24. Ibid.

25. A concept derived from the *Great Learning,* ch. 2, and the *Book of Changes,* Great Appendix, section 1, ch. 5.

26. A direct quotation from *Tu-shu lu,* 2:1b.

27. A direct quotation from *Tu-shu lu,* 5:7a.

28. For Hsüeh Hsüan's use of this term, see *Tu-shu hsü-lu* 2:8a.

29. For Ts'ui Hsien, see *DMB,* v. 2, 1431.

4.　The San-yüan[1] School

The schools of Kuan-chung[2] generally admired Hsüeh Hsüan. These included the San-yüan school as an offshoot. Many of Wang Shu's disciples became known for their nobility of character. They had a favored native environment as well as the benefit of learning.

NOTES

1. San-yüan was a prefecture belonging to the present province of Shensi in northwestern China. The school was led by Wang Shu, a native of that place.

2. The schools of Kuan-chung were those deriving their teachings from Chang Tsai.

Wang Shu

Wang Shu, *tzu* Chung-kan, *hao* Chieh-an, later also called Shih-ch'ü (1416–1508),[1] was a native of San-yüan in Shensi. A *chin-shih* of 1448, he was selected a Hanlin bachelor. Wang's purpose in life was to help with the governing of the country. He was sent away [from the Hanlin post], made a judge, and then a deputy justice at the grand court of revision before his promotion to prefect of Yangchow (1454). While there, he requested relief aid for a famine but did not await a reply before distributing grain to the needy. In addition, he freed the population from forced labor on public works, such as digging dikes. For his accomplishments he was raised several grades to junior administrative commissioner of Kiangsi (1460) and transferred to Honan as senior administrative commissioner (1464). Because the many steep mountains of Honan had attracted, from the far west and nearer provinces, a migrant population who had turned to banditry, a new provincial administration was created with Wang as governor, with the rank of junior vice censor-in-chief. In this capacity he put down many raids, even those of [the rebels] Liu T'ung[2] and the monk Shih. After doing so, he sent out a proclamation to the migrants, asking them to return to their usual occupations. Then he had to go home to mourn his mother's death, after which he became governor of Honan and senior vice-minister of justice in Nanking (1468). Mourning for his father's death (1496) obliged him once more to return home, after which he was made senior vice-minister of justice (1471), this time also in charge of conservation work on the Grand Canal. Next, he was transferred to vice-minister of revenue in Nanking and senior assistant censor-in-chief and governor of Yunnan.

[In this last post] he found that the eunuch Ch'ien Neng [sent to purchase gems][3] was abusing his powers and ordering his subordinate Kuo Ching to make secret pacts with Annam. So Wang sent someone to pursue Kuo, until he killed himself in a well. He then made a disclosure of the eunuch's corruption and arrogance, so that the emperor dismissed Ch'ien from the post. But Wang was called back to Nanking, as junior censor-in-chief, to head the censorate at the southern capital. He was later made minister of war in Nanking (1478) and a member of the governing triumvirate.[4] He also took on the posts of assistant censor-in-chief and governor of Nan Chih-li.

From the time the governorship of this area had been established, Wang and Chou Ch'en were actually the only ones who did good and removed abuses. There he had to deal with the eunuch Wang Ching, who, relying upon his battalion commander, Wang Ch'en, obtained an imperial order by unsavory means and began collecting from the market various rare books and pictures and other antique gems, with much arrogance and ado. Wang Shu set forth their crimes, had the eunuch put into the Imperial Guard prison and Wang Ch'en condemned to death. Two years later, he returned to the office of grand adjutant at Nanking, this time with Ch'ien Neng serving as chief eunuch and therefore as a colleague of his at the triumvirate. Wang Shu generously overlooked the past [and extended every cooperation], leading Ch'ien to tell others, "Wang Shu is an angel. I have only to serve him with respect." Wang was also honored with the title of junior guardian to the heir-apparent. When Lin Chün[5] was put in prison for impeaching the corrupt monk Chi-hsiao, Wang rescued him and obtained his release. With increasing frequency he memorialized the throne on affairs of the world, until the ruler felt ill at ease. Eventually the title of junior guardian to the heir-apparent was removed from him, and he was made to retire with the status of chief minister (1486).

When Emperor Hsiao-tsung came to the throne (1487), Wang Shu was recalled as minister of personnel and senior guardian of the heir-apparent. On an occasion at which the emperor had to perform sacrifices at the Confucian temple, Wang requested that His Majesty wear leather and offer an ox in order to show more solemnity, and the emperor agreed.[6] As Wang was a scholar with great respect for men of propriety and righteousness, many younger members at court, such as Tsou Chih, the Hanlin bachelor, T'ang Nai, the censor, and Li Wen-hsiang, the secretary—in all, about a dozen or more people—served generously and joyfully under his tutelage. While waiting upon the emperor at a lecture on the classics held at court, Wang Shu once

noticed that the emperor was suffering from the intense summer heat.
So he requested that the lectures be halted. On that occasion, T'ang
intervened, saying that the emperor was just showing interest in his
studies and should not be prevented by Wang's petition. Wang then
begged pardon, acknowledging his mistake. He added that there were
men impatient in desiring good government who witnessed the honors
granted to himself and reproved him too severely, as they desired that
he take charge of business at court and accomplish great things in the
manner of Ssu-ma Kuang (1019–86) of the Sung dynasty. But Wang
said that he did not dare to emulate Ssu-ma Kuang and did not consider
their own time as similar to Ssu-ma Kuang's. The emperor replied to
him with gentleness.

After that incident, T'ang Nai impeached the ministers Wang An,
Liu Chi, and Yin Chih and was told by the eunuchs that his memorials
had reached their office of transmission. But T'ang complained loudly
that if the memorials were not answered, he would even impeach the
eunuchs—who, hearing this, went into hiding. Soon afterwards, Wang
and Yin were dismissed from office. T'ang and Li Wen-hsiang continued day and night to celebrate their victories by drinking, believing that
they had successfully promoted gentlemen and dismissed small men
from government and that the continued presence of Liu Chi at court
was not important. So Liu Chi sent his retainers, Hsü P'eng and Wei
Chang, to spy on T'ang. T'ang then received a letter from Liu Kai,
prefect of Shou-chou (Nan Chihli), his native place. Liu related to him
a dream, in which Liu was an old man trying to drag a buffalo into
water but was being prevented by T'ang, who rescued the animal. Now
since the word "buffalo" *(niu)* was close to that of the imperial surname
(Chu),[7] Liu regarded that dream as signifying T'ang's role in saving the
state from dire straits and restoring it to peace. T'ang was very pleased
and showed the letter to his guests. So Wei Chang impeached him for it,
causing both T'ang and Liu to be put into the imperial prison. Then the
censor-in-chief Ma Wen-sheng, who had also been impeached by
T'ang, wanted to accuse him of greater abuses. Only the intervention of
Wang Shu rescued T'ang from further dangers, until the affair was
resolved. In cases where eunuchs and other favorites received excessive
rewards, Wang Shu often intervened and, even when the emperor had
already given permission, he would insist upon certain limitations.

The minister of rites, Ch'iu Chün, was formerly below Wang Shu in
rank. When Ch'iu was made a grand secretary, Wang continued to consider himself as Ch'iu's senior and often placed himself above Ch'iu at
court functions as a senior minister.[8] Ch'iu was displeased with this and
rebuffed him secretly on every occasion. Ch'iu even ordered his friend
Liu Wen-t'ai, head of the imperial academy of medicine, to accuse
Wang Shu of having published certain memorials that Ch'iu had not

announced,[9] and in that way, of having put the emperor in the unfavorable light of having rejected good advice. Wang Shu responded by saying that what he included had all shown that the deceased emperor had been eager to take advice and could not be used to show the opposite. Besides [he pursued the question], Liu was a small man, incapable himself of writing such a cunning piece of discourse, unless someone expert in the letters had conspired with him. He requested that [Liu be made to tell] who was behind the whole affair. Liu was put into the embroidered guard prison, where he disclosed that Ch'iu Chün had indeed led him to the accusations. But the emperor decided that Wang Shu was trying too hard to build his own reputation for justice, ordered the printing blocks and manuscript to be destroyed, and released Liu from prison. After this, Wang begged to be permitted to retire and returned home. Ch'iu died two years later (1495). When Liu Wen-t'ai went to offer condolences, Ch'iu's wife sent him away, saying, "You involved my husband in such a controversy [against Wang Shu. You are a] despicable man! Why come here with your condolences?" Those who heard approved of her action.

During his retirement, Wang Shu spent his time at home compiling memorials of famous ministers of past dynasties into a work of 124 *chüan*. He also studied classics and commentaries, pausing on points of difficulty, making many efforts to understand them, offering his own opinions on those points that remained difficult, and calling the book *Shih-ch'ü yi-chien* (Private Opinions)[10] to show their tentative nature, as he did not dare regard them as certain. This was done at age eighty-three. At eighty-five, he compiled the *Shih-yi* (Supplements); at eighty-seven, the *Pu-ch'üeh* (Further Supplements). And so he remained studious in his old age.

Wang Shu's learning[11] was generally applied to affairs as much as possible. It was what assured him peace of mind, and therefore it could be found in every place. As to what concerns the great roots of learning, he probably did not achieve them. In his ninetieth year, the emperor sent a messenger to ask after him. He died after another three years and was awarded the posthumous title of grand preceptor and the honorific Tuan-yi.

(MJHA 9:1a–2b)

NOTES

1. See Wang Shu's biography by Chaoying Fang, in *DMB*, v. 2, 1416–20.

2. Liu had the nickname "Thousand Catties" (Ch'ien-chin) on account of his strength in lifting things. See *DMB*, v. 1, 534–36.

3. Ch'ien was there collecting precious stones for the emperor's favorite consort, Lady Wan (*DMB*, v. 2, 1417).

4. The triumvirate was composed of one civilian member (in this case Wang Shu), one eunuch, and the central military commissioner (*DMB*, v. 2, 1417).

5. Lin Chün, *hao* Chien-su, 1452–1527.

6. For these sacrifices, see *Ming-shih*, ch. 66.

7. This involves a disrespectful pun, since the imperial surname Chu looks like the written character *niu* (buffalo) in Chinese. This is made worse by the fact that another Chinese word, which sounds like Chu, means "pig."

8. As a minister's basic rank was 2A and a grand secretary without concurrent title ranked only 5A, Wang Shu placed himself above Ch'iu. See *MS*, ch. 72.

9. The memorials were included in an early work of Wang's, purporting to give his own biography (c. 1486).

10. The *Shih-ch'ü yi-chien*, presenting his notes on classics, was included in a collected work of 9 ch. But they also existed in a separate edition, 4 ch., with 2 supplements, each in 2 ch.

11. Wang Shu's thought is presented in extracts from his *yi-chien* and included in *MJHA*, ch. 9. They express certain departures from Chu Hsi's known ideas but can hardly establish Wang himself as a thinker of great merit. His accomplishments lie rather in his life of virtuous service in government, a generally faithful reflection of northern Neo-Confucianism, following the footsteps of Hsüeh Hsüan, also a studious man and an independent official.

5.   The Yao-chiang[1] School

The path of Ming learning was opened by Ch'en Hsien-chang but became brilliant only with Wang Yang-ming. The earlier custom was to memorize the known sayings of the former scholars, without reflecting carefully in oneself or seeking to develop their hidden points. This is the meaning of the statement that each man is only repeating Chu Hsi. Kao P'an-lung said:[2] "The recorded dialogues of Hsüeh Hsüan and Lü Nan are without evidence of much real enlightenment." This is what he means also.

Since Wang Yang-ming pointed out *liang-chih* as that principle of self-realization present in all, accessible to all through contemplation, the road to sagehood was opened to everyone. Thus, without Yang-ming, the learning of the ancients would have died out. But the formula, the extension of *liang-chih*, came from his old age. He did not have enough time to explore its significance with the help of others. Later on, his many followers mixed it with their individual opinions, giving it an aura of mystery in what resembles a word-game of guessing, to the point of losing the master's intended meanings.[3]

Yang-ming's doctrine of the investigation of things (*ko-wu*) taught the extension of the principle of Heaven (*T'ien-li*), present in the *liang-chih* of one's mind, to affairs and things, thus assuring that these all fulfill their principles. He regarded the teaching of the sages to be one of action, as extensive learning, careful questioning, cautious reflection, and clear discernment all refer to action. He who acts earnestly only carries these points out unceasingly. Yang-ming extended *liang-chih* in affairs and things—the word "extend" *(chih)* is equivalent to the word "act" *(hsing)*. In this way, he offered an alternative to the prevalent abstract quest for principles. But later scholars, using their own powers of imagination in a quest to discover *pen-t'i* (ultimate reality), based their opinion only on knowledge *(chih-chih)*, regarding this as *liang-chih*. If that were the case, why did the master refute the old teachings of searching for principles and investigating things, of knowledge first and action afterwards, and insist on starting a doctrine of his own?

In the Conversations at T'ien-ch'üan, Yang-ming said:

> The absence of good and evil characterizes the mind in itself *(hsin-t'i)*.
> The presence of good and evil characterizes the movement of intention.
> The knowledge of good and evil is *liang-chih*.
> The doing of good and ridding of evil is the investigation of things.[4]

Today, people explain it in this way:

> The mind in-itself, without good and evil, is human nature.
> From this is aroused the intention, which may be good or evil.
> This, in turn, makes possible the differentiation of good and evil.
> And with this differentiation, one can do good and avoid evil by the investigation of things.

Thus, each step becomes a movement from the interior to the exterior, and the whole process is quite superficial. For *liang-chih* has become something posterior and is no longer in possession of its prereflective naturalness. For these reasons, Teng Yi-tsan considers the [T'ien-ch'üan] teaching to represent a doctrine of expediency.

Actually, the absence of good and evil in the intention refers also to the presence of good and evil thoughts *(nien)*. It does not mean that human nature is without good and evil. [In the second of the Four Sentences], the presence of good and evil in the intention also refers to the presence of good and evil thoughts. These two sentences only describe activity and quiescence. On another occasion, Yang-ming said to Hsüeh K'an: "The absence of good and evil refers to principle *(li)* in quiescence; the presence of good and evil refers to the movement of *ch'i*."[5] He was then referring also to these two sentences. And knowing good and evil does not mean that the activity of the intention may be good or evil, while the differentiation of such is knowledge. For knowledge is only discerning between the attractions and repulsions experienced in making the intention sincere. The attractions are necessarily for good, the repulsions against evil. That which is able to discern right from wrong is nature-in-itself, an empty spirit and quite unobscured. To do good and avoid evil is to act according to nature; it is naturally without an admixture of good and evil. This is what Yang-ming meant by extending the *liang-chih* of one's mind in affairs and things.

Therefore, the Four Sentences are quite without fault in themselves. Scholars have understood them incorrectly, taking what is said about nature as being neither good nor evil to mean that the supreme good is neither good nor evil. But the good is one. If there is a good that is good and another good that is not good, would this not destroy the foundation of nature itself? Those who seek *liang-chih* in activity regard the state of mind posterior to emotions *(yi-fa)* to be the prior state *(wei-fa)*. They teach others to make efforts to extend knowledge. This is like the man who points to the moon, not by pointing to the moon in the sky but by pointing to the reflection of light on earth, and so departs further and further from what he is looking for.[6] If the reader would only listen to my explanations here and reflect upon them, he will understand how Yang-ming himself was not mistaken.

NOTES

1. Yao-chiang refers to Wang Yang-ming's native place.
2. For Kao's opinions on these men, see *Kao-tzu yi-shu* (Surviving Works of Kao P'an-lung), 5:20b. We made use of the microfilm copy from the Peking Library collection.
3. For Wang Yang-ming's philosophy, see J. Ching, *To Acquire Wisdom*.
4. See *Ch'uan-hsi lu*, part 3. The English translation is our own. For the discussion on this, see also J. Ching, *To Acquire Wisdom*, ch. 6.
5. See *Ch'uan-hsi lu*, part 1. English translation adapted from W. T. Chan, trans., *Instructions for Practical Living*, 63–4.
6. Pointing to the moon is a favorite parable among the Buddhists, referring especially to the error of mistaking the finger to be the moon and thus missing the nature both of the moon and of the finger. See *Śūraṅgama Sūtra* in *TSD*, no. 945, XIX, 2:111a.

Wang Shou-jen

Wang Shou-jen, *tzu* Po-an (1472–1529),[1] called Master Yang-ming by scholars, was a native of Yüyao (Chekiang). His father, Wang Hua, the *optimus* of the *chin-shih* examinations of (1481), rose to be minister of personnel in Nanking. Yang-ming was born after a fourteen-month pregnancy. His grandmother, *née* Ts'en, dreamed that a spiritual being delivered her grandson from the clouds, so [Shou-jen's grandfather] gave him the name Yün (cloud). Until age five he was unable to speak. An unusual monk passed by and said, "A pity that the secret was divulged!" At that his name was changed [and he began to speak.] He was carefree and unrestrained. At fifteen he rode outside the border fortifications, returning after several months. At eighteen he passed through Kuang-hsin (present-day Shang-jao, Kiangsi) to call upon Lou Liang and expressed eloquently the belief that one could reach sagehood through learning.[2] In 1499 he passed the *chin-shih* examinations and received an appointment in the ministry of justice (1500). This was changed to the ministry of war (1504).[3]

The traitor Liu Chin forged an edict, arresting the Nanking officers of scrutiny and circuits (Tai Hsien and Po Yen-hui). Wang memorialized against him to save them. Then came an edict ordering his imprisonment. He received forty strokes of the cane in the palace and was banished to serve as head of the Lung-ch'ang dispatch station in Kweichow. Liu Chin sent someone to follow and assassinate him. Wang feigned suicide by jumping into a stream and escaped. He was able to reach Lung-ch'ang. Liu Chin was executed (in 1510), and Wang was appointed magistrate of Lu-ling (Kiangsi). Then he was appointed in succession to the posts of secretary, vice-director, and director of a bureau in the ministry of personnel. He was promoted to vice-minister of the court of the imperial stud (1513)[4] and chief minister of the court of state ceremonial (1514) [in Nanking]. At that time, Kiangsi and Fukien were restless with rebel activities, and the minister of war, Wang Ch'iung, especially recommended Wang Yang-ming to the positions of left assistant censor-in-chief and governor of southern Kiangsi. Soon afterwards, he pacified the bandits of Chang-nan (south of Changchou, Fukien), Heng-shui (southwest Kiangsi), T'ung-kang (near Ch'ung-yi, Kiangsi), Ta-mao (southern Kiangsi), and Li-t'ou (northern Kwangtung).

In the sixth month of 1519 he received an imperial order to put down a rebellious army in Fukien. When he reached Feng-ch'eng (Kiangsi), he heard the news of the rebellion of Chu Ch'en-hao (the prince of Ning) and quickly turned back to Chi-an (Lu-ling Prefecture) to raise troops against him. Ch'en-hao had then surrounded An-ch'ing (on the Yangtze River in southern Anhwei), but Yang-ming defeated his forces at Nan-ch'ang, whereupon the rebel prince sent troops back to the rescue, encountering Yang-ming's forces at Ch'iao-she (a dispatch station outside Nan-ch'ang).[5] After three battles, Yang-ming captured Chu Ch'en-hao. However, Emperor Wu-tsung (r. 1506–21) had set out personally at the head of an army to fight Ch'en-hao. A multitude of small men, including [the eunuch] Chang Chung and the commander Hsü T'ai, wanted Yang-ming to release Ch'en-hao on the Po-yang Lake so the emperor could join in the battle and declare victory afterwards. Yang-ming refused to comply, passed Yü-shan (on the border of Kiangsi and Chekiang) at night,[6] assembled the three provincial officers of Chekiang, and handed over the captive Ch'en-hao to the eunuch Chang Yung, a favorite of the emperor who was feared by the multitude of small men.

Yang-ming was then made provincial governor of Kiangsi (1519).[7] The following year (actually, 1521), [Emperor Shih-tsung] made him minister of war in Nanking and then invested him as earl of Hsin-chien

(1522). That same year, he mourned the death of his father, Wang Hua, the minister of personnel at Nanking. In 1527 he was restored to his office and appointed concurrently senior censor-in-chief. He launched an expedition against the rebels in Ssu-en and T'ien-chou (Kwangsi),[8] which was completed successfully, and then defeated rebels at Pa-chai (southwest Kwangsi) and Tuan-t'eng Hsia (Kwangsi).[9]

As a child, Wang Yang-ming once dreamed that he visited the temple of General Ma Yüan (14 B.C.–49 A.D.) and wrote a poem on the wall. In 1522, his path went by Ma's shrine, and he felt as though he were still in a dream.[10] Being already ill, he submitted a memorial requesting permission to retire and then went on to Nan-an (Kiangsi). His disciple Chou Chi,[11] who attended him in his illness, asked if he had any last words. Yang-ming replied, "My mind is bright and clear. What more is there to say?"[12] Shortly afterwards, he passed away. It was January 9, 1592. His age was fifty-seven.

Wang's learning began with wide reading in prose and poetry, which was followed by a thorough reading of the works of Chu Hsi.[13] He followed the steps of the investigation of things but observed that the principles of things and the mind remained dual, providing no entry-point [into sagehood].[14] Then he drifted in and out of Buddhism and Taoism for a long time until his exile among the aborigines[15] and the difficulties surrounding this experience stimulated his mind and strengthened his nature.[16] He wondered how a sage would behave under these circumstances and was suddenly enlightened to the meaning of the investigation of things and the extension of knowledge. He then said: "My nature possesses all it needs for acquiring the way of sageliness. I need not look for help outside."[17] Thus his learning changed three times before he discovered the gate to wisdom. From then on, he eliminated entirely the leaves and branches and focused his mind on the roots [of learning]. [First,] he concentrated on sitting in meditation and purifying his mind, believing that only after attaining the equilibrium of consciousness that exists before the rise of emotions could one acquire the harmony of due proportion accompanying the rise of emotions.[18] Such cultivation consisted generally in keeping a disciplined watchfulness over seeing, hearing, speaking, and acting, and allowing oneself to become relaxed only when absolutely necessary.

But after his sojourn in Kiangsi, he only talked of the words "extending *liang-chih*";[19] one did not have to rely on meditation to acquire stillness nor did one's mind require purifying. Without exercise or reflection, one naturally behaved according to natural norms. This was because *liang-chih* was identical to the equilibrium [of consciousness] prior to the rise of emotions, since such a state could not precede *liang-chih;* it was identical to the harmony of consciousness posterior to the rise of emotions, since such harmony could not be subsequent to *liang-*

chih. Liang-chih could exercise discipline *(shou-lien)* of itself and did not require that one attend to it. *Liang-chih* also could relax of itself and did not require that one attend to relaxation. The exercise of discipline was the very substance of response, the shift from tranquility to activity. Relaxation was the manifestation of stillness, the shift from activity to tranquility. Knowledge in its genuine and earnest aspect was action, as action in its intelligent and discerning aspect was knowledge.[20] These were not two separate entities.

After Wang Yang-ming went to Chekiang, he redoubled his efforts and further transformed his achievements. At each moment he knew what was right and what was wrong and yet transcended both right and wrong. Whenever he opened his mouth, he spoke from his original mind. There was no need to borrow ideas from others and patch things together. All phenomena were illuminated as if by the red sun in the sky. This shows that after completing his learning, he further underwent three changes.

Wang Yang-ming was concerned with the fact that, since the Sung philosophers, scholars had considered knowledge as the knowledge of information, on the theory that the human mind had nothing but a faculty of perception, while principle *(li)* was shared by Heaven and Earth and all things. They therefore considered it necessary to investigate exhaustively the principles of Heaven and Earth and all things before the perceptive faculty of the mind could enter into communion and harmony with these. They denied any separation between the inner and outer realms but relied actually upon information gathered from outside through seeing and hearing, to make up for their lack of noumenal understanding. Wang Yang-ming held that the learning of the sages was itself the learning of the mind *(hsin-hsüeh)* and that the mind was identical to principle *(li)*.[21] As to the extension of knowledge and investigation of things, he had to assert that one must extend the heavenly principle of one's mind to things and affairs. For when the knowledge of information was taken to be true knowledge, one ran the risk of becoming superficial and insubstantial and needed therefore to exert much effort in cultivation. But the responses of *liang-chih* were quick and subtle, requiring no waiting; the clarity of the original mind was itself knowledge and to refrain from deceiving it would be action. Thus one had to say that knowledge and action were one. Such were the essentials of the doctrines he established. They did not go beyond these.

Although some people have claimed that the Buddhist theory of the original mind was quite close to the learning of the mind [as taught by Wang Yang-ming], they do not know that the word *li* (principle) sets the line of demarcation between Confucianism and Buddhism. The Buddhists regard the principles of Heaven and Earth and all things to be entirely beyond their quest and so say nothing about them, holding exclusively to the perception [of the mind]. The worldly Confucians, on the other hand, do not rely on this perception and seek principles among Heaven and Earth and all things. They say they are different from the Buddhists, but they are actually one with the Buddhists since they ally principle with Heaven and Earth and all things, and the perceptive faculty alone with the mind. Looking outside for principles, they could only find a stream with no source or a tree with no roots. Even if they accorded with original reality *(pen-t'i)*, it could only be indirectly. After all, begging for light from door to door does not differ much from closing one's eyes in the dark. But when it is pointed out that what constitutes mind as mind is not the perceptive faculty but heavenly principles, then the golden mirror [i.e., mind] that had been dropped is retrieved, and the difference between Confucianism and Buddhism shows itself like that between mountain and river; anyone with eyes can see it. To prove this with the words of Confucius and Mencius, when one extends one's *liang-chih* to things and affairs, then things and affairs will all have their principles. Is this not what is meant by "man making the Way great"?[22] But if principle were only in things and affairs, the Way would be what makes man great. Kao-tzu put righteousness in externals[23] but did not suppress and overlook righteousness. He too looked for it in things and affairs. This is also what worldly Confucians call the exhaustive investigation of principles. Why then did Mencius not approve of it and insist instead that the four beginnings of virtue reside in the mind? Alas, when the rice chaff is caught in the eye, the four directions seem to change their positions.[24] Only then could one doubt Wang Yang-ming's teachings.

In the beginning of the Lung-ch'ing period (1567), Wang Yang-ming was honored posthumously with the title of marquis of Hsin-chien and the honorific Wen-ch'eng. During the Wan-li period (1584), he was included in the sacrifices of the Temple of Confucius and was called "the late [honored] Confucian scholar, Master Wang."

(MJHA 10:1a–4b)

NOTES

1. For Wang Shou-jen (Yang-ming), see his biography by Wing-tsit Chan, *DMB*, v. 2, 1408–16. There is also a "psychobiography" of his youth by Wei-ming Tu, *Neo-Confucian Thought in Action: Wang Yang-ming's Youth* (Berkeley, 1976) and a study of his mature philosophy by Julia Ching, *To Acquire Wisdom* (New York, 1976).

2. See also Yang-ming's *Chronological Biography (Nien-p'u)*, in his *Collected Works, Wang Wen-ch'eng kung ch'üan-chu (WWKC)*, SPTK ed., ch. 32, 904–5.

3. Ibid., 32, 905–6.

4. Ibid., 32, 917.

5. See Chang Yü-ch'üan, "Wang Shou-jen as a statesman," *Chinese Social and Political Science Review* 23 (1940), 41.

6. Ibid., 74–5.
7. *WWKC*, 33, 933.
8. Ibid., 34, 973–81. See also Aoyama Sadao, *Chūgoku rekidai chimei yōran* (Tokyo, 1933), 253.
9. Chang, op. cit., 52–65. Chang also gives precise locations for the events.
10. *WWKC*, 34, 988b.
11. Chiao Hung, *Kuo-ch'ao hsien-cheng lu*, 105:58. Chou Chi was then prefectural judge of Nan-an.
12. He had been in Nan-an for exactly one month. See J. Ching, *To Acquire Wisdom*, 34.
13. *WWKC*, 32, 906.
14. Ibid.
15. See also his poems written in exile, 10:41b. An alternative translation here is "living in adversity" *(chü-yi)*.
16. Allusion to *Mencius* 6B:15.
17. *WWKC*, 32, 909. See also J. Ching, *To Acquire Wisdom*, 31.
18. J. Ching, *To Acquire Wisdom*, 71–72.
19. See Wang's letter to Tsou Ch'ien-chih (Tsou Shou-yi), in Julia Ching, trans., *The Philosophical Letters of Wang Yang-ming* (Canberra, 1972), 101.
20. *Ch'uan-hsi lu*, part 1. W. T. Chan, trans., *Instructions for Practical Living*, 93. J. Ching, *To Acquire Wisdom*, 66–69.
21. J. Ching, *To Acquire Wisdom*, 120–24.
22. *Analects* 15:28.
23. *Mencius* 6A:1–2.
24. Allusion to *Chuang Tzu*, ch. 14.

6. The Che-chung[1] School

The teachings of the Yang-ming School spread from near to far. Its first adherents were all from the same prefecture (Shao-hsing or Yüeh). After his experience at Lung-ch'ang, Yang-ming started to accept disciples from all over. Ch'ien Tê-hung and Wang Chi were the only two from his native prefecture who became famous for learning; the others remained minor figures.

At the moment of highest interest in his teaching, our town of Shao-hsing vibrated with the sound of discussions and recitations, of ritual music and songs sung with accompaniments, and the number of scholars was beyond count. For example, there was Fan Huan of Shan-yin, *tzu* T'ing-jan, *hao* Li-chai, who first studied with Wang Wen-yüan and Hsü Chang,[2] finishing his education under Yang-ming. He made a wide investigation of the many classics, had a sudden enlightenment, and considered that Confucius' and Mencius' authentic teachings had been inherited only by Chou Tun-yi and Ch'eng Yi, while all those from Chu Hsi and Lu Chiu-yüan down did not reach their level. He did not worry about poverty at home, saying: "There is a treasure under Heaven, the possession and enjoyment of which can help us to forget poverty." He composed twenty poems in the ancient genre, recounting the transmission of the Tao and the teachings on *T'ai-chi*. His teaching is deep and difficult to fathom.

There was also Kuan Chou, *tzu* Tzu-hsing, *hao* Shih-p'ing, of Yüyao, who served as a chief clerk in the ministry of war. Whenever on duty, he would sing lines of praise and blame, astonishing the minister. When a frontier alarm was sounded, the minister was afraid. But Kuan said: "The ancients always measured their strength and their virtues. Since you regard your own talents and strength as limited, why don't you retire from office to give place to a worthier man?" The minister responded listlessly with words of thanks, but Kuan was sent home on the occasion of the evaluation of Peking officials. Chao Chen-chi had a poem entitled "Sleeping in the Four Patriarchs' Mountain," with the line: "The Four Masters come here specially and with ceremony." He was referring actually to Ts'ai Ju-nan, Shen Ch'ung, Wang Chi, and Kuan Chou.[3]

There was also Fan Yin-nien, *hao* Pan-yeh, who taught at Ch'ing-t'ien and had many friends and disciples. There was Hsia Ch'un, *tzu* Wei-ch'u, *hao* Fu-wu, who passed his provincial examination and rose to be vice-prefect of Ssu-ming, where he died. When Wei Chiao[4] was teaching the doctrine of heavenly root and heavenly mystery, Hsia said: "To refer to the quiescent as heavenly root and the active as heavenly mystery is possible. But if one takes quiescence to be that which nurtures heavenly root and activity to be that which observes heavenly mystery, one would be separating activity and quiescence. This would be no way of speaking of nature." There were Ch'ai Feng, *tzu* Hou-yü, who was master of T'ien-chen Academy with many followers from Ch'ü-chou and Yen-chou Prefecture; Sun Ying-k'uei, *tzu* Wen-ch'ing, *hao* Meng-ch'üan, who served as assistant vice censor-in-chief and regarded [Yang-ming's] *Ch'uan-hsi lu* as his rule and directed the T'ien-chen Academy;[5] Wen-jen Ch'üan, *tzu* Pang-cheng, *hao* Pei-chiang, who compiled and published Yang-ming's writings together with Ch'ien Te-hung.[6] In my own clan, there were Huang Chi, *tzu* Te-liang, whose accounts of Yang-ming have been recorded by Yu Hsi-shan; and Huang Wen-huan, *hao* Wu-nan, the instructor of K'ai-chou (Szechuan), to whom Yang-ming sent his own son as a student. Huang Wen-huan also compiled the *Tung-ko shih ch'ou*, recording what he had heard. There was also Huang Chia-ai, *tzu* Mou-jen, *hao* Ho-hsi, *chin-shih* of 1508, who rose to be prefect of Ch'in-chou (Kwangtung). There were Huang Yüan-fu, *hao* Ting-shan, and Huang K'uei, *tzu* Tzu-shao, *hao* Hou-ch'uan,[7] who were both earnest and open, keeping faithfully to the master's teachings. From this, one can imagine how many others studied [with Yang-ming] but have been forgotten by the world.

NOTES

1. Che-chung refers to central Chekiang. In this introduction to the central Chekiang branch of the Yang-ming school, Huang Tsung-hsi names a list of

minor thinkers, giving their formal as well as other names. It is a practice he follows elsewhere, as in the preface to the Nan-chung school. For this reason, the translation also includes the multiple names of the persons concerned. It has not, however, been possible to find other biographical references to some of the figures he has included.

2. For Fan Huan, see also Chiao Hung, *Kuo-ch'ao hsien-cheng lu* 114:101–2. As to Wang Wen-yüan and Hsü Chang, both are mentioned in *MJHA* 10:4–5. Both were semi-eremitical scholars who never entered official life.

3. Ts'ai Ju-nan was a disciple of the school of Chan Jo-shui (*MJHA* 40:10a). For Shen Ch'ung, *hao* Ku-lin, d. 1571, see *MS* 216:523b. Wang Chi has his own biography in this book.

4. We have little that is important to add to Hsia Ch'un, but one can refer to *MJHA* 3:1 for Wei Chiao, a private disciple of Hu Chü-jen.

5. We have nothing to say about Ch'ai Feng. Sun Ying-k'uei's biography is in the *Pen-ch'ao fen-sheng jen-wu k'ao* (Ming Regional Biographical Directory), comp. by Kuo T'ing-shün (1622 ed., Taipei reprint, 1971), v. 14, 4453.

6. For Wen-jen Ch'üan, Wang Yang-ming's relative, see J. Ching, trans., *The Philosophical Letters of Wang Yang-Ming*, 46–47. See also the gazetteer *Shao-hsing fu-chih* 33:436.

7. For Huang Chi, see *Pen-ch'ao fen-sheng jen-wu k'ao*, v. 30, 9969. We have nothing to add to the information about Huang Wen-huan, Huang Chia-ai, Huang K'uei, and Huang Yüan-fu.

Hsü Ai

Hsü Ai, *tzu* Yüeh-jen, *hao* Heng-shan (1487–1517),[1] a native of Ma-yen Village in Yüyao, was *chin-shih* in 1508 and became prefect of Ch'i-chou (Shansi) and deputy bureau director in the ministry of war in Nanking before being transferred to bureau director in the ministry of works in Nanking. In 1516 he went home to visit his family[2] and died the following year on June 5, at age thirty. Hsü was the son-in-law of Wang Hua, hence Wang Yang-ming's brother-in-law. When Yang-ming left prison to return home (1510), Hsü became his disciple, so no one followed Yang-ming earlier than he.[3] After that he and Yang-ming both served as officials in Nanking and never left each other's company morning or evening. When other scholars had their doubts about Yang-ming, Hsü served as an intermediary between them, so that Yang-ming's disciples grew close to him. Yang-ming said, "Hsü Ai is my Yen Yüan."[4] When Hsü visited Mount Heng (Hunan), he dreamed of an old monk who caressed him on the back, saying, "You have Yen Yüan's virtue; you also have the same life span as he." Hsü woke up very astonished. Yang-ming was in Kan-chou (Kiangsi) when he heard of Hsü's death and wept bitterly over it. But Yang-ming never forgot Hsü, even during lecture hours, though he was dead. In conversation with disciples, whenever he met with little understanding, he would say, "This is something I discussed with Hsü, but then, he is difficult to emulate." One day, after a certain lecture, Yang-ming paced around the columns of the house, saying, "If only I could raise Hsü from the dead to hear this!" So he went with his disciples at once to Hsü's tomb and offered him libation, telling him of what happened.

When Hsü first heard Yang-ming and realized his divergences from earlier scholars, Hsü was very surprised, without knowing how to take it. Only after having been for some time with Yang-ming, when he had reflected upon himself and practiced accordingly, did he believe Yang-ming to be teaching the authentic way of the Confucian school, whereas other paths were sidetracks leading nowhere. Yang-ming changed his teachings several times after his exile to Lung-ch'ang (1507). During his sojourn in Nanking, Yang-ming generally emphasized gathering oneself together, regarding dispersal in action to be a necessary evil, so that quiet-sitting to purify the mind was the goal of learning. But after his sojourn in Kiangsi, Yang-ming spoke of the extension of *liang-chih* in particular. Hsü recorded part I of the *Ch'uan-hsi lu,* giving what he heard in Nanking. In that case, he would not have heard of the doctrine of the extension of *liang-chih.* Yet he did say, in the *Ch'uan-hsi lu,* that knowledge *(chih)* is the *pen-t'i* of the mind—that the mind naturally knows [for example] that on seeing one's father, one naturally knows filial piety; on seeing one's elder brother, one naturally knows brotherly respect; on witnessing an infant falling into a well, one naturally knows compassion. All this is *liang-chih.* When *liang-chih* fills the mind and flows from it, what is effected is extension.[5] This shows that Yang-ming had mentioned the words "extension of *liang-chih*" long before his sojourn in Kiangsi, although he made it his main teaching after the Kiangsi period. So Hsü really got the true teaching of Wang Yang-ming.

Nieh Pao[6] said, "People today who follow the teaching of *liang-chih* often neglect part I of *Ch'uan-hsi lu,* which records important points. They construct generalities in a vacuum, appearing to be saying things close to Yang-ming's teachings while pursuing objects outside. Yet they regard themselves as having accomplished much." So he too lamented the loss of Hsü Ai.

(MJHA 11:3a–b)

NOTES

1. See also *MS* 283:700b.
2. The text of the *MJHA* includes here a parenthesis, claiming that Hsü's position with the ministry of war and his request for a home visit were not factual and this, according to Hsü's biography. [This biography cannot be located.]
3. The text of the *MJHA* includes here a parenthesis, claiming that it is not correct to say that Ch'ien became Wang's disciple after his return from exile in

Lung-ch'ang, and this, according to Teng Yüan-hsi's *Huang-Ming shu* (Ming History). [Teng's dates are 1529–93. His book is not available in North America.]

4. Yen Yüan, Confucius' favorite disciple, died young.

5. See *WWKC* 1:56a–58b. For the English translation, see W. T. Chan, trans., *Instructions for Practical Living*, 6–8. See also J. Ching, *To Acquire Wisdom*, 58–67, *passim*.

6. For Nieh Pao, *hao* Shuang-chiang, see his biography. An important letter he received from Wang Yang-ming in 1528 is included in *Ch'uan-hsi lu*, part 2. See also W. T. Chan, trans., *Instructions for Practical Living*, 172ff.

Ch'ien Te-hung

Ch'ien Te-hung, *tzu* Hung-ju, *hao* Hsü-shan (1497–1574),[1] was a native of Yüyao in Chekiang. On Wang Yang-ming's return to Chekiang after his defeat of Ch'en-hao (1521), Ch'ien and his fellow countrymen Fan Yin-nien, Kuan Chou, Cheng Yin, Ch'ai Feng, Hsü Shan, and Wu Jen, as well as several dozen others, assembled at Chung-t'ien-ko and all became Wang's disciples. The following year Ch'ien received his *chü-jen* degree. At that time, such a multitude of disciples flocked to Wang in Chekiang that Ch'ien and Wang Chi first had to explain to them the principal tenets of Wang's teachings before they could study with Wang personally. Thus [Ch'ien Te-hung and Wang Chi] were called tutors. In 1526, the two went to the metropolitan examinations but returned home without taking the palace examinations.[2] When Wang Yang-ming set off on his campaign to Ssu-en and Tien-chou (1529), Ch'ien and Wang Chi remained home to attend to the affairs of the academy in Shao-hsing. In 1529 Ch'ien traveled to Kuei-hsi to attend Wang Yang-ming's funeral.[3] He asked Shao Chu-feng there what kind of mourning apparel he ought to wear. Shao replied, "When Confucius died, his disciple Tzu-kung mourned as for a deceased father but without wearing special apparel, and that, in accordance with the rituals." Ch'ien said, "My master died on the wayside with no one to preside over his funeral. As a disciple I ought to don mourning robes. But my parents are still alive, and I dare not put on sackcloth and ashes." So he built a hut near the grave to satisfy the dictates of his heart. Only in 1532 did he take the palace examinations and receive his appointment as instructor in the Soochow prefectural school. In 1535 he mourned his mother's death. On completing the prescribed mourning, he was transferred to proctor in the National University, then promoted to secretary and to vice-director of the Shensi bureau in the ministry of justice.

When Emperor Shih-tsung visited Hsi-shan one night, he summoned Marquis Wu-ting, Kuo Hsün,[4] to see him, but in vain. Kuo was then impeached by the supervising secretary, Kao Shih, sent to the Imperial Guard Prison, and then to the ministry of justice. On account of his arrogance and arbitrary actions, Kuo was hated by all the court ministers, who desired to see him punished on the charge of treason. Ch'ien followed the law and recommended a death sentence for Kuo, citing ten counts related to his disobedience [to the imperial summons]. Although submitted, this recommendation was not acted upon. The court ministers thought this was due to the lightness of the sentence and impeached Ch'ien for his lack of understanding of the penal codes. But the emperor withheld announcing it, because he thought the sentence too severe. After the impeachment, Kuo was put into prison. Actually, the Emperor still held Kuo in favor, wished only to humiliate him somewhat, and so disagreed with the judgments of the court ministers. Even in shackles and cuffs, Ch'ien continued to discuss the *Book of Changes* with other imprisoned officials—the associate censor, Yang Chüeh, and the commissioner-in-chief, Chao Po-lou.[5] He was released only after Kuo's death. When the temples of the imperial ancestors were completed, he was restored to his former rank. In the reign of Mu-tsung (1567–72), he was promoted to the rank of fourth-grade retired official. During the early years of the Wan-li reign (1573–1619), he was further promoted one grade.

During his thirty years as a private citizen, Ch'ien never passed a day without teaching. [He visited] lecture halls throughout the famous sites of Kiangsu, Chekiang, Anhwei, Kiangsi, and Hukuang. Indeed, Ch'ien Te-hung and Wang Chi took turns presiding at these assemblies. At the age of seventy, Ch'ien finally announced his intention to retire, which he circulated everywhere. After that he stopped traveling. He died on November 10, 1574, at age seventy-seven.

Wang Yang-ming's doctrine of the extension of *liang-chih* came from his later life. In the beginning he had taught his disciples quiet-sitting to purify the mind. He found that they tended to prefer tranquility to activity. Knowing the source and what flows from that, one tends to take too much from it. But to say that *liang-chih* is the Mean [of consciousness] before emotions are manifest and to say that practicing vigilance in solitude is the same as extending *liang-chih*[6] is to continue to regard inner composure as essential. That is why Tsou Shou-yi's caution and apprehension and Lo Hung-hsien's tranquility both represent Wang Yang-ming's true transmission.[7]

Ch'ien and Wang Chi had both studied longest under Wang Yang-ming and frequently heard those teachings he particularly emphasized. Wang Chi regarded stillness *(chi)* as the original substance *(pen-t'i)* of the mind. Stillness takes reflection as its function *(yung)*. To keep to its empty knowledge and abandon reflection is to abuse its function. Ch'ien inquired as to where the state of consciousness before emotions are manifest can be discovered, since it is impossible to leave the state of consciousness after the emotions are manifest and seek the prior state.

This shows that both speak of *liang-chih* as actual consciousness, which has nothing to do with that upon which sages and worthies dwelt so long. It cannot but indicate an infinitesimal departure from their master's teachings. Only Wang Chi starts with actual consciousness to reach enlightenment regarding the substance *(t'i)*, which is changing and unstable, while Ch'ien polished his mind in affairs and things. That is why Ch'ien's enlightenment is not as penetrating as Wang Chi's, while Wang's cultivation is not as good as Ch'ien's. But Wang Chi eventually drifted into Ch'an Buddhism, while Ch'ien never departed from Confucian norms. Why is this so? For Wang Chi dared to go to the very brink of the cliffs and could not be restrained by his master's teachings, while Ch'ien's more cautious behavior resembled that of a man who held to the ropes while sailing his boat. And so, if his catch was not vast, neither were his losses.

Lo Hung-hsien said, "Ch'ien's learning changed several times. In the beginning he recognized doing good and avoiding evil as exterior to *liang-chih.* Later he said, "*Liang-chih* is neither good nor evil. How can I take good as something to be done and evil as something to be avoided?" Still later he said, "How could I have been so confused! That which is neither good nor evil is not *liang-chih.* I merely need to do what I know to be good and avoid what I know to be evil. That is possible to me." And again, "My earlier words were still dualistic. The master said, 'The mind-in-itself is characterized by the highest good.' Only with the movement [of intention] does what is not good emerge. I cannot insist that there be nothing that is not good. I can only remain without activity. What he calls intention is activity. What I call activity is also activity. I need merely not act and thus I remain constant and at one."

What Ch'ien calls "without activity" is precisely what Yang Chien calls "without deliberate thought" *(pu-ch'i-yi).*[8] And is this not the same as [the state of consciousness] prior to the manifestation of emotions? But then to say that the prior state of consciousness *(wei-fa)* is not found outside the posterior state of consciousness *(yi-fa)* cannot be what Ch'ien means.

(MJHA 11:5b–6b)

NOTES

1. See Ch'ien's biography by Julia Ching, *DMB,* v. 1, 241–44.
2. They were angered by the official disapproval of Wang Yang-ming's philosophy. See Wang Chi's biography, *MJHA* 12:1a–2a.
3. Wang Yang-ming had died at Nan-an (Kiangsi).
4. See Kuo Hsün's biography by Lien-che Tu Fang, *DMB,* v. 1, 771–73.
5. Yang Chüeh, *hao* Hu-shan, biography by Lien-che Tu Fang, *DMB,* v. 2, 1506–8. I have no information on Chao Po-lou.

6. J. Ching, *To Acquire Wisdom,* ch. 2–3.

7. Huang Tsung-shi maintains throughout this book that the school of Kiang-yu (particularly Kiangsi), represented by Tsou Shou-yi and Lo Hung-hsien, has best adhered to the authentic teachings of Wang Yang-ming.

8. For Yang Chien, *hao* Tz'u-hu (d. 1226), a disciple of Lu Chiu-yüan, who manifested more Buddhist influence than even Lu himself, see *SYHA* 74. See also Fung Yu-lan, *A History of Chinese Philosophy,* v. 2, 579–83. For a more recent biographical account of Yang Chien, by W. T. Chan, see *Sung Biographies,* ed. by H. Franke (Wiesbaden, 1976), v. 3, 1218–22. Yang Chien's teaching of *pu-ch'i-yi* refers to keeping the mind free of deliberate thought so that it may become manifest in a state of pure consciousness.

Wang Chi

Wang Chi, *tzu* Ju-chung, *hao* Lung-hsi (1498–1583),[1] a native of Shan-yin in Chekiang, passed his provincial examinations at the age of twenty-one (1519). In 1523, after failing his *chin-shih* examinations, he returned to study with Wang Yang-ming. In 1526 he did not want to go to take the examinations. Wang Yang-ming said to him, "I do not consider it a glory for you to pass examinations. But people are reacting to my teaching with a mixture of belief and doubt. If you go to the capital you can make it better known." So Wang Chi went there and passed the metropolitan examinations that year. At that time, the people in authority did not like Wang Yang-ming's teachings. Wang Chi told Ch'ien Te-hung, "This is no time for you and me to be officials." So they returned south without taking the palace examinations.

As Wang Yang-ming was always getting more disciples and could not teach all of them, he sent many to Wang Chi and Ch'ien Te-hung. Wang Chi was supple and approachable, and the disciples grew daily closer to him. When Wang Yang-ming left on his campaign to Ssu-en and Tien-chou, Wang Chi saw him off to Yen-t'an. The following year Wang Yang-ming died in Nan-an. Wang Chi had left for the palace examinations, but when he heard the news, he went to Kuang-hsin for the funeral. He wore the heaviest mourning, as for a parent, to complete the funeral affairs and then kept mourning of the heart.[2]

Only in 1532 was he free for the palace examinations, which he passed. He was appointed secretary of a bureau in the ministry of war in Nanking but resigned later, on account of sickness, and returned home. Restored afterwards to his original position, he was then transferred to be a bureau director in the ministry of war.

Wang Chi was disliked by the grand secretary Hsia Yen.[3] When fire burned down three throne halls [*sic*] (1541),[4] the supervising secretary, Ch'i Hsien, sent a memorial to the throne recommending Wang Chi as a distinguished scholar who could give good counsel. Hsia Yen responded by criticizing Ch'i Hsien as a mediocre man following a false doctrine and irresponsibly recommending others of his own clique to the court. He demoted him to an outer province (Shantung). Wang Chi begged also to resign but was told that he should await the evaluation of capital officials. The following year, Hsüeh Ying-ch'i,[5] director of the bureau of evaluations in the ministry of personnel in Nanking (also a follower of Yang-ming's philosophy), who differed from Wang Chi in his teachings, wanted to use his case to correct the course of learning. So he gave Wang an unfavorable evaluation. Wang Chi returned home and, for the following forty and more years, taught daily without cease, visiting lecture halls in an area stretching from Peking and Nanking to Kiangsu, Hukuang, Fukien, and Chekiang, being recognized everywhere as the senior member [of the Yang-ming followers]. Even at age eighty he went around tirelessly. He died on July 25, 1583, at age eighty-five.

In *T'ien-chüan cheng-tao chi,*[6] Wang Chi said that the master, Wang Yang-ming, frequently referred to the Four Sentences in his teachings:

- The absence of good and evil characterizes the mind-in-itself.
- The presence of good and evil characterizes the movement of its intentions.
- The knowledge of good and evil characterizes its innate capacity for knowledge and wisdom *(liang-chih)*.
- The doing of good and ridding of evil characterizes its investigation of things.

Ch'ien Te-hung regarded this formula as representing a fixed teaching that could not be changed. Wang Chi called it an expedient doctrine. According to him, reality *(t'i)* and its manifestations *(yung)*, however minute and subtle, derive fundamentally from one dynamic source *(chi)*, and mind, intention, knowledge, and things are actually all one thing *(wu)*. When a person awakes to the understanding that the mind is neither good nor evil, he also realizes that intention, knowledge, and things are also neither good nor evil. Together, the two disciples questioned Wang Yang-ming about it. Wang said: "I have actually two ways of teaching. The Four Negatives[7] are for men of superior gifts of understanding. The Four Positives[8] are for men of medium gifts or less. The superior gifts refer to the understanding that reality itself *(pen-t'i)* is nothing but its manifestation *(kung-fu)* or effort. This is the teaching of sudden enlightenment. Those with medium gifts or less should devote themselves to the effort of doing good and ridding themselves of evil, in order to recover gradually the original reality *(pen-t'i)* [within themselves]." This proves to us that Wang Chi's interpretations belong generally to the category of the Four Negatives.

To take the rectification of the mind as the learning of the natural *(hsien-t'ien)* and the sincerity of intention as the learning that comes afterwards *(hou-t'ien)* is to fix one's roots in the mind. The mind that is neither good nor evil is also the intention that is neither good nor evil. This is a case of the natural controlling what comes afterwards. But should one fix the roots in the intention, one would not be able to avoid the choice between the two extremes of good and evil. The mind also cannot be free from involvement. This is the natural being restored by that which comes afterwards. Such are the general tenets of Wang Chi's teachings. When such tenets are spread throughout the country, scholars could not overlook certain difficulties. Speaking from the point of view of the Four Positives, the good alone is what the mind originally possessed, so the good of intention, knowledge, and things arises from the equilibrium *(chung)* of consciousness, while evil comes in from the outside. If the mind-in-itself is neither good nor evil, then the evil of intention, knowledge, and things is also delusion, and even good itself is delusion. If the effort and manifestation *(kung-fu)* is delusion, how can one speak of restoring the original reality *(pen-t'i)?* Such words cannot be found in Yang-ming's daily teachings. Wang Chi is the only person who gives them. Yet he once replied to Wu Shih-lai,[9] saying, "The mind-itself is characterized by the utmost good, without any evil. The movement of intention is characterized by the presence of good and evil. The innate capacity for knowledge *(liang-chih)* is that which knows good and evil. Investigation of things refers to doing good and ridding oneself of evil." This shows that his own teaching is not consistent. Speaking from the point of view of the Four Negatives, the effort of rectifying the mind, as given in the *Great Learning,* begins with the sincerity of intention. To say now that one should fix the roots in the mind is to say that one need not worry about the intention, and that to fix the roots in the intention is something meant for those of medium gifts or less. Has the *Great Learning* really two such teachings about the efforts of cultivation, or does it only offer a teaching for those of medium gifts or less? Wang Chi also said that *liang-chih* is something that is produced by nothing, being the Mean of consciousness before the emotions arise *(wei-fa)*. There is no other such prior state before such knowledge outside the harmony of emotions in due proportion, and there is no posterior state of consciousness *(yi-fa)* following such knowledge. One can naturally gather one's composure *(shou-lien)* without forcing it, and one can naturally manifest emotions without deliberation. Thus self-realization can happen at once, without reliance on effort and cultivation. By the same reasoning, the extension of *liang-chih* was taught for the sake of those who had not yet attained enlightenment. Those who could believe in *liang-chih* could come and go by themselves, as the bead travels across the abacus, without need of any control, keeping naturally from waywardness. Thus earnest fidelity and cautious behavior, as well as all action that flows from the concern for reputation, are to be considered artificial behavior.

T'ang Shun-chih[10] said that Wang Chi was excessively self-confident, that he did not restrain his wild behavior and was without moral discernment. That was why he provoked innumerable criticisms. Since *liang-chih*[11] flows from consciousness itself *(chih-chüeh)* with no determination of space or direction, doctrine or law, effort in cultivation cannot but be troublesome to the reality of emptiness and nothingness. Such teaching is necessarily close to Ch'an Buddhism. Manifestation and process *(liu-hsing)* is nothing but the source and center of consciousness *(chu-tsai)*. When one lets fall one's hands while climbing a precipitous cliff, one is without any hold on [solid reality]. To take the mutual interdependence of mind and breath (yoga) as contingent teaching is necessarily close to Taoism. Even though Wang Chi talks about the manifestation of true nature, which of itself reveals natural laws *(t'ien-tse)*, his doctrines disclose certain divergences from the Confucian norms of practice. However, Wang Chi personally inherited Yang-ming's last instructions and frequently gave voice to some of the master's subtle words. Just as Lu Chiu-yüan had to be followed by his disciple Yang Chien, so Wang Yang-ming had to be followed by Wang Chi. If we are to judge from the rise and fall of certain teachings, then Yang Chien served as a catalyst to Lu Chiu-yüan and his teachings, while Wang Chi clarified certain things for the Yang-ming school, to which he contributed with his own explanations and discoveries.

(*MJHA* 12:1a–2a)

NOTES

1. See his biography by Julia Ching, *DMB,* v. 2, 1351–55.
2. This means he did not continue to wear heavy mourning robes after the funeral.
3. See Angela Hsi's biography of Hsia Yen, *DMB,* v. 1, 527–31. Hsia was Grand Secretary from roughly 1537 to 1548. He has been described as ambitious and power-driven, constantly involved in factional struggles.
4. The building that burned down in 1541 was the Imperial Ancestral Shrine and not the throne halls, which were destroyed sixteen years later in the fire of 1557, an even more spectacular event. This is another example of Huang Tsung-hsi's historical errors, probably attributable to his excessive reliance on memory alone.
5. Hsüeh's biography by Mou Jun-sun and L. C. Goodrich, *DMB,* v. 1, 619–22.
6. *WLHC* (1822 ed.), ch. 1, 1a. This book relates Wang Chi's testimony about Yang-ming's teaching at T'ien-ch'üan.
7. The Four Negatives refer to Wang Chi's interpretation of the Four Sentences, as given briefly above. See *WLHC* 1:2a.
8. The Four Positives refer to Ch'ien Te-hung's interpretation of the Four Sentences. See also Ch'ien's biography in *DMB,* v. 1, 241–44.
9. See the latter, given in *WLHC* 10:23a.
10. For T'ang Shun-chih, see his biography in this volume.

11. What follows appears to be Huang Tsung-hsi's judgment of Wang Chi, summing up his biography for the *Ming-ju hsüeh-an*.

7.   The Chiang-yu[1] School

The Chiang-yu (Kiangsi) school alone acquired the true transmission of Wang Yang-ming. Tsou Shou-yi, Lo Hung-hsien, Lo Lun, and Nieh Pao were its best representatives. These transmitted the teaching to Wang Shih-huai and Wan T'ing-yen. All of them were able to make explicit Yang-ming's intended meanings. At this time, the Shao-hsing (Chekiang) school[2] had developed many errors, and the members appealed to their master's authority as support for their own opinions in the face of their critics. Only the Chiang-yu school could point that out, thus preventing the Way of Wang Yang-ming from decaying. After all, Yang-ming had spent his whole life and energy in Kiangsi. It was reasonable and natural that his influence should be most felt there.

NOTES

1. Chiang-yu, literally, right bank of the Yangtze River, refers to the region centering around Kiangsi where Wang Yang-ming spent many years as censor-in-chief and grand coordinator of the border regions of Kiangsi, Kwangtung, and Fukien (1516–22).

2. Yüeh refers especially to Shao-hsing, the prefecture of Wang Yang-ming's birth.

Tsou Shou-yi

Tsou Shou-yi, *tzu* Ch'ien-chih, *hao* Tung-kuo (1491–1562),[1] was a native of An-fu District in Kiangsi. At age nine he followed his father (Tsou Hsia) when the latter served as an official in Nanking. Lo Ch'in-shun saw him there and was impressed by him. In 1511 he ranked first in the metropolitan examination, third in the palace examination, and was named a Hanlin compiler. After one year he had to mourn his mother's death. When Chu Ch'en-hao revolted, Tsou followed Wang Yang-ming in his campaign. After Emperor Shih-tsung succeeded to the throne (1521), Tsou was summoned back to his official duties. On the occasion of the great ritual controversy[2] he offended the emperor with his memorials and was put in prison and exiled to Kuang-te (Anhwei) as assistant magistrate. There he destroyed the temples dedicated to strange deities and established the Fu-ch'u Academy. Promoted to director of receptions in the ministry of rites in Nanking, he stayed there until his term was over and then went home. Made director of the bureau of evaluations in the ministry of personnel in Nanking, he was later transferred to Hanlin librarian and lecturer-in-waiting. He sub-

mitted to the court [thirteen] pictures of exemplary emperors.³ Shih-
tsung was still chagrined over his earlier memorial on the ritual question and took this occasion to cause Tsou to be investigated by the ministry of rites. But this matter was not further pursued. Tsou was then
made vice-minister of the court of imperial sacrifice (1540) and reader-
in-waiting in charge of the Hanlin Academy in Nanking. When fire
broke out in the imperial ancestral temples in Peking (1541), the
emperor decreed that ministers should make confessions. Apprehen-
sively, the officials accused themselves of various charges. Tsou submitted a memorial on the duty of mutual respect between ruler and minister, and this cost him his office. After years of retirement, he died in
1562 at age seventy-one. In 1567 he was posthumously awarded the title
of vice-minister of rites and the honorific Wen-chuang.

When Tsou first saw Wang Yang-ming at the governor's office (Kan-
chou), it was to request of him an epitaph for Tsou's father, with no
intention of studying with Yang-ming. But Wang Yang-ming was then
preoccupied day and night with teaching, and Tsou was suddenly
struck, saying, "I used to doubt Ch'eng Yi and Chu Hsi because they
amended the *Great Learning,* giving priority to the investigation of things
and the exhaustion of principles,⁴ while the *Doctrine of the Mean* emphasizes vigilance in solitude, so that these two texts no longer tallied. Now
I realize that investigating things and extending knowledge mean vigilance in solitude." So he called himself Wang Yang-ming's disciple.
Later he saw Wang Yang-ming again in Shao-hsing and stayed over a
month. After his departure, Wang thought of him, saying, "Tsou is the
kind of man who is gifted and able himself, yet asks questions of those
who are less able."⁵ And when Tsou went from Kuang-te to Shao-hsing,
Wang admired his detachment in not taking his banishment hard. Tsou
said, "An official has to watch his steps just as an actor takes whatever
comes." Wang kept silent for a long while and said, "The *Book of History*
describes Yao as 'intelligent, respectful, accomplished, and thoughtful.'⁶
I believe you are respectful and thoughtful. How about being intelligent
and accomplished?" Tsou realized then that his past respect and
thoughtfulness were not entirely free from cynicism.

Tsou's learning was especially strong in reverence. Reverence refers
to *liang-chih* being bright and clear without a speck of dust. Moving in
the midst of daily relations and affairs, my nature-in-itself makes no distinction between activity and tranquility, day and night, and never
stops. What is called good refers to those places where the flow of consciousness (*liu-hsing*) is proper; what is called evil refers to those places
where this is hindered and blocked up. For once caution and apprehension are forgotten, all will be hindered and blocked up. So one should
make sure that wherever caution and apprehension are present, in those
directions nature-in-itself will go. Outside of caution and apprehension,

one cannot find nature. Outside of nature, one cannot find daily relationships and affairs. That is why we say the metaphysical (Tao) and the
physical *(ch'i)* are not two, and nature is present in physical endowment
(ch'i-chih).[7]

At that time, Nieh Pao was reflecting on the substance of stillness,
considering the function of our [emotional] responses as effects. Tsou
said that Nieh was partial to the inner realm of consciousness and so
split mind and its substance into two things. Chi Pen disliked the natural and emphasized alertness. Tsou said that he was stubborn and
unyielding, rather than "directing [things naturally], without giving
trouble." After Confucius, the source of learning became distant, its
tributaries separating from one another. After Wang Yang-ming, those
who kept his authentic transmission could not but regard Tsou as
Wang's legitimate heir. To regard the flow of consciousness *(liu-hsing)* as
nature-itself is what even Buddhists can do. But their dislike of external
things and their ways of attributing to emptiness right and wrong, good
and evil, in order not to obstruct the flow of self-consciousness, shows
no insight into the oneness and wholeness of all things. As to principles
of origin in what concerns daily relations and affairs, these can no
longer be clearly distinguished. Vagueness and lack of conciseness are
things that scholars ought to criticize.

Tsou's *Ch'ing-yüan cheng-ch'u*[8] recorded that during Wang Yang-
ming's campaign in Kwangtung and Kwangsi, Ch'ien Tê-hung and
Wang Chi each gave expression to what they considered Wang's essential teachings. Ch'ien said that the mind was neither good nor evil, the
intention either good or evil, while *liang-chih* (literally, knowledge of
good) knows good and evil, and investigation of things means doing
good and avoiding evil. Wang Chi said that mind, intention, knowledge, and things are neither good nor evil. Wang Yang-ming laughed
and said, "Ch'ien Tê-hung should learn about metaphysical reality
(pen-t'i) from Wang Chi, while Wang Chi should learn cultivation *(kung-
fu)* from Ch'ien Tê-hung." This refers to the same incident given in
Wang Chi's *T'ien-ch'üan cheng-tao chi,* but the two accounts are very different. My teacher Liu Tsung-chou used to suspect that what Wang
Yang-ming said at T'ien-ch'üan [i.e., the Four Sentences] differed from
his ordinary teachings. Wang usually referred to mind-in-itself as being
characterized by the good, and this good means fulfilling to the utmost
the principle of Heaven, without a speck of human passion. He also
said *liang-chih* is the principle of Heaven. And the *Ch'uan-hsi lu* refers
many times to the principle of Heaven. Even if there is a reference to *li*
in tranquility being neither good nor evil, Wang Yang-ming never said
there that the mind-in-itself was neither good nor evil. Now that we
read Tsou's account, we discover that the Doctrine of Four Positives
regards the mind as being characterized by the highest good, without

any evil, but that this doctrine comes from Ch'ien Te-hung and is what Wang Yang-ming himself taught.[9] I wonder whether those who follow the T'ien-ch'üan account and criticize Wang Yang-ming for teaching a doctrine of absence of good and evil have ever studied Tsou's records. Tsou Shou-yi's son was named Tsou Shan. His grandsons were called Tsou Te-han, Tsou Te-p'u, and Tsou Te-yung.[10]

(*MJHA* 16:3a–4a)

NOTES

1. For Tsou Shou-yi, see his biography by Julia Ching, *DMB,* v. 2, 1310–12.
2. Reference to Emperor Shih-tsung's endeavors to bestow imperial honors on his natural parents, the deceased prince of Hsing and his surviving wife, Lady Chiang (d. 1518), which divided the ministers of the court into two parties: those opposing the honors and those supporting them. See the emperor's biography by Lien-che Tu Fang, *DMB,* v. 1, 315–22.
3. This was done as a help for the education of the heir-apparent.
4. Reference to Chu Hsi's amendment of the *Great Learning,* adding to it a paragraph on "exhausting principles" *(ch'iung-li),* as an expansion of the investigation of things and extension of knowledge.
5. Reference to *Analects* 8:5.
6. Reference to *Book of History,* "Canon of Yao," in J. Legge, trans., *The Chinese Classics,* v. 3, 15.
7. Huang Tsung-hsi approves here of Tsou's teaching, especially his integration of human nature. The Sung philosophers, Ch'eng Yi and Chu Hsi, had explained the rise of evil in human nature in terms of the conditioning of man's originally good nature, which he received from Heaven and Earth with his physical endowment *(ch'i-chih),* that is, the quality of his existential endowment.
8. See *MJHA* 16:7b.
9. For the Four Positives, see Ch'ien's biography in this volume.
10. For Tsou's son and grandsons, see *MJHA* 16:4a–b.

Ou-yang Te

Ou-yang Te, *tzu* Ch'ung-yi, *hao* Nan-yeh (1496–1554),[1] a native of T'ai-ho in Kiangsi, passed the provincial examination shortly after he had been capped as an adult. He studied at Ch'ien-t'ai with Wang Yang-ming, twice refraining from taking the metropolitan examinations. Wang Yang-ming called him fondly "the talented youth." He acquired the *chin-shih* in 1523, became successively magistrate of Liu-an-chou (Anhwei), vice-director of a bureau in the ministry of justice (1526), Hanlin compiler (1529), and, a year later, director of studies in the National University of Nanking, director of the seal office in Nanking (1535), vice-director of the court of the imperial stud (1536), and director of the court of state ceremonial in Nanking. He took time off to mourn his father's death, after which he was restored to office. When his request for permission to retire was not granted, he was transferred to director of the court of imperial sacrifices in Nanking (1547) and then called back to Peking as chief minister of the court of imperial sacrifices with responsibilities as chancellor of the National University. He was then promoted to vice-minister of rites, moved from there to the ministry of personnel, and became Hanlin chancellor in charge of the supervisorate of imperial instruction (1549). He then went home to mourn the death of his mother but, before the period was over, was called back (October 1552) as minister of rites and Hanlin chancellor, on duty in the Wu-yi Hall. He died in office on April 24, 1554, at age fifty-eight and was awarded the title of junior guardian of the heir-apparent and the honorific Wen-chuang.

Ou-yang Te's greatest contribution at court concerned the problem of the succession to the throne. At the time, the emperor [Shih-tsung] had avoided making any decision about this, having succumbed to the foolish theory of the perverse man T'ao Chung-wen,[2] who told him that two dragons should not see each other (meaning that it would not be propitious for a reigning emperor to meet with the future emperor). So he did not wish to designate another heir after the death of the heir-apparent, Chuang-ching (1549). Instead, he wanted to make both his sons feudal princes.[3] As minister of rites, Ou-yang raised the issue, but his memorial was not answered. When the two princes were instructed to marry away from court in their outside residences, Ou-yang reminded the emperor that Emperor T'ai-tsu (the dynastic founder, r. 1328–98) had arranged the weddings of his sons when they were all residing in the Imperial Palace, while Emperor Hsiao-tsung (r. 1488–1505) arranged for his younger brothers to wed in their own outside residences. He pointed out clearly that the precedent set by Emperor T'ai-tsu should be followed in similar circumstances, and the princes should not be sent away. The emperor disapproved, and ordered the two princes to move out of the Imperial Palace (1553). Ou-yang then referred to the Taoist prayers for special services in the *Hui-tien*,[4] which spoke of [the "designation" of the eldest son as] "the presiding person in sacrificial rites" *(chu-chi)* as "succession" *(ch'eng-tsung),* and of enfeoffment as "inheritance" *(ch'eng-chia),* and asked what ought then to be followed. The emperor, displeased, replied that the designation of feudal princes should follow proper ceremonials since otherwise one might as well proceed to the installation of an heir-apparent. Ou-yang Te seized upon this occasion to submit the ceremonials immediately for the installation of an heir-apparent, with their commentaries. The emperor was furious. The ceremonies for the princes were then held, with no differentiation made. When the lady-mother to [the future] Emperor Mu-tsung[5] died, Ou-yang Te submitted the ceremonials for mourning and funerals, with their commentaries, proposing that the precedent set in the Ch'eng-hua period (1465–87) after the death of the Lady Chi, mother of Emperor Hsiao-tsung,[6] be followed. The emperor once more disagreed, burying her with the dignity of an ordinary consort. These incidents show that Ou-yang Te was faithful to the proper rituals and ceremonials, without regard to the pleasure or displeasure of the emperor. His insistence upon rightful precedents in the rituals regarding feudal princes of royal blood was actually only a minor example.

Ou-yang Te considered the teaching of philosophy *(chiang-hsüeh)* as his work. Scholars of the time all knew well the doctrine of the extension of *liang-chih;* indeed, half the world called themselves Ou-yang's disciples. Together with Hsü Chieh,[7] Nieh Pao, and Ch'eng Wen-te,[8] he presided over the assemblies at the imperial capital, which took place in the Taoist Ling-chi Temple in 1553 and 1554. These assemblies gathered up to a thousand followers in one place and stood out as big events the like of which had not been known for many centuries.

Lo Ch'in-shun,[9] who did not agree with the teaching of *liang-chih,* said that the Buddhists, because they had some understanding of the mind but no understanding of nature, considered consciousness *(chih-chüeh)* to be nature. According to him, to speak of the *liang-chih* of one's mind as the principle of Heaven *(T'ien-li)* would also be to consider consciousness as nature. Ou-yang Te responded that consciousness and *liang-chih*[10] appear similar but remain different. Consciousness comprehends our faculties of seeing, hearing, speaking, and moving, which are not necessarily all good. *Liang-chih* refers to our capacities for commiseration, shame, respect, and for discerning between right and wrong, all of which represent what is called original goodness. This original goodness is constituted by knowledge *(chih)* as its substance *(t'i)* and can have no other substance. Our true heavenly nature is clearly aware of the natural, and responds to it with penetration. Having its own principles of organization, it is called *liang-chih* and *T'ien-li* (heavenly principle). One might also say that heavenly principle serves as the organizing principle of *liang-chih,* while *liang-chih* serves as the spiritual intelligence *(ling-ming)* of the heavenly principle. It cannot be adequately described as consciousness.

Lo Ch'in-shun also brought up the point that there cannot be two faculties of human knowledge. But if Mencius calls that which knows without reflection *liang-chih,*[11] it is not because there is still another cognitive faculty. Hence, Lo said, those who refer to commiseration, shame, respect, and discernment of right and wrong[12] as *liang-chih,* and seeing, hearing, speaking, and moving as consciousness, would be making the same distinction as does the *Laṅkāvatāra Sūtra*[13] between true perception *(chen-shih)* and discriminating perception. Ou-yang Te responded that there are not two kinds of cognitive faculties. The knowledge that arises from commiseration, shame, respect, and discerning between right and wrong cannot be isolated from seeing, hearing, speaking, and moving, although seeing, hearing, speaking, and moving do not necessarily possess the original goodness of commiseration, shame, respect, and discernment between right and wrong. One refers therefore to consciousness in seeing, hearing, speaking, and moving, but perceives the good that arises when commiseration, shame, respect, and discernment between right and wrong are experienced. Consciousness should not be called nature or principle *(li);* only the knowledge of the good may be called the principle of Heaven. This is similar to the distinction between the moral mind *(Tao-hsin)* and the human mind *(jen-hsin).*[14] There is no question of two minds, just as the distinction between heavenly nature and physical endowment does not constitute two natures.[15] Lo Ch'in-shun also raised the difficulty that, when *liang-chih* is regarded as the heavenly principle, the principles of Heaven and Earth and the myriad things are then put outside our speculations and never discussed, with the result that one could no longer achieve a penetrating and unitary understanding of all reality. Ou-yang Te responded that *liang-chih* could only manifest itself through our seeing and hearing, reflections and deliberations, while our seeing and hearing, reflections and deliberations could only become manifest through our interactions with Heaven and Earth, humans and things. These represent an unlimited realm for knowledge; seeing, hearing, reflections, and deliberations may also assume unlimited forms. The same may be said of *liang-chih.* There can be no *liang-chih* in isolation from Heaven and Earth and the myriad things.

What Ou-yang Te calls *liang-chih* relies upon the knowledge in solitude *(tu-chih)* of right and wrong. Its substance is always manifest, and there is no prior moment *(wei-fa)* before its responses are made. What is called *wei-fa* usually refers to what precedes the manifestation *(fa)* of joy, anger, sorrow, and pleasure. [In Ou-yang's case], the two states, prior and posterior, are explained [paradoxically] in terms of the hidden becoming manifest.[16] His fellow disciples, who also taught *liang-chih,* differed naturally in their depths of understanding or in details of expositions. But Ch'ien Te-hung, Wang Chi, Tsou Shou-yi, Huang Hung-kung, and Ch'en Chiu-ch'uan[17] all insisted that the prior *(wei-fa)* and the posterior *(yi-fa)* do not refer to two different moments, and that the achievement of the harmony of manifest emotions is also the achievement of the pristine equilibrium *(chung,* or the Mean) of consciousness. Only Nieh Pao[18] emphasized the return to stillness *(kuei-chi),* concentrating his efforts on achieving equilibrium as that which brings with it harmony of emotions. This led to much questioning on the part of the fellow disciples. Nieh Pao had much difficulty in coping with these problems. Only after he met Lo Hung-hsien was he no longer alone.

All this happened because Wang Yang-ming developed the teaching of the extension of *liang-chih* in his later life, without having had opportunity to discuss it in depth with other scholars. When we read the *Ch'uan-hsi lu,* we come upon the passage in which he said,

> When I was in Ch'u-yang I saw that my students were mostly concerned with intellectual knowledge and spent time debating, which did them no good. So I taught them quiet-sitting, enabling them to experience a purer form of consciousness, which brought some immediate results. But in time they developed a fondness for silence and a disgust for action, thus falling into the pitfall of becoming like lifeless dry wood. . . . But I expound now only the doctrine of extending *liang-chih.* If *liang-chih* is clear, one can either try to attain truth through quiet reflection or through efforts made in the midst of activity. *Liang-chih* in itself is originally neither active nor tranquil. This is the gist of our learning.[19]

His general meaning can be seen from this. Later scholars knew only how to make efforts in the midst of activity, so that consciousness becomes *liang-chih;* they drifted into the secret pitfall of externalizing righteousness and forcing the work of cultivation.[20] Its injuries were worse than those coming from fondness of tranquility and disgust for action. For these persons did not make efforts on *liang-chih* but only on activity and tranquility, or rather, only on activity. In Yang-ming's words, they clearly became one-sided. Although Ou-yang Te and Nieh Pao did not reach the same conclusions in their discussions, Nieh Pao's return to stillness did not make him like a piece of dry wood, while Ou-yang Te's investigation of things avoided fragmentation [of learning]. In making clear Wang Yang-ming's teachings, they needed to have no further regret, since they did not get in each other's way.[21]

(MJHA 17:1a–2b)

NOTES

1. For Ou-yang Te, see his biography by Wei-ming Tu, *DMB,* v. 2, 1102–4.
2. See T'ao's life by Liu Ts'un-yan, *DMB,* v. 2, 1266–68.
3. The prince, Chu Tsai-jui, posthumously honored by the title Chuang-ching, died at age thirteen. His two younger brothers, including Chu Tsai-hou, later Emperor Mu-tsung, were next in the line of succession. They were named feudal princes at very early ages and made to wed in February, 1553. See Chu Tsai-hou's biography, by Lien-che Tu Fang and Chaoying Fang, *DMB,* v. 1, 365–67.
4. This refers to the unpublished edition of the *Hui-tien* (Collected Institutes) of 1529, which Ou-yang himself participated in compiling.
5. Reference to the death of Chu Tsai-hou's natural mother (1554), who was buried without the pomp due to the mother of an heir-apparent. This displeased Ou-yang Te and others, who desired a clear designation of the heir to the throne. This succession question was a recurrent source of conflict between

ministers and sovereigns, especially later between the men of Tung-lin and Emperor Shen-tsung. See *DMB*, v. 1, 365.

6. For the poignant story of the way Emperor Hsiao-tsung honored his deceased natural mother, who was of low birth, see his biography by Chaoying Fang, *DMB*, v. 1, 376.

7. Hsü Chieh, *hao* Shao-fu, served as grand secretary. See his life by Chaoying and Lien-che Tu Fang, *DMB*, v. 1, 570–76.

8. For Ch'eng Wen-te, *hao* Sung-hsi, (1497–1559), see *MJHA*, ch. 13.

9. Some of the problems Lo raised were discussed with Wang Yang-ming. See *Ch'uan-hsi lu*, part 2, for Yang-ming's letters to Ou-yang and to Lo. English translation in W. T. Chan, trans., *Instructions for Practical Living*, 120–57, 157–65.

10. The word *chih* is common to "consciousness" *(chih-chueh)* and *liang-chih*.

11. *Mencius* 7A:15.

12. Reference to the "four beginnings of virtue" *(Mencius* 2A:6).

13. See *Laṅkāvatāra Sūtra, TSD* XVI, no. 670, ch. 4.

14. Reference to the formula considered to contain the sacred teaching of the sages: "Man's mind is prone to error; the mind of the Way is subtle. Remain discerning and single-minded: keep steadfastly to the Mean *(chung).*" See the *Book of History*, "Counsels of Great Yü," in J. Legge, *The Chinese Classics*, v. 3, 61.

15. Reference to the Ch'eng-Chu explanation *(ECCS, Yi-shu* 18:5b) of moral evil in spite of human goodness, in terms of a difference between "heavenly nature" (man's essential goodness) and his "physical endowment" *(ch'i-chih)*, by which the essential goodness of his original nature is conditioned. The best account of this theory is given in Fung Yu-lan, *Chung-kuo che-hsüeh shih*, 861. English translation, *A History of Chinese Philosophy*, v. 2, 488. See also W. T. Chan, "Neo-Confucian Solution to the Problem of Evil," in *Neo-Confucianism etc.: Essays by Wing-tsit Chan* (New Haven, 1969), 99–112.

16. Reference to the importance of striking a balance between interior cultivation and active involvement in affairs. Those who are for *wei-fa* prefer quiet-sitting and contemplation; those who are for *yi-fa* plead for action as an expression of manifest contemplation.

17. Ch'en Chiu-ch'uan, *hao* Ming-shui (1495–1562), is regarded by Huang Tsung-hsi as a member of the Chiang-yu branch of the Yang-ming school. See *MJHA* 19:15b–19b. See also Chan, *Instructions*, p. 187, n. 1. Chen was the disciple who recorded the early sections of *Ch'uan-hsi lu*, part 3, which give largely his discussions with Wang Yang-ming. See Chan, *Instructions*, 187–99. For Huang Hung-kan, *hao* Lo-ts'un, 1492–1561, see *MJHA*, ch. 19.

18. For Nieh Pao, see his biography in this volume. He also exchanged letters with Wang Yang-ming. Two answers from Yang-ming are included in *Ch'uan-hsi lu*, part 2. See English translation in W. T. Chan, trans., *Instructions for Practical Living*, 165–82.

19. See *Ch'uan-hsi lu*, part 3. An English account is in Chan, *Instructions*, 217. But the translation here is our own.

20. Allusions to *Mencius* 2A:2, 15–16. The opposition is drawn between cultivation of righteousness as an interior disposition and practicing it only incidentally as an act of external conformity to social mores. Mencius also insists that the work of self-cultivation should not be forced *(chu-chang)*, although it requires constant alertness, because it ought to grow by a natural rhythm.

21. Huang Tsung-hsi gives an even-handed appraisal of Ou-yang Te and Nieh Pao, while pointing out that the former preferred action to meditation, and the latter preferred meditation to action.

Nieh Pao

Nieh Pao, *tzu* Wen-yü, *hao* Shuang-chiang (1487–1563),[1] a native of Yung-feng (Kiangsi), acquired the *chin-shih* in 1517 and was made magistrate of Hua-t'ing (Nan Chihli). He checked the accounts and recovered eighteen thousand taels of silver, which he used to make up for taxes that evaded collection, to repair irrigation systems, and to start schools. He also recognized the talents of Hsü Chieh,[2] then a local government student. Nieh was summoned (1525) to Peking and made a censor, in which capacity he impeached a powerful eunuch [Chang Tso] and some high officials, earning a reputation as a bold ombudsman. He became prefect of Soochow (1530) and then mourned the deaths of his parents, staying home for ten years, until he became prefect of P'ing-yang (1541, in Shansi). There he repaired fortifications and trained soldiers, taking precautionary measures to keep away frontier raiders. When Emperor Shih-tsung heard of it, he told his ministers-in-waiting, saying, "What a man is this Nieh Pao to be able to do all this!" and promoted him to be surveillance vice-commissioner of Shensi. But the displeasure of the grand secretary, Hsia Yen,[3] was such as to lead to his being relieved of his office and going home, after which Hsia even caused him to be arrested. At the time, Nieh was in the midst of discussing the *Doctrine of the Mean* with other scholars. When the men arrived suddenly and placed him under arrest, Nieh waited for them to put on his shackles and then finished his discussion with the other scholars before leaving. He was put into the Imperial Guard Prison, where Hsia Yen came to see him. Nieh expressed no complaint, which shamed Hsia extremely. He was eventually freed after a year's lapse. Then, in 1550, when the capital was preparing to defend itself against a military attack, Hsü Chieh, as minister of rites, recommended Nieh Pao to the court. He was subsequently made grand coordinator of Chi-chou (Chihli) with the rank of junior assistant censor-in-chief and transferred to vice-minister of war with the charge of assisting in the training of troops at the capital. When Ch'iu Luan, who was in charge of the training, requested that the troops at Hsüan-fu and Ta-t'ung be transferred to the capital guards, Nieh refused permission. Later, he was promoted to minister of war (1553), with the title of junior tutor to the heir-apparent, a reward for his contributions to frontier defense. When pirates *(wo-k'ou)* raided the southeast, Chao Wen-hua asked that he himself be sent to the coast to supervise the troops, and Chu Lung-hsi petitioned that land taxes be differentiated and maritime trading centers be reopened. They were supported by the grand secretary, Yen Sung.[4] But Nieh Pao disapproved of all these suggestions. As a result, he was demoted in rank and salary by two grades (1555), and then allowed to retire on the pleas of sickness and age (1556). He died on

November 19, 1563, at age seventy-six. In 1567, he was posthumously awarded the title of junior guardian and given the honorific Chen-hsiang.

When Wang Yang-ming was in Chekiang, Nieh Pao was performing censorial duties in Fukien and passed through Hangchow, wanting then to cross the river to visit Wang. The people around him advised against this, but Nieh refused to listen. When he eventually met Wang, he was much pleased and commented: "What the gentleman does may not be understood by many people." But he still wondered whether Wang was receiving people indiscriminately, and so he wrote to Wang about this. Yang-ming answered,[5] "In my teaching, I do not seek to awaken faith in myself. I only do what my mind and heart tells me I must do. Should I fear disbelief and so exercise more selectivity in receiving others, I would be going against my own mind." This impressed Nieh Pao very much. When Wang went on his campaign to Ssu-en and T'ien-chou (1529), Nieh asked him about the effort [of cultivating the mind] that should "neither be forgotten nor unduly helped."[6] Wang answered, "I talk only about 'always doing something' and not of 'neither forgetting nor helping.'[7] Should I talk only about 'neither forgetting nor helping,' it would be like putting an empty skillet on the fire." At the time of Yang-ming's death, Nieh was prefect of Soochow and said, "If I had not formally become his disciple, it was in the hope of seeing him again. This has now become impossible." So he set up a tablet in Yang-ming's name and prostrated before it, facing north. From then on, he called himself a disciple, Ch'ien Te-hung having served as his witness to assure that the ceremony was duly performed. He even had the two letters he received from Yang-ming inscribed in stone.

Nieh Pao's learning developed in prison, where he had plenty of tranquility and nothing to do, until he suddenly perceived the reality of the mind-in-itself, in its radiance and brightness, as that which contains all things. He said joyfully, "This is the equilibrium (or Mean) prior to the rise of emotions. Should I only be able to keep this and not lose it, I would possess the source of all the principles under Heaven." After his release from prison, he regulated a method of quiet-sitting that he taught those who studied with him, guiding them to return to stillness for the sake of attaining harmony with themselves and a composure that enabled them to respond perfectly to events and happenings, so that in practical life they might be in accord with their [minds]. At the time, those of his fellow students who also followed the teaching of *liang-chih* regarded the prior state [before rise of emotions] to be present in the posterior—[a moment at which] emotions were rising and yet not arisen, so that the effort of achieving such a prior state could be made manifest in the posterior state, and the effort of the natural (*hsien-t'ien,* literally, before Heaven, preconscious) could be made manifest in the conscious (*hou-t'ien,* literally, after Heaven).

Those who disagreed with Nieh expressed three kinds of doubts. First: if the Tao were that which should not be abandoned even for one instant, then to say that no effort need be applied to activity would be to abandon it. Second: if the Tao were beyond activity and tranquility, then the effort of maintaining tranquility would separate it into two modes. Third: if mind and affairs ought to be one, and mind ought to be present everywhere, in every affair, to say then that one might forgo efforts in one's conscious responses while these are in the flow of process *(liu-hsing)* would be to abandon affairs and to draw near to Ch'an Buddhist doctrines of enlightenment. Thus did Wang Chi, Huang Hungkang, Ch'en Chiu-ch'uan, Tsou Shou-yi, and Liu Wen-ming each raise difficulties, as Nieh sought to resolve them one by one. Only Lo Hunghsien agreed profoundly with him, saying that Nieh's teaching resembled a thunderbolt that struck at the ambiguity of many would-be heroes [of the sagely Way], until he made available to all a wide and open road, and no further doubt need remain. Much later, Liu too came to believe him and admitted, "Nieh Pao was right in what he said."

For the mind-in-itself[8] is that which is always in an unending flow of process, moving from tranquility to activity, activity to tranquility. The "prior" state refers to tranquility, the "posterior" state to activity. To apply effort to the posterior state is to follow activity, to apply effort to the prior state is to follow tranquility. Each shows partiality. But the *Doctrine of the Mean* speaks of "the great root,"[9] referring to the prior state, because the mind-in-itself is also Heaven-in-itself. The circumference of Heaven[10] measures 365.25 degrees. In the middle [of the celestial globe] stands the heavenly axis. Heaven does not cease revolving for an instant. Yet its cardinal axis is grounded in eternal stillness, a tranquility to which it must always return.[11] For this reason Chou Tun-yi[12] said that the Human Ultimate is established by concentrating on tranquility, and Yang Shih's[13] disciples regarded the experiences of the state [of consciousness] prior to the rise of joy, anger, sorrow, and pleasure as their secret transmission. Nieh differs from Buddhists because he said that one should return to stillness in order to respond to the harmony of the universe; this is not the same as the Buddhists' regard of such response and harmony as earthly troubles and their seeking to eliminate all and return to absolute stillness. So Nieh did not thoroughly adopt Buddhism. For Buddhists[14] take the manifestation of consciousness to be nature and dislike talking about reality itself *(t'i)*. They talked of the moment before one's birth, of the moment preceding Heaven *(hsien-t'ien)*, and of concentrating on the middle as essential. All such talk refers to the flow of process, a process not attached to things and affairs, but rather to consciousness only. And when they talked of the moment following Heaven *(hou-t'ien)*, of the great manifest immediate, and of objectivity *(pin,* literally, guest), they referred to those affairs present in the flow of process as consciousness. Their understanding of actual reality is partial to the side of activity, and so they say, "Without abiding anywhere and yet producing the mind," which is directly opposite to the teaching about preserving mind and developing nature. For the mind-in-itself is always in the flow of process, but it is a flow that takes place without transgressing certain laws [of nature], centering upon the constant and eternal, what is called tranquility and stillness. The Confucian effort to preserve mind and nurture nature[15] is applied to this place and so differs from the Buddhists. Should one merely make distinctions on the basis of whether there is concern for a response to events, then even the Buddhists have not neglected the realm of responses.

Wang Yang-ming started to speak of *liang-chih* after moving to Kiangsi. When he was still in Nanchung, he regarded quiet-sitting to purify the mind as the goal of learning and inner composure to control our dispersed self as necessary.[16] Only with the equilibrium (or Mean) prior to the rise of emotions could there be the harmony of due proportions following the rise of emotions. After that, his students showed the mistake of preferring tranquility to activity, so he taught the extension of *liang-chih* as a remedy. However, he still said that *liang-chih* was itself present in equilibrium prior to emotions, so actually he continued to teach as before. Nieh Pao did not really diverge from Yang-ming's teachings and should not have been criticized by so many people. In [*Shih-miao*] *shih-yü lu*, Hsü Hsüeh-mo[17] records that Yang Chi-sheng[18] impeached Yen Sung for making false reports of frontier victories, and that this matter was sent to the ministry of war for a proper investigation. But since Yen Shih-fan had himself drafted the report that was sent to the ministry, all Nieh Pao did was to follow the submitted draft and prepare the records. But if we check the *Shih-hsiao p'ien*, we find that Nieh Pao counseled Yen Sung[19] to decline the military awards and not submit the memorial of reply, giving all credit rather to Chang Shih-ch'e. If that were true, then the false accusation that Nieh had recorded entirely according to Yen's draft would become clear of itself.[20]

(*MJHA* 17:8b–10a)

NOTES

1. For Nieh Pao, see his biography by D. W. Y. Kwok, *DMB*, v. 2, 1096–98.
2. For Hsü Chieh, *hao* Ts'un-chai, see *MJHA*, ch. 27 and his biography by Chaoying and Lien-che Tu Fang, in *DMB*, v. 1, 570–76.
3. For Hsia Yen, see his biography by Angela Hsi, *DMB*, v. 1, 527–31.
4. For Yen Sung, see his biography by Kwan-Wai So, in *DMB*, v. 2, 1586–91.
5. The two letters that Wang Yang-ming wrote to Nieh in reply to Nieh's are collected in *Ch'uan-hsi lu*, part 2. See also the English translation in W. T. Chan, *Instructions for Practical Living*, 165–82. Mention is made in these letters of

the questions Nieh raised before Yang-ming proceeded to answer them. In rendering the excerpts here, however, we have translated from the *MJHA* itself, without following Chan's English.

6. *Mencius* 2A:2.

7. With these allusions to Mencius, Wang Yang-ming talks about the work of cultivation, placing emphasis upon the need of "always doing something," that is, of acting righteously. See W. T. Chan, trans., *Instructions for Practical Living,* 173.

8. What follows appears to be Huang Tsung-hsi's account of Nieh's philosophy.

9. *Doctrine of the Mean,* ch. 1, refers to equilibrium as the great root *(ta-pen)* from which arises all human activity.

10. Reference here is to the movement of the sun across the horizon and around the celestial sphere, that which is accessible to our observation and was the basis of the calendrical year. See Joseph Needham, *Science and Civilisation in China* (Cambridge, 1959), v. 3, 182.

11. Obviously, Nieh subscribes to the microcosm/macrocosm beliefs, here even paralleling the inner dynamics of our psychic processes to the outer dynamics in the celestial sphere. It is a belief derived from the *Doctrine of the Mean.*

12. For Chou Tun-yi, see *SYHA,* ch. 11–12.

13. For Yang Shih, see *SYHA,* ch. 25.

14. Buddhists are here criticized for not interesting themselves properly in the external affairs and activities making up human life. The Buddhist allusions are to well-known concepts of Ch'an Buddhism, which regard seizing ultimate reality or the Buddha-nature, that which is present "before the birth of our parents."

15. Reference to *Mencius* 7A:1.

16. See J. Ching, *To Acquire Wisdom,* 46–47.

17. Hsü's dates are 1522–93. See *Shih-miao shih-yü lu* (Notes on Shih-tsung's Reign) (n.d., Taipei reprint, Kuo-feng Press, 1965), 17:12a–14a.

18. Yang Chi-sheng, posthumous honorific Chung-min, 1516–55. See his biography by Sun Yuen-king and L. C. Goodrich, *DMB,* v. 2, 1503–5.

19. For an account of Yen's coping with frontier defenses, see his biography, *DMB,* v. 2, 1589.

20. Huang Tsung-hsi does not hide his partiality for Nieh, as he seeks to clear his name here. I have not, however, located *Shih-hsiao p'ien.*

Lo Hung-hsien

Lo Hung-hsien, *tzu* Ta-fu, *hao* Nien-an (1504–64),[1] a native of Chi-shui (Kiangsi) had as his father Lo Hsün, surveillance vice-commissioner of Shantung. He was a serious youth. At age four he dreamed that the main street of the town was filled with a great crowd. He cried aloud [in his dream], saying, "You people coming and going are all in my dream." After he woke up, he told this to his mother, a woman *née* Li. Those who knew him realized that he was no ordinary person. At age ten, he studied ancient prose and admired Lo Lun's character in particular, developing for himself an ambition for sagehood. In 1529 he was the *optimus* of the *chin-shih* examination. His father-in-law, Tseng Chih, the minister of the court of the imperial stud, heard the news and rejoiced, saying, "How happy I am that my son-in-law should accomplish something so great!" Lo replied, "A real man must do more than that. It is hardly a great accomplishment to come out first in an examination taking place once every three years." He was named a Hanlin compiler, but he had to return home a year later to mourn his father's death. During that time he slept on a pillow of straw and ate only vegetables, refraining for three years from entering his room.[2] This was followed by his mother's death, which he mourned as he did the earlier bereavement. In 1539 he was summoned to the post of senior director of instruction and adjutant but arrived in the capital only a year afterwards. At that time the emperor [Shih-tsung] seldom met with his court ministers. During the last month of the year, Lo, together with the censor T'ang Shun-chih and the [Hanlin] corrector Chao Shih-t'ai, requested that the heir-apparent appear on New Year's Day at the Wen-hua Palace to receive the good wishes of the ministers. The emperor said, "I have just been taken ill, and these people already want my heir to appear at court. They must think that I will not recover." So he reduced all the petitioners to the status of commoners. In 1558 the grand secretary, Yen Sung, raised T'ang Shun-chih[3] to secretary in the ministry of war and thought next of Lo. Lo responded by telling [Yen] of his determination to remain in retirement, but T'ang insisted that he also return to an official career. Lo told him, "There are things to be done in the world, if not by one person, then by another. Whatever I should like to do but cannot, you may do it. Why must it be me?" He died in 1564 at age sixty. After the accession to the throne of Emperor Mu-tsung (1567), he was posthumously made an assistant minister of the court of imperial entertainments and given the honorific Wen-kung.

In his learning, Lo began by applying his efforts to the practical realization of his beliefs, then took the road of stillness, and later achieved a penetrating enlightenment in the understanding of the substance of *jen* (*jen-t'i*). In his youth, when he heard that Wang Yang-ming was lecturing in Kan-chou (Kiangsi), he was already drawn to him in admiration. After the appearance of the *Ch'uan-hsi lu* (1518), Lo read it to the point of forgetting sleep and food. His fellow countryman, Li Chung, taught the learning of Yang Chu.[4] Lo became his disciple and learned all he could. Then Nieh Pao taught his fellows the doctrine of returning to stillness,[5] and Lo alone agreed with him wholeheartedly. At the time disciples of the Yang-ming school were all saying that *liang-chih* referred to the knowledge of good and evil, so that the extension of *liang-chih* referred to following one's discernment [between good and evil]. But Lo said, "*Liang-chih* is the name for the supreme good. The good of my mind and heart, I know. The evil of my mind and heart, I also know. I cannot therefore talk about not knowing. Since good and evil are mixed together, is there anything that could serve as a controlling principle in the middle? And if there were nothing serving as a controlling principle in the middle, the talk of knowing the roots and being constantly enlightened would not be possible. And if one's knowledge were not yet enlightened, but one acted in accordance with it, saying that this knowledge was without the influence of [emotions] that had been aroused, this would also not be possible. For, unless one has had the training of absolute stillness, exercising restraint of all his senses and permitting the principle of Heaven to radiate, one could not easily achieve [the extension of *liang-chih*]. Nieh Pao's words had the effect of a thunderbolt. They pointed out the defects of many would-be heroes and made possible a clear and wide path to sagehood that was beyond all doubt.'

Lo Hung-hsien carved out for himself the Rock Lotus Cave,[6] where he practiced quiet-sitting on a bed with his legs crossed. He stayed there for three years without venturing out and acquired an extrasensory knowledge of events before they came to pass. When people showed astonishment, he replied, "It is only chance and not worth mentioning." Wang Chi, being afraid that Lo was too concentrated on a dry stillness and was unable to reach a wondrous state of spontaneity, visited him at Sung-yüan and asked, "How do you find yourself now, in comparison with yourself in the past?" Lo answered, "In the past I often followed [distracting thoughts], but for a while now I have had no more distractions. And as these decrease, I naturally feel more spontaneity and harmony as I respond to things and events. This is like the work of equalizing the burden of taxation.[7] From the sixth month until now, already for half a year, I have been paying attention all day long, without daring to tire myself of it, or to become too attached to things, or to let myself loose, or to make too much fuss over myself. I only fear that, all alone, I might not get my sense of direction; even when distractions are not allowed entry, I might still not realize the two states of activity and tranquility and yet tell myself that this is the work of entering into *samādhi (ching-ting)*. It is not the moment when one is settled in quiet-sitting, but rather the moment when tranquility is turning into activity, that permits no attachment to tranquility itself."[8] Wang Chi sighed in admiration and left.

Lo Hung-hsien had at first admired the teaching of Wang Yang-ming. Later, when he observed that Wang's disciples were making the work of achieving ultimate truth *(pen-t'i)* look too easy, he began to have his doubts. Then when his own efforts at cultivation reached their maturity, he experienced the way Wang's instructions regarding various stages in the progress of self-cultivation became clear of themselves. Many scholars in the world acquired Wang Yang-ming's true spirit through Lo's teachings, while others who made much noise quoting Wang's words and arousing the world did not share [in these insights].

After Lo had compiled Wang Yang-ming's *Chronological Biography (Nien-p'u)* (1563), Ch'ien Te-hung said to him, "The reason you call yourself a 'later student,' rather than a disciple, is that you never formally became Wang Yang-ming's disciple during his lifetime. But would you regard this title of discipleship, past and present, to be restricted to those who actually went through a formal ceremony during the master's lifetime? When you were thirteen years old, you wanted to visit Wang Yang-ming at Kan-chou (Kiangsi) but could not obtain your parents' permission. This shows that you have always desired to become his disciple. By now you have spent three times twelve years studying his teachings and need have no further regret. Why hesitate to call yourself his disciple?" So Lo changed the wording at the head of the *Chronological Biography,* calling himself also a disciple of Wang Yang-ming. Ch'ien Te-hung and Wang Chi served as witnesses [at a formal ceremony held in front of Wang's portrait].

Lo Hung-hsien regarded Chou Tun-yi's[9] teaching on desirelessness and tranquility as the true transmission of the teaching of the sages. To those who claimed that receiving office and retiring, giving and taking, were trivial affairs, Lo said that this could be most injurious [to self-cultivation]. On his home leave, when he passed through Yi-chen (Nan Chihli), he nearly died of sickness. A fellow student of his, Hsiang Ch'iao,[10] was concerned about his poverty. There was then a rich man condemned to death, ready to redeem himself with a bribe of ten thousand taels of silver, who awaited only a word from Lo. Lo declined and departed. But then, remembering that the rich man did not really deserve death, he instructed Hsiang to show compassion and commute his sentence, without ever telling him of this intervention. Lo also gave away to his younger brother the farmhouse he had inherited and built for himself a dwelling for shelter from rain and wind, which was eventually destroyed by flood water. After this he lodged with a farmer. The grand coordinator, Ma Shen, gave him several thousand taels of silver, taking it from the money due to him that he had declined, to allow him to remarry,[11] but Lo refused to accept this. His disciples built him a house, called the Hall of Correct Learning. When he was on the point of dying, visitors went into his room to find it quite bare and asked why he should be so poor. For this reason he very much disapproved of the gatherings for lectures assembled by Wang Chi and others, which were held near cities and placed certain burdens on the public authorities. He said such action used the solemn mission of teaching as an excuse for allowing large retinues to feed on the public, thus encouraging people to take bribes and have no sense of shame.

In addition to his practice of quiet-sitting, Lo also traveled widely, looking for teachers and friends without worrying whether these persons belonged to acceptable society *(fang)*. He begged humbly for instruction from anyone with something to teach him, just as a sick man would act toward a physician, and again, without giving attention to the status and conventions surrounding his own position as a scholar-official. He went about all alone, suffering cold, hunger, and fatigue, running the risk of drowning in a lake, and bearing the humiliations of rough words received in small inns without uttering any complaint. Some said he never abandoned Buddhism and Taoism. Actually, Lo did read the *Sūraṅgama Sūtra* and learned from it the teaching of inward hearing.[12] He felt as though his body were in the Great Void and saw and heard things outside this world. People who saw him then marvelled at his expression. But he reflected upon this and said, "I made the mistake of entering into a state of *samādhi*." So he stopped these efforts and climbed up the peaks of Mount Heng, where he met a monk, Ch'u-chih, who offered him lessons in [the quest of] the outer elixir.[13] Lo said, "I have nothing to do with this." Fang Yü-shih,[14] the Mountain Man of Huang-p'o, was proud of his own secret knowledge regarding the calming of the mind and said that even disciples of sages should learn from him to discover what help tranquility might bring them. Together with Wang Chi, Lo went to Huang-p'o to take lessons from him. Wang departed earlier, while Lo stayed on, becoming ever more skilled in nightly meditations and telling himself, "I have entered the depths in the deep mountains; let no wild goose bring me any letter from home."[15] For Lo, there was no place where he could not learn something and no person who could not be his companion in learning. Even bedfellows have different dreams.[16] Why should he be said to be under Buddhist and Taoist influence?

Keng Ting-hsiang[17] told the story of Lo being deceived by Fang Yü-shih, resenting it until he got ulcers and went home, only to find his wife had died, which made him hate Fang all the more. But when we read his poems on "Sitting at Night" and so on, describing all he had acquired at Huang-p'o, and the insights he personally acquired that were not accessible to Fang, we cannot believe that he could have been so affected by his wife's death as to be shaken in his resolutions. So this only goes to show that Keng did not really know Lo. Teng Yi-tsan said, "Wang Yang-ming was certainly a teacher of the school of sages, although many of his disciples manifested contradictions. But among those who learned from him in private and had some insight, none could excel Lo." This is a mature judgment.

(*MJHA* 18:1a–2b)

NOTES

1. For Lo Hung-hsien, see *MS*, ch. 283.
2. The reference seems to be that Lo lived in a hut near his father's grave and refrained from an intimate relationship with his wife.

3. For T'ang Shun-chih, see his biography in this volume.

4. For Li Chung and Yang Chu, see *MS,* ch. 203.

5. For Nieh Pao, see his biography in this volume.

6. Presumably, he did this some time after being relieved of his official duties (1540).

7. As an analogy for spiritual cultivation, Lo refers here to the work of equalizing land taxes that he had done. See *MS,* ch. 283.

8. Presumably, the reference is to the moment near the end of the meditation period.

9. For Chou Tun-yi, see *SYHA,* ch. 11–12.

10. Hsiang Ch'iao, *hao* Ou-tung, had passed the examination at the same time as Lo. Presumably, Hsiang then held an office like that of a magistrate and could exercise discretion regarding the bribe. Although such action could hardly meet the approval of a modern reader, it should be pointed out that Ming officials, especially those in the lower, provincial ranks, received very meager compensation from the government for their services, so that many were reduced to accepting bribes as a means of making ends meet.

11. We have translated "marry" as "remarry," presuming that this occurred some time after Lo had lost his first wife, which was after his return home from Huang-p'o.

12. Literally, turning inward and hearing. It refers to a state of consciousness in which a person sublimates his sense of hearing to a spiritual level, as described by the Bodhisattva Avalokiteśvara, in the *Śūraṅgama Sūtra,* ch. 6: 128b–130c. See also Charles Luk, trans., *Śūraṅgama Sūtra* (London, 1966), 135–143.

13. Reference is to the Taoist practice of outer alchemy.

14. For Fang Yü-shih, also known as the Mountain Man of Huang-p'o, see the preface to the T'ai-chou school in this volume.

15. This appears to be a quotation from one of Lo's poems.

16. A well-known Chinese proverb.

17. See Keng Ting-hsiang's biography in this volume. Judging from here and elsewhere, Huang Tsung-hsi did not much approve of Keng Ting-hsiang.

Hu Chih

Hu Chih, *tzu* Cheng-fu, *hao* Lu-shan (1517–85),[1] was a native of T'ai-ho in Chi-chou (Kiangsi). In 1556 he obtained the *chin-shih* degree. He was at first given the position of secretary in the ministry of justice. In 1560 he left to become assistant surveillance commissioner in Hukuang and intendant of the Hupei Circuit. [In 1562] he advanced to become assistant administrative commissioner of Szechuan. Subsequently, as a surveillance vice-commissioner, he directed the work of education. At his own request he retired for a while. Later, he was put in charge of education in Hukuang by imperial order. [In 1570] he was transferred to administrative vice-commissioner of Kwangtung. [In 1573] he requested to retire from office to take care of his aging mother.[2] But he was later raised to surveillance commissioner of Fukien (1584). He died in office at age sixty-eight, in June 1585.[3]

When young, Hu was carefree and preferred to write in the style of ancient prose [rather than follow the style of examination essays]. At age twenty-six, he began his inquiries into Confucian learning with Ou-yang Te, who instructed him in the difference between the Way and practicalities. Hu had a relentless hate for evil.[4] Ou-yang Te told him, "Is there anyone who does not feel attractions and repulsions regarding others? How can this ability to love or hate be attributed only to the gentlemen? Should one not attain his original mind *(pen-hsin)*, he might be burdened by his love and hate. And when one is indignant or distraught over too many things, one has already lost his original humanity *(jen-t'i)* and fallen into evil." Hu listened, as though lost, and found himself bathed in perspiration.[5]

At age thirty, Hu turned to Lo Hung-hsien and studied with him.[6] Lo taught him quiet-sitting. When Hu was leaving for Szechuan, Lo said to him, "You talk about your views, not realities. Only when one contemplates truth constantly, from dawn to dusk, without distractions and without attachments, without even a moment of interruption, can one talk about realities. When one's knowledge is more than adequate, but one's practice is not enough, and one always feels as if he had a void inside that is never quite satisfied, then one can speak of having views." But Lo was unable to know Hu's later progress, made after his return to Szechuan [since Lo died that year, 1564].[7]

Hu wrote a book[8] emphasizing the clarification of the goal of learning. His general idea was that principle *(li)* was in the mind and not in Heaven and Earth and all the myriad things. He further clarified Wang Yang-ming's basic assumptions that what is called *li* is the *ch'i* that flows in process *(liu-hsing)* without losing order. In the Great Void there is no place without *ch'i* and no place without *li*. When Mencius says, "All things are complete within me,"[9] he is referring to the self being one with Heaven and Earth and the myriad things through the one *ch'i* that penetrates everywhere. Therefore the *li* of the human mind is also the *li* of Heaven, Earth, and the myriad things; these are not two things. If selfishness has not yet disappeared, and it gets into physical form, then we cannot encompass the myriad things within us. If we are not able to encompass the myriad things and instead seek *li* outside in the myriad things, then these have nothing to do with us. Therefore it is said that *li* is in the mind and not in Heaven and Earth and the myriad things, which is not to say that Heaven and Earth and the myriad things are without *li*.

Hu also said, "My mind is what creates Heaven, Earth, and the myriad things. If this were not so, Heaven, Earth, and the myriad things would become extinguished, and there would only be chaos."[10] Therefore "the flight of the hawk and the swimming of fishes"[11] can be called mindless, as they are caused by physical instinct coming from material form and *ch'i* and not by the ability of hawks and fishes to follow the

Way step by step. But this is not compatible with Wang Yang-ming's teaching of the penetrating *ch'i*. Hu's teachings are not so different, after all, from the Buddhist's teachings: "The three worlds are only Mind; mountains and rivers of the world exist within the wondrous, purified mind."[12] Where he differs from them is that while Buddhists know Heaven, Earth, and the myriad things to be not external to the mind, they insist upon abandoning the world. So their teaching stops with understanding the mind. When there is understanding, the mind reflects Heaven, Earth, and the myriad things, but in the end all is said to be nonbeing. [In Hu's opinion], Confucians should concentrate on serving the world. Their tradition of learning is to exert the mind fully and to become able to observe Heaven, Earth, and the myriad things while remaining fixed on reality.[13] For him, the only difference is that between exerting the mind and not exerting the mind. But in my opinion [says Huang Tsung-hsi], this is not the case. The Buddhists correctly perceive that *li* is in Heaven and Earth and the myriad things and is not something one can personally acquire. So they regard it as a hindrance and reject it. The reason for their saying that mountains, rivers, and earth are all [projections of] the mind is that they do not recognize the existence of mountains, rivers, and earth. If mountains, rivers, and earth are not to be a hindrance to what they call emptiness, then mountains, rivers, and earth must be the things of the wondrously purified mind. And then the worldly Confucian searching for *li* and the Buddhist who does not seek it differ only in scholarship but are one in their agreement that *li* is in Heaven and Earth and the myriad things.

(MJHA 22:1a–b)

NOTES

1. For Hu Chih, see the biography by D. W. Y. Kwok, *DMB*, v. 1, 624–25. See also Keng Ting-hsiang, *Keng T'ien-t'ai wen-chi*, ch. 12 (Taiwan reprint, pp. 1225–43). His autobiography is given in *K'un-hsüeh-chi*, which is appended to the *Heng-lu ching-she hsü-kao* (1902 ed.). See R. L. Taylor, "Journey into Self: The Autobiographical Reflections of Hu Chih, *History of Religions* 21 (1982), 321–38.

2. Hu cared for his mother until her death in 1581, his father having died when he was only seventeen. (His father had been close to Wang Yang-ming.)

3. *Keng T'ien-t'ai wen-chi*, 1226; *K'un-hsüeh chi*, 221.

4. A fuller account of the relation between Ou-yang Te and Hu is given in *K'un-hsüeh chi*, 221.

5. *K'un-hsüeh chi*, 221–22; *Keng T'ien-t'ai wen-chi*, 1228.

6. Hu visited Lo Hung-hsien at Chi-shui, Kiangsi, where Lo had built a retreat for meditation and study. See *K'un-hsüeh chi*, 221.

7. Hu spent the time studying Taoism and Ch'an Buddhism and gives an extensive account of his eventual experiences of enlightenment in *K'un-hsüeh chi*, 222.

8. *Hu-tzu heng-ch'i,* 8 ch. (reprinted in *Yü-chang ts'ung-shu,* 1916).

9. *Mencius* 7A:4.

10. *Hu-tzu heng-ch'i,* ch. 2.

11. This is taken from the *Book of Poetry* (No. 239, Mao version) and quoted in the *Doctrine of the Mean,* ch. 12.

12. The earliest form of the idea is found in *Avataṃsaka Sūtra, TSD,* no. 278, ch. 25, IX, 558c. The initial part of the phrase is found in various versions of *Laṅkāvatāra Sūtra, TSD,* no. 16; 489c, 555b, 618a, 599c, 567a, 626b. The "three worlds" *(san-chieh, trailokya, triloka)* refer to the worlds of desire, of form, and of spirit.

13. *Hu-tzu heng-ch'i,* ch. 2.

8.   The Nan-chung[1] School

Famous disciples from Nan-chung (Nan Chihli) who knew Wang Yang-ming in his lifetime included Wang Ken, Huang Hsing-tseng, Chu Te-chih, Ch'i Hsien, Chou Chung, and Feng En.[2] After Yang-ming's death, Ch'ien Te-hung and Wang Chi taught everywhere they went. Hence the circles they started included the Shui-hsi Assembly in Ching-hsien (Anhwei), the T'ung-shan Assembly in Ning-kuo (Anhwei), the Chün-shan Assembly in Chiang-yin (near Nanking), the Kuang-yüeh Assembly of Kuei-ch'ih (Anhwei), the Chiu-lung Assembly of T'ai-p'ing (Anhwei), the Fu-ch'u Assembly of Kuang-te (Anhwei), the Nan-ch'iao House in the area north of the Yangtze River, the Ch'eng Ancestral Temple Club in Hsin-an (Anhwei), and the Hsin-chai Lecture Hall in T'ai-chou. It was as though each house were ready for enfeoffment.[3] Besides, Tsou Shou-yi, Ou-yang Te, and Ho T'ing-jen[4] each served for a term as an official in Nanking and attracted quite a few disciples. I shall record their teachings later but include here those who have left behind no available recorded dialogs.

Ch'i Hsien, *tzu* Hsiu-fu, *hao* Nan-yüan, a native of Ch'üan-chiao (Anhwei), north of the Yangtze, *chin-shih* of 1526, rose to be chief supervising secretary in the office of scrutiny for justice. He recommended Wang Chi for office, lost the favor of Hsia Yen[5] and, degraded, resigned from service. When Yang-ming was in Ch'u-chou (Anhwei), Ch'i was just one of the students in his company. He did not then know what he believed. Later he became magistrate of Kuei-an (Chekiang). In reading certain texts on learning, he began to understand [Yang-ming's] teaching. So he asked for instruction by correspondence. Afterwards he addressed a group at the An-ting Academy discussing the learning of the sages, which he regarded to be that of *hsin* but said that it might be lost when the person is opinionated and self-indulgent. However, he said that one could rediscover the original mind after repentance and return [to truth]. Whenever he was at the assemblies at the capital, he always prevented people from discussing Buddhism and Taoism. Once, Wang Chi suddenly cited the riddle *(kung-an)* about the leaf stopping the child from crying.[6] Ch'i said angrily, "You are a leader of our group. One careless allusion you made can do untold injury." Wang Chi thanked him in shame. In his own teaching, Ch'i never spoke of anything except *liang-chih*. He was full of energy and expounded it well.

Feng En, *tzu* Tzu-jen, *hao* Nan-chiang, a native of Hua-t'ing and a *chin-shih* of 1556 [*sic*],[7] served as messenger and brought a dispatch to Yang-ming when the latter was fighting in Ssu-en and T'ien-chou (1527). He became Yang-ming's disciple and later rose to be a censor in Nanking. He was put into prison for criticizing the censor-in-chief Wang Hung and the grand secretary Chang Fu-ching. During his trial, Wang was holding the writing brush, while Feng stood arguing his own case. Although he was condemned to death, his sentence was commuted to exile; he was pardoned and allowed to go home.

Kung An-kuo, *tzu* Yüan-lüeh, *hao* Shou-lan, was a native of Hsüan-ch'eng (Anhwei) and a disciple of Ou-Yang Te and Wang Chi. He presided over the assemblies of Shui-hsi and T'ung-shan. In a letter, Ch'ien Te-hung said to him: "Formerly people said, 'Mandarin ducks[8] may be shown after they are embroidered, but the Golden Needle should not be given to another.'[9] Our Golden Needle came to us from the ancients. If we are unable to embroider the mandarin ducks but proudly hold on to the Golden Needle in order to teach others, people who only see the Golden Needle and not the mandarin ducks will not only disbelieve but also lose their desire to learn to embroider the mandarin ducks." Kung became later the prefect of Lü-chou in Shantung and also lectured at the Chih-hsüeh Academy.

Cha Tuo, *tzu* Tzu-chin, *hao* Yi-chai, was a native of Ching-hsien (Anhwei) and a *chin-shih* of 1565. He served as supervising secretary in the supervising office of justice but was disliked by Kao Kung and so transferred to vice-surveillance commissioner of Kwangsi. A disciple of both Wang Chi and Ch'ien Te-hung, he said that *liang-chih* represents a simple and straight principle, surpassed by no other doctrine. According to him, vacuity *(hsü)* means being unattached to one's own opinions, stillness *(chi)* means being uncontaminated by passionate desires, and joy means not being ensnared by things. There is neither being nor nonbeing, neither beginning nor end, neither grades nor steps. One need only work hard at [extending *liang-chih*] every day, for one's whole life.

Shen Ch'ung, *tzu* Ssu-wei, *hao* Ku-lin, was a native of Hsüan-ch'eng and passed the provincial examination in 1537. His highest offical rank was as assistant administration commissioner in Kwangsi. He was a disciple of Kung An-kuo, who had been a disciple of Ou-yang Te and Wang Chi before returning to his native place. Kung told Shen that the learning of Wang Yang-ming's school was to be found especially in Nanking, advising him to go there. So Shen studied also under Ou-yang Te and Wang Chi. He then established the Yang-cheng Academy in Fukien and the Ts'ung-cheng Academy in Ch'i-huang (Hupei). When Lo Ju-fang gathered the K'ai-yüan Assembly in Hsüan-ch'eng, both Shen and Mei Shou-te presided there. When gravely ill, Shen was asked how he felt at heart and answered, "There is nothing *(wu)* there any more."

Mei Shou-te, *tzu* Ch'un-fu, *hao* Wan-hsi, held the highest official rank as senior administration vice-commissioner in Yunnan. When he was prefect of Shao-hsing, he restored Wang Yang-ming's lecture hall and asked Wang Chi to be in charge there. He also called upon [the hermit] Yang K'o, known as [the Mountain Man of] Mi-t'u.[10] He was really no ordinary bureaucrat.

Hsiao Yen, *hao* Nien-ch'ü, was a vice-minister of revenue and had the posthumous honorific Ting-su. He was a native of Ching-hsien and a disciple of Ch'ien Te-hung.

Hsiao Liang-kan, *tzu* Yi-ning, *hao* Ch'uo-chai, held his highest official rank as administration commissioner in Shensi. He was a disciple of Ch'ien Te-hung and Wang Chi. It was mostly through his efforts that the Shei-hsi Assembly to discuss learning succeeded so well.

Ch'i Kun, *tzu* Pu-chih, *hao* Chu-p'o, was a native of Hsüan-ch'eng and a magistrate of Hsiang-ch'eng (Honan). He first studied under Tsou Shou-yi and Ou-yang Te, then finished his courses under Wang Chi, who told him, "What is called resolve *(chih)* cannot be taken away, although vitality or enthusiasm *(yi-ch'i)* may know moments of weakness. But *liang-chih* is that which one need not acquire or reflect upon, the clear consciousness of the natural and the substance of desirelessness. We cannot be completely without desire, so we need to make effort in extending knowledge. Our studies are directed to restoring the substance that is beyond learning; our reflections are directed to restoring the substance that is beyond reflection. That is why one should learn extensively while keeping to some general truths, reflect upon a hundred things and yet extend only one thing. This is not relying upon the externals. As to the knowledge of seeing and hearing, of inferences and references, such come from outside and are not of the originalness *(pen-jan)* of *liang-chih*. We have to be careful about the steps we take, keeping properly to norms and regulations that are called essential. The learning of extending knowledge is one that embraces all kinds of changes and processes, but such changes need not affect the internal control within the self, while the norms and regulations naturally exceed the possiblities of application. This is the infinitesimal difference [between true and false learning]. Ch'i associated with teachers and friends, seeking to improve himself for about seven or eight years. Only then did he begin to know that enthusiasm was not the same as determination, that the knowledge of information was not true knowledge, that external forms are not to be adhered to [as sacred truths]. His determination became more firm and his application more precise, while his influence over others extended further.

Chang Ch'i, *tzu* Chih-yi, *hao* Pen-ching, was a native of Ching-hsien (Anhwei). At the age of five he was able to understand the various books that were taught to him orally. At night when he heard the cock crow, he called his mother, saying: "According to *Elementary Learning*,[11] when one waits upon father and mother, one should get ready by washing one's face and mouth when one hears the first cock crow. Now that the cock is crowing, why don't we get up?" His mother laughed and said: "You only have to continue your studies to understand its real meaning."

He answered, "I shall certainly do so and do better than just understanding." When Ou-yang Te was chancellor at the National University, Chang went to study with him and did not return home for many years. Then he studied under Tsou Shou-yi, Ch'ien Te-hung, and Wang Chi, after which he went home and taught his own disciples. He regarded the composure of spirit *(shou-lien)* as essential, the polishing of mind as real effort, and the consciousness of the oneness of all things as the final goal. He was able to move many hearts with his enthusiasm and eloquence.

Chang Shih-luan, *hao* Meng-ch'üan, was a native of Ch'ing-yang (Anhwei) and a vice-commissioner of Honan. He studied under Tsou Shou-yi.

Ch'eng Ta-pin, *tzu* Ju-chien, *hao* Hsin-ch'uan, was a native of She (Anhwei) and an administration vice-commissioner of Kweichow. He studied under Ch'ien Te-hung, who told him, "The learning of the ancients never left the realm of working on the seven emotions, although their anguish also came frequently from the seven emotions."

Ch'eng Mo, *tzu* Tzu-mu, was a native of Hsiu-ning (Anhwei) and a vice-prefect of Canton (Kwangtung). He went away to study under Wang Yang-ming. At time of his death, he pointed to the Six Classics and said to his son, "You can find me in these books. Do not think they are just old words."

Cheng Chu, *tzu* Ching-ming, was a native of She and assistant prefect in Ho-chien (Chihli). He was a disciple of Tsou Shou-yi. People noticed that he wore clothes of a plain material and considered that he was practicing simplicity. He said, "It is not easy to speak of practicing simplicity. One must first know what the word means."

Yao Ju-hsün, *tzu* Hsü-ch'ing, *hao* Feng-lu, was a native of Nanking and *chin-shih* of 1556. He served as magistrate of Chia-ting. Lo Ju-fang once discussed the teaching of making virtue manifest. Yao pointed to the sun and said, "Virtue resembles a mirror.[12] Without dust it is not obscured; without polishing it does not become bright." Lo laughed and said, "Clear virtue has no substance *(t'i)* and cannot be compared to things. Besides, you are only one person. How can you possibly serve as mirror and dust and then act as polisher?" After hearing this, Yao had real insights and gradually entered the realm of enlightenment. When an irresponsible person criticized Wang Yang-ming for his alleged mistakes, Yao asked him what he meant. The man replied that he did not like Wang's teaching of *liang-chih*. Yao said, "The world considered the sage to be someone descending from Heaven and sagehood as beyond the access of human efforts. This went on for a long time. Only when the doctrine of *liang-chih* emerged, did people know that everyone originally possessed the seed of sagehood and that even foolish men and little children all have that by which they could gain entrance into the Way. This is a historical contribution. Why should you criticize Wang Yang-ming for it?"

Ying Mai, *tzu* Shih-hsün, *hao* Ch'iu-min, was a native of Liu-shou-wei (Nanking) and served as vice-minister of rites. He was a friend of Ho T'ing-jen and heard him speak of Wang Yang-ming's teachings. He wrote treatises concerning the correction of anger and the control of passions.

Chiang Pao, *tzu* T'ing-shan, was a native of Tan-yang, and served as minister of rites in Nanking. He was a disciple of T'ang Shun-chih.

NOTES

1. Nan-chung, literally "south central," refers to the large region of southern (Nan) Chihli, which includes much of today's Kiangsu, Chekiang, and Anhwei. Nanking is the center of this region.

2. See *MJHA,* ch. 25, for Huang Hsing-tseng, Chou Chung, and Chu Te-chih, and see Feng En's biography in *DMB* by Chaoying Fang and L. C. Goodrich, v. 1, 445–48. Ch'i Hsien and Feng are not discussed elsewhere in the *MJHA.* Chou's biography is in *MJHA,* ch. 16.

3. Allusion to Wang Ch'ung's *Lun-heng,* ch. 2. The reference speaks of the people of the sage kings of the past who were all deserving of enfeoffment or "being made noble."

4. See *MJHA,* ch. 19, for Ho's biography.

5. Hsia Yen, 1482–1548, was grand secretary from 1537 to 1542 and 1545 to 1548. See his biography by Angela Hsi, *DMB,* v. 1, 527–31. He is called Kuei-hsi, after his native place in Kiangsi.

6. Reference to the story of a man stopping a child from crying by giving him a yellow leaf in place of gold. The alleged moral is that heavenly joy can cure all earthly sorrows. See *Mahāparinirvāṇa Sūtra, TSD,* no. 374, XII, 20:475.

7. Huang Tsung-hsi gave the wrong date, 1556, instead of 1525.

8. Mandarin ducks are proverbial for their conjugal fidelity and happiness.

9. The Golden Needle refers originally to the needle of the legendary Weaving Girl. It represents some treasure—in this case, the legacy of the sages. Perhaps it stands for the key to sagehood, since the Needle is used in embroidering the ducks. The verse quoted comes from the poet Yüan Hao-wen

(1190–1257?). See his *Complete Works, Yüan Yi-shan hsien-sheng ch'üan-chi,* 1881 edition, 14:8b.

10. Mei's visit to Yang K'o, who refused three times to see him, is recorded in the *Pen-ch'ao fen-sheng jen-wu k'ao,* comp. by Kuo T'ing-hsün (1622 ed.), v. 10, 3081.

11. See *Hsiao-hsüeh chi-chieh,* CYTC ed., 2:1b–2b.

12. Allusion to the mind as a mirror, an analogy made famous by the Ch'an patriarch Hui-neng and his poem. See P. B. Yampolsky, trans., *The Platform Sutra,* (Chinese text, p. 4; English trans., p. 132). That he should point to the sun and speak of the mirror should cause little surprise, since the old Chinese mirror, made of bronze, was usually round in shape.

T'ang Shun-chih

T'ang Shun-chih, *tzu* Ying-te, *hao* Ching-ch'uan (1507–60),[1] a native of Wu-chin (Nan Chihli), came out first in the metropolitan examination of 1529 and was appointed a secretary in the bureau of personnel of the ministry of war. He went home to mourn his mother's death, was subsequently appointed to the bureau of records, then to the bureau of evaluations in the ministry of personnel. He was then moved to the office of Hanlin compiler to do the checking of the *Veritable Records* of the dynasty. But he did not want to work with Chang Ts'ung[2] and requested permission to return home, thus earning Chang's hatred. He retired with the rank of his earlier position in the ministry of personnel. After the heir-apparent was named, a search took place for his palace personnel, and T'ang was appointed an advisor in the directorate of instruction (1539). As the emperor (Shih-tsung) seldom met with his ministers at court, T'ang joined Lo Hung-hsien and Chao Shih-ch'un[3] in requesting that the prince meet his ministers on New Year's Day (January 27, 1521) at the Wen-hua Palace. This enraged the emperor, who relieved him of his post and reduced him to the status of a commoner. When the southeastern coasts suffered harassment from pirates,[4] T'ang worried over the country's problems and offered strategies to those in charge, who in turn recommended him to the court as someone knowledgeable in military affairs. He was made a secretary in the bureau of equipment in the ministry of war in Nanking. Before going there, he was raised to assistant director of the bureau of operations in the ministry of war in Peking. He went to the imperial capital and was promoted to the directorship of that bureau, first with the task of surveying the frontiers and then of inspecting troops in Chekiang and Nan Chihli.

T'ang reflected that pirates should be dealt with on the seas, saying that such "whaleback" activities should not be decided upon in luxurious buildings.[5] So he sailed out to sea to acquire familiarity with the routes and defeated the pirates at the Ch'ung-ming shores. Promoted to junior minister of the court of the imperial stud and vice-commissioner of transmission, he hardly had time to reach Peking before receiving a further promotion to assistant censor-in-chief and grand coordinator of the areas around the River Huai and Yang-chou. Later, while fighting pirates at San-sha (Nan Chihli), T'ang received word that the area north of the Yangtze was in danger, so he delegated powers to his commander Lu T'ang, who stayed behind. He personally attacked the pirates of the Yangtze, defeating them at Yao-chia-tang and Miao-wan, until they nearly collapsed. He returned afterwards to San-sha as the pirates fled further north up the Yangtze. T'ang pursued them across the river. But when they were eventually overcome, the regions around Huai River and Yang-chou suffered a great famine, and T'ang had to feed a starving population of several hundred thousand. He died in a boat on his way to T'ai-chou, on the first day of the fourth month (April 25), in 1560, at age fifty-three.

Since T'ang had emerged into public light in later life on Yen Sung's recommendation, he was criticized by many people. He once asked counsel of Lo Hung-hsien on this subject and received the reply, "Anyone whose name was once on an official register no longer belongs to himself. It would be selfish of him to engage in debates with others about how retired scholars are summoned to office, especially in time of war when difficulty is no excuse. Besides, what efforts have you been making in the cultivation of character?" This settled the question for T'ang. Actually, we know that Yang Shih [the Sung philosopher] even answered the summons of Ts'ai Ching, although he was then in retirement. Many excuses have been offered for Yang's action. How much more sympathy does T'ang deserve!

T'ang's first love was the vain prose and poetry [of Li Meng-yang],[6] which he recited by heart, and which he always imitated in everything he wrote. But Wang Shen-chung[7] told him, "Even the art of writing has its own 'orthodox treasure of the dharma-eye.'[8] Why do you only learn the superficial trappings?" After that, T'ang turned to imitating Ou-yang Hsiu and Tseng Kung[9] and acquired the subtle skills of Ssu-ma Ch'ien.[10] After some practice, and from the abundance of his knowledge, T'ang was able to compose spontaneously, even when he had no intention of doing so. Yet, compared to Wang Shen-chung, he was still too intent upon writing for its own sake. His essential works are classified in five sections, under the headings: Scholarship, Left, Right, Essays, and Miscellaneous. He owed the most to Wang Chi; it is even said that he is beneath Wang Chi by only "one prostration."[11]

T'ang regards creativity (*T'ien-chi*) to be the essential of learning, desirelessness to be effort, and he calls the mind the live locus of creativity. It responds to events and returns to stillness naturally, without needing the intervention of human effort, so that one has only to follow the way of creativity. But creativity is hindered by desire. If one purifies the roots of one's desires, creativity will operate of itself, without requiring any control. It is said that King T'ang and the Duke of Chou sat waiting for the dawn,[12] that Kao-tsung kept respectful silence for three years,[13] and that Confucius refrained from eating and sleeping [for three months] without knowing the taste of meat.[14] Such hardships are endured by those who seek the Way in quiet solitude. And even sages feel that the mind may not be the pure locus for the smooth flow of creativity, so that such effort and exertion would be needed.

T'ang distinguishes Confucians from Buddhists, saying that the Confucians desire the manifest harmony of the emotions of joy, anger, sorrow, and pleasure, while they realize that Heaven and Earth and the myriad things are the seat of convergence and penetration for joy, anger, sorrow, and pleasure. But the Buddhists desire to go against and diminish their manifest emotions of joy, anger, sorrow, and pleasure, since for them, Heaven and Earth and the myriad things have nothing to do with joy, anger, sorrow, and pleasure. So the difference between Confucians and Buddhists is marked by their following the course of creativity or going against it.

Now what is called creativity is nothing other than the ceaseless flow of the mind-in-itself. The Buddhists "produce a mind that abides nowhere"[15] so they too follow the course of creativity. "To go against" and "to flow with" are opposites; what is flowing cannot be against the current. The Buddhists regard emotions of joy, anger, sadness, and pleasure, as well as Heaven and Earth and the myriad things as the rise and fall of projections in emptiness that do not hinder the flow of consciousness, and which cannot be recaptured when it passes over. It has a source, but no tributaries or differentiations, and resembles the waters of Mount Huai and Hsiang-ling (Honan). The Confucians' "flow" fills up all holes and proceeds in an orderly fashion. Its routes are clear; there is a source and there are many tributaries, like river water that flows into the ocean. Buddhists and Confucians do not differ in the following of nature. [Confucians] speak of the three thousand rules of demeanor,[16] and [Buddhists] speak of the eighty thousand fine points of behavior. For the Buddhists have not refrained from making differentiations, even though they frequently separate the mind-in-itself and affairs into two realms. In the end, Buddhist monastic rules differentiate and fine points of behavior have nothing to do with the ultimate truth or [mind]-in-itself *(pen-t'i)*. Hence, in my judgment, one should not lightly compare Confucians and Buddhists and regard them as the same.

(MJHA 26:1a–2a)

NOTES

1. For T'ang Shun-chih, see his biography by Ray Huang, *DMB*, v. 2, 1252–56.

2. Chang Ts'ung, *hao* Lo-feng, 1475–1539, was then grand secretary.

3. Chao Shih-ch'un, *hao* Ch'in-ku, 1509–67.

4. The pirates were referred to as Wo-k'ou, traditionally identified as Japanese, although historians say that many of the later ones who raided the coasts were Chinese pirates.

5. "Whaleback" is used as a parallel to "horseback," referring to naval battles.

6. Li Meng-yang's dates were 1472–1529. He had been a popular writer, admired also by Wang Yang-ming for a time. But he objected to the writing of poetry merely to express philosophical thought, as did the Sung thinkers. See his biography by Chaoying Fang, *DMB*, v. 1, 845.

7. Wang Shen-chung, *hao* Tao-ssu, 1509–59, was known as a stylist and imitated the works of Tseng Kung and Ou-yang Hsiu, in opposition to Li-meng's preference for works of the Ch'in and Han periods. See Wang's biography by Chin-tang Lo, in *DMB*, v. 2, 1398–99.

8. "Orthodox treasure of the dharma-eye" refers to the heart of the Buddha's message, that which is not transmitted by the texts but understood by his favorite disciple, Mahākāśyapa, who smiled when the master showed a flower. "Dharma-eye" (*fa-yen*) is literally that which looks into the depths of truth. Wang Yang-ming also used this expression to describe *liang-chih*, in *WWKC* 5: 198a; English translation in J. Ching, *The Philosophical Letters of Wang Yang-ming,* 62. The expression itself can be found in *Ching-te ch'uan-teng lu, TSD,* no. 2076, 205b–c. See also J. Ching, *To Acquire Wisdom,* 121 and 303, notes 90–91.

9. Ou-yang Hsiu (1007–72) and Tseng Kung (1047–1107) were great stylists. See their biographies by James T. C. Liu and S. Aoyama, in *Sung Biographies,* v. 2, 808–16; v. 3, 1066–69.

10. Ssu-ma Ch'ien (145–86 B.C.?) was author of the *Historical Annals.*

11. T'ang was inferior only to Wang Chi, his teacher.

12. Reference here is to the rigorous self-restraint and reverential attitude of King T'ang, the founder of the Shang dynasty. According to the *Book of History,* as translated by J. Legge, *The Chinese Classics* (v. 3, pp. 201–2), the wise minister Yi-yin counseled the deceased king's grandson and successor by reminding him that King T'ang (d. 1753 B.C.) used to rise before dawn "in order to have large and clear views." This has been interpreted in the sense that the king continually kept his eye on Heaven's requirements. But there is no mention of the Duke of Chou here, although he is presented in the same classic as a man who was always reverentially obedient to Heaven.

13. Reference here is to Wu-ting, known also as King Kao-tsung of the Shang dynasty, whose capital was at Yin (r. 1273–1214 B.C.). According to the *Book of History,* as translated by J. Legge, ibid., p. 248 and p. 466, Wu-ting did not speak for three years. In *Analects* 14:43, Tzu-chang asked Confucius about it, and the Master replied that the ancients all kept silence during the three-year mourning period for their sovereigns. (J. Legge, *The Chinese Classics,* v. 1, 291.) But this interpretation can be challenged, as the references in the classic appear to speak of the silence as occurring after the mourning period. In his *Ch'ing-t'ung shih-tai* (The Bronze Age) (Shanghai, 1951), Kuo Mo-jo offers the hypothesis that Wu-ting was sick with aphasia and so unable to speak. He sees no precedent here for the three-year mourning period either. See pp. 140–42.

14. *Analects* 7:13; Legge, *The Chinese Classics,* v. 1, 199. The reference here is specifically to Confucius' love of *shao* music, which took away all taste for meat.

15. Reference to the passage from the *Diamond Sūtra,* which was reportedly the occasion of enlightenment for the monk Hui-neng, sixth patriarch of Ch'an Buddhism. See P. B. Yampolsky, trans., *The Platform Sutra,* 94, note 18. This

statement and what follows appeaɾ to give Huang Tsung-hsi's opinions rather than T'ang Shun-chih's.

16. The *Doctrine of the Mean,* ch. 27, refers to the three thousand rules of demeanor. The eighty thousand fine points of behavior refer to Buddhist monastic rules.

9.   The Ch'u-chung[1] School

The Ch'u [Hukuang] school flourished especially because of Keng Ting-hsiang and his followers, whose teaching was received from T'ai-chou. During Yang-ming's lifetime, he had very few followers from this area. There were then only Chiang Hsin, Chi Yüan-heng, and Liu Kuan-shih,[2] all of whom came from the one place, Wu-ling, so that the students from Wu-ling formed the largest group in the Ch'u region. According to Hsü Ai's poem, "On Visiting Te-shan,"[3] there were also other men: Wang Wen-ming [*tzu*] Ying-k'uei, Hu San [*tzu*] Ming-yü, Liu Hsien-te [*tzu*] Ch'ung-yang, Yang Yüeh [*tzu*] Chieh-ch'eng, Ho Feng-shao [*tzu*] Ju'hsieh, T'ang Yen [*tzu*] Ju-yüan, and Lung Ch'i-hsiao [*tzu*] Cheng-chih. These have all been recorded. But Chiang Hsin was the one who really received Yang-ming's transmitted teaching. Keng Ting-hsiang had many followers, but his group did more to injure the teachings of *liang-chih.* How can they be compared [to Chiang Hsin]?

NOTES

1. Ch'u-chung refers to the Hukuang region south of the central Yangtze.

2. For Chiang, see his biography in this volume. For Chi, see *MJHA,* ch. 28. Chi was victimized by the eunuchs who tried to find fault with Wang Yang-ming in 1519 after his victory over the rebel, Prince Ch'en-hao. For all of them, including Liu Kuan-shih, see J. Ching, trans., *The Philosophical Letters of Wang Yang-ming,* 7.

3. For Hsü Ai, see *MJHA,* ch. 11.

Chiang Hsin

Chiang Hsin, whose *tzu* was Ch'ing-shih and whose *hao* was Tao-lin (1483–1559),[1] was a man of Ch'ang-te, Hunan. In youth he was sedate and serious; even at the height of summer, he never rolled up his sleeves. He did not believe in the art of geomancy; when his mother died, he himself selected a dry, elevated place and buried her. He passed the *chin-shih* examination of 1532 and was appointed a bureau secretary in the ministry of revenue. Later he was transferred to vice-director of a bureau in the ministry of war and sent out to Szechwan as an assistant surveillance commissioner. There he initiated beneficial services and eradicated harmful measures with energy and enthusiasm. In one case, he found a Taoist priest intimidating the people with the art of sorcery, so he summoned him to a performance. But the priest's art did not work, and Chiang judged him according to the law. When he was promoted to vice surveillance commissioner in charge of education in Kweichow, he built two academies, one called "Correct Learning" and the other, "Cultured Brilliance." He selected from among the students those who were talented and outstanding, educated them in these academies, and showed them the proper direction so that they would not be submerged in the customs of the times. At Lung-ch'ang, there was a shrine to Wang Yang-ming,[2] for which Chiang purchased some sacrificial land[3] in order that the burning of incense at the shrine would be maintained permanently. The students of the Five Guards of Ch'ing-lang in Hukuang[4] had to travel long and dangerous roads to their provincial capital in order to take examinations. Many were unable to get through. Therefore Chiang increased the quotas for the Kweichow provincial examination and allowed those students to participate there. Shortly afterwards he went home on account of illness and was accused by a censor of leaving his post without authorization. His name was removed from the register of officials. Later, on the occasion of an amnesty, he was allowed [to purchase the restoration of his rank and] wear his official cap and sash in retirement.

Chiang Hsin built an academy at T'ao-hua kang (in Hukuang), to which students flocked. With revenues received from the school land assigned to the academy, he provided for those who came from afar. The students studied without interruption, with him as their master, sitting with dignity in their midst. Only at times of family sacrifice did Chiang leave the academy and go into town. Occasionally, he went out on a tour. He was then invited everywhere to give lectures. He died at age seventy-six, in December 31, 1559. Just before his death, he had composed a poem saying,

> For us Confucians, to transmit nature is to transmit spirit,
> How can we let wind and dust detain this body?
> O moon over the mountain of ten thousand peach blossoms,[5]
> I bid you, shine on all tonight!

Chiang had no teacher to begin with. In the company of Chi Yüan-heng,[6] he sought for knowledge in books. He said, "The phrase 'to know where to abide'[7] of the *Great Learning* ought to refer to the substance of humanity *(jen-t'i).*" Chi jumped up saying, "If that is so, then [the words] calm, tranquility, peace, and deliberation[8] simply refer to preserving the substance of humanity with sincerity and reverence."[9] While at Lung-ch'ang, Wang Yang-ming saw Chiang's poems and praised them. Subsequently, Chiang and Chi both studied under Wang Yang-ming. When Chiang later went to the imperial capital as a tribute student, he also studied under Chan Jo-shui.[10] And when Chan was at the National University in Nanking, numerous students came to him, and he ordered Chiang to assist in teaching them. After Chiang had given up his office and returned home, Chan traveled to Mount Nan-yüeh,[11] and Chiang was with him for about a month. Four years later, he went to Kwangtung to visit Chan. Another eight years later Chan revisited Nan-yüeh, and Chiang was again with him. This shows that Chiang had much to learn from Chan.

On first reading the *Analects,* [Ch'eng Hao's] letter on calming one's nature,[12] and [Chang Tsai's] *Western Inscription,*[13] Chiang realized that the foundation of the teaching of the sages rests on [the doctrine] of the oneness of all things. At age thirty-two or so, he developed a lung dis-ease and went to the Tao-lin Monastery to practice quiet-sitting. After a while, both the fear of death and the thought of his mother ceased. One day he had the sudden feeling that the whole universe was one with himself. Thereupon he came to believe that this was what Ch'eng Hao meant by the line "infinitely impartial, without any differentiation between self and other" and also, "regarding the self and other as equal." He began to realize that in the past his understanding had been basically a matter of discursive reasoning and quite removed from the silent remembrance[14] [it had come to be]. He also realized that his past practice of quiet-sitting had only brought him some impression of clar-ity, even though there had been moments of deep quiet.

This experience of enlightenment brought Chiang to a penetrating understanding of *li* and *ch'i,* mind and nature, self and other, which he no longer regarded as two. He pointed out that the Six Classics[15] were there for all to see and asked, "Where is it ever said that there is a *li* and also a *ch'i?*" He maintained that all talk about destiny, the Way, sincer-ity, the Great Ultimate, and humanity refers to *ch'i,* and that the uni-verse is entirely *ch'i.* Of itself *ch'i* is without delusion, harmonious, cor-rect, pure, concentrated, and participates ceaselessly in the process of creativity. He said that if one would only experience one's own mind, then one would know that this mind is the mind of the life-giving *ch'i* and is one with the "nature conferred by Heaven." So he asked, "How can there be one thing that is mind and another that is nature?" More-over, according to him, this *ch'i* fills the universe without the slightest deficiency. Heat and cold, wind and rain, dew and thunder as well as ears, eyes, mouth, nose, limbs, bones, and the whole spiritual con-sciousness of men and things are all the transformation of this life-giv-ing *ch'i.* And so, [he asked,] "How could self and other be separate?"

Chiang considered the universe to be nothing but the one *ch'i.* In its totality it is the Great Harmony. Within it, however, are many differen-tiations of clarity and turbidity, hardness and softness. So, [he noted,] if we viewed the universe after forms were produced, the spirit aroused, and the five natures stimulated,[16] we would know that there were naturally many differences between the foolish and the worthy, the hard and the soft, the good and the evil. But these all emerge from the same Great Harmony, and if what is intelligent is nature, how can what is stupid not also be nature? If what is good is nature, how can what is evil not also be nature? [According to Chiang] this cannot be understood unless effort and heavenly destiny are one. [He maintained that] movement without moving, quietude without being quiet, and that which is between movement and quietude are the original substance of heavenly destiny, the reason creation and transformation are spiritual. Therefore, [he said,] when effort reaches the state of "neither neglecting nor aiding" [self-cultivation], it becomes the very substance, and the head and face of pure and utmost goodness reveals itself. Then does one know nature and Heaven, what is soft and what is hard. Then do the [four feelings] of compassion, shame, deference, and knowing right and wrong respond properly. [According to him] this is precisely where Mencius' teaching of the goodness of nature may be perceived. Chiang further maintained that the essence of the two ch'i [yin and yang] and the five agents is li and that the genuineness of the Non-Ultimate in its circulation and change becomes the essence of the two ch'i and the five agents. When the essence of the two ch'i and the five agents wondrously combines and concentrates, the way of Ch'ien (Heaven) becomes male and the way of K'un (Earth) becomes female. As a result comes the transformation and generation of the myriad things. If, according to him, one knows that the two ch'i and the five agents, the male and the female, and the myriad things originally come from nonbeing, then one knows that the ultimate of the Mean, of correctness, humanity, and righteousness is established on the foundation of quietude.

Chiang holds essential that which is between movement and quietude or activity and tranquility. So he considers what is in motion but without form, what is between being and nonbeing, and what is known as the origination point (chi) of the intention to be the very place to which sages and worthies applied their efforts of caution and apprehension and single-mindedness. It is also the place where harmony is realized, where the equilibrium existing before the emotions arise (wei-fa) prevails. And what Chou Tun-yi calls movement refers to that which is not destructible in the midst of nonaction.[17] This is the mind of Heaven and Earth that gives life without cease. Sincerity, spirituality, and the point of origination are different in name but the same in reality. Because it is nonbeing, it is called sincerity. Because it is nonbeing and yet actually existent, it is called origination. And because it does not fall into [the categories of] either being or nonbeing, it is called spirituality. Chiang takes the place where thoughts arise to be the point of origination. As soon as thoughts arise, there is form and being. And when there is being there is also extinction. [With regard to these thoughts] even though the best efforts are made to realize their meaning, it is yet a matter regarding differentiation and not of his intention of returning all to the oneness of *li*. In discussing *li*, *ch'i*, mind, and nature, Chiang may be said to have acquired the essential. And yet in his efforts, why should he have been so wide [of the mark]?[18]

(*MJHA* 28:2a–3b)

NOTES

1. For Chiang Hsin, see his biography by Julia Ching in *DMB*, v. 1, 227–30.
2. Lung-ch'ang, Kweichow, was the place of Wang Yang-ming's exile as well as enlightenment.
3. I.e., land the produce of which could be assigned to the sacrifices offered at the shrine.
4. Ch'ing-lang is in the modern province of Kweichow.
5. Allusion to the name of his academy: T'ao-hua Kang means literally, the Peach Blossom Heights. "Peaches and plums" also represent "students."
6. Chi Yüan-heng, *hao* An-chai, was to die in prison in 1521 after an unjust accusation regarding his implication in the rebellion of Prince Ch'en-hao, defeated and captured by Wang Yang-ming, to the chagrin of Emperor Wu-tsung and the eunuchs.
7. From the *Great Learning*, a text attributed to Confucius.
8. Ibid.
9. Sincerity is a central concept of both the *Great Learning* and the *Doctrine of the Mean*. Reverence comes from the commentary to the hexagram *K'un* in the *Book of Changes*.
10. See Chan Jo-shui's biography in this volume.
11. I.e., Mount Heng in modern Hunan.
12. Ch'eng Hao's famous letter in his *Collected Writings*, *ECCC*, *Ming-tao wen-chi*, 3:1a–b. For an English translation, see W. T. Chan, *A Source Book of Chinese Philosophy*, 525–26.
13. Chang Tsai's famous essay. See *CTCS*, 1:1a–6b. For an English translation, see W. T. Chan, *A Source Book of Chinese Philosophy*, 469–70.
14. Reference to *Analects* 7:2.
15. "Six" because of the inclusion of the lost *Classic of Music*.
16. Chiang Hsin shows here the influence of Chang Tsai's philosophy of *ch'i*. For Chang on the Great Harmony, see *Cheng-meng* (Correcting the Ignorant) in *CTCS*, ch. 2.
17. Chiang shows here the influence of Chou Tun-yi. He is referring to Chou's *T'ung-shu* (Penetrating the Book of Changes), ch. 4. See *Chou-tzu ch'üan-shu*, SPPY ed.
18. Huang Tsung-hsi appears to agree largely with Chiang's theoretical discussions and yet criticizes him, quite abruptly, for his efforts *(kung-fu)*. The reason is difficult to surmise, unless it be Chiang's partiality to Chan Jo-shui. Indeed, he is sometimes supposed to be a follower of Chan's school.

10. The Northern School

Few among northerners were disciples of the Yang-ming school. Of these, Mu K'ung-hui[1] left no dialog; Wang Tao,[2] *tzu* Ch'un-fu, although a student of Yang-ming, was corrected by Yang-ming for being opinionated and without desire for improvement. Later on, Wang Tao did tend in a different direction and should therefore not be classified under the Yang-ming school. [Thus], aside from followers of the two Mengs (Meng Ch'iu and Meng Hua-li),[3] the few worthy men mostly repeated an exterior learning that they had seen and heard. Few among these had personal insight.

NOTES

1. For Mu K'ung-hui, see *MJHA*, ch. 29.
2. For Wang Tao (1487–1547), *chin-shih* of 1511, see *MJHA*, ch. 42. See J. Ching, trans., *The Philosophical Letters of Wang Yang-ming*, 18.
3. For the two Mengs, see *MJHA*, ch. 29.

Mu K'ung-hui

Mu K'ung-hui, *tzu* Po-ch'ien, *hao* Hsüan-an (1479–1539),[1] a native of T'ang-yi (Shantung), was *chin-shih* in 1505 and moved from the position of Hanlin bachelor to that of corrector. Having incurred [the eunuch] Liu Chin's displeasure, he was moved to Nanking as a secretary in the ministry of rites. After Liu's fall from power, Mu was restored to his former office, became director of studies [of the National University], lecturer-in-waiting, director of instruction [for the royal princes], Hanlin chancellor, and chief minister of the court of imperial sacrifices. He died in the middle of 1539, at age sixty, and was posthumously awarded the title of right vice-minister of rites and the honorific Wen-chien.

Mu K'ung-hui came out first in the Shantung provincial examinations, which were administered by Wang Yang-ming (1504).[2] Mu had first studied ancient prose and poetry before turning to philosophy. In teaching he said that the ancients pursued *li* exhaustively, developing their natures and destinies, while the moderns seek from the sources of nature and destiny by reviewing the writings of the ancients, but without making any personal discoveries. Even when they claim insight, who knows but that it might be some commonplace reflection? He also said that the mirror reflects both the beautiful and the ugly,[3] but that the beautiful and the ugly do not remain on the mirror, just as the mind follows affairs and things without affairs and things leaving traces on the mind. For these come and go naturally, while the mind responds [to them] and returns to stillness, just as a bird crosses the emptiness [of the skies] without hindering the substance of emptiness[4] itself. He said too that there is no distinction in nature between what is thought to be Buddhism or Taoism. At the point of death, he left behind a *gāthā* saying, "Only at this point [am I] a man of understanding." For while Mu studied with Wang Yang-ming, he drifted later to Ch'an Buddhism, without having been through the rigorous training of the Yang-ming school. That is why we find no mention of him in Yang-ming's dialogs. Huang Tso[5] even said that, although Mu was examined by Wang Yang-ming as a scholar-candidate, he did not really follow Yang-ming's teachings, nor did he reject the Sung thinkers. But this is unfair to Mu. Besides, had Yang-ming himself really rejected the Sung thinkers? Is this comment not also unfair to Yang-ming? It merely illustrates what is meant by the saying that one sentence is sufficient to demonstrate ignorance.

(*MJHA* 29:2a–b)

NOTES

1. See *MS,* ch. 183.
2. See *WWKC,* ch. 31b.
3. He appears here to be repeating Wang Yang-ming. See *Ch'uan-hsi lu,* pt. 2, English translation in W. T. Chan, trans., *Instructions for Practical Living,* 148–49.
4. The play is on the word "emptiness" *(k'ung),* which, in Chinese, is also the word for "sky."
5. Huang Tso *(hao* T'ai-ch'üan), 1490–1566. See *MJHA* 51:1a–b. Huang Tsung-hsi appears here to be defending Mu against Huang Tso.

11.   The School of Yüeh and Min[1]

Of the scholars from the southeastern coastal region, Fang Hsien-fu[2] was the first to study under Wang Yang-ming. When Yang-ming began his period of office in Kan-chou (Kiangsi), he received many disciples. He said then that although Ch'ao-chou was only one prefecture at the edge of the Southern Sea, yet, from that one prefecture came the Hsüeh brothers, sons, and nephews; this was already enough to make learning flourish. Then there were also the Yang brothers and, besides, several dozen other intelligent, talented people firmly committed to the Way. Today, however, only the Hsüehs are really known for their learning.

Fang Hsien-fu, *tzu* Shu-hsien, *hao* Hsi-ch'iao, became *chin-shih* as a young man of twenty and served as secretary in the ministry of personnel, rising to vice-director. At the time Yang-ming was recalled from his place of exile, Wang was a secretary, lower in rank than Fang. As they conversed together one day, Fang acquired some insight and at once requested discipleship. Soon after, Fang had to return home on account of sickness. More than ten years afterwards, the controversy regarding the rites arose. Fang submitted a memorial from his home, begging that the emperor's natural parents be honored posthumously as emperor and empress. For this, he was summoned and promoted to lecturer-in-waiting and minister of rites with the title of grand tutor to the heir-apparent. Once more he returned home on account of sickness. He was then recalled as grand secretary of Wu-ying Palace. Soon he begged for leave to return home and died some ten or more years later. He was given the posthumous title of grand guardian and canonized Wen-hsiang.

Hsüeh Shang-hsien[3] was known in his native place for his learning and conduct. When Hsüeh K'an came home from Kan-chou (Kiangsi) and related to him what he had personally heard from Wang Yang-ming, Hsüeh Shang-hsien liked this report and also became his disciple. Later he served as an assistant lecturer at the National University.

Yang Chi, *tzu* Shih-te, was first a disciple of Chan Jo-shui and later finished his studies under Yang-ming. When Yang-ming was conduct-ing the battle in Heng-shui, he wrote to Yang Chi saying, "It is easy to defeat the bandits in the mountains but difficult to defeat the bandits in the mind."[4] Soon afterwards Yang died. Chan Jo-shui said that Yang approved of the inner but not of the outer [dimensions of learning] and so lost the naturalness of ultimate truth *(pen-t'i)*. He also wrote an essay to mourn Yang's death.

Yang [Hsi-yen], *tzu* Shih-ming,[5] studied in the company of his elder brother. When he first took notes of what he heard, he recorded what Yang-ming had said. But Yang-ming regarded him as not having prop-erly understood his meaning. Later Yang noted down what he himself had acquired as insights in learning, which strangely met with Yang-ming's approval. When Shih-ming discussed the effort of daily learn-ing, he said that each person need only follow his own *liang-chih*, remov-ing its obstacles, expanding it to the fullness of its substance *(pen-t'i)*, and not yield to the habits of one's physical nature by conforming to the fashion of the times. He also asked Tsou Shou-yi: "When you were pre-paring for your examinations, did you give the best of your capacity *(ts'ai)?*" Tsou replied, "No, I have not been able to do so." He then said, "Unless one exerts oneself to the utmost, how can one perceive the sublime? The two words, *chieh-ts'ai* (giving to one's capacity), constitute the goal of my learning." Tsou Shou-yi often quoted this conversation to others. But Yang Shih-ming died not long afterwards.

Liang Ch'o, *tzu* Jih-fu, was a native of Nan-hai (Kwangtung) and a *chin-shih.* He served as a secretary in the bureau of operations [in the ministry of war] and was punished with a beating at court for counsel-ing the emperor against going south. Emperor Wu-tsung also used for-eigners as carriage drivers. Liang applied the laws [of the land] to them too, without partiality. Liang once passed through Kiangsi and studied with Yang-ming, asking him questions about abiding in reverence and investigating principles *(li).* He received much light in return. When his fellow disciple Chi Yüan-heng died in the imperial prison, Liang saw to giving him a proper burial.

Cheng Yi-ch'u, *tzu* Ch'ao-so, was a native of Chieh-yang (Kwangtung) and a *chin-shih* of 1505. He lived on Mount Tzu-mo, cultivating quiet contemplation in solitude at home, but was summoned by the government to the position of censor. Yang-ming was then at the ministry of personnel. Cheng asked Ch'en Shih-chieh to request Yang-ming to accept him as a disciple. When he heard Yang-ming's teachings, he recognized that formerly he had followed the side paths [to truth] but that now he had been shown the great Way. At that time, Cheng was already sick. Others counseled him not to study too hard; he replied, "I am ready to die any evening."[6] He passed away in Chekiang.

Of the people in Fukien, outside of Ma Ming-heng,[7] there was no one really well known. Ma Ming-heng, *tzu* Tzu-hsin, was a native of P'u. His father, Ma Ssu-ts'ung, died during the rebellion of Prince Chu Ch'en-hao (1519).[8] Ma Ming-heng was bold and ambitious. He practiced writing prose in the ancient style with Cheng Shan-fu. Yang-ming said [of him]: "A flower with many leaves frequently yields no fruit; a tree with many flowers yields little fruit." In 1524, when Ma Ming-heng was censor, he criticized the emperor for adding honorific titles to his mother, exalting her above [his aunt] the dowager.[9] He was put into prison, relieved of his office, and later sent home.

NOTES

1. Yüeh refers to Kwangtung and Min to Fukien. (This "Yüeh" is different from another, referring to Chekiang.)

2. Fang exchanged many letters with Wang Yang-ming. See J. Ching, trans., *The Philosophical Letters of Wang Yang-ming*, 54, 62.

3. For Hsüeh Shang-hsien, see also ibid., 47.

4. For this letter written by Wang Yang-ming to Yang Chi, see J. Ching, trans., *The Philosophical Letters of Wang Yang-ming*, 45.

5. For Yang Shih-ming, see ibid., 63.

6. Allusion to *Analects* 4:8, "If a man hears of the Way in the morning, he may die without regret in the evening." Eng. tr. adapted from J. Legge, *The Chinese Classics*, v. 1, 168.

7. For Ma Ming-heng, see J. Ching, trans., *The Philosophical Letters of Wang Yang-ming*, 115.

8. Reference to Emperor Wu-tsung's reckless expedition to the south, personally directing a campaign against the rebel Prince Ch'en-hao (1519).

9. Reference to Emperor Shih-tsung's repeated acts to honor his own mother as well as his deceased father. This was in spite of the opposition of many scholars, who considered these acts excessive in view of the fact that he had succeeded to the throne as the heir of his uncle, Emperor Hsiao-tsung. This is related to the so-called Great Ritual Controversy. See *MS*, ch. 17, part 1.

Hsüeh K'an

Hsüeh K'an, *tzu* Shang-ch'ien, *hao* Chung-li (d. 1545),[1] a native of Chieh-yang (Kwangtung), became *chin-shih* in 1517 and begged permission to return south to care for his parents. He studied with Wang Yang-ming in Kiangsi for four years before going home. In 1521 he was made a messenger but had to mourn his mother's death and went to Peking only afterwards. When he heard of Yang-ming's death (1529), he met with Ou-yang Te[2] and other fellow disciples around Yang-ming's tablet and wept with them. On a mission to Shantung, he visited Confucius' and Mencius' temples and had the ceremonial for the Almond Terrace[3] lectures inscribed. He was promoted to head of the office of messengers. At the time, [the junior tutor] Chang Fu-ching was using Ch'eng Min-cheng's[4] earlier proposal to make changes in the Confucian sacrifices. Hsüeh requested that both Lu Chiu-yüan and Ch'en Hsien-chang[5] be added to these sacrifices. Lu was accordingly included (but not Ch'en). After the death of Prince Chuang-ching, the heir-apparent,[6] the succession long remained undecided. Hsüeh drafted a memorial citing ancestral institutions and asking that a choice be made of a worthy imperial clansman, to be brought to Peking and kept there as protector of the city until the emperor's younger son grew up. Then, [that clansman] could be sent off to a large feudal state.[7] He showed it to Huang Tsung-ming, chief minister of the court of imperial entertainments. Huang counseled him not to submit it. But Hsüeh had also shown it to his fellow graduate, P'eng Tse, chief minister of the court of imperial sacrifices. P'eng was a crafty man. At the time, Chang Fu-ching was on bad terms with [the grand secretary] Hsia Yen. P'eng was attached to Chang and wanted to use this material to attack Hsia. So he took the draft memorial to Chang in secret, saying, "This touches what the emperor considers a taboo. And since Hsüeh and Hsia are fellow graduates of the same year, could one not say that the memorial had been inspired by Hsia and thus also throw him under suspicion of guilt?" Chang agreed, had the memorial copied and submitted to the emperor, saying, "Hsia and Hsüeh are plotting such-and-such, but we should not do anything until the memorial is really submitted." Then P'eng told Hsüeh, "Chang liked your memorial. You may submit it." Hsüeh did so, thus enraging the emperor, who had him arrested at the imperial palace and assembled officials there to interrogate him, asking who had inspired him in this action. As Hsüeh refused to comply, P'eng then hinted that he should implicate Hsia. Hsüeh stared at P'eng, saying, "You said that Chang Fu-ching liked my words, and you encouraged me to submit the memorial. What has it to do with Hsia Yen?" But the censor-in-chief Wang Hung, also Chang's friend, held Hsüeh's arm, insisting that Hsia was behind the whole affair. Hsia then banged the table and rebuked him, almost wanting to hit Wang. So the interrogation stopped. The emperor then ordered the earl of Wu-ting, Kuo Hsün, and the grand secretary, Chai Luan, together with the judiciary, the nine chief ministers, the offices of scrutiny and circuit, and the Imperial Guard Prison to reopen interrogations with the use of torture. Hsüeh then said, "If such an intelligent sovereign as His Majesty can be deceived by P'eng Tse, how much more a fool like myself?"

The emperor then showed Chang's two memorials to all the ministers, reproved him for fraudulence and ordered him to retire from office, while P'eng was exiled from court as a frontier soldier. Hsüeh himself was reduced to commoner's status after making a large payment. He reached the River Lu (near Peking), on the occasion of the imperial birthday. The reader-in-waiting, Hsiang Ch'iao, was then performing the celebrations in his own boat. On being told that an unknown commoner in a small boat was also offering incense and performing the ceremony, Hsiang said, "This must be Hsüeh K'an," and visited him. After his return home, Hsüeh assembled over a hundred disciples. In 1536, he visited Nanking (Kiangsu) and Chekiang, met Lo Hung-hsien at Ch'ing-yüan Academy (Kiangsi), and then went to [Mount] Lo-fou (Kwangtung) and lectured at the Yung-fu Monastery. Only in 1545 did he return home. His disciples recorded what they heard in a book entitled *Yen-chi lu*. In his *Sheng-hsüeh tsung-chuan*,[8] Chou Ju-teng recorded that, after Hsüeh's release from prison, he saw Wang Yang-ming in K'uai-chi (Chekiang) and that Yang-ming asked him how things had been during his troubles. Hsüeh replied, "I had only my *liang-chih*. It was bright and clear with nothing [tarnishing] it." Wang Yang-ming [according to Chou Ju-teng] approved of this. However, Hsüeh was released in 1531 and Yang-ming died in 1529 [three years earlier]. So how could that meeting have taken place?

Those who regard Wang Yang-ming's philosophy to be Buddhistic point out three things: his neglect of books, his divergence from Chu Hsi, and his discussions of the void *(hsü)*. Hsüeh refuted each point, without really answering their objections adequately. Such critiques actually show only superficial doubts. Others with serious doubt say this: Since *li* is present in Heaven and Earth and the myriad things, and I am one of the myriad things, I should not take *li* as being only in the self. Now Yang-ming taught that *li* is in the mind; he neglects Heaven and Earth and the myriad things, saying, like the Buddhists, that if one knew the mind, one would realize that not an inch of the earth exists. They do not understand that, for Yang-ming, *li* is in the mind because the principles *(li)* of Heaven and Earth and the myriad things are all in the mind; abiding by and following the mind is therefore abiding by and following Heaven and Earth and the myriad things. On the contrary, should one take *li* to be in Heaven and Earth and the myriad things and then abide and follow it there, the Tao (truth) would be enlarging man and not vice versa. The Buddhists regard the no-mind *(wu-hsin)* as mind and the transformations of Heaven and Earth and the myriad things as all transformations of the mind. Take water, for example. The Buddhists are like the tributaries that flow out sideways, while the Confucians are like the source of the spring, which rushes out, flowing without cease, day and night. Further, what is subject to doubt is Yang-ming's statement about absence of good and evil. When we examine the *Ch'uan-hsi lu,*[9] we read about the occasion when Hsüeh K'an asked Yang-ming about removing weeds from among flowers. Yang-ming said that the absence of good and evil characterizes the tranquility of *li,* and the presence of good and evil characterizes the movement of *ch'i.* So he calls tranquility that which is without good and evil, rather than *li.* For *li* is nothing but the good. In the same way, Ch'eng Yi said that man is born in a state of tranquility, and the state preceding that could not be discussed.[10] Chou Tun-yi added the Non-Ultimate to the Great Ultimate.[11] Only in the *T'ien-ch'üan cheng-tao chi* is it recorded that the absence of good and evil characterizes the mind-in-itself, and the presence of good and evil characterizes the movement of its intention.[12] Now the mind-in-itself is *li,* but the mind-in-itself is beyond activity and tranquility. Should it be neither good nor evil, then *li* too is neither good nor evil, and Yang-ming should not speak of it as such only in the mode of tranquility. The Buddhists talk of the absence of good and evil to deny *li.* The names for good and evil are established from the reality of *li.* So if there is *li,* how can one speak of absence of good and evil? Having checked what Yang-ming said about removing weeds, we can tell that the words at T'ien-ch'üan [attributed to him] may not come from Yang-ming.[13] Now that both kinds of doubts [the superficial and the serious] are resolved, to insist that Yang-ming's teachings resemble Buddhist teachings would be unscholarly. Why should we go on disputing with such people?

(MJHA 30:3a–4a)

NOTES

1. For Hsüeh K'an, see *MS* 207:497d. Hsüeh published the first collection of *Ch'uan-hsi lu.* See W. T. Chan, trans., *Instructions for Practical Living,* 53, 58, 239. See also J. Ching, trans., *The Philosophical Letters of Wang Yang-ming,* xvii, 45, 48, 83.

2. For Ou-yang Te, see his biography in this volume.

3. The Almond Terrace refers to the place where Confucius allegedly taught his disciples in his native Ch'ü-fu, Shantung.

4. Ch'eng Min-cheng, *hao* Huang-tun, was born in 1445. He suggested making changes involving the so-called worthies who also received sacrifices at the Temple.

5. Ch'en Hsien-chang and Hsüeh K'an both came from the province Kwangtung.

6. *MS* 120. He died in 1549.

7. The submission of such a memorial would be an impolitic act, given the imperial suspicion of fellow clansmen with undue ambitions.

8. See *Sheng-hsüeh tsung-chuan,* 15:30a.

9. *WWKC* 1:79a. See English translation in W. T. Chan, trans., *Instructions for Practical Living,* 63–65.

10. This reference came originally from the *Book of Rites,* chapter on music. See J. Legge, trans., *Li Ki (SBE,* v. 27), pt. 1, 96. Ch'eng Hao refers to it in *ECCS, Yi-shu,* 1:7b–8a. See W. T. Chan, *A Source Book of Chinese Philosophy,* 528.

11. Reference to Chou's *Explanation of the Diagram of the Great Ultimate (T'ai-chi t'u-shuo).* See *SYHA* 12:1a–b.

12. Wang Chi, *WLHC,* ch. 1.

13. This is Huang Tsung-hsi's constant reminder. See also the biographies of Ch'ien Te-hung and of Wang Chi in this volume.

12.   The Chih-hsiu[1] School

Li Ts'ai studied under Tsou Shou-yi; hence he was also a follower in the Wang Yang-ming school. But he established his own independent ideas and so needs to be considered separately. Today there are many who teach and discuss Li's ideas. Since he sought to remedy the problems connected with the philosophy of *liang-chih,* he was also a filial son of the Yang-ming school.

NOTE

1. The formula *chih-hsiu* (rest and cultivation) is taken from the *Great Learning:* "knowing where to rest" *(chih-chih)* and "cultivation of self" *(hsiu-shen).* For Li's philosophy, see his biography by Julia Ching, *DMB,* v. 1, 874–77.

Li Ts'ai

Li Ts'ai, *tzu* Meng-ch'eng, *hao* Chien-lo (1520–1606),[1] a native of Feng-ch'eng (Kiangsi), was the son of Li Sui, who rose to be minister of war in Nanking and was posthumously honored with the name Hsiang-min. Li Ts'ai became *chin-shih* in 1562 and was named secretary in the ministry of justice. Later he served as surveillance commissioner in Yünnan (1584). At that time, the region of Chin-ch'ih and T'eng-chung was often troubled by Mien-tien (Burma), but the land in between was under the control of the aboriginal chiefs of Meng-yang and Man-mu, who alternated between rebellion and submission. Li used the strategy of attacking barbarians with barbarians. He sent envoys to Man-mu, persuaded them to join with Meng-yang and invade Yi-hsi (in Meng-yang), and killed Ta-lang-chang, who was close to the Burmese. The ruler of Burma then counterattacked. Meng-yang requested urgent help, and Li sent troops to his aid. So the aboriginal chiefs defeated the Burmese on the Che waters, made obeisance to the Chinese court in gratitude, and offered two elephants as tribute.[2] For this accomplishment Li was promoted to governor of Yün-yang (Hukuang) and right assistant censor-in-chief. There he taught disciples, who, following the advice of geomancers, persuaded him to transform the local comman- der's headquarters into an academy and move the headquarters to the old school premises. Li gave permission for this change. After this, the commander, Mi Wan-ch'un, a [former] government student, arrived, and stirred his soldiers to mutiny. As Li was attending to his public duties, Mi and others came in to threaten him. But the captain, Wang Ming-huo, held a knife to Mi and said severely: "If you kill him, I'll kill you." Li was therefore saved. But when this affair was reported to the throne, Li was dismissed from office, although Mi continued in his.

The following year (1588) the Yünnan regional censor, Su Tsan, in an attempt to please the government (i.e., the emperor), attacked Li's report of victory over Burma for giving an exaggerated account of his accomplishments, for taking credit himself for the achievements of the aboriginals, and even for giving a false count of the number killed. An imperial order then threw Li into prison to await investigation, and the emperor desired to see him killed. The ministry of justice first sentenced him to a prison term and then to exile, but neither was approved. Indeed, the more perseveringly the minister insisted, the firmer became the emperor, to the extent that the officials of justice were all frightened. Kao Ts'ung-li, director of a bureau in the ministry of justice, then said, "An intelligent ruler should listen to reason." So he took a brush and wrote a memorial, saying that Li Ts'ai did well to use aborigines to defeat the Burmese and was not without merit in expanding the coun- try's frontiers. That he exaggerated his merits in his reports was a crime of deception against the sovereign. But although a minister might deserve more than death for such a transgression, the sovereign who would pardon such and overcome suspicions would encourage his sub- jects to give their lives in his service. The emperor was visibly moved when he read this memorial. So Li was imprisoned for over ten years[3] and sent as an exiled soldier to the Fukien coast (1593), where he died.

Li Ts'ai first studied with Tsou Shou-yi and learned the teaching of the extension of *liang-chih*. Later he modified this teaching, saying that the extension of knowledge refers to extending the substance of knowl- edge *(chih-t'i)*, while *liang-chih* refers to the knowledge that is manifest without adding anything to that substance and is not the substance of knowledge itself. So he changed [the teaching regarding *liang-chih*] to the teaching of nature and consciousness. After some time, he sighed and said, "This is like the mouse moving into the hole without really leaving its nest." So he brought out the two words *chih-hsiu*, regarding this as the authentic transmission of Confucius and Tseng-tzu. *Chih-hsiu* (literally, "rest" and "cultivation") assumes that human nature is born in a state transcending tranquility, which is the highest good. Thus, nature manifests itself in the four beginnings of virtue, such as in the heart of compassion.[4] However, when there is good, there is also what is not good. Even knowledge is a thing that flows and derives from nature and belongs to the posterior state of consciousness. Should one extend such knowledge, one would daily recede from [the nature] in-itself that is born in a state transcending tranquility. To comprehend knowledge in rest *(chih)* is to rest in this nature-in-itself that is born in a state transcending tranquility. Besides, the authenticity ordained by Heaven (the word refers here to nature) reveals itself in the person's seeing, hearing, in his speech and action. All this refers to what is called the self *(shen)*. Should one constantly be able to maintain an attitude of rest *(chih),* then one's sight, hearing, words, and actions would all be in accordance with proper norms, so that one need not speak of cultivation and yet would be practicing cultivation. Even if one might sometimes depart from the norms, one would need only a slight effort of simple restraint and composure *(shou-lien)* to return all to the state of rest. That is why one may speak of investigation of things, extension of knowledge, sincerity of intention, and rectification of mind as four things that should be evenly developed. Should there be some defect in one of these four, this is what one should attend to in cultivation, proceeding according to the defect that is discovered. Li Ts'ai wrote lengthy volumes generally giving the above opinions.[5]

The *Great Learning*[6] regards personal cultivation as the root of all learning. But it says that the method of personal cultivation lies in investigation of things and extension of knowledge, making clear therefore that this is where the task should begin. Thus, when one views it from the point of giving the world peace and the country order, then the root lies in personal cultivation, and when one views it from the point of personal cultivation, then the root lies in investigation and extension. Instead of this, Li Ts'ai wants to attribute everything to personal cultivation, uniting the root of all learning and that of personal cultivation and conflating them. In the last analysis, this remains clumsy and difficult to accept. The two words, nature and emotions, are always hard to separate. So the *Book of Changes* says that nature and emotions are to be correlated to *li* and *chen*.[7] Without emotions, how can one find nature? Mencius says that compassion, shame, modesty, and discernment between right and wrong are the beginnings of humanity, righteousness, propriety, and wisdom—but not that there is a superior level of humanity, righteousness, propriety, and wisdom above that of compassion, shame, modesty, and discernment between right and wrong.

At the court of the sage king Shun it was said that the moral mind *(Tao-hsin)* is the Mean of emotions.[8] But how can the moral mind also be that which proceeds from the Mean? Such a statement already diverges from the teachings of the former worthies. Li Ts'ai went on to separate [nature and emotions], adding therefore to his divergence from the for-

mer worthies. Even in what Li calls cultivation, how can something outside of compassion, shame, modesty, and discernment between right
and wrong serve as the controlling principle *(chu-tsai)* [of human
nature]? Is it something to be sought in the realm of the unknown and
unknowable? The operation of Heaven above proceeds entirely without
sound or odor. But can the four beginnings of virtue be described as
having sound and odor? And is that which is without sound and odor
not adequate to serve as nature-in-itself? Is that not the state transcending tranquility in which man is born? Must one talk like the Buddhists,
who claim that speech injures the Way *(Tao)* and that one may discuss
nature only before the birth of one's father and mother? The two words
chih-hsiu move in two directions, offering something quite superfluous.
Should Li Ts'ai have spoken only of "knowing where to rest" *(chih-chih)*
as what is essential, then he would be directing knowledge to rest and
meeting Nieh Pao's teaching of returning to stillness *(kuei-chi)*. But Li
was afraid of getting too close to the Ch'an Buddhist doctrine of stillness
and so sought to give substance to his own teaching by emphasizing personal cultivation. Should he have merely taken personal cultivation as
his essential, then he would have given too much attention to external
demeanor, even that which proceeds naturally. Li was afraid that this
would be a mere exterior righteousness and decided for rest and cultivation. In actuality, his teaching takes "rest" to mean gathering together
and nourishing the mind and "cultivation" to mean self-examination
and watchfulness. He merely gave new names [to these teachings],
making some fuss over them though not differing very much from the
Sung scholars.

Hsü Fu-yüan said that Li Ts'ai speaks of the moral mind *(Tao-hsin)*
and the human mind *(jen-hsin)* as both belonging to the realm of the
operations of the mind, while intention and knowledge cannot be said to
belong to the substance [of the mind]. [According to Hsü], such teachings cannot avoid being too exaggerated. The Mean is of course the
perfect virtue of [human] nature. Outside of the subtleness of the *Tao-
hsin,* there is no place where one might find the Mean. The good is of
course the restful abode of the Way *(Tao)*. Outside of mind, intention,
and knowledge, where else can one understand the good? If nature
transcends distinctions of the inner and the outer, mind also transcends
these distinctions, and then there is no way in which one may speak of
reality or substance *(t'i)* and its manifestations and functions *(yung)*.

Kao P'an-lung[9] said that "investigation of things and extension of
knowledge" in the *Great Learning* is nothing but the teaching of "understanding the good" in the *Doctrine of the Mean*. It is given to help students
discover their own resolutions and set upon their tasks, discerning
between the realm of self and that of the other, investigating carefully
the limits of differences between righteousness and profit, right and

wrong. What is essential is to make the mind bright and radiant, without the slightest confusion or doubt in any hidden corner that might lead to self-deception. Otherwise, even if one desires rest and cultivation, one's physical endowment of *ch'i* and one's material desires *(wu-yü)* might reverse all the beginnings of virtue, so that knowledge would never be perfect. The effort of cultivation must always be firm and concrete, never easy and relaxed or described in such terms.

Hsü and Kao have both given incisive criticisms of Li's teachings. It has also been said that when Li Ts'ai left prison for banishment to Fukien as a simple soldier, he continued to use the insignia of office of a surveillance commissioner. When Hsü Fu-yüan was governor of Fukien, he and Li met outside the city gates. Hsü greeted Li with much consideration and to the point of tears but then warned him seriously: "You have been freed from prison by the grace of the emperor, but your status is that of a banished person. You ought to practice humility and reflect upon your faults and not continue to glorify yourself." On hearing this, Li Ts'ai was displeased and called Hsü old-fashioned and petty. For Li Ts'ai always regarded himself as having a mission as a teacher and could not change in a time of adversity. Those who do not know him say that he could not forget the glories of his former office. They really misjudge him.[10]

(*MJHA* 31:2a–3b)

NOTES

1. For Li Ts'ai, see his biography by Julia Ching, in *DMB*, v. 1, 874–77.
2. For these battles, see *MS*, ch. 315. At that time, Burma (Mien-tien) was also regarded as a border area under an aboriginal chief *(t'u-ssu)*. The battles appear to have occurred in the northeastern region of present-day Burma.
3. Huang Tsung-hsi appears to be mistaken here. Li was in prison barely five years (1588–93) before his exile.
4. *Mencius* 2A:6.
5. "The above" is of course Huang Tsung-hsi's account of Li Ts'ai's philosophy. Li has left behind an account of military exploits of earlier dynasties, a treatise on the meaning of the old text of the *Great Learning*, treatises on questions of human nature, etc. They are difficult to locate today, although the Naikaku Bunko appears to possess some of his surviving writings. See *DMB*, v. 2, 877.
6. What follows is Huang Tsung-hsi's interpretation of Li's philosophy in the light of his own.
7. The *Book of Changes*, Hexagram 1, *Ch'ien*. The two words are translated by Legge as "advantageous, correct." See J. Legge, trans., *Yi King*, in *SBE*, v. 16 (Oxford, 1882), 57.
8. Reference here to the "sixteen characters" taken out of the "Counsels of Great Yü," of the *Book of History*. They constitute the formula of faith considered as the sacred legacy transmitted from the sage king Shun to his successor Yü. For further reference, see J. Ching, *To Acquire Wisdom*, Introduction.

9. For Kao P'an-lung, see *MJHA*, ch. 57.

10. Huang Tsung-hsi appears to condone Li Ts'ai's strange action. Indeed, the placing of Li's school of thought between the Kwangtung and Fukien followers of the Wang Yang-ming and those of the T'ai-chou persuasion shows that he regards Li to be also a Yang-ming follower, whose teachings are largely those of the Yang-ming tradition.

13.   The T'ai-chou[1] School

The teaching of Master Yang-ming became popular everywhere under Heaven on account of Wang Ken and Wang Chi. But it gradually lost its transmission in part due to Wang Ken and Wang Chi. Wang Ken and Wang Chi were frequently dissatisfied with their master's teachings, seeking all the while to unveil more of the Buddha's mysteries and attribute them to the master. Thus they pressed Yang-ming into the ranks of Ch'an Buddhism. In Wang Chi's case, no disciple emerged who was stronger than himself, and his teaching was balanced and remedied by the Chiang-yu school. So there was no total disintegration effected. In Wang Ken's case, many of his disciples could fight the dragon and the snake with their bare hands.[2] By the time his teaching passed down to men like Yen Chün and Ho Hsin-yin,[3] it was no longer within the boundaries of Confucian moral philosophy. Ku Hsien-ch'eng said: "Ho Hsin-yin and his like were attached to profit and passion like [men] sitting in a basin of paint. They were able to exercise influence over others only through their petty cleverness, which was their strong point." However, in my opinion, what attracted others to them was not their so-called cleverness but rather their teachings. What we call Patriarch Ch'an[4] is the teaching that regards transformation of consciousness as direct perception of nature. These men turned Heaven and Earth upside down. There has been no one like them among the ancients and the moderns. The Buddhists practiced beating and yelling, acting wildly according to the situation; however, once the stick was laid down, they were like fools. But these men bore everything with their bare bodies, never letting down their stick, for which reason they have caused so much harm.

People today who discuss these men of T'ai-chou refer usually to Wang Shih-chen's[5] *Kuo-ch'ao ts'ung-chi*. But Wang had summarized everything from the judicial records of the time and could not be completely relied upon. I have done research into this matter and list here below the best-known followers of this school:

Yen Chün, *tzu* Shan-nung, native of Chi-an (Kiangsi), had first studied under Liu Pang-ts'ai without acquiring much. He went over to Hsü Yüeh and received the transmission of T'ai-chou. He regarded man's mind to be more mysterious than anything, indeed quite inscrutable. Human nature is like a bright pearl, without any defilement originally.

So what can it see or hear? What can it fear or be anxious about?[6] On ordinary days one need only follow one's nature, acting completely spontaneously and naturally. This is what is called the Way. Only in moments of excess need one practice caution, fear, and apprehension in order to rectify it. All experiences, doctrines, and formulas reported by earlier scholars can become hindrances to the achievement of the Way. Such is his chief message. He once said: "Among my disciples, one can speak with Lo Ju-fang of following nature or with Ch'en Yi-ch'üan of following the mind. The others only speak of following the emotions." Yen Chün was a knight-errant and always ready to help others out in emergencies. He accompanied Chao Chen-chi to his place of exile, thus earning his deep gratitude. After the death of Hsü Yüeh at the battlefield in Yüan-chiang, Yen Chün found his remains and brought them home for burial. He wanted very much to do something worthwhile in the world and fulfill his ambition of becoming one with all people and all things. He once sent a poem to Chou Yi, saying:

> The misty, drizzling rain envelops the River Bank,
> Fishermen on the river fight over the Fishing Terrace.
> In the quiet night, having caught a fish, I send for wine:
> Rapid stream and peaceful moon are gathering together—
> Should the spring breeze only breathe over the Nine Heavens,
> Where in the world will one find a Terrace of Three Returns?[7]
> When ruler is kind and minister just, the common people are content,
> Rabbit hunters and fuel-gatherers can go and come back.[8]

The men of the times noticed his eccentricities: all disliked him, both the worthy and the unworthy. For some reason or other, he was put into prison in Nanking, where the authorities wanted to kill him. Lo Ju-fang[9] tried his best to save Yen, refraining from attending palace examinations for six years. Lo said to Chou Yi: "I have been close to Yen for over thirty years. He is of a great delicacy of mind and intention and quite unable to practice deceit. I dare say that his learning can be traced back to Confucius and Mencius directly and awaits the coming of future sages with certainty. If I, lacking in virtue and talent, have deserved your kind reception and friendship, I should dare say that knowing a hundred persons like myself is not as important as giving Yen Chün a fair trial." Yen Chün was then exiled and lived until over eighty.

Liang Ju-yüan, *tzu* Fu-shan, changed his name later to Ho Hsin-yin. He was a native of Yung-feng, Chi-chou (Kiangsi). In his youth, he filled the vacancy of a student and then went to study under Yen Chün. From Yen Chün he heard Wang Ken's doctrine of establishing roots. At that time, there were three or four "bigwigs" from Chi-chou who were well known for their learning. Ho Hsin-yin was proud of his personal knowledge and information and often mocked these persons. He said

that the *Great Learning* speaks first of ordering the family. So he constructed a great hall to assemble his clan together, with himself governing the whole clan, supervising cappings, weddings, funerals, and sacrifices, and paying taxes and supplying the government with labor. He
did every task communally, assessing the haves to make up for the have-
nots, and did it successfully. When the local magistrate decreed an extra
tax, Ho Hsin-yin wrote him a letter to reproach him. The magistrate
was angered and accused him falsely to the authorities, who put him in
prison. Ch'eng Hsüeh-yen of Hsiao-kan (Hupei) was then a counselor
to Hu Tsung-hsien, the supreme commander [of Nan Chihli, Chekiang, and Fukien], and [advised Hu to] order the governor of Kiangsi
to free Ho Hsin-yin. When Hu finally met Ho, he told others, "This
man is quite useless, but having him around does bring exhilaration."
Ho went with Ch'eng to Peking, where he associated with Lo Ju-fang
and Keng Ting-hsiang. One day (1560), he met Chang Chü-cheng in a
Buddhist monastery. Chang was then the director of studies of the
National University. Ho asked Chang bluntly: "You are at the National
University. Do you know the Tao of the National University?" Chang
pretended that he heard nothing but stared at Ho and said: "You would
like very much to fly, but you cannot even leave the ground." After
Chang's departure, Ho was very discouraged and said: "This man will
one day be in charge of the country and will then kill me."

At the capital, Ho opened a hostel at each gate to collect men from all
over, including those [of lower classes] and questionable trades. At that
time, the Yen clique was in power, and many faithful ministers suffered
the death penalty for trying to remove Yen, but all failed. A man called
Lan Tao-hsing had the emperor's favor for his ability as a diviner. Ho
Hsin-yin taught him a secret plan. They found out that Yen Sung had
prepared a memorial, so Lan claimed that he had received a message
from the gods, which told him: "Today, an evil minister will submit a
memorial." As the emperor was hesitating over the possible meaning [of
such a message], Yen's memorial arrived. From then on, the emperor
suspected Yen Sung. The censor Tsou Ying-lung followed up with his
impeachment of Yen Sung and caused him to lose power. But the
emperor could not yet forget Yen Sung and later had Lan Tao-hsing
killed in prison. Ho Hsin-yin escaped to the south, passing Nanking on
his way to visit the vice-minister of justice, Ho Ch'ien, who, as governor of Kiangsi, had released him from jail (1599). Ho Ch'ien, however,
belonged to the Yen clique and, because of Yen, hated Hsin-yin. So Ho
Hsin-yin disappeared from public view, going halfway around the
empire.

After the rise of Chang Chü-cheng to power, Ho was impeached by
the censors Fu Ying-chen and Liu T'ai, both of whom were also men of
Chi-an. Chang therefore developed a hatred for men from Chi-an and

especially for Ho Hsin-yin, whose craftiness had effected the fall of the earlier grand secretary. Ho was gathering disciples and teaching at Hsiao-kan, when Chang commanded the governor Ch'en Jui to arrest him. Before finding Ho, Ch'en left office and was replaced by Wang Chih-yüan, who finally caught him. Ho Hsin-yin told Wang: "You would not dare to kill me and have no power to kill me. The man who wants me killed is Chang Chü-cheng." Eventually he died in prison.

The teachings of Ho Hsin-yin[10] do not project any sound or shadow. For him, where there is *li* (principle), there is an affair *(shih)*. [*Li*] is without sound or odor. Affair is hidden in *li*. [Affairs] have their shapes and forms and give manifestation to *li*. So he said: "The person who believes in *Wu-chi* (the Non-Ultimate) accepts neither sovereign nor father. And also the *Changes* must have a Great Ultimate in order that we may not perform such base acts as killing the sovereign or our fathers and become men who are without sovereign and father. For *Ch'ien* and *K'un* refer to sovereign and minister, *Ch'ien* and *K'un* refer to father and son." He also said: "What Confucius and Mencius call 'desirelessness' *(wu-yü)* is not what Chou Tun-yi calls 'desirelessness.' One need only have a few desires to adhere to the mind, for the mind cannot be without desires. To want to have a fish or a bear's paws is a desire. To give up the fish and choose the bear's paws is to have fewer desires. To want to have life and also acquire righteousness is a desire. To give up life for the sake of perfecting righteousness is to have fewer desires. Is not wanting *jen* a desire? To want nothing more once one has acquired *jen,* is that not having fewer desires? Is not 'following the desires of one's mind' a desire? And is not 'without transgressing the norms' having fewer desires? Is this not what the Buddhists call mysterious being *(miao-yu)*?" For [Ho Hsin-yin] has transformed his learning to that of Su Ch'in and Chang Yi.[11]

Teng Hao-ch'ü's original name was Teng Hao, *hao* T'ai-hu. He was a native of Nei-chang in Szechuan. When he was a young student, he did not discuss philosophy. At that time, Chao Chen-chi, also a student, was discussing the learning of the sages in the east room, while Teng was instructing others in the art of writing examination essays in the west room. They could hear each other's voices all day long but did not ask questions of each other. After some time he had some insight and humbly became Chao's disciple. One day, he left his family and went about traveling, seeking for men who were known for their learning. He regarded nature and destiny as important and did not think one could achieve much by having worldly involvements. So he had his hair shaved to become a Buddhist monk and went to see Li Yüan-yang in Ta-li (Yunnan), Tsou Shou-yi and Liu Pang-ts'ai in Kiangsi, Wang Pi in T'ai-chou, Chiang Hsin in Wu-ling, and Keng Ting-li in Huang-an. But he had heard nothing from Chao Chen-chi for several dozen years.

When Chao, recalled to government service, passed Wei-hui on his way to Peking, Teng happened to be there and went out of the city to meet him. Chao was astonished, descended from his carriage, took his hand, and walked with him for several miles. Together they wept for a while. Chao said to him, "I have really missed you. For I used to speak of such exalted things and so caused you to go to such lengths [as becoming an itinerant monk]. My crimes are really great. I had earlier thought you were dead and so could not make up for my crimes. Now that I know you are yet alive, I want you to return home and spend the rest of your life at the side of your father's grave. Let me give you from my holdings enough land to yield an annual rent of one hundred piculs of grain." So he signed the deed over to Teng. At that time some people came to ask Chao questions on learning. Chao asked Teng to give them answers. But then, after hearing Teng's discussions, Chao was very unhappy and said: "I was doing this to try to find out what your think-ing has been like recently. So it is as ridiculous as that!" Chao went to the capital, while Teng traveled in Shantung without any intention of returning home. When Chao became Grand Secretary, Teng went to the capital to ask for an interview. But Chao refused to see him and asked an official traveling to Szechuan to take him back home. He reached Cho-chou and died in an abandoned monastery.

Teng related his own learning by saying: "In the *chi-hsi* year (1539), I paid my respects to the master and heard the teaching of *liang-chih* but did not understand it. So I went into the Ch'ing-ch'eng Mountain to practice Ch'an meditation for ten years. In 1548, I went to Mount Chi-tsu [in Yunnan]. There I awakened to the fact that outside of human emotions and contingent affairs, there is an ineffable truth. At the time, without the instruction of a good master, I was unable to acquire sudden understanding. In the *kuei-chou* year (1553), I reached T'ien-ch'ih and paid my respects to [the priest] Yüeh-ch'üan, telling him what I had learned at Chi-tsu. He told me that the second truth is also the first truth. So I thought that I knew that which is presently bright and intelli-gent—[the Tao] that ordinary people use every day without realizing. In 1554 I went to Mount Lu to pay my respects to [the monk] Hsing-k'ung; in 1558 I was at Li-chou. For about eight years, I felt that I was not making any progress from day to day. So I went to Huang-an, stay-ing in Keng Ting-li's cottage. Only then did I understand the meaning of that which is prior to my birth and my parents, even to the creation of Heaven and Earth, that which is beyond the waters and the mountains, beyond the hundred-foot pole. This is called that which belongs neither to being nor to nonbeing, neither to truth nor to illusion, neither to life nor to extinction, neither to words nor to speech. It resides always in the true mind and has no connection with profane affairs. I suddenly understood everything I had learned at Chi-tsu about human emotions and contingent affairs, realizing that I had been misled for over twenty years by Yüeh-ch'üan. After 1566 my learning became daily more pro-

found and abstract, to the point that there was no longer self, no longer
Tao, [and all was] as free as an empty boat or a floating tile with no
attachment. [What people call] coming out of the womb and changing
one's bones is really this."

Teng's mistakes are due to his emphasizing insights into nature but
without insisting upon rules and regulations. [Thus], that which is natural *(hsien-t'ien)* is natural, that which is artificial *(hou-t'ien)* is artificial,
the first principle is the first principle, the second principle is the second
principle.[12] The body and nature are two different things. Words are
outside of the world, actions are inside the world. People could only
remark that he followed his emotions without knowing that what he
calls the natural, first principle, is nothing other than the one word,
nothingness *(wu)*. Alas, is that only Teng's mistake and nobody else's?

Fang Yü-shih, *tzu* Chan-yi, was a native of Huang-p'o. At about
twenty he was a salaried student but left everything suddenly and went
to Mount T'ai-ho, where he practiced control of his mind. After a long
period of silence he developed clairvoyance and learned the secret of
yellow and white alchemy[13] from a priest. So he went to Ching-shan
and met Wang Chi and Lo Hung-hsien, both of whom regarded him as
an unusual technician. Wherever his carriage went, notables would
offer welcome. Old teachers and high officials all were content to regard
him as a superior. But he liked abstractions and indulged in long discussions. Keng Ting-li first studied with him; after a long time he realized
that Fang's learning was not real and so left him. One day he told Lo
Hung-hsien, "We people who have left the world to learn by ourselves,
we have our secret formulas too and transmit them only to the right persons. How can the learning of the sages be so easy?" Lo agreed with
him. So Fang invited Lo to his own village in Mount Tao-ming.
Together they sat up all night talking. After a long time, Lo learned
nothing and so returned home. When Ch'eng Hsüeh-yen and Ho Hsin-
yin called a big assembly on Mount K'uang, the place was filled with
horses and carriages. Fang went in a sedan chair carried by two young
boys. After the bows, Ho took his arm and said, "Lend me a hundred
pieces of silver." Fang yielded by saying, "As you wish, even should it
be a thousand pieces of silver." Later he went to the capital, desiring to
use his technique to influence the emperor. Chang Chü-cheng heard
about it and said, "Fang's drum will soon be broken." After a short
time, Yen Shih-fan heard of his skill at the furnace and favored him, but
Fang avoided Yen and went home. When Hu Chih was in charge of the
school in Hukuang, he remembered that Fang had earlier deceived Lo
Hung-hsien and so sent men to arrest him. Fang escaped to join the
retainers of Kao Kung. When Kao fell, Fang went into hiding in
Mount T'ai-ho and died there of sickness.

Ch'eng Hsüeh-yen, *tzu* Erh-p'u, *hao* Hou-t'ai, was a native of Hsiao-kan (Hu-kuang). He served as assistant minister in the court of the imperial stud. Seeing that his own learning was lagging behind, he cried in secret, so fervent was his desire for improvement. After Ho Hsin-yin's death, Hsüeh-yen's brother Ch'eng Hsüeh-po said, "Master Liang (Ho Hsin-yin) regarded his friends as his own life. But among those of his friends who are known to scholars, besides Ch'ien T'ung-wen there is only my brother. Liang's soul will not leave my brother's." So he opened up the graveyard and buried the two together.

Ch'ien T'ung-wen, *tzu* Huai-su, was a native of Hsing-hua in Fukien. He was magistrate of Ch'i-men and then served as secretary in the ministry of justice and, after frequent transfers, became a prefect. He was friendly with Ho Hsin-yin. Ch'ien once said that although there were numerous people studying the Tao, they all belonged to a peer group, as did brothers. He had not yet seen anyone who was worthy of being [regarded as] a parent.

Kuan Chih-tao,[14] *tzu* Teng-chih, *hao* Tung-ming, was a native of T'ai-ts'ang in Soochow and a *chin-shih* of 1571. He was made a secretary in the ministry of war in Nanking and then changed to the ministry of justice. When Chang Chü-cheng was grand secretary, Kuan submitted a memorial with nine items, criticizing the government, with the intention of taking away from Chang his great influence and returning it to the sovereign. Of these items, there was one on regulations of the censorate that said that in early Ming times the two top provincial offices were equal [in power] to the censor inspectorate, and that the practice in his own time was no longer correct. So Chang sent him out as assistant surveillance commissioner in Kwangtung to get him into trouble so that he might harm himself with his own law. Sure enough, soon after, he was impeached by the censor Kung Mou-hsien and degraded to salt distribution superintendent. The following year, at the triennial examination of provincial officials, he was adjudged to be too old and sick, and he retired. He died in 1608 at the age of seventy-two.

Kuan studied under Keng Ting-hsiang and wrote a book of several hundred thousand words. Generally speaking, he attempted to merge Confucianism and Buddhism [in a philosophy that is] vast and intangible. He said that *Ch'ien* (Heaven), the beginning, was the head without head and no different from the "sea of nature" as this is taught in Hua-yen Buddhism; that the way of change is equal to Heaven and Earth and so is naturally though unexpectedly in accord with [the teachings] of the patriarchs of Buddhism and Taoism. He also said that Confucianism regards the other two teachings as rivals, and therefore that they run into conflict with Buddhist and Taoist followers. According to him, the principles of a teaching must be "round," while the substance *(t'i)* of a teaching must be "square";[15] hence, one can make use of the roundness of [the original teachings of] Confucius to round out the squareness of the Sung Confucians, so that Confucianism may not become an obstacle to Buddhism or Buddhism an obstacle to Confucianism. And one can make use of the squareness of Confucius' teaching to render square the roundness of the later Confucians, so that Confucianism may not change Buddhism or Buddhism change Confucianism. As he explained, from the time of T'ang and Sung on, Confucians have either insisted upon the supremacy of Confucius, while subjugating Buddhist claims, or exalted Buddhism at the expense of Confucianism, for they had erected boundaries [between the two teachings] in *Ch'ien* [i.e., hexagrams] and in [Hua-yen's] "sea of nature." He suggested that *Ch'ien,* the beginning, be put in control of Heaven, to resolve two problems at one stroke.

He expounded ten things about Confucius, as follows. First, Confucius was responsible for the transmission of literature *(wen-t'ung)* and not for the transmission of doctrine *(tao-t'ung).* Second, Confucius adhered to the way of the minister, not the way of the teacher. Third, the editing of the Six Classics and the collecting of his seventy-two disciples may not be the full and true story of Confucius. Fourth, had Confucius changed places with Po-yi and Liu-hsia Hui, he would have acted as did Po-yi and Liu-hsia Hui.[16] Fifth, Confucius knew the ordinance of Heaven and did not insist especially upon principles *(li),* but he also understood the cyclical movements of *ch'i.*[17] Sixth, while his all-pervasive teaching[18] belonged yet to the realm of enlightenment, he had to actualize it in the realm of action. Seventh, his work of education penetrated the order of nature while its concrete influences penetrated the order of action. Eighth, Confucius was once a disciple of Lao-tzu. Ninth, Confucius regarded as "men of former times"[19] the Yellow Emperor and even earlier persons. Tenth, had Confucius attained high office, he would have modeled himself upon Duke Huan of Ch'i and Duke Wen of Chin.[20]

Now the kind of things Kuan said were only superficial things about the Three Teachings. He was especially fond of telling stories of ghosts, spirits, and of dreams. One can see from all this that he did not attain the Tao in his learning. Wang Ken excitedly talked about "the dragon appearing," which Kuan exposed as false. But in seeking to overcome the tensions between Confucianism and Buddhism, Kuan showed himself still to be a member of T'ai-chou.

(*MJHA* 32:1a–4b)

NOTES

1. It is obvious from this critical account of the T'ai-chou school that Huang Tsung-hsi, like his teacher Liu Tsung-chou, blames it for the later ills of the intellectual movement that was initiated by Wang Yang-ming.

2. The metaphor is used to show their daring.

3. For Yen Chün, see Ho Hsin-yin's biography by Wu P'ei-yi and Julia Ching, *DMB*, v. 1, 513–15.

4. This refers to the school of sudden enlightenment founded by Hui-neng.

5. For Wang Shih-chen, *hao* Yen-chou (1526–90), see the biography by Barbara Yoshida-Kraft, *DMB*, v. 2, 1399–1405.

6. Allusion to the *Doctrine of the Mean*, ch. 1.

7. Allusion to *Analects* 3:22, which refers to an extravagant terrace built by Kuan Chung, chief minister to Duke Huan of Ch'i (683–642 B.C.).

8. Allusion to *Mencius* 1B:2, where he describes how King Wen of Chou shared his garden with the people.

9. For Lo, see his biography by Julia Ching, in *DMB*, v. 1, 975–78.

10. See Ronald Dimberg, *The Sage and Society: The Life and Thought of Ho Hsin-yin* (Honolulu, 1974), especially ch. 3.

11. Su Ch'in and Chang Yi were diplomatists of the Warring States period. Metaphorically, their teaching refers also to a contingent and relativist learning, even a kind of opportunism.

12. In Buddhist vocabulary, the first principle *(ti-yi-yi)* refers to ultimate truth, the second principle *(ti-erh-yi)* to secondary truths.

13. Allusion to the alchemists' attempt to make gold out of base metals.

14. For Kuan Chih-tao (1536–1608), see Chiao Hung, *Kuo-ch'ou hsien-cheng lu* 99:164.

15. "Square" refers to that which is independent, while "round" refers to that which blends easily with other teachings.

16. Po-yi was a hermit, while Liu-hsia Hui was an official to an unworthy ruler. See *Analects* 5:22, 7:14, 15:13, 16:12, 18:2, 18:8.

17. Literally, *ch'i-yün*. It refers to times and fortunes in terms of the cyclical operations of *ch'i*.

18. Allusion to *Analects* 4:15, where Confucius described the all-pervading unity of his teaching.

19. Allusion to *Analects* 11:1, where Confucius described the "men of former times" *(hsien-chin)* as "rustics" in matters of rites and music.

20. Duke Huan of Ch'i (r. 681–643 B.C.) and Duke Wen of Chin (r. 631–628 B.C.) were two hegemons during the Spring and Autumn Period.

Wang Ken

Wang Ken (1483–1541),[1] *tzu* Ju-chih, *hao* Hsin-chai, was a native of An-feng-ch'ang, T'ai-chou Prefecture. At the age of seven he enrolled in a village school, but because of the poverty of his family, he was unable to complete his education. Accompanying his father, a trader, to Shantung on business, he made a practice of carrying with him in his sleeves the *Classic of Filial Piety,* the *Analects,* and the *Great Learning.* Whenever he met someone [qualified to discuss them] he would ask about the difficult passages. For a long time he discoursed on these texts in a free and unpremeditated manner, as though someone had revealed their meaning to him. One winter his father was called to fulfill *corvée* duties. In the chill of the morning he would rise and wash with cold water. Wang Ken saw this and wept bitterly, saying, "As a son, how can one see his father [suffer] like this and still call himself a man?"[2] Thereafter, he took his father's place whenever he could and so was unable to devote his efforts solely to his studies. Nevertheless, he continued to practice a type of silent cultivation, using the classics to verify his insights and, conversely, using these same insights to interpret the classics. In this fashion he persevered for many years, without others being able to discover his achievements.

One night, Wang Ken dreamed that the heavens were falling upon him. As thousands of people ran screaming and begging for rescue, he raised his arms and lifted the heavens. Then, noting that the sun, moon, and other heavenly bodies had strayed from their orbits, he raised his hands again and restored them to their proper positions. When he woke, sweat was pouring from his body like rain, and he achieved a penetrating insight into his mind-in-itself *(hsin-t'i).*[3] Later he would record, "In the sixth year of the Cheng-te era (1511), I lived in accordance with *jen* for three and one-half months."[4] From then on, whether moving or standing still, talking or remaining silent, he remained ever conscious of this. Having also carefully studied the *Book of Rites,* he now set about fashioning according to prescription a hat, an informal robe, a sash, and tablets. Putting these on, he said, "How can I speak the words of [the sage] Yao and act as Yao did without also wearing his clothes?"[5]

At that time Wang Yang-ming, grand coordinator of Kiangsi, was lecturing on the doctrine of *liang-chih.*[6] Scholars from south of the Yangtze flocked to him and became his disciples. But Wang Ken was far away and had not yet heard of him. A certain Hung Wen-kang, a native of Chi-an living in T'ai-chou, heard Wang Ken's teachings and said in surprise, "This teaching is very similar to that of Grand Coordinator Wang." Wang Ken was pleased with this and said in reply, "Is that so? Master Wang expounds the doctrine of *liang-chih* and I discuss the investigation of things *(ko-wu).* If they are indeed the same teaching, Wang will stand as Heaven's legacy to future generations, but if they are different, I will stand as Heaven's legacy to Wang." That very day he set out for Kiangsi. Taking with him his specially fashioned dress, he went to seek an audience with Wang Yang-ming. When he arrived at the middle gate of Yang-ming's official residence, he stood with raised tablets. Yang-ming came out and greeted him beyond the gate and they entered the house together. Taking the high seat (the one reserved for guests), Wang Ken debated with Yang-ming for a long time. But gradually his heart yielded [to Yang-ming's brilliance] until finally he retired to a seat on the side. When the discussion was over, Ken sighed and said, "Here is a simplicity and directness that I have not yet attained." Leaving his seat, he bowed before Yang-ming and declared himself his disciple.

After Wang Ken had withdrawn and pondered over the things he had heard, he realized that there were still issues on which he and Yang-ming did not agree, and he said with regret, "I have been rash." The next day he again sought an audience with Yang-ming in order to tell him of his regret. Yang-ming said, "It is wise of you not to be swayed so easily." Only after Wang Ken had returned to the high seat and had resumed his lengthy discussions with Yang-ming did he yield to the other's arguments. Subsequently, he became Yang-ming's disciple once again. Yang-ming told his other students, "At the time that I captured the rebel prince Ch'en-hao, I was not in the least affected. Today, however, I have been moved by this man."[7]

When Yang-ming returned to Shao-hsing, Wang Ken followed him. Many students in attendance studied with Ken. But later Wang Ken sighed, saying, "This kind of learning was interrupted for a thousand years. Now Heaven has again revealed it to my teacher. How can the world be allowed not to hear of it?" So he asked Yang-ming about making a carriage like the one in which Confucius had traveled. Yang-ming smiled but would not answer, so when Ken returned home he constructed such a vehicle by himself. Traveling this way, he stirred up a lot of attention on the roads. As he was about to reach the capital, an old man dreamed that a headless yellow dragon had walked in the rain to the Ch'ung-wen gate, transformed himself into a man, and stood there. At daybreak this old man rose and proceeded to the gate, only to find Wang Ken approaching.

At that time, criticisms of Yang-ming's teachings were rising like a swarm of bees. Moreover, as Ken's hat, dress, words, and deeds were unlike those of other men, the people of the capital looked upon him with suspicion. [Fearing that his outlandish behavior was bringing discredit upon them,] his fellow disciples urged him to quit the capital. Yang-ming himself sent a letter reproving him, and so Ken began his return to K'uai-chi. Yang-ming considered Wang Ken's self-esteem too high and his demeanor too outlandish and thus decided to discipline him. For three days Ken waited at the gate, unable to gain an audience with him. When Yang-ming finally came out to the gate to see a guest off, Ken prostrated himself by the roadside and said, "I now know my fault." But Yang-ming, re-entering his quarters, would not even turn around. Only after Ken had followed him as far as the courtyard and had cried out severely, "Confucius himself would not go to such extremes!"[8] did he bid Ken to rise.

When Yang-ming died in the midst of a campaign [and his body was being shipped down the Ch'ien-t'ang River], Ken went in tears to T'ung-lu [a port on that river about seventy kilometers southwest of Hangchow] to meet the hearse.[9] He took care of Yang-ming's affairs and then returned to his own home. There he opened a school to which pupils came from far and wide. When Yang-ming's students gathered together for discussion, they always invited Ken to preside. For although Wang Chi's skill as a debater was considered second only to that of Yang-ming, nevertheless there were some who lacked faith in his teachings. It was Wang Ken who, through even his glances and facial expressions, was capable of inspiring the greatest number.[10] He taught that the daily activity of the common people was the Tao, and he pointed in illustration of this to the unfailing naturalness of domestic servants in the midst of their every activity. Those who heard him were pleased and uplifted. Later, the censor Wu T'i sent a memorial recommending him for office, but in vain.[11] Wang Ken died on January 4, 1541, at the age of fifty-eight.

Wang Ken regarded the investigation of things *(ko-wu)* as referring to the fact that things have roots and branches. He taught that one's self, the world, the state, and the family all make up one substance. The investigation of things, the extension of knowledge *(liang-chih)*, and making the self secure *(an-shen)* constitute the root. Regulating the family, ordering the state, and giving peace to the world constitute the branches.[12] Therefore, if in one's actions there is some deficiency, one must turn and look for it within oneself. This reflexive moment is the fundamental effort *(kung-fu)* of the investigtion of things. Should one wish to regulate one's family, order the state, and give peace to the world, one must first make secure the self. According to the *Book of Changes,* "When the self is secure, the world, the state, and the family can be preserved."[13] But when the self has yet to be made secure, the root is not firmly established.

Now, one who knows how to give security to the self cannot but love and respect himself. One who loves and respects himself cannot fail to love and respect others. If I am able to love and respect others, others must love and respect me, and my self shall be secure. In the same way, if the entire family loves and respects me, then the family will be regulated. If the entire state loves and respects me, then the state will be ordered. And if the whole world loves and respects me, then the world will be at peace. Therefore, should others fail to love and respect me, it is not particularly a case of others' lacking humanity *(jen)* or respect. Rather, it is my own lack of humanity and respect that may be discerned. This became known as the Huai-nan doctrine of the investigation of things.

[Commenting upon this,] Liu Tsung-chou said: "Among the doctrines of the investigation of things propounded by later Confucian scholars, the Huai-nan doctrine ought to be regarded as the correct one; but it stands in need of a minor modification. It is certainly correct to say that the investigation of things, the extension of knowledge, and making sincere the will are the root, and that proper cultivation, ordering the state, and giving peace to the world are the branches. But when we speak of making the self secure we refer only to the securing of the mind *(hsin)* and not to a security that derives from the zealous attempt to protect one's body. Should one live in a country in crisis or enter a state in rebellion and see what is to be done and yet [out of concern for the safety of the body] not act, then neither self nor mind is secure. Sometimes, there is a no alternative but to sacrifice one's life in order to establish *jen,* as in the cases of King Wen's imprisonment at Yu-li,[14] or the voluntary starvation of Po-yi and Shu-ch'i.[15] For if the mind is secure then there is never a case of the self being insecure." Wang Ken himself said, "To make secure both one's self and the mind is best. To make secure only one's mind and not one's whole self is less good. And to fail to make secure either self or mind is worst. Should we not regard the singing bird as a model for securing the self and in this way establish opportunities for escaping from danger?"[16]

Wang Ken regarded the attitude expressed in the *Book of Changes,* "Dragon appearing in the field, it benefits one to see the great man,"[17] as the correct one. Confucius cultivated himself, taught pupils, and thus became known to the world. Not for a single day did he hide himself in seclusion. Therefore, when people praised Wang Ken as [a modern-day] Yi Yin or Fu Yüeh, he would say, "I have not the ability to do what Yi Yin or Fu Yüeh did; nor am I of the same lineage. That Yi Yin and Fu Yüeh each found service with a wise lord may certainly be considered fortuitous. Nevertheless, had they failed to do so, they would simply have lived out their days practicing virtue in solitude."[18] But Confucius was different. That was why he traveled ceaselessly from state to state in his carriage. This example, the imitation of which Yang-ming wished to curb, proved difficult for Wang Ken to forget. And thus [the knowledge so bitterly acquired by Ken on the occasion of Yang-ming's rebuke] is still not the same as the wisdom of having no regret at all even when one is unknown to the world.[19]

Wang Ken also said, "The sage rules the world with Tao; what he prizes most is Tao. The ordinary man can extend the Tao;[20] what he prizes most is the self. But if the Tao is prized then the self is prized; and if the self is prized then the Tao is prized. That is why those who follow this learn to become teachers, elders, or princes. The world and all the things in it depend upon the self; the self does not depend upon the world. To ignore this is the way of women!"[21]

Even should a sage return, he would not change these words.

(MJHA 32:6a–7b)

NOTES

1. For Wang Ken, see his biography by Julia Ching, *DMB,* v. 2, 1382–85. See also his *Collected Writings (Wang Hsin-chai ch'üan-chi,* 1846 Japanese edition,

reprinted in Taipei, 1975) for the chronological biography in *chüan* 1. This volume has appeared in a new series of reprints of Japanese editions of Chinese collected writings, entitled *Chin-shih Han-chi ts'ung-k'an*. It belongs to the "Section on Thought," New Series, number 13. The collection has been compiled by Okada Takehiko and Araki Kengo of Fukuoka.

2. See *Wang Hsin-chai ch'üan-chi* (hereafter *HCCC*), 1:2b.

3. *HCCC* 1:3a.

4. *Analects* 6:5 refers to Yen Hui, Confucius' favorite disciple, as having lived in accordance with *jen* for three months.

5. Cf. *Mencius* 6B:2–5.

6. *HCCC* 1:4b.

7. *HCCC* 1:5a–b. Reference also to the rebellion of Chu Ch'en-hao, suppressed by Wang Yang-ming in 1519.

8. *Mencius* 4B:10.

9. *HCCC* 1:9a.

10. *HCCC* 2:4a–b.

11. Wu T'i (*hao* Shu-shan), 1502–68. See his biography by Julia Ching and Huang P'ei, *DMB*, v. 2, 1495–97.

12. See the *Great Learning*.

13. See the *Book of Changes, Hsi-tzu,* part B, in J. Legge, trans., *Yi King* (*SBE*, v. 16), 392.

14. Chou, the last Shang king, acceded to the throne in 1145(?) B.C. His reign has been held up to history as an example of Heaven frowning on the unvirtuous. He had several chief ministers. One, the prince of Ch'u, was killed because his daughter refused to enter the harem. Another, the man later known as King Wen, remonstrated with Chou and was then imprisoned at Yu-li. There, tradition relates, he composed parts of the *Book of Changes*. Freed some years later, he went on to counsel the king and succeeded in curbing the more exotic enormities of his rule. When the Chou (different word) dynasty established itself in 1123, King Wen was apotheosized as its founder. See the *Book of History*, trans. by J. Legge as *The Book of Historical Documents,* in *The Chinese Classics,* v. 3, 268–70.

15. According to tradition, Po-yi and Shu-ch'i were sons of the lord of Ku-chu. At their father's death both abjured the throne and went into retirement. When King Wu defeated the last Shang king and established the Chou dynasty, Po-yi and Shu-ch'i secluded themselves on Mount Shou-yang and died of starvation rather than live by eating the grain of the new royal household, for they believed King Wu guilty of ritual impropriety concerning the disposition of his father's remains. See *Shih-chi,* ch. 61.

16. See the commentary to the *Great Learning,* chapter 3, "In the *Book of Poetry* it is said, 'The twittering yellow bird rests on a corner of the mound.' The master said, 'When it rests, it knows where to rest. Is it possible that a man should not be equal to this bird?' " Quoted in J. Legge, trans., *The Chinese Classics,* v. 1, 362. Here, the singing yellow bird is used as a metaphor for spontaneity and naturalness: When the bird wishes to take his rest, the means by which he does so (the mound) is immediately at hand. So too with man, as the means by which he rests (making the mind tranquil) is likewise constantly accessible. The bird takes no special thought to his resting place, landing freely and spontaneously when he is in need of rest. Man's rest too, requires no special cultivation, merely a spontaneous and direct tapping of his creative wellspring, the mind. Thus in whatever situation one finds oneself, even in one of extreme danger, tranquility does not lie in frantic efforts to flee the situation but rather in a return to the self.

17. *Book of Changes,* hexagram *Ch'ien.* See J. Legge, trans., *Yi King,* 57.

18. Yi Yin was teacher and chief minister to T'ai-chia of the Shang; Fu Yüeh served as chief minister under Wu-ting (Kao-tsung). Both men are considered exemplary models of virtuous ministers. See *Shih-chi,* ch. 3.

19. See the *Book of Changes,* ". . . he would do nothing merely to secure his fame. He can live, withdrawn from the world, without regret; he can experience disapproval without trouble of mind." J. Legge, trans., *Yi King,* 409.

20. *Analects* 15:28.

21. *Mencius* 3B:2. Here the correct course for women is described as one of obedience and submission. This is contrasted with that of the great man *(ta-chang-fu),* whose aims are engagement in the world and the promotion of righteousness.

Wang Pi

Wang Pi, *tzu* Shun-tsung, *hao* Tung-ya (1511–87),[1] was the second son of Wang Ken. At age eight he followed his father to K'uai-chi. At times of [large] assemblies he used to sing poetry aloud with his child's voice, which harmonized with metal and stone. Wang Yang-ming asked about it, found that he was Wang Ken's son, and said, "I had suspected that this was no child from Shao-hsing." So he made him study with Wang Chi and Ch'ien Te-hung. Wang Pi thus remained about twenty years in Shao-hsing. When his father, Wang Ken, started to teach in the region south of the River Huai, Wang Pi assisted him. After his father's death, he continued the work, traveling back and forth as he took charge of teaching. Whenever he returned home to the village, he would spend time boating, while the voice of his singing shook the woods, creating an atmosphere that reminded people of [the passage in *Analects* 11: 25 describing Tseng Tien's desire to] sing and dance near the altars of rain. He died on November 4, 1587, at age seventy-six.

Wang Pi's learning[2] regarded lack of self-restraint as good. For him, the singing of birds and falling of flowers, the firmness of mountains and movements of waters, to eat when hungry and to drink when thirsty, to wear light dress in summer and heavy furs in winter: all this perfectly reveals the Tao. Should one be able to cultivate this [sense of the Tao], Heaven and Earth will go on transforming themselves and trees and woods will grow prosperously. Should one not be able to cultivate this, Heaven and Earth will fold up and worthy men will go into hiding. [He said that] the men of his days started getting ideas with the mere mention of the word "learn." In discussions of learning and the rigors of self-regulation, the more effort they applied, the wearier grew their minds; the more diligent they became, the clumsier appeared their activities. They held back their desires in the hope of earning a good name and yet boasted of a love of the good. They were attached to their thoughts while hiding the evidence and yet called this correction of faults. Their minds and spirits were shaken, their blood and energy were disturbed. They did not know that there was originally not one thing, that [the Tao] realizes itself naturally. As long as one did not hin-

der the flow of process *(liu-hsing),* true joy would appear of itself, and the
student should complete this joy, since, without joy, there was no learning. Although this insight was derived from Wang Ken's song on the joy
of learning, Wang Chi's contribution should also not be denied. Ch'en
Hsien-chang[3] had said:

> Let everything alone! There is no need for you to busy your hands and
> feet. Dancing at the rain altar in groups of two and three[4] is somewhere
> between 'neither forgetting nor helping.'[5] Tseng Tien's lively impulses,
> when disciplined by Mencius, resemble hawks flying and fishes leaping.[6] But
> without Mencius' insistence on effort, Tseng's preferences strike one as
> dream-talk. For Confucius' sight at the river bank [*Analects* 9: 16] gave us the
> heavenly principle-in-itself that is always in a state of dynamic flow. Tseng
> translated this into singing and dancing in late spring;[7] Shao Yung perceived
> it as cyclical changes in terms of "Origin," "Epoch," "Revolution," and
> "Generation."[8] For unless learning brings with it great joy, it does not
> deserve the name of learning.

Such a spirit of spontaneity made itself manifest in Ming times in
Ch'en Hsien-chang's straw-cloaks (i.e., contentment in poverty) and in
the songs and echoes of Wang Ken and his son Pi. These words are full
of savor, and yet they are also extremely difficult to comprehend properly. A slight error could lead one onto the path of madness and eccentricity. For this reason Chu Hsi said that Tseng Tien could not be imitated,[9] while Ch'eng Hao said that with all his admirable and heroic
stature, Shao Yung did not keep his feet on the ground. Even Ch'en
Hsien-chang himself cautioned others against dream-talk. So when we
examine carefully Wang Pi's learning, we find that he also was only
indulging himself in certain moods and projections.

(MJHA 32:11b–12a)

NOTES

1. For Wang Pi, see Wang Ken's biography by Julia Ching, *DMB,* v. 2,
1383–85.
2. There is doubtless much of the romantic in Wang Pi, as also in others of
the T'ai-chou branch of the Yang-ming school, a romanticism that may be
traced, as also in the case of Ch'en Hsien-chang, not only to Ch'an Buddhist,
but also to Taoist influences.
3. This is a direct quotation from a letter written by Ch'en to his disciple Lin.
See *Po-sha-tzu ch'üan-chi* (1612 edition), 3:22b. The passage is highly allusive
and even elliptical, almost impossible to understand unless one knows the classical references and the philosophical perspectives of Ch'en himself.
4. Allusion to Tseng Tien, Confucius' disciple, who expressed his desire in
life in terms of singing and dancing at the rain altars in late spring. See *Analects*
11:25.
5. Reference here to *Mencius* 2A:2, regarding the cultivation of the mind,
which should be undertaken with proper seriousness, "neither forgetting," and

yet also proper detachment, "nor helping," or, without forcibly busying oneself. See Glossary, *wu-wang wu-chu*.

6. Allusion to the *Doctrine of the Mean*, ch. 12. This expression is a frequent reference in Neo-Confucian writings and refers to the natural, as opposed to the artifical.

7. *Analects* 11:25.

8. Shao Yung, the Sung philosopher, wrote about grandiose schemes of cyclical processes in his work, *Huang-chi ching-shih* (Supreme Principles for the Governance of the World). See *Huang-chi ching-shih shu*, SPPY ed., ch. 6.

9. See Chu Hsi's *Ssu-shu chi-chu* (The Four Books Annotated), SPPY ed., 3:6b, 7:24b; *Chu-tzu yü-lei* (Recorded Dialogues) (1473 ed.), 29:11a–13b.

Chu Shu

Chu Shu, *tzu* Kuang-hsin,[1] a native of Ts'ao-yen-ch'ang, T'ai-chou (Nan Chihli), collected firewood to support his mother. One day, while passing Wang Ken's lecture hall, he sang:

Ten *li* away from the mountain, the wood is at home,
One *li* away from the mountain, the wood is in the mountain.

Wang Ken heard this and told his disciples, "Listen to this, young men! The problem is not to look for the Tao. Should one not look for it, there is no easy way of getting it." The woodcutter also heard his words and listened with much interest. From then on, he would always pass by there whenever he went to collect firewood and listen to Wang's lectures. When hungry, he would beg for some broth to eat with the rice he had packed with him. After listening, he would sing out as he carried the firewood away with him. Wang Ken's disciples watched him in astonishment. One of them, by the name Tsung, called him over and said, "I have here several dozen taels of silver for you to find another means of living, so that you need not do this tiring work and may even spend your days and nights with us all." The woodcutter took the silver, bent down, and thought, then said angrily, "You do not really love me. Should I allow myself to start thinking now of how to use this [money], I would be giving up my whole life." So he returned the money to him. When Hu Chih became educational intendant, he summoned this man to him, but the man did not come. When Hu then gave him some work to do, the man arrived in work clothes and bare feet. Hu greeted him courteously before they took leave of each other.

(*MJHA* 32:12a)

NOTE

1. Chu Shu's name is included in the list of Wang Ken's disciples (p. 2b), given at the end of *HCCC*, referred to in note 1 to the translated biography of Wang Ken. See also Chou Ju-teng, *Sheng-hsüeh tsung-chuan*, 18:a–b.

Han Chen

Han Chen, *tzu* Yi-chung, *hao* Lo-wu,[1] a native of Hsing-hua (Nan Chihli), was a potter by trade. He admired the woodcutter Chu and became his student, eventually completing his studies under Wang Pi. He had a rudimentary knowledge of letters and gave up his three-room hut to cover his debts. After this, he lived in the potter's kiln and sang to himself,

> The three-room hut goes to the new master,
> The glaze of smoke stays as an old friend.

Although he was over thirty-six, he was yet unmarried. So Wang Pi's disciples collected some money for him to arrange a wedding. After quite some time, he felt that he had some insights and took upon himself the work of teaching the ignorant, doing this work as the occasion allowed him. Thousands of people, including farmers, artisans, and merchants, followed him. In the autumn, when farmers had more time, he would gather disciples for lectures, going from one village to another, as he sang and the others responded, so that the voice of songs filled the countryside. The magistrate heard of him and encouraged him, sending him two piculs of rice and six ounces of silver. He took the rice but returned the money. When the magistrate asked him about government, he replied, "I am a potter and cannot assist you personally. I just hope that those who are with me will not be involved in litigation that troubles the government. In this manner, I hope to return your kindness." When Keng Ting-hsiang[2] passed through T'ai-chou, he called for an assembly at the temple of Wang Ken. There he showed excessive emotions of pleasure and anger while talking in passing about the deceased grand secretary (Yen Sung).[3] Han knocked on the bed, and cried out, "Can you understand the meaning of this little thing [*liang-chih*] as I do?" Keng laughed, saying, "It is just as bad for a poor man to show arrogance." Wang Pi said, "Han understands what it means to regard officialdom and poverty with equanimity." Whenever Han heard people discussing worldly affairs during assemblies, he would cry out, "How much time have we in our lives, that we should waste it in such gossip?" When people looked for quotations in chapters and verses, he would exclaim angrily, "Why do you give up trying to understand your experience of the immediate and play with dead words instead? Could this be an old schoolhouse?" [Such words] served as caution to all those seated with him.

(*MJHA* 32:12a–b)

NOTES

1. For Han Chen, see also Chou Ju-teng, *Sheng-hsüeh tsung-chuan*, 18:6b–7b.
2. For Keng Ting-hsiang, *hao* T'ien-t'ai, see his biography in this volume.
3. Keng had served under five Grand Secretaries: Yen Sung, Hsü Chieh, Chang Chü-cheng, Shen Shih-hsing, and Wang Hsi-chüeh. He had offended Yen Sung but always remained partial to Chang Chü-cheng. But, as Huang Tsung-hsi himself points out in Keng's biography, there had not been any major disagreement between him and any of these powerful men.

Hsü Yüeh

Hsü Yüeh, *tzu* Tzu-chih, *hao* Po-shih,[1] was a man of Kuei-hsi (Kiangsi) and a *chin-shih* of 1532. He had served in a ministry as a bureau director and had also been sent out as a surveillance commissioner. In 1552, he was elevated to senior administration commissioner in Yunnan. At the time, Na Chien, an aboriginal chief in the Yüan-chiang prefecture (Yunnan), had killed the prefect Na Hsien and had attacked several subprefectures and counties. The imperial court decided to launch an expedition against him. The regional commander, Mu Ch'ao-pi,[2] and the provincial governor, Shih Chien, mustered some troops, divided them into five routes, and advanced to fight him. Na Chien pretended to surrender, sending the registrar Chang Wei to Wang Yang-hao, assistant commissioner of Yunnan and censorial inspector for the expedition. Wang was suspicious and did not dare go to meet Na Chien. Hsü Yüeh, who had arrived at the headquarters with military supplies, volunteered magnanimously to go to meet Na Chien. But when he got outside the southern gate of the prefectural town of Yüan-chiang, Na Chien did not come out to greet him; so Hsü Yüeh angrily demanded to know why. Na Chien's troops, lying in ambush, then rose up and killed him. Kao Ku, the aboriginal official of Yao-an, had tried hard to rescue him but was also killed in battle. For several years, our government troops attacked Na Chien without conquering him. But when Na Chien died, the various aboriginal chiefs desired to atone for the crime of their rebellion with a gift of elephants. Emperor Shih-tsung (r. 1522–66), being weary of war, accepted this token. So the people of the time recalled the memory of Hsü Yüeh, saying, "How sad that a provincial administration commissioner, a high official of the second rank, should be only worth eight elephants from Yüan-chiang!" They grieved that the criminal Na Chien was not apprehended.

In their youths, Hsü Yüeh and Hsia Yen (later grand secretary) had roughly equal reputations for their talents. Hsü studied first under Wang Yang-ming and then completed his education under Wang Ken as the latter's disciple. He was very strict with himself. He often took walks with Wang Ken under the moon, examining himself constantly, so that he provoked Wang to say to him harshly, "Are not Heaven and Earth in communion?"[3] On another evening, they came to a small stream. Wang jumped across and looked at Hsü, saying, "Why are you so hesitant?" Hsü then crossed the stream and felt suddenly as though lost. He later sighed and said, "In the past I wasted all the energy that this old man spent on me."

Hsü said that the six realms[4] are the outer limits of the mind, the four seas are the boundaries of the mind, and the myriad creatures are the forms and color of the mind. He also maintained that there is only this mind, past and present, vast, profound, and unfathomable. According to him, it can hear and see, from dawn to dusk. It is also able to be filial and brotherly, day and night. Without need of rational calculation, it is naturally bright and conscious, attuned to Heaven. Once it enters the order of sound and smell, it becomes what is called a deliberate thought (*yi-nien*) and is selfishness. He asked whether any of the human activities, such as rising, going about one's affairs, eating, and resting, were not natural. For him, they all refer to real knowledge and real perception. If one tries to add to these, another knowledge, another perception, one would be creating two kinds of knowledge and perception. Moreover, there is no pain, no itch, no sight, nor hearing, of which the mind of man is not conscious. And so "outside of this consciousness can there be another?" Even the foolish and unworthy have never departed from this substance (*t'i*). For it is not that they are ignorant of this substance, but that they do not know its function (*yung*) is nature. That is why they are described as acting foolishly. For they regard their activity as consciousness, and their consciousness is dull. These are words explaining the realized *liang-chih* (*hsien-ch'eng liang-chih*). It regards not going against the natural as a wondrous formula.

Wang Ken once asked Hsü Yüeh, "What is the supreme good?"[5] Hsü replied, "The supreme good is the goodness of nature." Wang continued, "Which is worthier of respect, the Way or the self? And what difference is there between the Way and the self?" He replied, "They are one and the same." Wang pursued, "Is your self worthy of respect right now?" Hsü stood up and implored, "Sir, what do you mean by respect for the self?" Wang said, "The self and the Way are originally one. This Way is most worthy of respect. This self is also most worthy of respect. If one respects the self but not the Way, that cannot be called respecting the self. If one respects the Way but not the self, that cannot be called respecting the Way. Only when both Way and self are respected is it the supreme good. Hence it is said that when the world possesses the Way, the Way may be made to accord with the self, and that if the world is without the Way, the self is to accord with the Way. To have the Way accord with man is the Way of the concubine. If you yourself cannot respect and believe in yourself, how can you make others do so?" Then Hsü prostrated himself, expressing thanks, "Your teaching shames me greatly."

If we judge Hsü Yüeh by his accepting Na Chien's surrender, we should recall that Hsü's job of supervising supplies did not entitle him to accept surrender. Yet he went there out of impulse. Even if one dare not criticize him for vanity, one might still say that he was imperfect in the Way of self-respect.

(MJHA 32:14b–15b)

NOTES

1. For Hsü Yüeh, see Chou Ju-teng, *Sheng-hsüeh tsung-chuan,* 16:26b.
2. See Mu's biography in *MS,* ch. 126.
3. An allusion to the *Book of Changes.* J. Legge, trans., *Yi King (SBE,* v. 16), 223.
4. Heaven, Earth, and the four compass points.
5. Allusion to the *Great Learning,* the Text of Confucius.

Lo Ju-fang

Lo Ju-fang, *tzu* Wei-te, *hao* Chin-hsi (1515–88),[1] was from Nan-ch'eng (Kiangsi). He received the *chin-shih* degree in 1553, served as magistrate in T'ai-hu (Anhwei), was chosen as secretary (of a bureau) in the ministry of justice, and then went to Ning-kuo-fu (Anhwei) to serve as prefect. He made use of lecture assemblies and rural compacts in his government. After a mourning period for his father, Lo returned to public service. When Chang Chü-cheng [the grand secretary] asked about his studies in the mountains,[2] Lo said, "I am reading the *Analects* and the *Great Learning* and find them somewhat more interesting now than before." Chang was silent.[3] He made Lo fill a vacancy in Tung-ch'ang (Shantung) and then transferred him to Yunnan as surveillance vice-commissioner. Lo made a complete overhaul of the irrigation system within that territory. When the aborigines raided the frontier lands in the far west and emergency was reported, Lo instructed his six pacification commissioners to annihilate them and divide up their territories. This intimidated the aborigines, who begged to surrender. Lo was then transferred to administration vice-commissioner. In 1577 he went to Peking to give reports. He lectured at the Kuang-hui temple and had a large following among the scholars of the court. Chang Chü-cheng was displeased with his popularity. Then the supervising secretary, Chou Liang-yin, impeached Lo for not leaving after completing his duties and lingering on at the capital. Lo was then made to resign from office. He went home, and, with his disciples, traveled about in An-ch'eng (Chi-an, Kiangsi?), then down the River Chien (Kiangsi), and on to the area in Chekiang and Nanking, wandering back and forth between Fukien and Kwangtung. Such travels helped to spread his teachings. Everywhere, disciples crowded the halls, but Lo never occupied for himself the teacher's seat. In 1588, a landslide occurred in the Ts'ung-ku Mountain (Kiangsi) and a hurricane uprooted trees there. Lo predicted that he would pass away on the first of the ninth moon (October 20), but his disciples asked him to stay on one more day. So he died the following noon, at age seventy-three.

In his youth, Lo had read these words of Hsüeh Hsüan:[4] "My mind has long been confused by the endless waxing and waning of selfishness. I must now completely remove it in order to render clear and peaceful the mind's substance."[5] He determined to put these words into practice. So he locked himself in the Lin-t'ien Temple, placing a basin of water and a mirror on a table and sitting opposite it in silence, with the aim of making his mind one with the water and mirror. After some time he became sick at heart, as though burning inside. Once he happened to pass by a Buddhist temple (1540, in Nan-ch'ang) and saw a sign: "Emergency help for sicknesses of the heart." He thought it referred to some famous doctor but went in to find an assembly and a lecturer. After listening in the crowd for some time, Lo exclaimed with delight, "This can truly cure my sickness." Upon inquiry, he discovered the lecturer to be Yen Chün, *hao* Shan-nung, who was from Chi-an (Kiangsi) and had received instruction from Wang Ken,[6] of the T'ai-chou school. Lo explained to him that his mind could remain unmoved by thoughts of life and death, gains and losses. Yen said, "What you have done is to control your passions rather than to realize perfect virtue *(t'i-jen)*." Lo replied, "One must eradicate selfishness to recover the principle of Heaven. Without controlling the passions, how can one realize perfect virtue?" Yen said, "Have you not read Mencius' discussion of the four beginnings of virtue?[7] [It says, 'Since all men have these four principles in themselves], let them know how to give them full scope for development and completion, and the issue will be like a fire that has begun to burn or a spring that has begun to find vent.' In this way one might achieve personal realization of virtue. It is quite simple and direct. But you worry about now knowing the meaning of the present and immediate in daily living. Do not vainly doubt the creative processes of heavenly nature, as though they would come to a stop occasionally." At that time, Lo felt as though he had awakened from a long dream. The following day, during the fifth watch of the night, he went to present himself as a disciple, after which he learned all he could from Yen. Yen then told Lo, "From now on, your sickness should cure itself, your preparations for examinations should work themelves out, and success in the examinations should come of itself. If this does not happen, you are not truly my disciple." And in time, Lo's sickness was indeed cured.

Later, when Yen was imprisoned at the capital for some reason, Lo sold all his land in order to free him and waited on him in prison for six years without going to take the palace examinations. When Lo returned home, he was already quite old. But he welcomed Yen's visit and would not leave his side, serving him personally every meal and every refreshment. His grandsons thought it too tiring, but Lo said, "I cannot leave it to you to wait on my teacher."

Hu Tsung-cheng of Hupei was formerly a disciple of Lo's. When Lo heard that Hu had gained insight into the *Book of Changes,* he in turn sought to study with him. Hu asked, "Why did Fu-hsi draw this line on the plain ground?" Lo cited many annotations, but Lu did not agree with him. Only after three months did Lo understand his teaching.[8]

Lo had often suffered over the divergences in the theories of investigation of things. He was puzzled by these for a long time. One day it became clear to him that "the Way of the *Great Learning*" lies in first knowing its principal message. Should one know this first, then the whole text teaches nothing else. Everything in the *Great Learning* gives the roots and branches, the beginning and the end of this one central truth. All these roots and branches, beginnings and ends, are nothing other than the fine words and good deeds of the ancient sages, as related in the Six Classics. The meaning of investigation is nothing but the so-called method and program, the marvelous technique by which we might become great men. That night he rushed to the bedside of his father, telling him of it. His father said, "Does that mean that there is no difference between the text and the added commentary?" Lo replied, "The *Great Learning* is contained in the *Book of Rites* and originally makes up one text with it. It begins by giving the general ideas, follows up by giving a detailed exposition, and always gives carefully selected words of goodness and wisdom. This is in order to clarify and determine the greatest kind of learning." The father fully agreed.

Another time, Lo became seriously ill when passing through Lin-ch'ing (Shantung). In his delirium he saw an old man[9] who told him, "Throughout your life, whenever affected, your energy *(ch'i)* frequently does not respond; whenever fatigued, your eyes frequently know no rest; whenever disturbed, your thoughts cannot be dispersed; whether in a dream or awakening, you do not forget anything. All this points to a chronic sickness of the heart." Lo was alarmed and said, "If that is the case, are all my insights only symptoms of a sickness?" The old man said, "Man's mind-in-itself comes from the constancy of Heaven. It moves with things and responds to them without any fixed pattern. But you have exercised too strong a control over yourself in your life, so that a single thought could dazzle you, until you became entangled. Unless you awaken, you will gradually lose the heavenly substance of the mind. And not only will you be sick at heart, but your body will also fol-

low in its train." Lo awoke, greatly alarmed, and bowed in prostration
as his perspiration poured down like rain. From then on he gradually
relaxed his control over his interior movements, and his circulation and
pulse returned to normal.[10]

Lo set his mind on study at age fifteen,[11] under the guidance of
Chang Hsün-shui. At twenty-six, he developed his learning under Yen
Chün. At thirty-four, he understood the *Book of Changes* with the help of
Hu. At forty-six, he was confirmed in the Way by the old man of Mount
T'ai.[12] At seventy, he asked instructions of the mind from Master Wu-
yi.[13] Lo's teaching takes as its goal the recovery of the heart of the
infant, which requires neither learning nor exercise of thought,[14] and he
regards as essential becoming one with Heaven and Earth and the myriad things, the discarding of the body, and the forgetting of distinctions
between things and the self. He sees *li* as something that renews itself
without cease,[15] without needing strict control or development, but is
spontaneously smooth and harmonious. When it is difficult to fix one's
efforts, one should not seek to fix them and should regard such detachment as effort. When one's dispositions appear without support, then
one should take such absence of support as disposition. It is like untying
the cables and letting the boat float freely, the oars following the course
of the wind, and everywhere reaching the right shores. Scholars who
lack understanding vainly take the mind-in-itself to be clear and pure
and repress their feelings and dispositions out of attachment to a transient consciousness [received in meditation]. Such is just a means for
surviving, as in a demon's cave, and not heavenly enlightenment.

People have said that Wang Chi[16] wrote better than he spoke, while
Lo spoke better than he wrote. Both in subtle discussions and in intense
expositions, what he said had the effects either of spring breezes or of
thunderbolts. Even in cases of those who had no learning, Lo was able
to open up their minds and hearts in an instant, so that they could see
the Tao in front of their eyes. He swept away the superficial atmosphere
then prevalent in philosophic circles and made possible immediate
results. Obviously, there was not his like before him.

But what is called harmonious and smooth is precisely the immediate
realization that Buddhism talks about, and what is called surviving in
the demon's cave is also the [Buddhist] shortcut afforded by stillness,
which prevents one's entering into the land of the dead. All of that is
beyond the reach of concepts and of imagination. Thus Lo truly
grasped the best of patriarchal Buddhism.

The subtle creative forces of the universe that fill Heaven and Earth
are nothing other than the flow of consciousness *(liu-hsing chih t'i)*. This
[consciousness] is full of movement and yet comes to a point of restful
unity; as in the case of rivers and streams, where there is ebb and flow,
there is also transformation.[17] That is why the Confucian scholars who

discern oneness in the movement of flow can be said to know nature. Should they only see the creative energy of *ch'i* and play around on that level, they remain merely in the realm of *yin* and *yang*.[18] Hence Lo himself is not without some lack of understanding.

The difference between Buddhism and Confucianism rests on an infinitesimal point. To say that [Buddhism] is partial to introversion and cannot be used to govern the country or the world—to say that is merely selfishness, and to say that all may be decided on the basis of effects shows ultimately a lack of decisive judgment. According to my own humble opinion, what is called the flow of consciousness is that which Confucians and Buddhists have both acquired in their enlightenment. But there yet remains something important after this enlightenment, and that is, to penetrate into the flow. As we see now, why is disorder absent from this flow, why is there a myriad of differentiations and yet one source? Clearly present is a controlling principle *(chu-tsai)*. Should the Buddhists not proceed to further depths, then they would only attribute the flow itself to the rising and falling of dust particles raised perchance by wild horses. That is why I say the Buddhists are those who have studied the flow but have not yet arrived at an adequate understanding. What they have seen is not incorrect. For outside of this flow, there is no controlling principle either.

Should one consider Lo's philosophy to be too close to Ch'an Buddhism and so reject his teachings, one would be merely uttering vulgar opinions that are quite distant from the goal of sagehood. Hsü Fu-yüan said that Lo's learning is vast but without system, extensive but without clear mastery. He has hit well on the mark. Wang Shih-huai[19] said that Lo had, in his earlier years, dabbled in many Buddhist scriptures and teachings, accepting Buddhist monks and Taoist priests with no reservation. This is common knowledge. But what is not known is that Lo selected the best of Buddhist teachings and rejected the worthless, according to certain norms. The recorded conversations that date from his old age are based on the teachings of filial piety, brotherly respect, and parental affection, given in the *Great Learning,* and make no mention of either Buddhism or Taoism. Once when his grandson was reading the recorded dialogs of the Buddhist monk Chung-feng,[20] Lo ordered him abruptly to put it aside, saying, "Ch'an Buddhist teachings cause people to lose their way. Once you are caught, it is like falling into a trap. Only one or two out of a hundred is able to re-emerge and return to the teaching of the sages." This shows a real knowledge of Lo's achievements.

Yang Shih-ch'iao[21] sent up a memorial on the habits of scholars, saying that Lo studied under Yen Chün, dicussed philosophy with him, and then went to Hu Tsung-cheng to learn Taoist alchemy, the arts of finding the elixir and of levitation. Then he studied with the Buddhist monk Hsüan-chüeh,[22] talking about causation, direct transmission, and immediate realization [of the mind]. When he was in Ning-kuo,[23] he assembled disciples together in discussions and ordered litigants to sit cross-legged in the public hall to meditate and examine their minds. He used public funds to make offerings of food and money, attracting to himself a great crowd. When he was in Tung-ch'ang and Yunnan, he placed his seal in his public hall, where it was used by various subordinates. When he returned to the capital he begged for various favors and so annoyed the authorities. Whenever he met with scholar-officials, he would talk about the thirty-three Buddhist heavens, cite as authority the spirit at a séance,[24] and praise Lü Yen[25] for his letter from the Chungnan Mountain (Shensi). When his son died in Kwang-tung as a student of an alchemist, Lo said that his son was nonetheless by him all the time. Such was the extent of his irrationality. But this [information] came from mistaken rumors spread by his diverse following. Their blame and praise departed from the truth and could not conceal his earnest learning.[26]

(*MJHA* 34:1a–3a)

NOTES

1. For Lo Ju-fang, see his biography by Julia Ching in *DMB*, v. 1, 975–78.

2. A euphemism about his mourning period, spent in retirement. See his recorded dialog in Yang Ch'i-yüan et al., ed., *Lo Ju-fang yü-lu: Hsü-t'an chih-ch'üan* (Taipei reprint, 1967), 2:28a.

3. Ibid., 2:51a–52b. Chang himself would be criticized for cutting short his own mourning period for his father (1577).

4. See the account by Julia Ching, *DMB*, v. 1, 616–19. See also Hsüeh Hsüan, *Tu-shu lu*, 1827 ed., 1:23a.

5. See *Hsü-t'an chih-ch'üan*, 2:37a.

6. See Wang Ken's biography. See also the account in *DMB*, by Julia Ching, v. 2, 1382–85.

7. *Mencius* 6A:6 , J. Legge, trans., *The Chinese Classics*, v. 2, 203.

8. *Hsü-t'an chih-ch'üan*, 2:39a. Hu's question refers to the legendary sage Fu-hsi, to whom the invention of the hexagrams of the *Book of Changes* was attributed.

9. See Lo Ju-fang's *Complete Works*, *Lo Chin-hsi hsien-sheng ch'üan-chi* 1618 ed., 7:48a–b.

10. This incident happened early in 1553, while Lo was on his way to Peking for the palace examinations. It shows that his studies with Yen Chü had not entirely cured him of his earlier difficulties.

11. This account of Lo's evolution recalls that of Confucius, in *Analects* 2:4.

12. The old man of Mount T'ai is without doubt that of Lo's dreams in Shantung.

13. Master Wu-yi might be another name for the Buddhist monk Hsüan-chüeh, with whom Lo allegedly studied in later life.

14. Allusion to *Mencius* 4B:12.

15. Allusion to the *Book of Changes*, Great Appendix, part 1.

16. For Wang Chi, see his biography and the account in *DMB* by Julia Ching, v. 2, 1351–55.

17. Allusion to the *Doctrine of the Mean*, ch. 30. See J. Legge, trans., *The Chinese Classics*, v. 2, 427–28.

18. Allusion to Ch'eng Yi. *ECCS, Yi-shu* 15:13b–14b. See W. T. Chan, *A Source Book of Chinese Philosophy*, 557–58.

19. For Wang Shih-huai, *hao* T'ang-nan, see *MS*, ch. 283, and *MJHA*, ch.

20. Wang's biography of Lo is given in *Lo Chin-hsi tzu chi* (1587–1606 ed.), 1:8a–13b, and Huang Tsung-hsi has quoted verbatim the passage at 1:12b.

20. A work by the Yüan dynasty Buddhist monk Ming-pen, *hao* Chung-feng.

21. Yang Shih-ch'iao, *hao* Chih-an. See *MS*, ch. 224; *MJHA*, ch. 42.

22. I could find no information on Hsüan-chüeh.

23. Lo served there (Anhwei) from 1562–65.

24. Reference to a kind of séance to which certain spirits were invited. See Hsieh Chao-che, *Wu-tsa-tsu* (Kyoto, 1795) 15:20a.

25. Lü Yen, *hao* Ch'un-yang, of the T'ang dynasty (fl. 844), considered one of the Eight Immortals of religious Taoism. (Consult *SS*, ch. 457, p. 5648).

26. Huang Tsung-hsi gives here his own balanced and impartial assessment and appreciation of Lo Ju-fang.

Keng Ting-hsiang

Keng Ting-hsiang, *tzu* Tsai-lun, *hao* T'ien-t'ai (1524–96),[1] was from Huang-an in Hukuang (Hupei). He acquired the *chin-shih* degree in 1556 and was raised to censor in the censorate [in 1559]. From assistant minister in the grand court of revision (1567), he was demoted [in 1570] to assistant subprefecture magistrate [of Heng-chou, Kwangsi Province]. After successive promotions he became vice-minister of the court of the imperial stud and [in 1575] became right assistant censor-in-chief. After three years of mourning [for his mother], he was made governor of Fukien [in 1578]. After another three years' mourning period [for his father],[2] he was recalled to vice assistant censor-in-chief and rose to left vice censor-in-chief. He was transferred to vice-minister of justice [in 1585], censor-in-chief in Nanking [1587], and minister of revenue in charge of granaries in Nanking [1589]. After announcing his retirement [in 1589], he resided at home for seven years before dying [in July, 1596] in his seventy-third year. He was awarded the posthumous title of junior guardian of the heir-apparent and the honorific Kung-chien.

There were no major disagreements between Keng Ting-hsiang and the grand secretaries served successively by him: Yen Sung, Hsü Chieh, Wang Hsi-chüeh, Chang Chü-cheng, and Shen Shih-hsing.[3] When Chang Chü-cheng curtailed mourning *(tuo-ch'ing),*[4] Keng sent him a letter[5] comparing him to those like Yi Yin who, instructing their ages [in the Tao] and assuming the cares of the world as their personal responsibility,[6] "are bound to risk the criticism of the world."[7] Those who rebuked Chang for curtailing mourning, [said Keng], did so "because they simply did not understand this."[8] Even though his intention was to exculpate Chang of his misconduct, this was like reciting the Six Classics[9] in order to conceal evil words.

While Keng Ting-hsiang was in charge of the censorate in the southern capital, he regarded as [improper] disregard, for a court official, the censor Wang Fan-ch'en's impeachment of three provincial governors without notifying him [first]. He submitted a memorial censuring Wang. Those engaged in pure discussion considered that he was threatening a censor in order to curry favor with the grand secretary.[10] Ku Yün-ch'eng was chiefly responsible for calling Keng to account for this by writing *K'o-wen* (Questions of a Guest). Keng could not respond to this.[11]

In Keng Ting-hsiang's learning and teaching, mystification and speculation are discouraged. On Tao, the principle of life, he said that it is not true if it cannot also be understood by the common people and, in practice, if it cannot stand the test of nature or be thoroughly related to the people's affairs and needs.[12] Hence expending [words and explanations] on the Tao is to keep it hidden; making it an everyday practice is to keep it mysterious; preaching it in coarse and easily understood language is to have it remain refined and subtle.[13] This idea of Keng's cannot be deemed wrong. But his failure to perceive the original substance [of the Tao] makes him unavoidably fall into the ranks of the worldly. As the poem says, "We all travel on the same road of life, but who knows that achievement and failure can be as far apart as Heaven and Earth?" This is the reason thinkers of the past placed a high value on the learning [to develop the personality that could withstand all tests] of knives, saws, tripods, and cauldrons. For this reason those who aim at perfection (*chung-hsing*) in their learning, if they fail slightly to penetrate its essence, in the end fall behind the ardent and the cautious.[14]

Because Li Chih promoted "wildcat" Ch'an Buddhism and many scholars followed his lead, Keng frequently took what was practical as of chief importance. He made earnest exhortations to correct the evil and avert danger, but he in turn became muddled, half believing and half disbelieving the teachings of the Buddha. In the end he could not prevail over Li Chih. Li Chih developed a hatred for Keng because of the imprisonment of Ho Hsi-yin.[15] Keng was on close terms with Chang Chü-cheng.[16] Li Yu-tzu,[17] who advocated the killing of Ho Hsin-yin, was Keng's associate in conducting public discussion [in the independent academies]. It certainly would not have been difficult for Keng to have saved Ho Hsin-yin at this time, but he did not dare soil his hands [on Ho's behalf], lest by doing so he violate Chang Chü-cheng's prohibition against public discussion. Keng took "do not permit it to stop" (*pu-jung-yi*) as his basic principle, but in this case how could he stop trying?

Keng Ting-hsiang said[18] that one must cross three strategic mountain passes in the task of learning. The first is that the Tao is present in the mind.[19] The second is that the mind is cultivated in affairs. The third is the art of practicing caution.[20] The art of caution refers to *liang-chih* being already realized *(hsien-ch'eng)*. There is no one who does not have *liang-chih*. When it is used one way, it is realized one way; when it is used another way, it is realized another way. So, if it is used to make manifest clear virtue in the world,[21] there is no need to make special effort to regulate the mind. Indeed, no one will be without perfect virtue *(jen)*.

[As I, Huang Tsung-hsi, see it], *liang-chih* is nothing other than the Mean (or equilibrium) of consciousness before the rise of emotions. It is all good and not evil. It moves like water flowing downward, like the compass needle pointing always to the south. It is called *liang-chih* with the desire to manifest clear virtue in the world. There is no need of using it. Hence the knowledge *(chih)* that can be directed in one way or another belongs to the order of the emotions and of the senses and cannot be called good *(liang)*. Keng Ting-hsiang's understanding of *liang-chih* is not clear enough—partly because of the inaccurate records given of Wang Yang-ming's words in the last part of *Ch'uan-hsi lu*. Take, for example, the passage about Chang Yi and Su Ch'in[22] as also having had insights into the wondrous functioning of *liang-chih* but applying this to evil uses.[23] Keng Ting-hsiang was misled by this passage.

(MJHA 35:1a–b)

NOTES

1. See Keng's biography by Julia Ching, *DMB*, v. 1, 718–21.

2. Keng's father died in 1580.

3. See their biographies in *DMB*, 1586–91, 570–76, 1376–79, 53–61, 1187–90.

4. Literally, "violated feelings." It refers to Chang's refusal to leave office to observe the mourning period after his father's death in 1577.

5. See Keng's *Collected Writings, Keng T'ien-t'ai hsien-sheng wen-chi* (Taipei, 1970), v. 2, 609–13.

6. The sage minister of the founder of the Shang dynasty. See *Mencius* 5A:7, 5B:1.

7. *Keng T'ien-t'ai hsien-sheng wen-chi*, 610. (Although this book appears in 4 volumes, the page numbers throughout are continuous.)

8. Ibid., 611.

9. Literally, the "Six Arts," although the reference is clearly to the Classics.

10. Keng discusses the censor's role in two memorials. See ibid., 207–19.

11. Ku resigned from office because of his opposition to Keng's censuring of Wang. See also *DMB*, 736.

12. See Keng, op. cit., pp. 1000–9. *Doctrine of the Mean,* 12:2.

13. Ibid., pp. 1000–9.

14. Allusion to *Analects* 13:21.

15. Ho Hsin-yin was imprisoned in early 1579 and beaten to death six months later. See his life in *DMB,* 513–15, by Wu P'ei-yi and Julia Ching.

16. Chang Chü-cheng, senior grand secretary, was regarded as responsible for Ho's arrest.

17. Li Yu-tzu, i.e., Li Yi-ho, Chang's subordinate, was regarded as responsible for signing Ho's death warrant.

18. Keng, op. cit., 818.

19. Allusion to *Ch'uan-hsi lu,* part 2. See W. T. Chan, trans., *Instructions for Practical Living,* 139.

20. Keng, op. cit., 853. See *Great Learning,* ch. 4.

21. Keng, op. cit., 820.

22. Famous strategists and diplomats of the Chou dynasty who died in 309 B.C. and 317 B.C. respectively.

23. *Ch'uan-hsi lu,* part 3. Consult W. T. Chan, *Instructions for Practical Living,* 236. Huang Tsung-hsi criticizes here the section recorded by Huang Hsing-tseng, *hao* Mien-chih.

Keng Ting-li

Keng Ting-li, *tzu* Tzu-yung, *hao* Ch'i-K'ung (1534–84), was the younger brother of Keng Ting-hsiang.[1] When he was young he studied books, but to no avail, and was chastised by his father. He often walked alone in deserted mountain valleys, not knowing where to express his grief and anger. When he was asked [about his behavior], Ting-li said: "What can I do since I cannot understand? I am like a blind man who does not know what he cannot see and understand." Thenceforth he alternated between practicing quiet-sitting in a room without coming out for a year at a time and staying on the road searching for a friend to inquire with him into the Way and for several months forgetting even to return home. At first he studied with Fang Yü-shih. Finally he learned from Teng Hao[2] the principle that "everything is common and genuine" *(yi-ch'ieh p'ing-shih),* and he was able to refrain from looking and listening to see and hear his inner self with his interior senses.[3] From Ho Hsin-yin he learned the principle that "the darkness is impenetrable" and was quite content.

There were those who questioned him, saying, "We have heard that you wish to become an immortal. Is that so?" He said: "I want to become a heavenly immortal, not an earthly immortal or a human immortal." They said: "What is a heavenly immortal?" He said: "One who enters this state directly by means of the Great Ultimate *(T'ai-chi)* without descending into *yin* and *yang* and the five agents." When [his brother] Keng Ting-hsiang heard it, he scolded him, saying, "Aren't you trying to learn without going through the practice of serving your parents and obeying your elder brother?" Ting-li said: "Learning has its source. What Yao and Shun transmitted, one to the other, is the one word, 'middle' (the Mean, *chung*). Tzu-ssu commented on this word, saying: 'When joy, anger, sorrow, and pleasure are held in, on the verge of expression, this is called the Mean.[4] Among people of today, who would care to be a little more watchful over himself before these emotions are expressed?' "[5] Keng Ting-hsiang said: "The *Doctrine of the Mean* simply talks about ordinary speech and ordinary behavior,[6] the universal Way,[7] and the nine standard rules,[8] and that is all." Ting-li said: "But did you not notice that the final words [of the *Doctrine of the Mean*] are 'having neither sound nor smell'?"[9]

When Ting-li discussed learning he did not use many words. Just by indicating the point at the proper time, he enabled others to understand clearly. [On one occasion] Li Chih wanted very much to talk, but Ting-li did not utter a word. Only when he was on the verge of leaving did he address Li Chih, saying: "Why is it that people [stubbornly] consider themelves to be right, so that it is impossible to proceed with them to the Way of Yao and Shun?"[10] Li Chih was silent.

When Keng Ting-hsiang took Ting-li with him to see Liu Ch'u-ch'üan, he said [to Ting-li]: "Now do not say that we two are brothers." At that time Ch'u-ch'üan lay ill. Ting-hsiang said: "I have come here with a doctor." After Ting-li said only a few words in front of the bed, Ch'u-ch'üan was much impressed and rose up, for he already had discerned that Ting-li was Ting-hsiang's younger brother. He spoke to Ting-hsiang: "How can the Buddhist monk Hui-neng be regarded as a bumpkin hulling rice?[11] Here is a man of great vision. I am afraid you cannot just treat him as a younger brother."

Li Shih-lung came to visit Ting-li for instruction. When Ting-li did not utter a word of teaching, Shih-lung said in anger: "I braved danger for a thousand *li,* coming here over a month ago. But I have not heard a single word of instruction. Why do you exclude me [from your attention]?" Ting-li smiled but made no answer. When Li was about to leave, Ting-li accompanied him to the river bank and asked him this question: "Confucius spoke of people who do not say 'What about this? What about this?'[12] How would you go about explaining this?" Shih-lung mentioned Chu Hsi's commentaries [upon this point]. Ting-li said: "So those who understand correctly do not say 'What about this? What about this?' " Then Shih-lung himself understood.

At a great audience in the capital, someone raised the question about the meaning of "the Mean" *(chung).* Each gave his opinion. Ting-li was at first silent. Then he arose suddenly from his seat and, standing in reverence, said: "Please, all of you, look! This is the Mean." He then sighed and said: "If you leave the immediate present and talk about the Mean, if you complacently search for it in books, you will be wasting your whole life." Some in attendance at the audience then understood. Such was his quick and incisive mind!

(*MJHA* 35:7a–b)

1. For Keng Ting-li, see Keng Ting-hsiang's biography, *DMB*, v. 1, 720. This refers to the elder of Ting-hsiang's two younger brothers, both named Ting-li in romanization, although the Chinese *li* is a different word in each case. While *our* Ting-li in this biography had strong philosophical interests, the youngest of the three was more of a successful official, rising to be censor-in-chief and vice-minister of war in Nanking.

2. Teng Hao, *hao* T'ai-hu.

3. Reference to the powers of inner hearing discussed in the *Sūraṅgama Sūtra* and in Lo Hung-hsien's biography, in this volume, note 12.

4. *Doctrine of the Mean*, ch. 1, 4.

5. *Doctrine of the Mean*, ch. 1, 2–3.

6. *Doctrine of the Mean*, ch. 13.

7. *Doctrine of the Mean*, ch. 1, 4.

8. Ibid.

9. *Doctrine of the Mean*, ch. 33.

10. *Mencius* 7B:37. For Li Chih, see *DMB*, v. 1, 807–18. The biography there is written by K. C. Hsiao.

11. Alluding to Hui-neng's position as a monk doing menial tasks such as pounding rice, when he was at the monastery of Hung-jen, fifth patriarch of Ch'an Buddhism, in modern Hupei, near the Han River. Hui-neng was to become the sixth patriarch and the most celebrated Ch'an Buddhist. See P. B. Yampolsky, trans., *The Platform Sutra*, Chinese Text, section 3, English translation, 128.

12. *Analects* 15: 15.

Chiao Hung

Chiao Hung, *tzu* Jo-hou, *hao* Tan-yüan (d. 1620),[1] was a man of the banner-bearers' guard *(ch'i-shou wei)* in Nanking. He placed first in the *chin-shih* examination of 1589. In honor of this occasion, the Nanking metropolitan government offered to erect a triumphal arch at the gate of his residence. He declined and requested that the money be used for famine relief. His original place of registry was in Shantung, which offered to publicize his accomplishment at his native place. This money was also diverted to purchase charity land. He was appointed compiler in the Hanlin Academy.

In 1593, the history bureau was instituted to compile the Ming state history. The grand secretary, Ch'en Yü-pi,[2] intended that Chiao be the head of the bureau, and Chiao submitted a four-point proposal. Later when the project on Ming state history was interrupted, Chiao privately finished the *Record of Worthies (Hsien-cheng lu)* in 120 *chüan*.

In 1594, he was selected to be lecturer-reader to the heir-apparent. Once during a lecture, a chirping bird flew by. The heir-apparent watched it and Chiao immediately ceased his lecture. Thereupon, the heir-apparent rectified his countenance and listened again. Only then did Chiao resume the lecture. Taking those past events that were morally edifying, he presented them with illustrations to the emperor as a textbook for the heir-apparent in a volume entitled *Illustrated Thesaurus for Nurturing Correctness (Yang-cheng t'u-chieh).*

In 1597, Chiao was appointed to preside over the provincial examination in Peking.[3] He received the appointment even though the ministry of rites had recommended him to the emperor only as the second choice. He had always been disliked by Chang Wei [the grand secretary].[4] The person whom the ministry of rites had recommended as the first choice also schemed against him. As a result, the supervising secretaries Hsiang Ying-hsiang and Ts'ao Ta-hsien[5] censured him for passing papers that were seditious and grotesque. Chiao defended himself by saying, "The reading of the papers was divided among the examiners by classics, and what these two criticized were not what I had passed."[6] Nevertheless, he was demoted to the post of vice-magistrate at Fu-ning Subprefecture,[7] from where he was then transferred to the court of the imperial stud as assistant minister. Later he was promoted to director of studies at the National University in Nanking. By then, however, he was already seventy.

Chiao had a collection of books that came to several tens of thousands of *chüan*. He read nearly all of them. Nanking was a place where scholars converged. Chiao was regarded as their arbiter, and they came to him like water pouring into a valley. His proposition and promotion of Neo-Confucian philosophy *(li-hsüeh)* was a contribution that Wang Shih-chen could not match. He died in 1620 at the age of seventy-nine and was granted the honorific Yü-te. After the government moved south in 1644, he was given the posthumous title of Wen-tuan.

Chiao studied under Keng Ting-hsiang and Lo Ju-fang. He also firmly believed in the teaching of Li Chih and maintained that Li, though not necessarily a sage, might at least be considered as *k'uang* or ardent and deserved the seat next to the sage. Understandably, he considered Buddhism to be the same as the sages' learning and systematically sought to rebut Ch'eng Hao's refutations of Buddhism. Ch'eng's refutations of Buddhism are not exactly thorough, but they did not, by and large, fall so far outside the Buddhist realm as to be irrelevant. For instance, Ch'eng Hao said, "The Buddhists are determined to annihilate normal nature completely."[8] Chiao retorted by saying, "This is the heretical view of the two vehicles [of *śrāvakas* and *pratyekabuddhas*] that denies the law of *karma* and advocates extinction, but which the Buddha himself has condemned."[9] Now the reason the Buddhists speak of non-annihilation *(pu tuan-mieh)* is that they regard Heaven, Earth, and the myriad things as creations of one's own mind. True emptiness *(chen-k'ung)* is thus equated with wondrous being *(miao-yu)*. However, if distinctions are made with regard to Heaven, Earth, and the myriad things, then they become obstacles to one's mind. Have the Buddhists not desired to annihilate them completely as obstacles? We must read carefully the statement in the essay "On Calming Nature" *(Ting-hsing shu*)[10] that "having emotions in accord with the myriad affairs is having no emotion."[11] The lamentation of Confucius over Yen Yüan,[12] the anxiety of Yao and Shun,[13] and the anger of King Wen[14] are all known as "emotions in accord with the myriad affairs." If one is literally without emotions, then the inner and the outer are split in two; and that is precisely Buddhist annihilation.

Ch'eng Hao said, " 'To realize one's mind fully is to know one's Nature.'[15] This is what the Buddhists call perceiving mind and seeing nature. However, they have no teaching for preserving mind and nurturing nature."[16] In reply, Chiao said, "If one is truly able to know nature and Heaven, what need is there to talk further about preserving mind and nurturing nature? 'When a white film covers the eye, one sees illusory flowers fall in disorder from the sky.' "[17] Now, preserving mind and nurturing nature is simply the effort of fully realizing the mind. This is what the essay "On Understanding *Jen*" (*Shih-jen p'ien*)[18] has described as "mind being naturally bright after long preservation."[19] If one does not go through the process of preserving and nurturing, what one calls knowledge is nothing but imagination, which is like a mere flash of lightning or a spark from striking stones, and which one ultimately does not possess as one's own. In preserving and nurturing one's original substance, which is without the white film, one can be said to be preserving and nurturing only when there is no white film. But how can preserving and nurturing be regarded as a white film?

Ch'eng Hao said, "Of the thousand and seven hundred people mentioned in *Ch'uan-teng lu* (The Transmission of the Lamp), none ever reached the Way. At death, none of them could find a foot of cloth to wrap around his head."[20] Chiao rejoined, "Theirs are the customs of a foreign country, [but are not to be ridiculed as barbarian]."[21] Now, these thousand and seven hundred people were all born in China, but they practiced the customs of a foreign land. How can it be denied that they wore the clothes of the barbarians? Chiao also said, "Ch'eng Hao once sighed in praise of the Buddhists for having the decorum of the Three Dynasties.[22] He was not unaware of the virtues of the Buddhists. Rather, he deliberately discriminated against them."[23] Now, Ch'eng's sigh was over the inability of the Confucians to observe rituals, while the Buddhists still maintained a few. He did not really attribute to the Buddhists the rites and music of the Three Dynasties.

Chu Kuo-chen[24] once remarked that Chiao was certainly a true man, but he simply could not be rid of his biases. While in Nanking, Keng Ting-hsiang told Chiao's son that there were three people in the world who could not be persuaded by arguments and were difficult to get along with. When asked who they were, Keng said, "Sun K'uang,[25] Li T'ing-chi,[26] and your father."

(*MJHA* 35:8b–9b)

NOTES

1. See *MS* 188:713b–c. See also Edward Ch'ien, *Chiao Hung and the Restructuring of Neo-Confucianism in the Late Ming* (New York, 1986).

2. Ch'en Yü-pi (1545–97), grand secretary from 1594 to 1597, was also called Nan-ch'ung, the name of his native place (in modern Szechuan).

3. The metropolitan area around Peking, known as Shun-t'ien-fu.

4. Chang Wei, grand secretary from 1592 to 1598, was also called Hsin-chien, the name of his native place.

5. Ts'ao Ta-hsien (1555–1613).

6. This is a paraphrased version of Chiao Hung's memorial, which is printed in his *Tan-yüan chi* (Collected Writings) (Chin-ling ts'ung-shu ed.), 3: 4a–6a.

7. This is in modern Fukien.

8. A quotation from *ECCS, Honan Ch'eng-shih yi-shu,* 2:8b.

9. Quotation from *Tan-yüan chi,* 12:12a. Allusion is to the Lotus sūtra and its teaching that the so-called pratyekabuddhas (aiming at the salvation of self by its own efforts) and śrāvakas (aiming at the salvation of self by listening to a Buddha and taking his sermons to heart) "are either bodhisattvas putting on a show or bodhisattvas deceiving themselves." See *Saddharma-puṇḍarīka sūtra, TSD,* no. 262. Consult also Leon Hurvitz, trans. *Scripture of the Lotus Blossom of the Fine Dharma (The Lotus Sūtra)* (New York, 1976). See especially his Preface, xix–xx. See also the Glossary of Technical Terms, under *Erh-ch'eng* (Two Vehicles).

10. The essay was written by Ch'eng Hao. See English translation in Wing-tsit Chan, *A Source Book of Chinese Philosophy,* 525–26.

11. Quotation from the essay in *ECCS, Ming-tao wen-chi,* SPPY ed., 3:1a.

12. *Analects* 11:8–9.

13. *Mencius* 3A:4, 5A:1.

14. *Mencius* 1B:3.

15. *Mencius* 7A:1.

16. Quotation from *ECCS, Yi-shu,* 13:1b.

17. Not an exact quotation. See *Tan-yüan chi,* 12–12a. The statement "when a white film covers the eyes . . ." is a quotation from the *Ching-te ch'uan-teng lu,* SPTK ed., 10:14a. But the metaphor of a diseased eye seeing illusory flowers falling from the sky is a common Buddhist one. See, for instance, *Yüan-chüeh-ching (The Sūtra of Perfect Enlightenment), TSD,* no. 842, p. 913.

18. Quotation from *ECCS, Yi-shu,* 2–3b. An English translation of this essay is found in Chan, *Source Book,* 523–24.

19. Ibid., 1:2b–3a.

20. *Tan-yüan chi,* 12–13a. The insertion in brackets represents a summary of the rest of Chiao Hung's rejoinder.

21. *ECCS* 12:24b.

22. *Tan-yüan chi,* 12–13a.

23. This is Huang Tsung-hsi's opinion.

24. Chu Kuo-chen's dates are 1557–1632.

25. Sun K'uang, *hao* Yüeh-feng.

26. Li T'ing-chi, *hao* Chiu-wu.

Chou Ju-teng

Chou Ju-teng, *tzu* Chi-yüan, *hao* Hai-men (1547–1629),[1] was a man of Sheng-hsien (Chekiang). He was a *chin-shih* of 1577 and was selected to be a bureau secretary in the ministry of works in Nanking. Later he served successively in the ministries of war and personnel as a bureau director and, in his official career, reached the post of chief minister of the office of the seal in Nanking.

Chou had a cousin named Chou Meng-hsiu, who learned of the Tao from Wang Chi.[2] Following his cousin, Chou also began to turn toward learning. For seven days after meeting Lo Ju-fang,[3] he requested no special instruction. Then, he asked inadvertently, "What is the meaning of the phrase 'to choose goodness and to hold it firmly'?"[4] Lo replied, "It is to choose *this* goodness and to hold it firmly." Chou gained his initial enlightenment from his reply. Once Lo showed him the book, *Fa-yüan chu-lin*.[5] After looking at a page or two, Chou desired to say something. Lo stopped him and asked him to read on. Chou was as shocked as though he had been whipped on the back.[6] Until the end of his life, he venerated Lo's portrait, making sacrificial offerings to it [after Lo's death] on feast days.

In a scholarly assembly in Nanking, Chou expounded [Wang Chi's] *T'ien-ch'üan cheng-tao chi* [regarding the Four Sentences of Wang Yang-Ming].[7] Hsü Fu-yüan said that the absence of good and evil could not be considered as the essential teaching and so wrote the *Chiu-ti* (Nine Inquiries) to dispute him. Chou wrote the *Chiu-chieh* (Nine Explanations) to elucidate his theory. He maintained that since there was no good, there could be no evil, as a man without illness need not suspect illness. And since there is no evil, it is not necessary to establish the good, just as it is difficult to add another head on top of the one head. To reality itself *(pen-t'i)* one cannot have even the slightest particle of attachment; should there be any such attachment, it becomes curdled, incapable of becoming transformed. This was the gist of his teaching.

Wang Yang-ming's sentence "The mind-in-itself is characterized by the absence of good and evil"[8] differs originally from the idea that nature is neither good nor evil. For nature is described in terms of *li*, but *li* is without evil, so how can it be described as without goodness? The mind, on the other hand, is described in terms of *ch'i*, which in its movement is sometimes good and sometimes evil. But when the mind hides its substance in the midst of tranquility, it simply knows itself to be clear. How can one say that it has good and evil? Moreover, Wang Yang-ming said the above because the teachings of the investigation of things and of searching for principles[9] of the later generation were founded on an *a priori* goodness. Chou, however, established his own teaching, going so far as to consider nature to be without good and evil. He had missed the meaning of Wang Yang-ming's teaching. For he said that what is neither good nor evil is the supreme good. This is an added twist resulting from making unnecessary distinctions. The good is one. In maintaining that there is the goodness of the good and the goodness that transcends the good, Chou was seeking to be direct and clear-cut but became dualistic.

Chou's *Nine Explanations* only resolved the human side of the issue. The good originates in nature and so has a foundation. Even though it may have suffered injury over a long period, it may suddenly emerge. Evil comes from contamination and has no foundation. So even when in activity, it may suddenly disappear without leaving a trace. If there were indeed no good, then [the virtuous] Yao need not have lived and [the wicked] Chieh[10] would also have disappeared. The difference between Confucianism and Buddhism begins with this. Chou's doctrine of the absence of good and evil is precisely what Buddhists call emptiness. Ku Hsien-ch'eng and Feng Ts'ung-wu[11] both criticized Wang Yang-ming later for the teaching of the absence of good and evil. Did they realize that this had absolutely nothing to do with Wang Yang-ming?[12] So those who followed Wang Yang-ming and those who criticized him both missed the intent of his teaching. How can it be said that they made distinctions as fine as hair? Chou valued direct response in his teaching of others. He once asked a sudden question of his disciple, Liu Ch'iao:[13] "Do you believe at once or no?" Liu answered, "Yes." Chou continued, "Then are you a sage or not?" Liu said, "Yes, I am also a sage." Then Chou yelled, "A sage is a sage. The word 'also' is superfluous." He frequently instructed others in this manner. Such methods are all examples of the dynamic applications of [Ch'an Buddhist] doctrines.

(*MJHA* 36:1a–b)

NOTES

1. For Chou Ju-teng, see his biography by Julia Ching, *DMB,* v. 1, 271–74.
2. See Wang Chi's biography in this volume.
3. See Lo Ju-fang's biography in this volume.
4. *Doctrine of the Mean,* ch. 20.
5. A Buddhist work in 120 *chüan* by Shih Tao-shih (d. circa 668).
6. Chou appears to have been enlightened then and there.
7. See Wang Chi's biography in this volume.
8. See Wang Yang-ming's biography in this volume.
9. *Great Learning,* "Text of Confucius."
10. Reference to the sage King Yao of antiquity and the tyrant Chieh of the Hsia dynasty.
11. See Ku's biography in this volume. Feng Ts'ung-wu's *hao* was Shao-hsü. He was also a disciple of the school of Chan Jo-shui. *MJHA* 41:6b–7a.
12. According to Huang Tsung-hsi's repeated emphasis, here and elsewhere, it is a fabrication of Wang Chi's.
13. Liu's *hao* was Ch'ung-ch'ien.

14.   The Kan-ch'üan[1] School

Of the schools of Wang Yang-ming and Chan Jo-shui, each had its main doctrines. While Chan's disciples did not equal Wang's in number, many persons first studied under Chan and then finished under Wang or studied first under Wang and then went to Chan, just as did the disciples of Chu Hsi and Lu Chiu-yüan. Afterwards, the lineages they established continued to grow. Outside of the Yang-ming followers, there are still today those who call themselves students of Chan Jo-shui. Even if they may no longer follow his main doctrines, the line has not disappeared.

NOTE

1. Kan-ch'üan is the other name of Chan Jo-shui. See Chaoying Fang's biography of Chan Jo-shui and Julia Ching's contribution on his thought in *DMB,* v. 1, 36–42.

Chan Jo-shui

Chan Jo-shui, *tzu* Yüan-ming, *hao* Kan-ch'üan (1416–1560),[1] a native of Tseng-ch'eng, Kwangtung, studied with Ch'en Hsien-chang without taking the civil service examinations. Later he followed his mother's instructions and went to Nanking (1504) as a student of the National University. The chancellor, Chang Mou,[2] tested him on the passage regarding the gentleman having "mild harmony in countenance and a rich fullness in the back"[3] and was astonished at the results. He attained the rank of *chin-shih* in 1505. At that time, Yang T'ing-ho[4] and Chang Yüan-chen were examiners. When they got to his examination essay, they remarked, "This can only have been written by a disciple of Ch'en Hsien-chang." When the seal over his name was opened, they found their opinion confirmed. Chan was selected as Hanlin bachelor and compiler, while Wang Yang-ming was giving lectures in the ministry of personnel. Chan and Lü Nan (1479–1542)[5] supported his endeavors. After some time Chan went as envoy to Annam, to attend the king's investiture. He returned to his native place in 1515 to mourn his mother's death and stayed for three years near her grave. Then he purchased a site on Mount Hsi-ch'iao (southwest of Canton), where he built a lecture hall. He had all those who came to him first learn rituals before attending lectures, and he assembled many disciples. At the beginning of the Chia-ching period (1521) he went north to court as a reader-in-waiting, then served as chancellor of the National University in Nanking (1524), as assistant minister of rites (1533–36), and was promoted to minister of rites (1533–36), of war (1536–39), and of war in Nanking (1539–40), before finally retiring.

Wherever Chan went, he always built an academy with a shrine in honor of Ch'en Hsien-chang. His disciples increased and spread everywhere under Heaven. At the age of ninety (1560) he still traveled to Mount Heng (Hunan) to honor Ch'en Hsien-chang at his shrine. When he was about to pass Kiangsi, Tsou Shou-yi warned his friends, saying, "When Master Chan comes, we should honor his age but without asking him for instruction. Do not lightly engage him in debates." He died at age ninety-four, on May 16, 1560.

Chan Jo-shui[6] and Wang Yang-ming each taught many disciples. Wang's main focus was the extension of *liang-chih,* while Chan taught the realization of the principle of Heaven everywhere. Scholars regarded the two as having each started his own school of thought. Some tried to reconcile their teachings, saying: since the principle of Heaven is nothing but *liang-chih* and realizing is the same as extending, then what can one say about similarities and differences? But Chan's teachings on the investigation of things pointed out four matters in Wang's teachings of which he did not approve, while Wang also said that realizing the principle of Heaven everywhere refers to an external quest for truth. Clearly, then, they cannot be arbitrarily made alike. In general, Chan explained Wang as having identified "investigate" with "rectify," "things" with "thoughts" *(nien-t'ou),* and the investigation of things with rectifying thoughts. He said that unless Wang added to this the effort of learning and inquiry, of thought, discernment, and action, he could have no proof that the thoughts had been rectified.

However, Wang Yang-ming[7] meant by rectifying thoughts the extension of knowledge. If this does not refer to learning and inquiry, thought, discernment, and action, then how can the task of extension be accomplished? [So Chan's objections] cannot be sustained as having pointed out errors in Wang Yang-ming's doctrine of investigating things. Besides, Chan held that the mind embodies all things without missing any one of them, while Wang only pointed to that which is within the breast as mind. That is why people mocked [Wang] as affirming the inner and not the outer. Actually, the principles *(li)* of Heaven and Earth and the myriad things are not outside of our breast, and from this one can see the vastness of the mind. Should one take the principles of Heaven and Earth and the myriad things as the principles of one's own mind, and seek them in Heaven and Earth and the myriad things in the name of vastness, then one is still hampered by the old teachings. For the principle of Heaven is nowhere to be found, except in the mind, which is its real locus, and the mind is also nowhere to be found, except in the stillness of consciousness before the emotions are aroused. In the center of this stillness and motionlessness, one finds also the response [of consciousness]. Hence, realizing means only realizing in stillness. Should one speak today of "realizing everywhere," one would mean realizing [the heavenly principle] in the response [of stillness], which shows that Chan's words are, in the last analysis, not quite correct.

(MJHA 37:2a–b)

NOTES

1. See Chan's biography by Fang Chao-ying, in *DMB,* v. 1, 36–42.
2. See Chang's biography by R. G. Dimberg and J. Ching, in *DMB,* v. 1, 96–97.
3. *Mencius* 7A:21.
4. See Yang's biography by Chou Tao-chi, in *DMB,* v. 2, 1542–46.
5. See Lü's biography by Julia Ching, in *DMB,* v. 1, 1010–13.
6. For Chan's philosophy, see J. Ching, "A Contribution to Chan's Thought," in *DMB,* v. 1, 41–42. See also Julia Ching, *To Acquire Wisdom: The Way of Wang Yang-ming,* ch. 2.
7. Huang Tsung-hsi is eager to take Wang Yang-ming's side in this critique of Chan Jo-shui.

Hsü Fu-yüan

Hsü Fu-yüan, *tzu* Meng-ch'ung, *hao* Ching-an (1535–1604),[1] a native of Te-ch'ing in Hu-chou Prefecture, became *chin-shih* in 1562 and was appointed a secretary in the ministry of works in Nanking. He was transferred to Peking for the evaluation of officials, but as he could not get along with the minister of personnel, Yang Po,[2] he pleaded sickness and went home. Later, he was made a secretary in the bureau of evaluations, but, owing to the displeasure of Kao Kung, he was sent to Kwangtung as assistant surveillance commissioner. After he had successfully concluded the surrender of the pirates Li Mau and Hsü Chün-mei, he was moved to Fukien as surveillance commissioner. Then, because of the chief of the bureau of evaluations, Wang Chuan, who resented him, he was again subject to evaluation and then degraded to assistant magistrate for salt transportation. In 1574 he was [once more] promoted, this time to assistant minister of the court of the imperial stud in Nanking. He moved on to the post of director of the bureau of appointments and, after a short leave, became director of the bureau of equipment in the ministry of war. Hsü visited [the grand secretary] Chang Chü-cheng, who asked him about the management of horses and pleased Chang with his quick and clear explanations. So Chang desired to use him in an important position. But Wang Chuan attributed [Hsü's turn of fortune] to his own influence and sought to draw Hsü to himself. As Hsü did not respond, he was made prefect of Chien-ch'ang. Later, on the recommendation of Tsou Yüan-piao,[3] the supervising secretary, he was made assistant educational intendant in Shensi, then promoted to vice-magistrate of Ying-t'ien-fu (Nanking). However, for his attempt to save [his friend] Li Ts'ai,[4] Hsü was [stripped of his office] and returned home. Afterwards, he was once more made assistant surveillance commissioner of Kwangtung and surveillance vice-commissioner of Kwangsi. He then served as junior vice-commissioner of transmissions and as junior assistant censor-in-chief and grand coordinator of Fukien. When the consideration of the investiture of Japan[5] as a tributary kingdom arose, Hsü memorialized the throne, advocating war. He proposed attacking Japan as the best policy and defending against it as the next best, saying that [the gesture of] investiture was no policy. The court was to adopt his second proposal and summoned him to the post of minister of the grand court of revisions in Nanking, promoting him after that to junior vice-minister of war in Nanking. He died in the seventh month of 1594 and was posthumously given the title of a minister of war of Nanking.

Ever since his youth as a student, Hsü had admired in private the character of the ancient sages and worthies and refrained from petty competitions with his fellow-countrymen. At age twenty-three he was recommended to the authorities of his province, but he preferred to study with T'ang Shu.[6] At age twenty-seven, he became a *chin-shih* and befriended scholars from all over. He began then the task of self-reflection, for which he stayed home for three years. In the midst of poverty and tribulations, he seemed to have acquired some enlightenment. When assigned to southern Kwangtung, he devoted himself utterly to war duties, exposing his life to danger. This helped to rid him of all tendency to laziness and impatience. When he passed through Lan-hsi, Hsü Yung-chien[7] remarked that his words and actions still showed certain complexes and that any lack of gravity here and there would prevent communion with the Tao. Hsü Fu-yüan formally became his disciple, pointing to the waters as he swore perseverance. Hence his learning took as its essential the importance of self-conquest. He amended the doctrine of investigation of things, saying that anyone attached to physical instincts and intellectual knowledge was subject to sensual temptations; even if various injuries to his character were not immediately visible, the roots of sickness remain in the guise of "things." It was therefore necessary to work constantly on these roots, until every inch of ground was free from the slightest particle of dust. Only then might "things" be said to be "investigated."

Hsü Fu-yüan believed in *liang-chih* and disliked those who used it to preach Buddhism. He once cautioned Lo Ju-fang about the danger of setting bad examples for younger scholars, saying that a few flippant persons speaking recklessly of ridiculous things and confusing the listeners could lead to the disapproval and disgust of correct and earnest scholars, who would then refuse to believe in the teaching (of *liang-chih*). This might bring about serious consequences. In organizing the Nanking lectures, Hsü shared the chief responsibilities with Yang Ch'i-yüan[8] and Chou Ju-teng.[9] Chou and Yang were both Lo's disciples and held opinions differing from Hsü's. Chou regarded the absence of good and evil as the essential teaching. Hsü composed the "Nine Inquiries"[10] to question him. He said that Wang Yang-ming's doctrines did not originally diverge from the school of the sages, for Yang-ming had said that nature was not without good, and therefore that knowledge also was not without good; the knowledge of good *(liang-chih)* being the state of consciousness called the Mean and present before the rise of emotions *(wei-fa chih chung)*. Such teachings were very clear, although what Yang-ming said about the absence of good and evil characterizing the mind-in-itself[11] was meant to refer to the freedom and stillness present in such a state *(wei-fa)*. This merely describes the one word "quietude" or "tranquility." When joined to the other three sentences (in Yang-ming's Four Sentences), the statement might be understood without any trouble. Those persons therefore who considered that even mind, intention, knowledge, and things[12] could be described as without good and evil, did not belong to the true transmission of Wang Yang-ming's philosophy. This exchange took place around the year 1592. These lectures drew famous persons, stimulating impressive discussions. The disciples of the two masters (Hsü and Chou Ju-teng) also had their own disputes. Hsü Fu-yüan eventually lost his official post because of this.

Hsü was especially friendly with Li Ts'ai. When Li was imprisoned, Hsü tried everything to save him. But when Li was exiled as a simple soldier to Fukien, he continued to use the insignia of his former position as [administrative vice commissioner]. Hsü was then grand coordinator of Fukien and went personally outside the city walls to meet Li. After exchanging greetings accompanied by tears, Hsü put on a serious expression and said, "By the grace of the emperor, you were released from prison. But you remain convicted [of your charges] and ought to humiliate yourself in repentance of your faults rather than blow trumpets in vain glory. Can such behavior be appropriate to your status?" Li was quite annoyed and called him old-fashioned. Then Hsü grew gentler, so genuine was his friendship for Li!

(*MJHA* 41:1a–b)

NOTES

1. For Hsü Fu-yüan, see also Liu Tsung-chou's brief comments, given in *Shih-shuo*. Hsü was Liu's teacher, and through Hsü, Liu could trace his intellec-

tual lineage to the school of Chan Jo-shui. I believe it is Huang Tsung-hsi's opinion that disciples of the school of Chan Jo-shui joined with the disciples of the Kiangsi branch of the Yang-ming school to remedy some of the excesses introduced into Ming thought by the latter-day disciples of Wang Chi and Wang Ken, especially those claiming to belong to the T'ai-chou branch of the Yang-ming school.

2. For Yang Po (1509–74), see the biography by Angela Hsi and Chaoying Fang, *DMB*, v. 2, 1525–28.

3. For Tsou Yüan-piao, a follower of the T'ai-chou branch and a statesman, see his biography by Charles Hucker, *DMB*, v. 2, 1312–14.

4. For Li Ts'ai, see his biography in this volume.

5. This was shortly before the Japanese invasion of Korea (1592). Presumably, the Ming had to deal with Hideyoshi Toyotomi, then in power in Japan.

6. For T'ang Shu, *hao* Yi-an, see *MJHA* 40:1a–b.

7. For Hsü Yung-chien, *hao* Lu-yüan, see *MJHA* 14:7a–b. (His dates are 1528–1611.)

8. For Yang Ch'i-yüan, see his biography by Julia Ching and Huang P'ei, *DMB*, v. 2, 1505–06.

9. For Chou Ju-teng, see his biography in this volume.

10. The "Nine Inquiries" were answered by Chou's "Nine Explanations."

11. Reference to Wang Yang-ming's Four Sentences (or Four Maxims).

12. Reference to Wang Chi's teaching of the Four Negatives. See Wang Chi's biography in this volume.

15. The Miscellaneous Scholars

The Records of the Miscellaneous Scholars include three kinds of people: those who did not study under known teachers but acquired their learning from the extant classics; those who relied upon the support of friendly scholars and were prevented thus from falling away but could not be classified under their friends; and those who flourished for a time but had no disciples to continue the line. They are all listed under this heading.

Section 1 deals mainly with men of early Ming who still kept the Sung norms.[1] Section 2 presents those who both heard and were astonished by Yang-ming's teachings.[2] Their arguments with him gave further opportunity for clarifying Yang-ming's teachings, just as the saying goes: "The stones of those hills may be used to polish jade."[3] Section 3 includes mostly a group of my own contemporaries, half of whom ended their lives as martyrs to the cause of loyalty and righteousness and so gave the witness of their lives to this teaching.[4] Without such commitment, there is only falsehood.[5]

NOTES

1. The biographies of Fang Hsiao-ju and Ts'ao Tuan appear in this section.

2. The biography of Lo Ch'in-shun appears in this section.

3. *Book of Poetry*, pt. 2, bk. 3; J. Legge, trans., *The Chinese Classics*, v. 4, 297. The meaning is the usefulness of friendly admonitions.

4. The biographies of Lü K'un and Hao Ching appear in this section.

5. I.e., unless you are ready to die for your beliefs, your philosophy is worth nothing.

Fang Hsiao-ju

Fang Hsiao-ju, *tzu* Hsi-chih (1357–1402),[1] was a man of Ning-hai in T'ai-chou-fu (Chekiang). From youth on, he showed an unusual intelligence. At age seven, he began to read books. By fourteen, he was studying literary composition and was often praised by his father's friends. At nineteen, he traveled to the imperial capital and studied with the Hanlin scholar Sung Lien.[2] Sung said, "Many have come to my door, but none can compare to this student Fang." When Sung returned to Chin-hua (Chekiang), Fang followed him there. He was with Sung for six years all together and learned all he could from him.

Fang was summoned to the capital twice by the emperor. The first time, he was appointed instructor of Han-chung (Shensi) and then was invited by Prince Hsien of Shu[3] to be the teacher of his heir. The prince valued him greatly and gave the name "Correct Learning" (*Cheng-hsüeh*) to his study. Later, Emperor Chien-wen (Hui-tsung, r. 1399–1402) summoned him to be an "erudite" in the Hanlin Academy and promoted him further to the post of lecturer-in-waiting. Whenever the emperor had a doubt, he invariably summoned Fang to resolve it. The relationship between him and Fang, his minister, was like that between the student and the teacher. When the Chin-ch'uan Gate of the capital (Nanking) was lost to the rebels, Fang put on a garment of coarsest sackcloth, as if to mourn for his parents, and wept without ceasing. Emperor Ch'eng-tsu[4] summoned him to court, but Fang did not go. Then the emperor sent his disciple Liao Yung to summon him again. Fang said to Liao, "You have studied for several years, yet you do not recognize the word 'right' (*shih*)." As a result, Fang was put into prison.

Fang's writings were considered by all to be the best of the time. For this reason Yao Kuang-hsiao[5] enjoined Emperor [Ch'eng-tsu], "Fang will definitely refuse to surrender. But you must not kill him. If you did so, the seed of learning would be annihilated." The emperor, who was already ashamed of his own impious rebellion [which had led him to the throne], wanted Fang to draft for him an edict to help smother the resentment in the hearts of the people. Fang embarrassed him by talk of the Duke of Chou.[6] The emperor restrained his own temper and begged for the draft. But Fang rebuked him angrily without cease and was executed outside the Chü-pao Gate by being cut into pieces, at age forty-five. Those condemned to death in association with him numbered 847. After the imperial court moved south (1644), Fang was given the posthumous honorific of Wen-cheng.

Fang took firmly upon himself the responsibility of a sage and a worthy man. He was totally unconcerned with conventional affairs. To friends who asked him about literature, he invariably talked about the Way *(Tao)*, saying that literature was not worth pursuing. He considered entrance to the Way as understanding the distinction between universality and selfishness, righteousness and profit, [saying that] thoughts ought to be examined in quietude as they arose. Not to pay attention to this is like letting a robber loose in the house, so that nothing else can be done. He interpreted Chou Tun-yi's emphasis on tranquility, saying that with emphasis on humanity, righteousness, the Mean [of the emotions], and correctness, tranquility will also occur;[7] this is not a forcible control of one's original mind *(pen-hsin)* that makes it become like wood or stone, unable to respond to things. That is why (according to him) the sage is not without movement. He believed that the effort of becoming a sage begins with the Elementary Learning, so he wrote *Yu-yi* (Demeanor for the Young) in twenty parts. Asserting that the transformation of people begins with the ordering of the family, he also wrote *Tsung-yi* in nine parts.[8] Saying that an ideal kingly government exalts virtue but is mild in punishments, he wrote the *Shen-lü lun,* in ten parts.[9] And he expounded the view that the Way is embodied in affairs, and that it is present everywhere, listing a number of injunctions in a volume entitled *Tsa-chieh,* for his own use. His strict self-discipline and his strong spirit can campare well with Chu Hsi. He was truly the patriarch of learning in the Ming period.

Although Fang's learning came from Sung Lien, he also learned a lot from his own family. His father, Fang K'o-ch'in, did research on the history of the transmission of true learning among past scholars from his own neighborhood and worked so hard that he often neglected food and sleep. While Sung Lien dabbled in Buddhism and Taoism, Fang regarded none other than these two schools as the worst rebels aginst the Tao and singled out Buddhism especially for criticism. He was not afraid of attacking Buddhism openly, so that for a while, the monks and their disciples all hated him. Mediocre people criticized Fang on two grounds. First, they attacked him for gaining the confidence of the earlier emperor and yet being unable to save him from destruction. Formerly, the reinstitution of political feudalism had resulted in the rebellion of the Seven States, an event occasioned by the policy of Emperor Kao-tsu of Han (r. 206–195 B.C.).[10] In the same way, the Ming dynastic founder had inadvertently opened the way to the accession to the throne of [his younger son], Ch'eng-tsu. The second rebellion knew success where the first had known failure because Emperor Ch'eng-tsu was ten times as courageous and intelligent as Prince P'i of Wu of the Han dynasty. This shows that one should not use success and failure as a norm and blame failure entirely on the royal house. Besides, Fang was never in charge of state affairs. Emperor Hui-tsung had only consulted him about classics and history.

Fang was also criticized for having been so impulsive as to lead to the destruction of his ten clans of relations.[11] Actually this was due to Emperor Ch'eng-tsu's natural harshness. As one revered by all under Heaven, Fang refused to acquiesce and write the desired edict, so the emperor, resentful and cruel, reacted inhumanely without consideration for anything. It had nothing to do with Fang's supposed impulsive reactions. Have these critics of Fang not noticed that there had been others besides Fang who suffered similar misfortune? Had they all been excessively loyal, or should this be attributed only to inexorable fate? Ts'ai Ch'ing said, "A man like Fang Hsiao-ju appears only once in a thousand years. Heaven and Earth fortunately had given him birth and yet, unfortunately, did not protect him to the end or allow him to become of use to the world. Do Heaven and Earth really have intelligence?" These painful words make us feel like questioning and complaining against Heaven and Earth. From such words, we know that a firm judgment can be found about Fang among the upright men of the past.

(*MJHA* 43:1a–2a)

NOTES

1. For Fang Hsiao-ju, see the biography by F. W. Mote in *DMB*, v. 1, 426–33.

2. Sung Lien, *tzu* Ching-lien, 1310–81. See his biography by F. W. Mote, *DMB*, v. 2, 1225–30.

3. This prince, Chu Ch'un, was the eleventh son of the Ming founder, Chu Yüan-chang, and the most literary-minded of the imperial princes. He lived from 1371 to 1423. He was named Prince of Shu, and he established his residence at Ch'eng-tu (1391). See Chu Yüan-chang's biography by Teng Ssu-yü, *DMB*, v. 1, 389–90.

4. Emperor Ch'eng-tsu, uncle of Chien-wen, had rebelled against his nephew and finally usurped the throne. See Chu Ti's biography by L. C. Goodrich and F. W. Mote, in *DMB*, v. 1, 355–64.

5. Yao Kuang-hsiao, 1335–1419, was a Buddhist monk who served Chu Ti, counseled him in his pursuit of the throne, and advised him against killing Fang. See his biography by Eugene Feifel and Hok-lam Chan, in *DMB*, v. 2, 1561–65.

6. The Duke of Chou, a loyal regent to his young nephew, King Ch'eng, presented a direct contrast to the man who usurped the throne of his nephew.

7. Fang appears to give priority to the practice of virtues over an emphasis on tranquility and quietude.

8. Neither of these works—possibly poems, especially in the first case—is found in his extant writings (*Fang Cheng-hsüeh chi*, CYTC ed.).

9. Two parts of this essay are extant. See *Fang Cheng-hsüeh chi*.

10. The rebellion was led especially by Prince P'i of Wu. See *Han-shu*, ch. 35.

11. The story goes that Emperor Ch'eng-tsu carried out his threat to Fang by executing not only all those related to him by blood and marriage (nine clans) but also his disciples (the tenth clan).

Ts'ao Tuan

Ts'ao Tuan, *tzu* Cheng-fu, *hao* Yüeh-ch'uan (1376–1434),[1] was a native of Mien-ch'ih in Honan. Even as a child, he never spoke or acted recklessly. By the age of seventeen, he had already finished studying the Five Classics. He studied under Ma Tzu-ts'ai of Yi-yang and P'eng Tsung-ku of T'ai-yüan[2] and made some progress. In 1408, he passed the provincial examination. The following year he took the metropolitan examination, which he did not pass, although his name came out first on the secondary list. Appointed instructor in Huo-chou (Shansi), he served there for nine years and then returned home to mourn the death of his parents, living by their graves. In 1422, he was called out of his retirement to serve as instructor in P'u-chou, Shansi. During the review of officials in 1425, students from the schools in both Huo-chou and P'u-chou presented petitions requesting his reappointment to their schools. Because Huo-chou [presented its petition first], its request was granted. Ts'ao remained there for another ten years and died there on July 7, 1434, at the age of fifty-eight.

Earlier, Ts'ao had obtained a copy of *Pien-huo-p'ien* (Disputing Errors) by the Yüan scholar Hsieh Ying-fang, which he liked very much. It helped him to remain steadfast and unmoved by the prevalent teachings of transmigration, fortune-telling, sorcery, geomancy, and divination. His father, Hu Ching-tsu, did good works in the local area, diligently practicing what Buddhists and Taoists regarded as good acts. Ts'ao admonished his father day and night with the teachings of sages and worthies, which exalted correctness and censured heterodoxy. His father was finally moved and listened to him willingly. Ts'ao also selected from these teachings a number of items pertaining to human relationships and daily life that were especially worth practicing and compiled a volume entitled *Yeh-hsing chu* (Candle for Walking at Night).[3] It claimed that a man living in a vulgar and commonplace society resembled someone groping at night and that the book could serve as a candle to light his way ahead.

Once a Taoist devotional session was to be held in Ts'ao's village. Unable to stop it, he petitioned the leading people of the village not to attend. He also petitioned the magistrate to destroy certain improper shrines (*yin-ssu*). The magistrate, in turn, entrusted him with this task, and Ts'ao destroyed more than a hundred such shrines, leaving intact only the two temples, dedicated to the sage king Yu of the Hsia dynasty and to the Thunder God. In place of the other shrines, he established altars to the spirits of the earth and grain for Confucian rites of prayer and thanksgiving during the four seasons. When Hsing Tuan reconstructed the temple dedicated to the Five Sacred Mountains,[4] Ts'ao criticized him for violating the rituals (which reserved solely to the emperor the right to worship Heaven, earth, and the spirits of the major mountains and rivers).[5] Ts'ao also criticized his fellow officials for paying obeisance to the Taoist deity, Tzu-t'ung.[6] When these told him that Tzu-t'ung was the patron of culture, Ts'ao retorted, "If Tzu-t'ung is in charge of culture, then what is Confucius in charge of?" A disciple was going to a shrine festival commemorating the War God, Kuan Yü.[7] Ts'ao rebuked him severely.

Whenever a death occurred in the family of any of his students, Ts'ao always sent someone who knew the Confucian rites to assist at the funeral. One student had desired a Buddhist service. Ts'ao said to him, "Buddhists teach us to rescue our parents from hell [by procuring special funeral services]. This does not regard parents as superior persons *(chün-tzu)* but as mediocre persons who have accumulated evils and crimes. Are they not treating their parents rather harshly?" In response, the student said, "But the whole world keeps to these observances. Should I do otherwise, I would become a laughingstock." Ts'ao replied, "The people of the whole village are mired in these customs because they do not read books. You have read the Confucian books and understand Confucian rituals. Yet, instead of regarding it as wrong to violate Confucian rituals, you regard the violation of popular customs as wrong. This means you are not really a man of books."

Whenever repair or reconstruction work was to take place, Ts'ao never bothered to select a propitious date or time for the event. And when others would tell him about the position of Jupiter or the waxing of the agent of earth, he would expose their absurdity. The people eventually followed him and became converted to his ways. Once a woodcutter in Huo-chou picked up a lost gold bracelet and returned it to the owner. People considered him unusual. But the woodcutter merely said, "I would not want to shame Instructor Ts'ao." A certain Kao Wen-chih, on his way to see a play, turned back, saying, "How could I let Master Ts'ao know of this?"

Ts'ao emphasized earnest practice, to which he personally adhered with great care. He would not tolerate expediency in anything. However, he did not simply attend to the externals. He established the foundation of his learning in reverence *(ching)* and its experiential realization in desirelessness. He said, "To cultivate the mind in everything we did is the great path that led to the gate of Confucianism."[8] His learning may truly be said to have a foundation. In clarifying the concept of the Great Ultimate, he also said: "Master Chu stated that *li* riding on *ch'i* resembles a man riding on a horse and as the horse comes and goes, the man also comes and goes with it.[9] If this were true, then the man would be a dead man and not the most spiritual of creatures, while *li* too would be dead *li* and unable to serve as the source of all things. However, if we allow a live man to ride a horse, then the coming or going, beginning or ending, speed or slowness all depend on how he reins the horse. The live *li* is also like this."[10]

Such clarification is illuminating but remains dualistic, since it maintains *li* as directing *ch'i*. If *ch'i* must wait to be directed by *li*, then *ch'i* becomes a dead thing. Did he not know that the terms *li* and *ch'i* were created by man? Speaking of things as emerging and submerging, ascending and descending, one says *ch'i*. Speaking of things as emerging and submerging, ascending and descending, and yet without departing from regular norms, one says *li*. *Li* and *ch'i* are but two names for one thing. They do not refer to two things that have the same substance. Hsüeh Hsüan[11] (Ts'ao's contemporary) used the metaphor of sunlight and flying birds to describe the relationship between *li* and *ch'i*. Their contemporaries discussing *li* and *ch'i* said largely the same things.

(*MJHA* 44:1a–2a)

NOTES

1. For Ts'ao Tuan, see his biography by Julia Ching, *DMB*, v. 2, 1302–3.
2. It has not been possible to identify these persons.
3. Ts'ao Tuan's *Yeh-hsing chu*, 1 ch., is included in *Ts'ao-yüeh-ch'uan hsien-sheng yi-shu*. A Ming edition of the earlier-mentioned Hsieh Ying-fang's *Pieh-huo p'ien* is included in the Four Libraries series.
4. The mountains include Mount T'ai in the east, Mount Hua in the west, Mount Sung in the center.
5. See Ts'ao's chronological biography by Chang Hsin-min, in *Ts'ao Yüeh-ch'uan hsien-sheng chi* (Collected Writings) as preserved in the *Kuang-li-hsüeh pei-k'ao*, 1702 ed., 16a–b.
6. Tzu-t'ung was allegedly a Taoist deity who had earlier lived as Chang Ya-chih and died in battle some time during the Chin dynasty (265–316 A.D.). See *MS*, "On Rituals," ch. 50.
7. Kuan Yü was the famous warrior of the Three Kingdoms and a faithful friend and supporter of Liu Pei, founder of the state of Shu (r. 220–223 A.D.). See *San-kuo chih* (Three Kingdoms), "Book of Shu," ch. 36.
8. Quotations from *Ts'ao Yüeh-ch'uan hsien-sheng chi*, 17a.
9. *Chu-tzu yü-lei* (Taipei reprint of 1473 edition, 1970), 94:10a.
10. See Ts'ao's preface to the *Pien-li*, in *Ts'ao Yüeh-ch'uan hsien-sheng chi*, 25a.
11. Hsüeh Hsüan's posthumous honorific is Wen-ch'ing. See Hsüeh's *Tu-shu lu fu hsü-lu* (1827 ed.), 5:7a–b.

Lo Ch'in-shun

Lo Ch'in-shun, *tzu* Yün-sheng, *hao* Cheng-an (1465–1547),[1] was a native of T'ai-ho in Chi-an (Kiangsi). In 1492 he ranked first in the provincial examinations. The following year he placed third among those taking the *chin-shih* examination, and the rank of Hanlin compiler was conferred on him. Then he was selected to be a lecturer in the National University in Nanking. At that time Chang Mou[2] was chancellor. Through personal uprightness they established their leadership, and the university flourished during this period. [In 1504] Lo returned home with his father and subsequently memorialized requesting permission to serve his father for the remainder of his life. He met with the anger of Liu Chin,[3] was dismissed from office, and was made a commoner.

After Liu Chin was executed (1510), Lo was restored to office. He later become vice-minister of the court of imperial sacrifices in Nanking (1511), was promoted to junior vice-minister of personnel in Nanking (1515), and was transferred to junior vice-minister (Peking, 1519). At the beginning of the Chia-ching period (1522) he was elevated to vice-minister of personnel (Peking) and later was made minister of personnel in Nanking. Subsequently he entered the ministry of rites. [In 1523] he observed mourning for his father. When the period of mourning was over, he was recalled to the same office as minister of rites, but, before he went, the appointment was changed to minister of personnel. He submitted a memorial firmly declining, whereupon he received an imperial decree permitting him to retire. He died on May 13, 1547, at the age of eighty-two. An imperial edict granted him a state sacrifice and burial and the title of grand guardian of the heir-apparent. He was given the posthumous name Wen-chuang.

When he dwelled at home he arose every day at dawn, dressed himself correctly, and went up to the *Hsüeh-ku lou* (Hall for the Study of Antiquity), followed by his disciples. After receiving their greetings and obeisances he sat in a dignified posture and engaged in study. Even when he dwelled alone, he was never careless in his demeanor. He was frugal in his diet, had no pavilions or garden houses, and employed no music when he entertained. It was said by Lin Hsi-yüan[4] that, "From his initial service in the Hanlin to his service as a minister, his conduct both in and out of office was like pure gold and precious jade. One could find no flaws."

He himself described his endeavors in learning by saying:

> Formerly when I was employed in the capital, I encountered an old Buddhist priest and questioned him casually about how to become a Buddha. With equal casualness he drew on the language of Ch'an in his reply, saying, "The Buddha is in the pine tree in the courtyard."[5] I supposed that there must be something in what he said and gave it my undivided thought until dawn. As I grabbed my clothing and was about to arise, I became suddenly enlightened and was unaware that my entire body was bathed in perspiration. Later I obtained the "Song of Enlightenment."[6] I read it and found that it accorded perfectly with my own experience. I regarded this as most wonderful and mysterious and beyond all worldly wisdom. Later when I held

office in the National University in Nanking, I never put the books of the sages and worthies out of my hands for even a day. I entered the spirit of the books and savored them, gradually realizing their truth. Only then did I understand that what I had perceived on that former occasion was the mysterious activity of the mind's pure spirituality and not the principle of nature. Since then I have carried on my painstaking study and have verified through personal experience what I learned from books. Having spent several decades engaged in earnest effort, only when I was approaching the age of sixty did I finally attain insight into the reality of the mind and nature and truly acquire the basis for self-confidence.[7]

Lo's discussion of *li* and *ch'i* is very precise and accurate. He says:

That which penetrates Heaven and Earth and connects past and present is nothing other than the one *ch'i* (material force). *Ch'i* is originally one but it revolves endlessly through cycles of movement and tranquility, going and coming, opening and closing, rising and falling. Having become increasingly obscure, it then becomes manifest; through being manifest, it reverts to obscurity, making for the warmth and coolness and the cold and heat of the four seasons, the birth, growth, gathering in, and storing of all living things, the constant moral relations of the people's daily life, the victory and defeat, gain and loss in human affairs. That which for all the infinite complexity and bewildering diversity cannot ultimately be disturbed and which is so even without our knowing why it is so is called *li* (principle). *Li* is not a separate entity that depends upon *ch'i* in order to exist or that "attaches to *ch'i* in order to operate."[8] Owing to the phrase, "There is in the changes the Great Ultimate,"[9] there are some who suspect that there is a single entity that acts as a controlling power amid the transformations of yin and yang. This is not the case.[10]

Through these words even Master Chu Hsi's statements that *li* and *ch'i* are two things[11] and that *li* is weak and *ch'i* is strong[12] may be clarified so as to make further argument unnecessary.

But Lo's theory of the mind *(hsin)* and nature *(hsing)* and his theory of *li* and *ch'i* are mutually contradictory. That which in heaven is *ch'i*, in man is the mind. And that which in heaven is *li,* in man is nature. What is true of *li* and *ch'i* will also be true of the mind and nature, for there is definitely no question of a difference between them. By virtue of receiving *ch'i* from Heaven, man is born. He has only one mind but it revolves endlessly through cycles of movement and tranquility, pleasure, anger, sorrow, and joy. When he ought to feel pity and commiseration, he naturally feels pity and commiseration; when he ought to feel shame and dislike, he naturally feels shame and dislike; when he ought to feel reverence and respect, he naturally feels reverence and respect; and when he ought to have a sense of right and wrong, he naturally has a sense of right and wrong. That which for all the infinite complexity and bewildering diversity remains clear and cannot be obscured is what is called nature. It is not a separate entity that exists prior to the mind or that attaches to the mind.

Lo thought that man's Heaven-endowed nature originates when life is first engendered, but that consciousness arises only after one is born, and that consciousness is mind and not nature. In this view, nature is substance and the mind is function. Nature originates before a person is born and is tranquil. The mind moves when it is aroused by external things and is active. Nature is the principle of Heaven and Earth and the myriad things and is common to all *(kung)*. The mind is what one personally possesses and is particular to oneself *(ssu)*. Clearly this is first to set up nature as prior and to regard it as master of the mind. This is no different from the theory that *li* can engender *ch'i*. Isn't this in marked contradiction to his theory about *li* and *ch'i?* How could it possibly be that *li* and *ch'i* are *li* and *ch'i* and that the mind and nature are the mind and nature, the two separating the realms of Heaven and man, so that they cannot relate to each other? Yet Lo was hardly the first person to have difficulty in understanding mind and nature.

The mind is characterized by activity and tranquility. When it is tranquil, it is unmoving; when it is aroused, it becomes penetrating. This is the meaning of activity and tranquility. The emotions are constantly present in both activity and tranquility, and nature is likewise constantly present in both activity and tranquility. Therefore regardless of whether pleasure, anger, sorrow, and joy have already been aroused *(yi-fa)* or have not yet been aroused *(wei-fa),* they are still emotions. The attainment of a state of equilibrium and harmony constitutes nature. Now to consider the equilibrium before pleasure, anger, sorrow, and joy have been aroused as nature, and the harmony after they have been aroused as the emotions, is necessarily to put nature first and the mind after. If nature is put first and the mind after, the argument inevitably shows flaws.

Pity and commiseration, shame and dislike, modesty and deference, and a sense of right and wrong are mind. Humanity, righteousness, propriety, and wisdom indicate that this mind is also nature; it is not that there first exists a nature of humanity, righteousness, propriety, and wisdom that subsequently gives rise to a mind of pity and commiseration, shame and dislike, modesty and deference, and right and wrong. (Perceiving this, one realizes that Li Ts'ai's[13] discussion of the Way and nature is also partial.[14])

Anyone who sees a child about to fall into a well will feel alarm and distress.[15] One who is starving may, when offered food with an insulting voice, not condescend to accept it.[16] This is nature manifested in action. Even while one is in a state of tranquility, nature that reacts with alarm and distress and does not condescend is always potentially present. Activity and tranquility are both aspects of the mind and therefore nature is the nature of the mind. To reject the mind that has clear consciousness of the natural, that possesses its own sense of order, and to search elsewhere for something called nature is like abandoning the *ch'i* that expands and contracts and comes and goes and searching elsewhere for something called *li*. Although Master Chu Hsi spoke of the mind controlling nature and emotions,[17] in the final analysis he identified the state before the feelings have been aroused with nature and the state after the feelings have been aroused with the mind. When he used the terms "mind" and "nature," he spoke of *li* and *ch'i*, so that *li* and *ch'i* cannot be unified. Lo's discussion of *li* and *ch'i* does not agree with that of Master Chu, while his discussion of the mind and nature does agree with that of Master Chu, which shows that he was unable to achieve theoretical consistency.

Lo referred to the Buddhists' insight into the clear consciousness of the natural as "knowing the mind" and to their not understanding the principles of Heaven and Earth and the myriad things as "not knowing nature."[18] My view is that the Buddhists have no gradations in caring for one's kin, being humane toward people and loving things.[19] This is to lack the mind of pity and commiseration. They are indiscriminate about giving and receiving and practice begging and almsgiving. This is to lack the mind of shame and dislike. They hold that "in Heaven above and Earth below, I alone am to be reverenced."[20] This is to lack the mind of modesty and deference. They consider that there is neither good nor evil. This is to lack the sense of right and wrong. Their not knowing nature stems from their not knowing the mind. This being the case, what they know is a reflection of the mind rather than the real thing.

Master Kao P'an-lung[21] said, "Lo inquired deeply into Ch'an and demonstrated the reasons for its differences [from Confucianism]. From the T'ang until the present no one has been so clear and thorough as he in refuting Buddhism. His contributions were extraordinary!"[22]

(*MJHA* 47:1a–2b)

NOTES

1. For Lo Ch'in-shun, see his biography by Tu Ching-i in *DMB*, v. 1, 972–74.

2. For Chang Mou, *hao* Feng-shan (1437–1522), see his biography in *MJHA*, ch. 45. See also the biography by Ronald G. Dimberg and Julia Ching in *DMB*, v. 1, 96–97.

3. The notorious eunuch who held power at court during the first decade of the sixteenth century. See his biography in *MS*, ch. 304 (Kuo-fang yen-chiu yüan ed., 3421). See also the biography by Yung-deh Richard Chu in *DMB*, v. 1, 941–45.

4. *Tzu* Mao-chen, *hao* Tz'u-ai; he was a *chin-shih* of 1517.

5. See *Wu-men kuan* (The Gate Without a Door), *TSD*, no. 2005, 48:297c.

6. The "Song of Enlightenment" is generally attributed to the Ch'an master Yung-chia Hsüan-chüeh (665–713). See *TSD*, no. 2014. There are various translations of this work, including one by Charles Luk in *Ch'an and Zen Teachings*, Third Series (London, 1962), 116–45.

7. *K'un-chih chi* (Notes on Knowledge Painfully Acquired) (1622 ed., Library of Congress), 2:16b–17a.

8. An explicit denial of Chu Hsi's statement (*Chu Tzu ch'üan-shu*, 49:4b) that "*Li* attaches to *ch'i* in order to operate."

9. *Book of Changes*, "Appended Remarks." In *Chou Yi cheng-yi*, SPPY ed., 7: 17a.

10. *K'un-chih chi*, 1:6b–7a.

11. Chu Hsi, "Letter to Liu Shu-wen," in *Chu Wen-kung wen-chi*, SPPY ed., 46:24a.

12. *Chu Tzu yü-lei* (1970 Taiwan photographic reproduction of 1473 ed.), 4: 13b.

13. For Li Ts'ai, see his biography in *MJHA*, ch. 31.

14. Just as Huang Tsung-hsi criticizes Lo Ch'in-shun for his distinction between "substance" and "function," he scores Li Ts'ai on similar grounds, arguing (*MJHA*, ch. 31), "If nature transcends distinctions of the inner and the outer, mind also transcends these distinctions, and then there is no way by which one may speak of reality or substance *(t'i)* and its manifestations and functions *(yung).*"

15. Alludes to *Mencius* 2A:6. See J. Legge, trans., *The Chinese Classics*, v. 2, 202.

16. Alludes to *Mencius* 6A:10. See J. Legge, trans., *The Chinese Classics*, v. 2, 412–13.

17. In this, Chu Hsi was interpreting a statement by Chang Tsai in *Chang Tzu ch'üan-shu*, 14:2a. Chu alluded frequently to this formulation. See, for example, *Chu Tzu yü-lei*, 98:7a.

18. *K'un-chih chi*, 1:2b.

19. Alludes to *Mencius* 7A:45. See J. Legge, trans., *The Chinese Classics*, v. 2, 476.

20. Words attributed to the Buddha at his birth. See *TSD*, no. 184, 463b; no. 187, 613c; no. 202, 418c.

21. For Kao P'an-lung, *hao* Ching-yi (1562–1626), see his biography in *MJHA* 58 and the biography by Charles O. Hucker in *DMB*, v. 1, 701–10.

22. *"Lo Wen-Chuang kung chuan"* (Biography of Lo Ch'in-shun) in *Kao Tzu yi-shu* (Surviving Works of Kao P'an-lung) (1746 ed., Princeton University Library), 10A:6b.

Lü K'un

Lü K'un, *tzu* Shu-chien, *hao* Hsin-wu (1536–1618)[1] was from Ning-ling, Honan. He received the *chin-shih* degree in 1574, was assigned to the magistracy of Hsiang-yüan (Shansi), and then transferred to Ta-t'ung (Shansi). When Wang Chia-p'ing[2] of Shan-yin (Chekiang) wished to deal leniently with some prisoner awaiting trial for murder, Lü K'un would not listen to him. Then Wang went to the ministry of personnel, where he spread the word to others, saying, "No one surpasses the magistrate of Ta-t'ung in refusing illicit requests." He even sent in a special memorial of recommendation, so that Lü was promoted to secretary in the ministry of personnel and then, after several promotions, transferred to director of a bureau. He left this post to become an administration vice-commissioner of Shansi, administration commissioner of Shensi, vice censor-in-chief of the right [*sic*][3] at the same time as governor of Shansi. He was then recalled to assist in the administration of the censorate and was promoted to junior, and then senior, vice-minister of justice.

Whenever discussions on the state took place, he adhered to the correct course without wavering. This displeased the small men. [As it happened], he had also written a book,[4] the *Kuei-fan t'u-shuo* (An Illustrated Explanation of Model Women), which was circulating in the streets. Since Emperor Shen-tsung was fond of fiction, drama, and various illustrated books, the eunuch Ch'en Chu[5] presented him with a copy of this book to read, and Shen-tsung then gave it to his imperial consort, the Lady Cheng.[6] To exaggerate the significance of this gift from the emperor, she wrote a preface for the book and had it reprinted and circulated inside and outside the palace. At that time, the question of the imperial succession had not been settled, and the whole court was concentrating its attacks on Lady Cheng, so those who did not like Lü said that this could be used to involve him in some big trouble. The supervising secretary, Tai Shih-heng,[7] promptly accused Lü of relying upon the *Kuei-fan t'u-shuo* to harbor malicious intentions. And some busybody composed *Yu-wei hung-yi,* saying that Lü had secretly presented the book to the imperial concubine, who responded with fifty taels of silver and four rolls of multicolored silk, unfortunately providing evidence of the [rumored] plot to change the heir-apparent. But Lady Cheng's relative, the official Cheng Ch'eng-en, submitted a memorial[8] pointing out the injustice of this case. Tai was banished to the borders, but Lü was also retired from office permanently. He remained home for forty years and died at the age of eighty-two,[9] receiving posthumously the title of minister of justice.

By nature, Lü was slow-witted.[10] In youth, because he could not memorize the texts he studied, he cast them all aside, purified his mind, and sought interior knowledge. After a long time he was enlightened and never forgot anything he read. When he was fifty he read books on the philosophy of nature and principle and delighted in his understanding of these. So he wrote *Yeh-ch'i ch'ao* (Notes at Night) and a poem, *Chao liang-hsin.*[11] All his life he studied and taught diligently and acquired many insights. In general he applied special effort to thinking, believing that each bit of self-examination brings with it a little accomplishment. It was because he himself experienced worries and distress that he became so self-restrained.

(*MJHA* 54:5a–b)

NOTES

1. See Lü's biography by Chaoying Fang in *DMB*, v. 1, 1006–10. See also Joanna F. Handlin, *Action in Late Ming Thought: The Reorientation of Lü K'un and Others* (Berkeley, 1983).

2. Wang Chia-p'ing, *hao* Tui-nan, 1537–1604. See *MS*, ch. 217. According to one account, the man being tried for murder was Wang's brother-in-law.

3. Huang Tsung-hsi reports this by mistake. Lü had the rank of junior assistant censor-in-chief. For our information given here, see *Ming-shih-lu* (Veritable Records) (Taipei ed.) under Emperor Sheng-tsung, p. 4817.

4. This book was first published in 1590. It was based in large part on Liu Hsiang's *Lieh-nü chuan* (Biographies of Model Women), but Lü simplified the style, added anecdotes of his own choosing, and liberally appended his own critical comments to the stories.

5. For this eunuch, see *DMB*, v. 1, 151–52. For a more complete account of the controversy surrounding Lü's *Kuei-fan t'u-shuo*, see Ku Ying-t'ai, *Ming-shih chi-shih pen-mo* (Detailed Ming History) (Shanghai, 1937), 115–17. The *Kuei-fan t'u-shuo* is included in *Lü-tzu yi-shu* (Surviving Works), 1827 ed.

6. For Lady Cheng, see *DMB*, v. 1, 208–11.

7. For Tai, see *MS*, ch. 234.

8. See Lü K'un's *Collected Writings, Ch'ü-wei-chai wen-chi*, in *Lü-tzu yi-shu* 1: 5a–20b, for some of the things singled out for criticism by this memorial.

9. Clearly an error. Lü retired in 1597 and died in 1618.

10. Huang Tsung-hsi cites Lü's self-assessment here. See *Ch'ü-wei-chai wen-chi*, 9:47b.

11. For the poem, see *Ch'ü-wei-chai wen-chi*, 9:47b–48a and 10:15a–b. The term *liang-hsin*, literally, the good mind-and-heart, is frequently used as a substitute for *liang-chih*. It may also be translated as conscience. The title of the poem is *Chao liang-hsin* (Summoning the Conscience). The text of the *MJHA* has mistakenly given *K'uo* for *Chao*.

Hao Ching

Hao Ching, *tzu* Chung-yü, *hao* Ch'u-wang (1558–1639),[1] was from Ching-shan of Hukuang. He received the *chin-shih* degree in 1589, served as magistrate in Chin-yün (Chekiang), and was transferred to Yung-chia (Chekiang). He was then recalled to Peking to serve in the office of scrutiny for rites and as a supervising secretary, before being moved to the office of scrutiny for revenue. When Emperor Shen-tsung initiated the mining tax,[2] the eunuch Ch'en Tseng brought fraudulent charges against Yi-tu (Shantung) and had the magistrate Wu Tsung-yao arrested for questioning. Hao impeached Ch'en Tseng and tried to clear Wu. As Lu Pao and Li Tao, eunuchs in charge of taxes, had asked for power to supervise local officials, Hao said that local officials were established by the emperor to shepherd the people, while private aides were dispatched by the emperor to collect taxes from the people. It was bad enough when those who shepherd the people were not encouraged to control those who collected from them. How much worse would it be to use those who collected from the people to control those who shepherd the people? Would that not be like letting tigers and wolves loose into an enclosure and allowing them to strike and bite as they wished?[3] Hao also accused the senior grand secretary, Chao Chih-kao, of the policy of negotiating [with Japan the] appointment of [the Japanese ruler] as king [of Japan] and of permitting [Japan to trade with China] as a tribute nation. This policy failed but Chao was not punished for it. He had acted cunningly, like a mouse watching its prey, and had plotted disloyally against the state, therefore arousing the resentment of all inside and outside the court. After this incident came the grand review of Peking officials (1599).[4] Hao was described as a superficial and ill-tempered person, was demoted to vice-magistrate of Yi-hsing (Nan Chihli), and was later transferred to the magistracy of Chiang-yin (Nan Chihli). Since he had displeased important people, he was given the lowest grade and was once more demoted, whereupon he left office and returned home.

Hao built for himself a garden, wrote books, and refused to receive visitors. In addition to commentaries on the Five Classics, he wrote explanations[5] of each of these texts: the *Ceremonials (Yi-li),* the *Institutes of Chou (Chou-li),* the *Analects,* and the *Book of Mencius.* [His explanations] always clarified the meaning, proving every assertion made, and so washed away the accumulated gloss of commonplace commentaries. Of the Ming scholars who investigated the classics thoroughly, Hao was truly among the most important. He also believed that (Shun-yu K'un's) statement,[6] "He who makes [fame and merit] his first objects, acts with regard for others," is what Mo-tzu meant by universal love, while "He who makes [fame and merit] only secondary objects, acts with regard for himself," is what Yang Chu meant by benefiting the self.[7] During the time of the Warring States (403–221 B.C.), discussions of merit and profit, such as those by Chang Yi, Su Ch'in, and Master Kuei-ku,[8] belonged either to one or the other of these two roads, with Yang Chu and Mo-tzu as their starting points. That was why Mencius said, "If you listen to people's discourses throughout the country, you will find that they have adopted the views either of Yang or of Mo."[9] That was why chaos developed during the Warring States period. And that was why we should resist Yang and Mo. If these two thinkers had only left behind empty words with no concern for the way of the world, Mencius would not have condemned them so severely.

Such an explanation really revealed something that earlier scholars had not articulated. But, in my opinion, the ways of Yang and Mo have continued up to the present. Ch'eng Hao said, "The harm done by Yang Chu and Mo Ti was greater than that of Shen Pu-hai and Han Fei Tzu, while the harm done by the Buddha and Lao-tzu was close to reason. In this they cannot be compared to Yang and Mo."[10] Now, to practice humanity and righteousness naturally, without any ulterior motive, is the meaning of humanity and righteousness. But the Buddhists and Taoists think in terms of life and death, which is simply to act for oneself. Their vows to save all living creatures are merely motivated by the thought of action for others. No matter how profound and wonderful their words might be, they are limited in their actions to one of these two motives. What they call the Buddhism of the Tathāgata requires only that one hold on to his inner soul. Is this not motivated merely by regard for self?[11] What they call the Buddhism of the Patriarchs relies purely on useful activity. Is this not motivated merely by regard for others? Therefore the Buddhists are those who teach the doctrines of Yang and Mo at a deeper level. Where have they ever departed from the nest of Yang and Mo? Besides, is this only true of the Buddhists? Ever since study for civil examinations has become so important, has the school of Confucius anything else to show that is neither egoistic nor altruistic? That is why the way of humanity and righteousness has become extinct. In my opinion, there has been no other harm outside of that done by Yang and Mo. Yang Hsiung[12] said, "In ancient times, Yang and Mo blocked the road. After Mencius so eloquently exposed their fallacies, the road became wide open." Is this not like talking in a dream? People today do not know the true story about Buddhism, and they do not talk about Yang and Mo. So when they criticize Buddhism, they pay no attention to matters of government and only look at the surfaces. Those who only keep to their inner souls are like the trees and stones in the deep forests and the dragons and snakes of the huge swamps and need no denigration. Those who are only interested in useful activity have drifted into all kinds of manipulations and contrivances. These people now fill up the space between Heaven and Earth. For the ways of Yang and Mo are flourishing without any sign of coming to an end.

Alas! Hao took as his goal the study of the humble and the penetration of the sublime.[13] Recognition comes only with practice; understanding comes only with habitual action. One who truly knows how to practice and to act from habit will not fail to achieve recognition and understanding. For the study of the near is recognition, and the penetration of the sublime is knowledge. Therefore he considered the Sung philosophers'[14] emphasis on tranquility and the exhaustive investigation of principles to be ideas expressed in a vacuum hardly one inch removed from the Buddhist teachings of emptiness and nothingness. Yet what Hao means by the study of the humble is nothing but what he calls the investigation of things. And Hao also has something to say about the effort of knowing where to rest before the investigation of things. All this too concerns only thought and precedes its manifestation in affairs. How can this also be described as the "study of the near"? In this regard, one cannot but discern that his view lacks coherence.

(*MJHA* 55:1a–2a)

NOTES

1. See Hao Ching's biography by L. C. Goodrich in *DMB*, v. 1, 503–4.

2. For information on the mining tax, see *DMB*, v. 1, 331–32; *MS*, ch. 81, and Ku Ying-t'ai, *Ming-shih chi-shih pen-mo* (Shanghai, 1937), ch. 65.

3. Huang Tsung-hsi has only roughly paraphrased the memorial of Hao Ching as preserved in the gazetteer *Ching-shan-hsien chih* (1882), ch. 19, 20a–22b.

4. Huang Tsung-hsi erroneously calls this *ta-chi,* a term referring to provincial reviews of officials. The correct term is *ching-ch'a,* the review of officials at the capital.

5. Hao Ching wrote numerous commentaries on the Five Classics and other texts. See *DMB*, v. 1, 503.

6. Reference to *Mencius* 6B:6. J. Legge, trans., *The Chinese Classics,* v. 2, 432.

7. Reference to *Mencius* 3B:9. J. Legge, trans., *The Chinese Classics,* v. 2, 282.

8. These were politicians and diplomatists of the Warring States period.

9. *Mencius* 3B:9. J. Legge trans., *The Chinese Classics,* v. 2, 282.

10. See Chu Hsi's *Chin-ssu-lu,* English translation in W. T. Chan, *Reflections on Things at Hand* (New York, 1967), 279. Shen Pu-hai and Han Fei Tzu were Legalists.

11. Hao upholds the idea that virtue should be practiced for its own sake, rather than for reasons of egoism or altruism.

12. For more on Yang Hsiung (53 B.C.–18 A.D.), see Fung Yu-lan, *A History of Chinese Philosophy,* v. 2, 137–50.

13. *Analects* 14:37, J. Legge, trans., *The Chinese Classics,* v. 1, 288–89.

14. Reference to the teachings of Chou Tun-yi, the Ch'eng brothers, and Chu Hsi.

16.   The Tung-lin School

Today, when people talk about Tung-lin,[1] they associate the Tung-lin party's political disaster with the fate of the Ming house. So mediocre men use this as an excuse to accuse Tung-lin of causing the loss of our country to the Manchus and to refer to it as the Two Parties. Even those who know better say that although many men of Tung-lin were gentlemen, the group included certain political extremists, and their associates were not all gentlemen. In the end they were no better than the partisans of the Later Han period. Alas, this is all nonsense! The teachers of philosophy *(chiang-hsüeh)* associated with Tung-lin were only a few men, and their lecture hall stood only in one prefecture. Earlier, Ch'ien Tê-hung, Wang Ken, and Wang Chi preached to the masses, establishing schools everywhere in Kiangsu, Chekiang, and Southern Chihli. They may be called propagators [of the philosophy of Wang Yang-ming]. Tung-lin did nothing of the sort. The first assembly of philosophers, which took place at the Shou-shan Academy in the capital, was presided over by Tsou Yüan-piao and Feng Ts'ung-wu,[2] both of whom had nothing to do with Tung-lin. [And yet, for many people,] all who took part in discussions regarding the root of the country[3] were men of Tung-lin; all who attacked the traitor eunuch (Wei Chung-hsien) were men of Tung-lin; and even those who discussed [Chang Chü-cheng's] remaining in office during the mourning period of his father, those who criticized the Grand Secretaries as traitors[4] and those who clamored for war against the bandits—anyone who had a correct opinion in politics, anyone of independent mind who did not follow the crowd—were all called men of Tung-lin. In this way, the name Tung-lin became popular in the whole country, and its popularity lasted for several generations. What misfortune for Tung-lin that this should be so! And yet what good fortune for Tung-lin that this should be so! But then does the name Tung-lin really represent some reality, or is it only a name given to some people by mediocre men?

The critics say that Tung-lin attracted disaster by its promotion of "pure discussion."[5] Confucius said: "The way of the gentleman may be compared to dikes conserving that in which people are deficient."[6] Those who engaged in pure discussions were like the dikes of the world. Confucius also criticized Tsang for usurping a position that was not his by right and Chi for going to Mount T'ai.[7] Are these also not examples of pure discussions? Only with the disappearance of pure discussions do we find men who praised Wang Mang in their memorials and flattered the eunuchs' party.[8] That is why mediocre men hated pure discussions, just as the Yellow River dislikes Mount Ti-chu for standing in its way.

During the reign of Hsi-tsung, when the divining tortoise and the tripods were in danger of changing hands, the men of Tung-lin resisted these changes with their flesh and blood and restored the setting sun to its place of honor.[9] During the critical days of the reign of Yi-tsung (1645), men mourned the emperor's death and committed suicide.[10] Were these men of Tung-lin, or were they enemies of Tung-lin? For a few decades, the courageous burned their wives,[11] while the weaker lot went into hiding underground. The loyalty and righteousness we witnessed surpassed that which was ever manifested during the earlier dynasties. All this was the result of the lasting influence and example of Tung-lin. That a group of teachers and disciples belonging to one academy should give their blood to purify Heaven and Earth and that fools should criticize them in secret is cause for lament!

NOTES

1. The name Tung-lin (Eastern Grove) refers primarily to an academy first opened by Yang Shih in the Sung dynasty and reopened in the Ming dynasty by the group of scholars centering around Ku Hsien-ch'eng and Kao P'an-lung. It was situated in Wusih (Kiangsu). Huang Tsung-hsi argues that the name should refer only to these men and their scholarly activities rather than to the movement of political protest that went on during the reign of Emperor Shen-tsung (r. 1572–1620) and continued afterwards.

2. For Tsou, see *MJHA,* ch. 23; for Feng, see *MJHA,* ch. 41.

3. Reference is to the disputes surrounding the naming of an heir to the throne under Emperor Shen-tsung, who delayed this action on account of his partiality for his concubine, *née* Cheng, and for her son. See *Ming-shih,* ch. 20–21.

4. The reference is to Chou Yen-ju and Wen T'i-jen.

5. "Pure discussions" refers to political discussions within scholarly circles of persons dissatisfied with the state of affairs. "Pure" refers to the absence of any selfish motive.

6. *Book of Rites,* bk. 27. English translation adapted from J. Legge, trans., *Li Ki* (Oxford, 1885), pt. 2, 284.

7. *Analects* 15:13 and 3:6. J. Legge, trans., *The Chinese Classics,* v. 1, 298–99, 156.

8. Reference to the usurper of the Han throne (9–23 A.D.) and his flatterers.

9. Reference to the opposition to the eunuch Wei Chung-hsien, the emperor's favorite, who was amassing power and who executed a number of men connected with Tung-lin.

10. Literally, those who "climbed up the dragon's beard" (mourned the emperor's death) and "slept with ants" (died, or committed suicide). Reference is to Emperor Yi-tsung's suicide when Peking was about to fall to the rebels.

11. Reference to the resistance against the Manchu invaders.

Ku Hsien-ch'eng

Ku Hsien-ch'eng, *tzu* Shu-shih, *hao* Ching-yang (1550–1612),[1] was a native of Wuhsi, Ch'ang-chou Prefecture (Nan Chihli). His father, Ku Hsüeh,[2] had four sons, of whom Ku Hsien-ch'eng was the third; his younger brother was Ku Yün-ch'eng.[3] At age ten, Ku Hsien-ch'eng studied Han Yü's *Hui-p'ien* (On Name Taboos).[4] He followed its teachings so thoroughly that he avoided using his own father's name (Hsüeh, meaning "study"), and when he could not help referring to it (i.e., in writing), he became anxious and unhappy. His father said to him: "In ancient times, Prince Hsien-an of Han[5] told his son not to shun the use of the word Chung (the prince's given name, meaning loyalty). Now my name is Hsüeh, and if you avoid it to honor me you may as well forget all about learning."[6]

At ages fifteen and sixteen, Ku studied with Chang Yüan-lo. Yüan-lo taught the classics by avoiding the blind following of the [officially designated] commentaries, relying simply upon his own understanding of the meaning. Ku Hsien-ch'eng listened attentively and was in frequent agreement with him. They discussed the chapter of the *Analects* where a question is raised regarding the great sacrifice.[7] Ku Hsien-ch'eng said, "I regret that the questioner did not ask another question. For if the Master (Confucius) did not know the meaning of the great sacrifice [as he claimed],[8] then how could he say that he who knew it would be able to govern the world?" And when they discussed Mencius, "to nourish the mind there is nothing better than to make desires few,"[9] Ku said, "To make desires few, there is nothing better than to nourish the mind."[10] Chang Yüan-lo responded, "Studying for civil examinations cannot adequately satisfy your intellectual ambitions. Why don't you seek the Way from Master Hsüeh Ying-ch'i?"[11] [So Ku went to Hsüeh]. Hsüeh was delighted to see him, gave him a copy of the *K'ao-t'ing yüan-yüan lu* (A Record of the Chu Hsi School),[12] saying, "Everything between Confucius and Wang Yang-ming has been brought together in this book."

In 1576 Ku placed first in the provincial examination, and in 1580 passed the *chin-shih* examination and was appointed a secretary in the ministry of revenue. At that time, Chang Chü-cheng was in power. Ku Hsien-ch'eng made friends with Wei Yün-chung of Nan-lo (Pei Chihli) and Liu T'ing-lan of Chang-p'u (Fukien). The three agreed to do all they could to set standards of high ethical conduct at court and were known as the "three *chieh-yüan*."[13] They also sent letters to Shen Shih-hsing of Soochow,[14] discussing the right and wrong of state affairs, keeping nothing back. Chang Chü-cheng said to Shen, "I heard of the assembly of the three *chieh-yüan*, who were all graduates under you. Do you also know about them?" Shen replied that he knew nothing. When Chang Chü-cheng got sick, the officials all abstained [from meat] and offered prayers for his health. Ku's name was included on the list by his fellow officials.[15] When he heard of it, he hastened to have it removed. In 1582, he was transferred to the ministry of personnel and [after a year] requested a leave of absence to return home.[16] In 1586 he was appointed a secretary in the bureau of honors (in the ministry of personnel). The following year the senior censor-in-chief, Hsin Tzu-hsiu, employed unyielding rigor in the scrutiny of the metropolitan officials and thereby incurred the dislike of the grand secretary Wang Hsi-chüeh.[17] When the minister of works, Ho Ch'i-ming, was impeached,[18] someone advised him: "Why don't you attack Hsin and get him dismissed along with yourself? The grand secretary will thank you for it." Ho followed this advice; the supervising censors discussed both the cases of Hsin and Ho, and the two were both dismissed from office as predicted. [On that occasion], Ku Hsien-ch'eng submitted a memorial,[19] in which he distinguished between the gentlemen and the small men and criticized the way in which the chief grand secretary had handled the affair. For this, he was demoted to assistant magistrate of Kuei-yang (Hukuang). As Liu Tsung-yüan (773–819), Su Shih (1037–1101), and Chuang Ch'ang (1437–99)[20] had all been demoted to Kui-yang before him, Ku thought of it as a place that these former worthy men had visited and transformed. He erected a sign above his own dwelling, naming it "The Unworthy Pavilion."

In 1588 Ku was transferred to prefectural judge of Ch'u-chou (Chekiang) and the following year went into mourning for his mother. In 1591, he filled the same position in Ch'üan-chou (Fukien) and was then promoted to secretary of the bureau of evaluation (of the ministry of personnel). When an imperial order conferred princely fiefs on the emperor's three sons, Ku led the four bureaus of his ministry in opposing it, offering nine reasons why it should not be done.[21] The order was eventually cancelled.

In 1593 there was a scrutiny of metropolitan officials. The minister of personnel, Sun Lung,[22] and the director of the bureau of evaluations, Chao Nan-hsing,[23] saw to it that mediocre men were all removed and the imperial offices consequently cleared out. This angered the grand secretaries, and Chao Nan-hsing was himself demoted to a provincial post. Ku declared that he was equally involved in the matter with Chao, and that if Chao were to be punished, he should not alone be spared. His request was not answered, but he was transferred to the bureau of records (of the ministry of personnel). At that time, Tsou Yüan-piao[24] had just asked to be relieved of his office, but Wang Hsi-chüeh said that the dispatch office had sent down the edict granting the request. Ku said, "Not so. When dismissals are in order, the grand secretary ought naturally to carry to completion what the emperor regards as right, and each bureau ought to carry to completion what the grand secretary regards as right. But if the dismissals are not in order, the grand secretary should not carry to completion what the emperor has incorrectly decided, and the various bureaus should not carry to completion what the grand secretary has incorrectly decided." This put a stop to Wang Hsi-chüeh's excuses.

From the time of Yen Sung (1480–1565) on, the grand secretariat had usurped the authority of the six ministries. Ministers of personnel like Wang Kuo-kuang[25] and Yang Wei were treated like slaves by the chief grand secretary. With Lu Kuang-tsu[26] [in the ministry of personnel), however, good leadership began once again and Sun Lung maintained it without change. On this account, Wang Hsi-chüeh wanted to make Lo Wan-hua minister of personnel, but Ku would not agree to it.[27] Instead, Ch'en Yu-nien[28] was named. Wang said to Ku, "Something strange has been happening recently. Do you know about it?" Ku said, "What is it?" Wang replied, "What the grand secretariat considers to be right, the outside court always judges to be wrong; what the grand secretariat considers to be wrong, the outside court always judges to be right." Ku said, "Something strange can be found in the outside court too." Wang asked what that was. Ku said, "What the outside court considers to be right, the grand secretariat always judges to be wrong, and what the outside court considers to be wrong, the grand secretariat always judges to be right."[29] So they both laughed and that was the end of it!

Ku was then promoted to director of the bureau of appointments (of the ministry of personnel). He recommended many candidates to office but was unable to get them approved, while Wang Hsi-chüeh always put the blame for this on the emperor. Ku then availed himself of Wang's temporary departure from office to recommend those gentlemen who had long been neglected. His recommendations were promptly accepted, and there was nothing Wang could do about it. When the occasion arose to recommend officials to fill vacancies in the grand secretariat, Wang wanted once more to have Lo Wan-hua, while Ku once more disapproved. He and the minister of personnel (Ch'en Yu-nien) each submitted a list of seven names that they recommended. The two lists were identical. This pleased the minister of personnel very much, and he reported the concurrence. But the seven were not liked by those in power, and the recommendation to restore to office the former grand secretary Wang Chia-p'ing[30] particularly inconvenienced Wang Hsi-chüeh. So Ku was dismissed[31] and made a commoner.

In 1598 Ku began to hold meetings with his associates of the Soochow area in the Erh-ch'üan Academy. In 1604 the Tung-lin Academy was ready, and scholars from all over assembled there. It followed the rule of the White Deer Grotto Academy [of Chu Hsi].[32] Following its example, other academies arose; the Ching-cheng-t'ang[33] in Pi-ling (Kiangsu), Chih-chu-t'ang in Chin-sha (Kiangsu), Ming-tao Academy in Ching-ch'i (Kiangsu), and Wen-hsüeh Academy[34] in Yu-shan (Kiangsu). They all paid hommage to Ku, inviting him to attend their meetings.

In discussing learning, Ku regarded the world as the most important concern and used to say: "If the thoughts of the official at the capital are not of the ruler, and the thoughts of the official in the provinces are not of the people, and if [private citizens] group together in retirement to discuss questions of nature and destiny, to help one another cultivate virtue without thought of the needs of the world, then even though they have other qualities, they are not to be approved of by the gentlemen." So during the meetings of the Tung-lin scholars, discussions of particular persons [in office] and criticisms of government were made, all in the hope that those in power might hear their words and use them as a remedy. The gentlemen of the world came to regard Tung-lin as the center of "pure discussions" (ch'ing-yi), and even the court came to fear its judgments.

When Shen Yi-kuan[35] was abusing his power in government, those who attached themselves to him were especially criticized by the gentlemen. Shen found that he could not remain in office, but when he left, he brought down with him Shen Li.[36] The grand secretariat was then solely under the control of Chu Keng,[37] who was a weak man, very old already, and unable to elicit the respect he needed. So the small men schemed to summon back Wang Hsi-chüeh and had an imperial decree issued to this effect. That same day, Yü Shen-hsing, Li T'ing-chi, and Yeh Hsiang-kao[38] were also appointed to the grand secretariat. Li was the first to arrive, since he was already in the capital. Wang acted according to precedent by declining office. Ku then satirized Wang in two essays, entitled *Meng-yü* (Dream Talk) and *Mei-yü* (Waking Talk).[39] The administrative vice-commissioner of Kiangsi, Chiang Shih-ch'ang, came to Peking to offer congratulations [for some special occasion] and memorialized against Wang Hsi-chüeh's resumption of the position of grand secretary, saying that his narrow-mindedness, envy, and suspicion of others had led him to suppress others who were very gifted, and so disqualified him from returning to power. He also referred to Li T'ing-chi[40] and, generally, reflected Ku Hsien-cheng's own intentions. Yü Shen-hsing actually died on the very day he was to take up his duties (1608). Yeh Hsiang-kao, having no previous connections with the former grand secretary, was favored by the Tung-lin gentlemen and took up office.[41]

In 1608 the emperor wanted to make Ku the subdirector of the court of imperial entertainments in Nanking, but he declined the offer. Then the evaluation results were announced. Eighty to ninety per cent of the newly selected censors and supervising secretaries were partial to the Tung-lin scholars. They increased their criticisms of the grand secretaries, Wang Hsi-chüeh, Chu Keng, and Li T'ing-chi, forcing them to leave office and having almost all their followers chased out of Peking. So Yeh was left alone to hold the power in government. And the whole country put its hope in him, looking forward to the recall of the discharged officials, although all knew Yeh would not plead with the emperor on this matter, and even if he did so, he could not insist upon it.

Soon after came the controversy over the governor of Huai (Northern Kiangsu/Anhwei). This governor, Li San-ts'ai,[42] had endeared himself to the gentlemen [of Tung-lin] as a man of sublime ambition, and they wanted to see him as minister of personnel or chief censor. But the small men were especially fearful of him and attacked him with a cunning plan. Ku had long been a friend of Li San-ts'ai. But Sun P'ei-yang was recalled to become minister of personnel—the same Sun who had formerly contended with Shen Ssu-hsiao[43] regarding the dismissal of Ting Tz'u-lu over the merit evaluations (1585), an affair that had led to men dividing themselves into two factions. Ku wrote to Sun,[44] counseling him to make peace now with Shen, believing that if he would only [make a gesture], such as offering a toast to Shen, he could win him over, while those who were in league with him would then disband. He also wanted Sun to protect Li from becoming a victim of the plotters. Sun failed to understand this, while curious persons were able to make copies of Ku's letter and show it to the world. On this account, Tung-lin became more and more a target of resentment.

In 1611 after a metropolitan scrutiny, Sun sent away seven of the leaders of the Hsüan-ch'eng and K'un-shan factions.[45] The small men made much noise over this, although Ting Yüan-chien[46], of the bureau of ceremonies in the ministry of rites, supported his action and criticized those who wanted to help them. Ting was a disciple of Ku's.

Ku died in June of 1612, at age sixty-two. After his death, Yeh Hsiang-kao also resigned from the grand secretariat. Fang Ts'ung-che came to power and dismissed all censors and supervising secretaries with Tung-lin affiliations, punishing also others who took the side of Tung-lin and those who had criticized Shen Shih-hsing, Wang Chia-p'ing, Shen Li, and Chu Keng. These persons were no longer mentioned and Tung-lin itself became the outcast or taboo of the world.

At the beginning of the T'ien-ch'i reign (1621), some of the righteous men were gradually restored to office. Tsou Yüan-piao requested that the deceased worthy men be honored, so Ku Hsien-ch'eng was awarded with the posthumous title of chief minister of the court of imperial sacrifices. When the eunuch Wei Chung-hsien was misusing his powers, the small men drew up lists of names of the men of Tung-lin, called *Tung-lin tien-chiang lu, T'ien-chien lu,* and *T'ung-chih lu,*[47] to use as a reference. Indeed, all the just men of the world, whether actually affiliated with Tung-lin or not, were all considered members of the Tung-lin party. At the suggestion of the censor Shih San-wei, Ku was stripped of his posthumous honors. Only in 1629 was the title of junior vice-minister of personnel given him, together with the honorific Tuan-wen.

Ku was very worried about those scholars of recent generations who fancied the easy and feigned the natural.[48] So, to those who talked about that which required no thought or effort, he would require that they check the sources [of their insights] to see if these really represented reflections of nature and destiny and also examine the critical points of their developments to see if they had really earned these insights in their experiences. Ku was especially diligent in pointing out the difficulties inherent in Wang Yang-ming's statement regarding "the absence of good and evil," considering this to be the occasion of ruin for the world.

Wang Yang-ming had taught that:[49] "the absence of good and evil characterizes the mind-in-itself; the presence of good and evil characterizes the movement of intention; the knowing of good and evil is the task of *liang-chih;* the doing of good and avoiding of evil is the meaning of the investigation of things." But by the absence of good and evil, he simply means having no thought of good and no thought of evil and not that nature is neither good nor evil. As to the movement of intention being good or evil, he refers there to intention as thought; while knowing good and evil does not mean that the intention is moved by good and evil and so distinguishes between them, but rather knowing the love of good and the hate of evil—something that is naturally ordained by Heaven, a knowledge that is clear and without obstruction, that is, nature itself.

Wang Yang-ming had simply added the word "good" to [knowledge] (making up the term *liang-chih*) as a way of speaking of the goodness of nature. To do good and avoid evil means that what is not good is not ignored, but once known, it is not done again. *Liang-chih* is original reality *(pen-t'i)*; it is the Way of Heaven. The investigation of things is moral effort *(kung-fu)*; it is the Way of man. The former two sentences [in Yang-ming's Four Sentences] formulate these ideas in simple terms, while the latter two formulate them in subtle terms. Mind, intention, knowledge, and things are all one.

At present, Wang Yang-ming's ideas are misunderstood, and it is said that the mind that is neither good nor evil refers to nature. From this comes forth the intention that is characterized by good and evil. And from this in turn comes knowledge that distinguishes between good and evil and then the investigation of things that does good and avoids evil. And we go from the interior to the exterior, step by step, so that good and evil are seen as relating to each other, and Yang-ming can no longer distinguish himself from Kao-tzu.[50] But in fact, Wang Yang-ming frequently said that the mind-in-itself is characterized by the highest good, and that the highest good is simply the complete fulfillment of the principle of Heaven, without the tiniest speck of selfishness and, again, that *liang-chih* is the principle of Heaven. He uses the term principle of Heaven far more than once. So how can he take nature as being neither good nor evil and weaken his own teaching? Moreover, if nature-in-itself is neither good nor evil, then the knowledge of good and evil becomes superfluous, and how could he also say that *liang-chih* is the Mean of the emotions before they are manifest? For this reason the mind that is without good thoughts or evil thoughts and yet does not suppress the knowledge of good and evil continues to rest in the highest good.

Ch'ien Yi-pen[51] said, "All the talk of absence of good and evil has been clearly disposed of in recent times by Ku Hsien-ch'eng, Ku Yün-ch'eng, and Feng Ts'ung-wu and so has not spread much harm." Those who criticized Wang Yang-ming regarded this [teaching of absence of good and evil] as a major issue. They did not realize that it had actually nothing to do with Wang Yang-ming. Also, how much trouble has Wang Chi's *T'ien-ch'üan-cheng-tao lu*[52] caused Wang Yang-ming!

(*MJHA* 58:1a–5b)

NOTES

1. See Ku Hsien-ch'eng's biography by Heinrich Busch, in *DMB*, v. 1, 736–44.

2. Ku Hsüeh's dates are 1516–76.

3. For Ku Yün-ch'eng, see *MJHA*, ch. 60. His dates are 1554–1607.

4. For Han Yü (768–824), see *Hsin T'ang-shu* (New T'ang History), ch. 176. The essay is given in Han's *Complete Works, Han Ch'ang-li ch'üan-shu chiao-chu* (Taipei, 1972), ch. 1, pp. 34–35. For Ku's study of this work, see *Ku Tuan-wen kung nien-p'u* (Chronological Biography), in *Ku Tuan-wen kung yi-shu,* ed. by Ku Chen-kuan (1877), reprint edition, Appendix. The problem concerns the Chinese custom of refraining (out of respect) from mentioning the names of one's elders.

5. Probably the Sung general, Han Shih-chung (1089–1151).

6. This incident is related in detail in Ku's biography in *Tung-lin lieh-chuan,* ed. by Ch'en Ting (Taipei, Hsin-wen-fang, 1975 reprint of 1711 edition), 2:5a–b. See also his *Nien-p'u* (Chronological biography) in *Ku Tuan-wen-kung yi-shu* 2: 4a–b.

7. *Analects* 3:11. This refers to the sacrifice offered by the ruler of the dynasty to his earliest ancestor.

8. In the *Analects* 3:11, Confucius said that he did not understand the meaning of the Grand Sacrifice.

9. *Mencius* 7B:35.

10. Ku reveals here his obvious concern with things of the spirit rather than with mere scholarship.

11. Hsüeh Ying-ch'i, *hao* Fang-shan (1500–73), had studied with Wang Yang-ming's disciple Ou-yang Tê and is listed in the *MJHA* under the Nan-chung school. Huang Tsung-hsi's description of him is extremely brief; his importance appears to have been due to his relationship to Ku Hsien-ch'eng.

12. This work, originally by Sun Tuan-yi (1447–1501), was revised by Hsüeh himself. See *DMB,* v. 1, 621.

13. Like Ku himself, Wei and Liu placed first in their respective provincial examinations and so were called *chieh-yüan.*

14. Shen Shih-hsing (1534–1614), a native of Soochow (or Wu-hsien), obviously did not want to get into trouble with Chang Chü-cheng, the powerful grand secretary. They were telling him about the persons punished by Chang Chü-cheng and made ineligible for office. See *DMB,* v. 1, 737.

15. Ku's name was included in a list soliciting contributions for the sacrifice. *DMB,* v. 1, 737.

16. For the period that Ku remained at home, see *Ku Tuan-wen kung nien-p'u,* 2:15b–19b. He named his house *Hsiao-hsin chai.*

17. Wang Hsi-chüeh came from Lou-chiang, near T'ai-ts'ang, Nan Chihli. See his biography by Chou Tao-chi and Lienche Tu Fang, *DMB,* v. 2, 1376–79.

18. Huang Tsung-hsi uses the term *shih-yi,* referring to the situation in which someone has been accused by the censors but refuses to resign from office. See Heinrich Busch, "The Tung-lin Academy."

19. See *Ku Tuan-wen kung nien-p'u,* 2:20b–22b. The memorial is given in *Ching-kao ts'ang kao* (1847 ed.), 1:1a–9a.

20. Liu was the famous writer of T'ang times and Su was the great Sung poet. Chuang Ch'ang, *hao* Ting-shan (1437–99), had rebuked the emperor for preoccupation with sensual pleasures.

21. The emperor, Shen-tsung, had conferred fiefs on his three sons, an event that was regarded as an attempt to postpone the naming of the eldest as heir-apparent, as the emperor favored instead the younger son, on account of his mother, the consort Cheng Kuei-fei. For Ku's memorial, see *Ching-kao ts'ang-kao,* 1:9a–15b.

22. Sun Lung (1524–94) had as honorific the title Ch'ing-chien.

23. Chao Nan-hsing (1550–1628) had as honorific the title Chung-yi.

24. Tsou Yüan-piao had as honorific the title Chung-chih.

25. Wang was a *chin-shih* of 1544, Yang of 1547.

26. Lu Kuang-tsu, *hao* Wu-t'ai (1421–97); see *Ming-shih,* ch. 224.

27. See Ch'en Ting, ed., *Tung-lin lieh-chuan,* 2:9a. Lo was a Hanlin official and Wang's friend. So Ku feared the possible effects of Hanlin graduates dominating not only the grand secretariat, but also the ministry of personnel.

28. Ch'en Yu-mien, honorific Kung-chieh. See *Tung-lin lieh-chuan,* 2:9a.

29. *Hsiao-hsin chai cha-chi,* 17:4a–b; *Ku Tuan-wen kung yi-shu,* book 1. See also the correspondence between Ku and Wang, in *Ching-kao ts'ang-kao,* 2:12a–14a; 3:1a–2b.

30. Wang Chia-p'ing, a native of Shan-yin (1537–1604); see *DMB,* v. 2, 1377.

31. As director of the bureau, Ku was punished for what the emperor regarded as partisan nominations for the office of grand secretary.

32. *Ku Tuan-wen-kung nien-p'u,* 3:9a–b. The White Deer Grotto Academy, near Nan-k'ang, Kiangsi, was especially connected with the memory of Chu Hsi, who had served as prefect of Nan-k'ang. Chu's rules for the academy are especially famous.

33. See *Ching-cheng t'ang shang-yu,* in *Ku Tuan-wen kung yi-shu,* book 6, which gives the proceedings of the meetings.

34. *Yu-shan shang-yü* appears to refer to the proceedings of the Wen-hsüeh Academy; see *Ku Tuan-wen kung yi-shu,* book 6.

35. Shen Yi-kuan (1531–1615), a native of Yin-hsien, Chekiang, was also known after the place name Ssu-ming. See his biography of Chou Tao-chi in *DMB* (where his name is spelled Yi-kuan), v. 2, 1179–82.

36. Shen Li (1531–1615) was called Kuei-te (Honan), after his native place.

37. Chu Keng (1535–1609) was called Shan-yin (Chekiang), after his native place.

38. Yü Shen-hsing (1545–1608) was a native of Tung-o (Shantung). Li T'ing-chi was a native of Chin-chiang (Fukien) and Yeh Hsiang-kao was a native of Fu-ch'ing (Fukien).

39. They are given in *Ching-kao ts'ang-kao,* 3:2b–5b, 3:6b–8b respectively.

40. Li T'ing-chi remained in office, although he asked repeatedly to resign. See *DMB,* v. 1, 329.

41. Yeh served as the only member of the grand secretariat from 1609 to 1613, when Fang Ts'ung-che and Wu Tao-nan were appointed to it. See *DMB,* v. 2, 1568.

42. For Li San-ts'ai, see *MS,* ch. 232; *DMB,* v. 1, 847.

43. Shen Ssu-hsiao was also called Chi-ho. Ting Tz'u-lu was also called Yu-wu.

44. Ku wrote to both Yeh and Sun P'ei-yang, minister of personnel. Busch, "The Tung-lin Academy," 77.

45. The K'un faction was named after Ku T'ien-chun, from K'un-shan (Kiangsu), and the Hsüan faction was named after T'ang Pin-yin, of Hsüan-ch'eng (Anhwei).

46. Ting Yüan-chien was also called Ch'ang-ju.

47. See *DMB,* 709, for a discussion of the lists of Tung-lin partisans.

48. See *Ku Tuan-wen-kung yi-shu,* book 5. An abridged version of Ku's ideas is given in *MJHA,* ch. 58.

49. *Ch'uan-hsi lu,* part 3; English translation in W. T. Chan, *Instructions for Practical Living,* 243. The translation here is from the Chinese original. Ku's

major discussions of Wang Yang-ming are given in *Ku Tuan-wen kung yi-shu,*
book 2 and book 14.

50. Kao-tzu had argued with Mencius over human nature and maintained
that it was neither good nor bad. (*Mencius* 6A:1–4, 6.)

51. Ch'ien Yi-pen, *hao* Ch'i-hsin (1539–1610). *MJHA* 59:1a–2a.

52. Huang Tsung-hsi repeats his assertion that Wang Chi had misreported
Wang Yang-ming's teaching regarding the Four Sentences.

Kao P'an-lung

Kao P'an-lung, *tzu* Ts'un-chih, *hao* Ching-yi (1562–1626),[1] was a
native of Wuhsi in Ch'ang-chou (Nan Chihli). He received his *chin-shih*
degree in 1589. However, on account of the death of his foster father, he
was assigned a position as an emissary only at the conclusion of the
mourning period. At that time, the assistant surveillance commissioner
of Szechuan, Chang Shih-ch'e, submitted a memorial saying, "The
learning of Ch'eng Yi and Chu Hsi is incompatible with the doctrine of
sincerity of intention[2] and has ruined the mores of the Sung dynasty."
He presented his own work, the *Ta-hsüeh ku-pen ch'u-yi* (First Meaning of
the Old Version of the *Great Learning*), desiring its promulgation
throughout the realm in order to correct the old ways of teaching texts.
Kao submitted a memorial[3] arguing against him and was able to stop its
distribution.

When Wang Hsi-chüeh was recalled to become grand secretary, he
dismissed sixty or more persons who disagreed with him. But because
Chao Yung-hsien[4] had a high reputation, Wang suggested to Cheng
Ts'ai and Yang Ying-su that they accuse Chao of having broken off the
engagement of his daughter and so have him dismissed.[5] Kao accused
Wang of pretending to be sincere in his voice and laughter but of being
unable to overcome his selfish desires in the lowliness of his scheming
mind, doing good [to his friends] and evil [to his enemies].[6] Kao was
demoted to the position of supernumerary jail warden in Chieh-yang
(Kwangtung) but returned home after only half a year.[7] Together with
Ku Hsien-ch'eng, he then restored the Tung-lin Academy and taught
there. For three days of every month, several hundred persons would
assemble there from near and far. They considered it their task to bring
order to the world, basing this on clear distinctions between right and
wrong. The small men heard of them and hated them and labeled all
those at court who did any righteous deed or expressed any righteous
opinion as members of the Tung-lin party.

In the first year of T'ien-ch'i (1621), after Kao had already been in
retirement for twenty-eight years,[8] he was raised to the position of assistant minister of the court of imperial entertainment and then promoted
to acting minister of the same court. The minister of rites, Sun Shen-
hsing, understanding the intended meaning of the *Spring-Autumn An-*

nals,[9] brought accusations against the former grand secretary Fang Ts'ung-che. At the conference of high officials, Kao concurred with Sun and supported his position.[10] He was transferred to the court of the imperial stud. He petitioned, got a travel order, and returned home [at the beginning of 1623].

In 1624, while still with his family, he was raised to vice-minister of justice at a time when the corrupt Wei Chung-hsien was disrupting the government. Kao addressed his friends, saying: "For the affairs of today one cannot simply use a cathartic; only the existence of harmony between superiors and inferiors will diminish the poison." What he said was very similar to what my deceased father, Huang Tsun-su,[11] had said. On the occasion of a vacancy in the censor-in-chief's position, Huang Tsun-su submitted a memorial urging the immediate selection of the official and care in making the appointment. His intention was to recommend Kao. Kao was promoted to left censor-in-chief, in which post he was responsible for the investigation of the covetous censor Ts'ui Ch'eng-hsiu, who, in accordance with the law, was banished to the frontier.[12] In a short time, however, the corrupt Wei [Chung-hsien] plotted with Wei Kuang-wei,[13] taking the opportunity, in consultation on the selection of the governor for Shansi, to have so many expelled that it was like emptying the offices at court. Kao subsequenlty returned home.

The following year the *San-ch'ao yao-tien*[14] was completed and Kao was mentioned in the case of the removal of the imperial consort to another palace.[15] His name was deleted from the register, and he was made a commoner. His Tung-lin Academy was also destroyed.

In 1626, arrests were again made of those belonging to the heterodox Tung-lin party, seven persons in all, including Kao and Huang Tsun-su. Before the guardsmen of the imperial bodyguard arrived, Kao composed his last memorial in the middle of the night and then drowned himself in a pond. This was the seventeenth day of the third month (April 14), and he was sixty-four years old. His memorial said: "Although my name has been deleted from the register, I was formerly a high minister. I therefore do obeisance to the emperor and go the way of Ch'ü Yüan.[16] I have not yet repaid the emperor's kindness but hope to do so in the hereafter."[17]

In 1628, the corrupt Ts'ui Ch'eng-hsiu was put to death and Kao was given the posthumous titles of guardian of the heir-apparent and minister of war. Sacrifice was offered at his burial site, ranks were given to his sons, and the honorific title Chung-hsien was conferred upon him.

His own account of the stages of his learning is the following:[18]

"At age twenty-five, when I heard Magistrate Li Fu-yang discuss learning with Ku Hsien-ch'eng, I resolved to pursue the quest of sagehood.[19] I thought that there must be a way of becoming a sage, although

I was yet unacquainted with the methods. I had read the *Ta-hsüeh huo-wen,* where Master Chu said the essential disposition for entering the Way was reverence.[20] So I exerted all my efforts in keeping recollected, attentive, and respectful, containing the mind within the square inch of space in my chest.[21] But I was aware only of oppressing my vital forces and restraining my person and felt quite uncomfortable. And whenever I let things go, I became distracted as before. A long time passed before I could find any remedy. Then I suddenly remembered that Master Ch'eng had said, 'The mind must be retained within the bodily frame *(ch'iang-tzu).'*[22] I did not know what the term *ch'iang-tzu* referred to. Was it really that square inch of space or not? I searched without success for an explanation and then by chance found it in the *Elementary Learning:* 'The bodily frame refers simply to the body.'[23] I was very happy and relieved that the mind was not just contained in a square inch, but present in the entire body. Then Lo Mao-chung[24] of Chiang-yu (Kiangsi) came and spoke of Li Ts'ai's teaching that self-cultivation was the foundation of learning. It was in line with what I took to be my own guide. I was happier and had no doubts. During this period I spent all my effort working on 'knowing the root.'[25] This caused both body and mind to progress together and word and deed to be without error. After passing the examination of the *chi-ch'ou* year (1589), I was even more aware of making progress in this sense. When I found myself in mourning,[26] I studied the *Book of Rites* and the *Book of Changes.*

"In the *jen-ch'en* year (1592) I presented myself for appointment as a successful candidate.[27] Since, in my life, the sense of shame weighed most, I swore when I received my appointment: 'I have not yet perceived anything of the Way. I shall simply act upon my solitary knowledge *(tu-chih).* Right and wrong, good and bad: what follows without my having acted comes from Heaven.' In examining my life, I found it very near to this ideal. With limited insight into the mind, I vainly thought that whenever I saw what was righteous, I would also do it. In winter, I traveled to the Chao-t'ien Temple (Peking) to exercise myself in ceremonial rules. While meditating in a monk's room and searching for [my mind]-in-itself *(pen-t'i),* I thought suddenly of the sentence 'He does away with what is perverse and preserves his integrity.'[28] I felt immediately that there was nothing perverse in me, that all in me was sincere, and that there was no further need of seeking sincerity. For a moment I felt rapturous, as if casting off all fetters.

"In the year *kuei-ssu* (1593), I was banished for having spoken out on certain affairs. But this did not disturb my thoughts. After returning home I tasted the ways of the world and my mind became once more agitated. In the autumn of 1594 I headed for Chieh-yang (Kwangtung). I realized that principle and desire were waging battle within and felt quite uneasy. In Hangchow (Chekiang), I talked for several days with

Lu Tsui-ming and Wu Tzu-wang.[29] One day Lu suddenly asked, 'What is the *pen-t'i* like?' I answered vaguely, 'Without sound or smell.'[30] But this came only from my mouth and ears, not from a true understanding [of the heart]. The night before I crossed over the [Ch'ien-t'ang] river, the moonlight was very clear. I sat beside the Liu-ho pagoda. The mountains and river were bright and alluring. My friends urged me to drink more. In this most agreeable of times I suddenly felt unhappy, as if something were amiss. I tried to arouse some joy, but its spirit did not come. Late in the night when the others had gone, I went on board the boat and alerted them with this question: 'How is it today, that the landscape was one way and yet my feelings were another way?' After making a thorough investigation, I realized that I had seen nothing of the Way, and my mind and body had not been affected by it. So I resolved firmly, 'If I don't grasp it this time, my life is in vain.'

"The next day, I arranged thick mats in the boat and set up a strict daily order. For one half of the day I practiced meditation, while for the other half I read books. Whenever I felt ill at ease during meditation, I would just follow all the instruction of Ch'eng Yi and Chu Hsi—in all that concerns sincerity, reverence, concentrating on tranquility, observing joy, anger, sorrow, and pleasure before they arise, sitting in silence to purify the mind, realizing in myself the heavenly principle. I practiced these points one by one. Whether I was standing or sitting, eating or resting, I would not forget these thoughts. At night I did not undress and only fell asleep when dead tired. Upon waking I returned to meditating, repeating and alternating these various practices. When the *ch'i* of the mind was clear and peaceful, it seemed to fill all Heaven and Earth. But such consciousness did not last.

"For the whole two months of the journey, there was fortunately no distracting involvement with people. The landscape was beautiful; my servant and I stayed together in peace and solitude. In the evenings I ordered a little wine, stopped the boat before a green mountain and let it drift near a jade-like stream. I sat for a time on a large rock. The whispering of the water, the harmony of the birds, the lush trees, and tall bamboos, all these things pleased my mind, although it remained unattached to them. I passed by T'ing-chou (Fukien) and traveled further by land until I reached an inn. It had a small loft that faced the mountains, with a rushing stream behind. I climbed up there and was very pleased.[31] Quite by chance I saw a saying by Ch'eng Hao, 'Amid a hundred officials, a myriad affairs, and a hundred thousand weapons, with water as drink and a bent arm as a pillow, I can still be joyful.[32] The myriad changes are all man-made; in reality there is not a thing.'[33] Suddenly I realized the sense of these words and said, 'That is it. In reality there is not a thing!' And as this one thought lingered, all entanglements were broken off. It was suddenly as though a load of one hundred pounds had instantly dropped off, as though a flash of lightning had penetrated the body and pierced the intelligence, and I merged in harmony with the Great Transformation[34] until there was no differentiation between Heaven and man, the outer and the inner. At this point I realized that the Six Points[35] were all my mind, the bodily frame was their field, and the square inch of space was their original seat. But in terms of their spiritual and luminous character, there was actually no location one could speak of. I had always despised scholars who discussed enlightenment with great flourish. So now I could regard this experience as something quite natural, while knowing that from then on, I would have to apply my own efforts in a certain direction.

"In the spring of *yi-wei* (1595), as I was returning from Chieh-yang, I read both Buddhist and Taoist writings and saw how very nuanced were the differences between the Buddhists and the Confucian sages. But I thought that Confucian teachings already possessed those subtle points the Buddhist teachings have, that nothing goes beyond the two words *wu-chi* (limitless).[36] And earlier Confucian scholars had already pointed out the defects of the Buddhists; everything can be summed up in the words *wu-li* (without principle). Having studied the two schools [of Buddhism and Taoism], I appreciated all the more the Confucian teachings; without the Way of the sages there would be no way of nourishing the people. Even the followers of the other two schools depended on this Way for food, drink, and lodging, although they were not conscious of the fact.

"In the year *wu-hsü* (1598) I built the Water Dwelling[37] with the intention of practicing meditation and studying there. For during the years following *pin-sheng* (1596), I lost my parents, moved about, and saw my children marry.[38] Those years allowed me no peace. In the midst of these activities, I tried to continue my former discipline but was only too aware of the difficulties of transforming our physical endowment. In *chia-ch'en* (1604) Ku Hsien-ch'eng first set up the Tung-lin Academy. I was able to benefit from discussions with friends. As I slowly observed, I could do nothing without settling down peacefully and meditating. Everyone had different problems. Great sages and worthies must have a great spiritual capacity; they can concentrate on tranquility in their ordinary lives. But the scholar whose spirit is deficient and whose physical endowment is unstable needs several dozen years of effort in tranquility before he can achieve some depth. The worst is a lack of basic education during one's youth.[39] Worldly habits contaminate us and are difficult to root out. Only by burying one's head in study, allowing principle and righteousness to harmonize, and transforming one's vulgar flesh and bone, purifying the spirit in still meditation, can one cause worldly delusions to disperse. It is then possible to strengthen the right mind and the right *ch'i*. With my most inferior endowment, what use could any expansive insight be in the absence of exertion? Fortunately, ever since I have come into my own [by enlightenment],[40] I can follow a plan [to improve myself] and at once find the thing there.

"In the year *pin-wu* (1606) I came truly to believe in Mencius' doctrine that human nature is good. This nature transcends past and present, sages and ordinary men. It is one in Heaven, Earth, and man. But only those with the highest grade [of nature], which is immaculate and without any obscuration, can reach faith. Those with the next grade are entirely dependent upon the effort of learning.[41] If a single speck of dust intervenes, the goal might as well be ten thousand *li* away. That is why Mencius prescribes 'a medicine that makes people dizzy.'[42]

"In the year *ting-wei* (1607) I came truly to believe in Master Ch'eng's words, that 'hawks fly and fishes swim'[43] and also, that 'one must always do something.'[44] What is called nature is entirely spontaneous and not of human effort. 'Hawks fly and fishes swim,' but who caused them to do so? 'Do not forget it, but do not assist it.'[45] This is especially an admonition to students. But in the case of true creativity *(chen-chi)* that, [like water], flows and spreads, in the past and the present, with no moment of rest, what can be forgotten or assisted? One must therefore always do something, as, for example, in growing grain. The roots, sprouts, flowers, and fruit change and transform on their own, yet they are cared for, watered, and cultivated, without undue force. Should one leave everything to the natural, nothing will get done. And without change or transformation, there will not even be anything natural.

"In the year *hsin-hai* (1611) I came truly to believe in the *Great Learning* and its doctrine of 'knowing the root.' In *jen-tzu* (1612) I came truly to believe the teaching in the *Doctrine of the Mean*. Most surely words cannot describe this Way. Master Ch'eng called it the heavenly principle *(T'ien-li)*. Wang Yang-ming called it *liang-chih*. But neither designation is as good as the words *chung* (the Mean, centrality) and *yung* (normality). 'Centrality' is what is appropriate and fitting; 'normality' is what is ordinary and dependable. If a slight transgression occurs, nothing is subtle or fitting. If a slight affectation takes place, nothing is ordinary or dependable. This is the way with *pen-t'i*, and this is the way with *kung-fu* (effort). The sage cannot fathom the limits of Heaven and Earth; how much less, people like ourselves? How can we put a limit to our efforts? We should exercise [moral] effort, observe honor in human relationships, speak with care, and act intelligently with all caution, until the day of death."

Kao's achievements prior to 1614 were such as he has described. From this point on, his cultivation was increasingly refined and his efforts careful. At the pinnacle of his learning, he observed, "The mind is like a great void. It is originally beyond life and death."[46] My teacher

Liu Tsung-chou said, "Kao's mind was one with the Way. He lived to fulfill the Way; he died to fulfill the Way. That is the meaning of 'transcending life and death.' It is not what the Buddhists call transcending life and death (i.e., *nirvāṇa,* which transcends *saṃsāra*)."[47]

Kao's teaching, based on that of Ch'eng Yi and Chu Hsi, considers the investigation of things as essential. And yet investigating things meant for Ch'eng Yi and Chu Hsi that mind is the master of each person, while principle is dispersed in all things. Preserving mind and discovering principle must both proceed together. But Kao has said, "Only as one knows how to search within oneself, is it truly investigation of things."[48] In a sense this is close to what Yang Shih said, "If I reflect upon myself in sincerity, there is nothing in the world that is not close to me."[49] This is, of course, different from the teachings of Ch'eng Yi and Chu Hsi. Kao has also said, "When the human mind is made manifest, the heavenly principle is discovered and 'Only in reaching the point of no delusion does the principle become profound.' "[50] This lends some support to Wang Yang-ming's discussion of the extension of *liang-chih.* Yet he said that for those who discuss *liang-chih* the extension of knowledge does not reside in investigating things. Thus the function of the spiritual faculty is mostly in the consciousness of feelings and is not natural like the manifestation of the heavenly principle. This is indeed far from the highest good.

Our kind of investigation of things is the investigation of the highest good. We consider the good, not knowledge, to be fundamental. Now the good has neither form nor shape. It also refers not to any particular good, which, when followed upon, known to the utmost, becomes the highest good. To extend *liang-chih* is precisely to rest in the highest good. How can one say that they are far apart from each other? In sum, the extension of knowlege and the investigation of things cannot be spoken of in terms of what is prior and what is posterior. The investigation of things clearly explains the word "extend." It occurs in the midst of extending knowledge. There is nothing that can be extended but not also investigated. If Kao speaks of an extension of knowledge that is not an investigation of things, then what thing is being extended? If he means that exhausting principles externally in affairs and things is also investigation of things, then it is possible to speak of Yang-ming's extension of knowledge as not residing in the investigation of things. And yet if it is as Kao says, "When the human mind is manifest, it is this principle of Heaven,"[51] then Yang-ming's extension of knowledge is clearly also the investigation of things. Kao's view of things is basically not incorrect. He wanted especially to differentiate himself from Wang Yang-ming, but in so doing, he only created some contradictions for himself.

NOTES

1. See Kao's biography by Charles Hucker, *DMB*, v. 1, 701–10. See also his Chronological Biography *(Nien-p'u),* compiled by Hua Yün-ch'eng, in *Kao-tzu yi-shu* (abbrev. as *KTYS*) (Surviving Works of Kao P'an-lung), 1746 ed. See also his *hsing-chuang* by Yeh Mao-ts'ai, in *Tung-lin shu-yüan chih* (Record of the Tung-lin Academy), ed. by Hsü Hsien, 1881 edition, 7:47b–59b. Kao was one of seven sons and was given in adoption to a childless paternal granduncle. On his childhood, see *Nien-p'u,* 1b, *hsing-chuang,* 48a.

2. "Sincerity of intention" is a teaching of the *Great Learning.*

3. The memorial is given in part in Kao's biography, *MS,* ch. 243. It is given in full in *KTYS* 7:1a–8b. The *Ta-hsüeh ku-pen ch'u-yi,* mentioned earlier, is in *KTYS.*

4. See his biography by L. C. Goodrich and C. N. Tay, *DMB,* v. 1, 138–40.

5. The affair grew out of the triennial personnel evaluation of metropolitan officials (1593), when the so-called pure critics *(ch'ing-yi)* had control of the scrutiny process and sought to eliminate unworthy officials. But the grand secretary succeeded in dismissing a number of these pure critics from office.

6. *Nien-p'u,* 7b. Allusion to the *Book of History.* See J. Legge, trans., *The Chinese Classics,* v. 3, 331.

7. *MS,* ch. 243.

8. Kao retired from office, after returning home from Chieh-yang, on account of his parents' death in 1596. *Nien-p'u,* 11b.

9. Sun used the *Spring-Autumn Annals* as a basis for judging the guilt of Fang Ts'ung-che. See *MS,* ch. 243. See also Sun's biography in this volume.

10. Fang was to be punished for his purported role in the Case of the Red Pill, in which Emperor Kuang-tsung died after being administered the pills as medicine. See *DMB,* v. 1, 705, *ECCP* 176, and Sun's biography in this volume.

11. See Huang's biography in this volume.

12. Ts'ui would plead his case with Wei Chung-hsien, asking to become his adopted son. *MS,* ch. 243.

13. Wei Kuang-wei, see *MS,* ch. 306.

14. An anti-Tung-lin publication by Wei Chung-hsien's sympathizers, which condemned the Tung-lin position on the "three cases" surrounding Emperor Kuang-tsung's succession to the throne and his demise. See *DMB,* v. 1, 705–7.

15. The case of the removal from the palace concerned the young Emperor Hsi-tsung, who succeeded Emperor Kuang-tsung, but who appeared to be in danger of being isolated from the ministers by a certain palace lady, Madame Li, and the eunuchs. The pure critics wanted him independent of their custody and asked to have Madame Li removed from his palace. *DMB,* v. 1, 705–6.

16. The Warring States poet who drowned himself.

17. *Nien-p'u,* 29b.

18. What follows is from the *K'un-hsüeh chi* (On the Difficulties of Learning), *KTYS* 3:13b–17b. The title alludes to *Analects* 16:9. Chinese cyclical dates are used in the original text. For a translation and study of this text, see R. L. Taylor, "The Centered Self: Religious Autobiography in the Neo-Confucian Tradition," *History of Religions* 17 (1978), 266–83.

19. The first sentence alludes to *Analects* 2:4, where Confucius says of himself that he set his mind on learning at age fifteen. Kao compares himself unfavorably, since he was already twenty-five. Li Fu-yang, *tzu* Yüan-chung.

20. Kao appears to have paraphrased the text from *Ta-hsüeh huo-wen.* This passage is also found in Chu Hsi's *Chin-ssu lu,* where it is assigned to Ch'eng Yi. See W. T. Chan, *Reflections on Things at Hand* (New York, 1967), 133.

21. "A square inch of space" refers to the heart.

22. In the *Chin-ssu lu,* Ch'eng Yi is credited with the saying (Chan, *Reflections,* 137); in the *Elementary Learning (Hsiao-hsüeh)* it is assigned to Ch'eng Hao. See Chu Hsi's *Hsiao-hsüeh chi-chu,* SPPY ed., 5:17a.

23. *Hsiao-hsüeh chi-chu,* 5:17a. Kao quotes the passage to explain the term *ch'iang-tzu* (physical frame).

24. For Lo, see *KTYS* 878A:63b–64b.

25. "Knowing the root" is a concept derived from the *Great Learning.*

26. Kao mourning his foster parents: his foster mother died in 1584, his foster father in 1589. See *Nien-p'u,* 3b, 4b–5a, in *KTYS.*

27. Kao presented himself in 1592 after the mourning for his foster parents. Kao was appointed an emissary in 1592. *Nien-p'u,* 5b, in *KTYS.*

28. The passage comes from the *Book of Changes.* See *Chou-yi cheng-yi,* SPPY ed., v. 1, 2b.

29. Lu Ts'ui-ming, *hao* Ku-ch'iao, a follower of Ch'en Hsien-chang. Wu Chih-yüan, *hao* Tzu-wang. These names are given in the *MJHA* text itself.

30. Allusion to the *Doctrine of the Mean,* ch. 33, which quotes from the *Book of Poetry,* III. i., Ode I, stanza 7. See J. Legge, trans., *The Chinese Classics,* v. 1, 433. The Chinese words *wu-sheng wu-ch'ou* (without sound or smell) referred originally to the imperceptible working of Heaven in the overthrow of the Shang dynasty but came to represent Heaven, or perfect virtue, or the Absolute, especially for the Neo-Confucian philosophers.

31. In the *K'un-hsüeh chi* of the 1876 edition of the *KTYS,* a phrase is found that is not in the present edition: "In my hand I held a book of the two Ch'eng brothers." *KTYS* 3:15b.

32. The interior quotation is from *Analects* 7:15. Legge translates the passage: "With coarse rice to eat, with water to drink, and my bent arm for a pillow I have still joy in the midst of these things. . . " Legge, *The Chinese Classics,* v. 2, 200.

33. This saying is found in *ECCS* 6:3a.

34. The Great Transformation is the cycle of increase and decrease of *yin* and *yang* in the four seasons.

35. The Six Points are the four compass points combined with the zenith and nadir.

36. The Non-Ultimate is the beginning point of the "Diagram of the Great Ultimate," Chou Tun-yi's cosmogony.

37. Two short writings by Kao concern the Water Dwelling: *Shui-chu chi* (Recollections of the Water Dwelling), *KTYS* 10:48b–49a and *K'o-lou chi* (Recollections of the Suitable Loft), *KTYS* 10:49a–50a.

38. According to the *Nien-p'u* (in *KTYS*), Kao's mother and father were both seventy years old in 1596. His father died in the third month and his mother died in the seventh month of that year (*Nien-p'u,* 11b).

39. This may well refer to the *Elementary Learning* of Chu Hsi.

40. The phrase "ever since I have come into my own" may refer to Kao's enlightenment experience. If this is the case, Kao would seem to imply that a certain level of understanding, which could be returned to, resulted from the experience.

41. An allusion to *Analects* 16:9.

42. *Mencius* 3A: 1. Mencius is referring to the *Book of History,* IV, 8, 1, 8. See J. Legge, trans., *The Chinese Classics,* v. 3, 252.

43. *Locus classicus* of the phrase seems to be the *Book of Poetry,* III, I, 5 (Mao no. 239). See J. Legge, trans., *The Chinese Classics,* v. 4, *The She King* or *Book of*

Poetry, p. 445. The *Doctrine of the Mean* quotes this ode. J. Legge, trans., *The Chinese Classics*, v. 1, 391–93.
  44. *Mencius* 2A:2.
  45. *Mencius* 2A:2. The reference here is to *wu-wang wu-chu*.
  46. *Nien-p'u*, 28b.
  47. See the preface to the Chi-shan school in this volume.
  48. *KTYS* 1:1b.
  49. *Mencius* 7A:4.
  50. *KTYS* 1:5a.
  51. Ibid.

Sun Shen-hsing

Sun Shen-hsing, *tzu* Wen-ssu, *hao* Ch'i-ao (1565–1636),[1] was a native of Wu-chin in Ch'ang-chou Prefecture (Nan Chihli). In 1595 he placed third in the *chin-shih* examination and was appointed a second grade Hanlin compiler. When Shen Yi-kuan made use of the case of the subversive tract and manipulated it into a cause célèbre,[2] Sun argued with him on the basis of national polity *(kuo-t'i)*. After a few transfers and promotions he became vice-minister of rites. In 1613 he became acting head of the ministry.

At the time, it had been announced that the prince of Fu[3] was to proceed to his fief the following spring. But Emperor Shen-tsung was making things difficult for the officials concerned by granting the prince [an extravagant] forty thousand *ch'ing*[4] of farm land. Sun said that during the reigns of the emperor's ancestors there had never been a grant that exceeded one thousand *ch'ing*. Besides, the emperor's own younger brother, the prince of Lu,[5] had been granted less. How could the emperor grant more to his [younger] son than to his younger brother? [The prince's mother,] Lady Cheng, the imperial consort, was also begging the empress dowager to stop the prince from leaving, saying that the dowager would have her seventieth birthday the following year, and the prince should remain at the capital to celebrate it. So the emperor issued instructions to change the date of the prince's departure. But even the man in the street knew that the prince of Fu would be unwilling to leave and would only multiply excuses to silence the mouths of those who might speak out.

Sun told the grand secretary, Yeh Hsiang-kao: "If this matter is not properly settled, you and I must run risk of death." Yeh asked, "Why so?" Sun said, "How else would we fulfill our responsibility, except by dying?" So Yeh convened the nine high officials of the outer court to submit a joint appeal, and they waited in the court twenty days for the emperor's reply. Sun's howling and weeping reached the emperor. Meanwhile Yeh [on receiving a secret request from the emperor] resealed and returned the emperor's personally written note. Emperor Shen-tsung was moved [to change his mind and comply with them]. On

December 31, he ordered Lady Cheng to yield a certain document that was in her possession. She refused to do so, and the order was repeated the following day. That evening she could no longer withhold it and gave it up. The document was one in which Emperor Shen-tsung, cutting his own arm in a vow of lasting devotion, promised to make their son, the prince of Fu, heir to the throne. The document was then burned in front of the [ancestral] spirits. Six days later, the emperor issued a decree setting a definite date for the prince's departure to his hereditary fief.

While Sun was acting head of rites, he submitted a memorial on the matter in which the prince of Tai replaced his elder son with a younger one as heir.[6] He also requested changes to correct the corrupt practices revealed in the *chin-shih* examination of 1610, reported in the punishments of T'ang Pin-yin and Nan Shih-chung,[7] and saw to it that the Sung scholars Lo Ts'ung-yen and Li T'ung[8] began to receive sacrifices in the Confucian Temple. In the case of the descendants of the first prince of Ch'u,[9] he also recommended the release of the twenty-three persons imprisoned in the high-walled enclosure and the twenty-two others held under house arrest. All these actions he had performed in office. Then, in the eighth month of 1614, he returned to his native place. The small men in government had used the sexennial examination of the central government officials to attack him [and had him dismissed].

At the beginning of the T'ien-ch'i period (1612), Sun was summoned to become the minister of rites. At once he began by charging those involved in the Case of the Red Pill [that allegedly killed Emperor Kuang-tung in 1620].[10] His memorial attacking the corrupt grand secretary Fang Ts'ung-che [who had not punished the culprits] was sent to the nine ministers, the supervising secretaries, and the censors for deliberation. They decided to propose to remove Fang from office and to banish [the court physician] Li K'o-shao.[11] Not long after, Sun resigned and returned home.[12] But the traitor eunuch (Wei Chung-hsien) went ahead and made a great case out of the earlier incidents [involving the men of Tung-lin] and compiled a list of those of them whom he considered to have been at fault.[13] In the Case of the Attack with a Club,[14] Wang Chih-ts'ai[15] was accused of having been a chief culprit. In the Case of the Removal from the Palace,[16] Yang Lien[17] and Tso Kuang-tou[18] headed the list of the accused. In the Case of the Red Pill, Sun headed the list of the accused. The persons implicated in the first two cases died in prison. Sun was to be banished to Ning-hsia (Kansu), but the timely succession of Emperor Ssu-tung (1627) kept him from going. When the reign name was changed to Ch'ung-chen (1628), he was restored to his former rank and appointed an associate director of imperial instruction, an offer he did not accept. Eight years later, after a decree of selection for offices in the Grand Secretariat, Sun was summoned to Peking together with Liu Tsung-chou and Lin Han[19]. Shortly after he reached the capital, he died at age seventy-one and was posthumously awarded the title Wen-chieh.

Sun's learning first began with Buddhism. Together with the monk Ching-feng[20] from the T'ien-ning monastery, he examined many riddles *(kung-an),* and there was none that he failed to comprehend. Whenever he found himself in troublesome circumstances, the substance of his mind would suddenly manifest itself. But even then, he did not consider it an accomplishment and said that one could enter the Confucian way through enlightenment. For if a gentleman were to spend his entire day in study, inquiry, thought, discernment, and practice, he would be exercising caution and vigilance in solitude, and where could he get the leisure to seek these indeterminate experiences of the no-mind *(wu-hsin)?* That was why those who forsook study and inquiry, thought, discernment, and practice, and looked for another way of maintaining oneself in quietude and examining oneself in action, for the sake of cultivating equilibrium and harmony, had always drifted into the teachings of Ch'an Buddhism.

Sun brought forth several points that Confucians before him had not developed. [First,] in discussing Heaven and destiny *(t'ien-ming),*[21] people had said that besides moral destiny (literally, [destiny of] moral principles), there was also physical destiny (literally, destiny shaped by material force, *ch'i,* and cyclical change, *yün*), and these were intermingled but not in mutual accord. From this came [the distinction between] moral nature and physical nature. From this also came [the distinction between] moral mind and physical mind-and-heart (literally, "mind of physical form").[22] All three (destiny, nature, mind) are simply different designations of the same problem. But Sun referred to Mencius: "Although Heaven is so high and the stars are so distant, if we are to seek the former instances, we may be able to calculate the solstice of a thousand years ahead, without stirring from our seats."[23] [So he reflected that] the material force *(ch'i)* of Heaven and the movement of cyclical change *(yün)* are not in disaccord. And why should destiny and man, which stand between *ch'i* and *yün,* show any disaccord? True, in the actual flow of *ch'i,* in its coming and going, there are certain to be excesses and shortages. Thus heat and cold cannot but get mixed; order and disorder cannot but alternate. Of course, when the human mind's worldly fancies and desires had reached the crossroad between life and death, gain and loss, one can do nothing else but to consign all to cyclical change (i.e., chance) and destiny. How could there be then any principle of concurrence? However, Heaven rewards good and punishes evil, and the reason for this is [the principle of] highest good. It is so for the length of one breath. It is so for all eternity. Otherwise, the principle of life would become extinct. This true ruling principle *(chu-tsai)* in the midst of myriad discords is what Sun calls concord.

[Second,] Sun says that not only is human nature good, but also physical endowment *(ch'i-chih)* is good. He illustrates this with the example of barley. The intent to grow is the nature of barley. As this intention becomes silently pervasive, it can be compared to material force *(ch'i)*. As this intention manifests itself and assumes form, it can be compared to physical endowment. And how can one take a single grain of barley and divide it into two separate parts, called nature good and physical endowment bad? True, physical endowments are unequal. People are born either dull or bright, transparent or opaque, set upon two separate paths. So how can physical endowment be said to be always good? Yet, even the most foolish and opaque persons have usually known enough to love their parents and respect their elders. The good that is subsequent to their natures persists in spite of their dullness or opaqueness, proving that physical endowment in itself is not all bad. That is why Sun regards it as good.

[Third,] Sun also states that the mind of man and the mind of Tao are not two kinds of mind. It is mind that makes man act as man, and it is the Tao that makes mind act as mind. At the core of the human mind is this one mind of Tao, [a mind] of moral principles. It is not as though there were another kind of human mind, made of matter and form, outside the mind of Tao. But since people of later generations consider that they have a physical nature, they take whatever is manifest through this as the physical mind or heart. They consider the mind as possessing only consciousness, and only when moral principles fill this consciousness can it be called the mind of Tao. So it would be necessary to study exhaustively these principles of Heaven and Earth and all things. It is not enough just to follow one's own mind. If this were the case, then man would be born only with consciousness and not moral principles. There would be only the human mind and no mind of Tao. And even if this were not so, these two minds are born indistinguishable from each other. Judging from this, Sun's opinion would be preferable.

These three opinions had flooded the world for a long time,[24] but with Sun, clouds and mist began to part. He has truly done well by Mencius. The disciples of Wang Yang-ming—except for Nieh Pao and Lo Hung-hsien—consider the Mean of the emotions before they are aroused as equivalent to the harmony of the emotions after they are manifest. They suggest that moral effort consists only of seeking to attain this harmony, but they consider words inadequate to express the Tao, and the practice of mind itself insufficient for conducting one's Way. They call this the Mean [of consciousness] and say that little effort is possible on this point. So they simply instruct people to make some effort to attain harmony, saying that it acts naturally like spilled ink writing by itself. Sun states, however, that only when we regard pleasure, anger, sorrow, and joy can we find what is yet unmanifest. Yet one's ordinary everyday life is not necessarily all pleasure or anger, all sorrow or joy. The time that emotions are manifest is brief, while the time that they are not manifest is longer. The clearer becomes the mind-in-itself, the more effective are moral efforts. People always regarded humanity, righteousness, propriety, and wisdom as nature, and commiseration, shame, deference, and right and wrong as the emotions.

Li Ts'ai, for example, tries in his *Tao-hsing pien* to investigate the [Mean of the] unmanifest in terms of the manifest emotions. He said that one should not take the mind of commiseration, shame, deference, or right or wrong and yet pass over nature. He regarded himself to have hold of the essential, but did not know that only with commiseration does one have the beginning of the name humanity; only with shame does one have the beginning of the name righteousness; only with deference does one have the beginning of the name propriety; and only with a sense of right and wrong does one have the beginning of the name wisdom. Leaving commiseration, shame, deference, and right and wrong, the path of the mind and action will be severed and there will be no way to reach after nature. Sun thus said that desiring men to recognize their minds, Mencius selected the mind of commiseration as a beginning for humanity. Thus it is not that humanity was at the center while the mind of commiseration was simply its beginning. In such fashion we know without argument that Li's discussion is inaccurate.

The Master Liu [Tsung-chou] said: "Recently I looked at Sun Shen-hsing's writings; I think he has improved his arguments. He said that if from youth to old age there is not a single affair that is not in rapport with propriety, then one can nourish the 'overflowing' nature.[25] If there is an impropriety, then one departs from it. Actually Ku Hsien-ch'eng first established the source of Tung-lin learning. Kao P'an-lung refined it. Sun Sheng-hsing came along and opened another horizon."

(MJHA 59:6b–8a)

NOTES

1. See Sun's biography in *MS,* ch. 243, 591c–92a.
2. For Shen Yi-kuan, see *MS,* ch. 218, *DMB,* v. 2, 1179 (name spelled as I-kuan). In 1603, Shen and others had been against the emperor's eldest son and in favor of his younger brother, son of the imperial consort, Lady Cheng.
3. Chu Ch'ang-hsün (1586–1641), third son of Emperor Shen-tsung by his consort, Lady Cheng, was named prince of Fu in 1601. But he remained in the capital, and there was fear that he posed a potential threat to the heir-apparent, his eldest brother. After great pressure was exerted, the emperor announced that the prince of Fu would leave the capital in the spring of 1614.
4. A *ch'ing* is equal to one hundred *mou,* and a *mou* equals one-seventh of an acre.

5. The prince of Lu, Chu Yi-liu (1568–1614), had been given a domain in Honan.

6. *MS* 243:591c–d.

7. T'ang Pin-yin and Han Ching were dismissed from office after it was suspected that they had taken part in manipulating the *chin-shih* examination of 1610, in which Han Ching came out first. The Tung-lin scholars especially criticized T'ang. See Heinrich Busch, "The Tung-lin Academy," p. 150.

3. Lo Ts'ung-yen, also called Yü-chang (1072–1135), a disciple of Ch'eng Yi, was especially associated with Yang Shih. See *SYHA,* ch. 39. Li T'ung, also called Yen-p'ing (1093–1163), was a disciple of Lo Ts'ung-yen and a teacher to Chu Hsi. See *SYHA,* ch. 48. Lo Ts'ung-yen and Li T'ung were both placed in the Confucian temple in 1614. See John K. Shryock, *The Origin and Development of the State Cult of Confucius* (1932; reprinted, New York, 1966), 251, 257, 266.

9. It appears that the imperial clansman from Ch'u, Chu Yun-chen by name, had killed the governor of Wuchang in 1604. See Sun's biography in *MS,* ch. 243.

10. The Case of the Red Pill concerned accusations arising out of the sudden death of the young emperor Chu Ch'ang-lo (Kuang-tsung), who died after taking a medicine of red pills. Those who administered the medicine were charged with plotting his death with the intention of trying again to place the prince of Fu on the throne.

11. Li K'o-shao administered the red pills to the emperor.

12. The court was divided over Sun's accusation. The Grand Secretary, Han K'uang, argued that the emperor's death was a natural one and that Fang Ts'ung-che was innocent of wrongdoing. See *DMB,* v. 1, 483.

13. *MS* 243:591d.

14. The first of these three cases involved what appeared to have been an attack on the heir-apparent by a certain madman who got into his apartment carrying a club and hit a number of persons.

15. Wang Chih-ts'ai aroused animosity by suggesting that a plot was involved in this attack on the heir-apparent. See *ECCP,* 812.

16. See note 16 to Kao P'an-lung's biography in this volume.

17. Yang Lien's honorific is Chung-lieh (1571–1625).

18. Tso Kuang-tou's honorific is Chung-yi (1575–1625).

19. Lin Han, *hao* Huo-chao (d. 1636). The text of the SPPY edition gives the name Huo-t'ai, which appears to be a mistake.

20. I have not been able to identify this monk further.

21. The Chinese words *T'ien-ming* refer literally to Heaven and ordinance. In the Confucian Classics, particularly the *Book of History,* they acquired a technical meaning in the context of political change and are translated as "mandate of Heaven"—the mandate given by Heaven to the ruler, from which he derives his legitimacy. In the *Doctrine of the Mean,* ch. 1, they have a much broader meaning, as "what Heaven has conferred," and refer there to human nature. In the case of Sun's thoughts and the discussions here, the latter reference is more appropriate.

22. "The mind of physical form" sounds strange. Remember that the Chinese word *hsin,* usually translated "mind," refers to both mind and heart, sometimes more to one, other times more to the other. It can refer also to the physical heart.

23. *Mencius* 4B:26. This is adapted from D. C. Lau, trans., *Mencius,* 133.

24. The three opinions refer to those with which Sun differs, on each of the

three points discussed. The first was the dualistic position regarding destiny, nature, and mind. The second was the belittling of physical endowment as that which renders human nature itself susceptible to evil. The third was the division between the mind of man and the mind of Tao.

25. *Mencius* 2A:2.

Huang Tsun-su

Huang Tsun-su, *tzu* Chen-ch'ang, *hao* Po-an (1584–1626),[1] was a native of Yüyao, Shao-hsing-fu (Chekiang). A *chin-shih* of 1616, he was named a prefectural judge in Ning-kuo-fu (Kiangsi). Even the powerful princely family there had to practice self-restraint in order to avoid his judgments. At the time, the favors of the K'un and Hsüan faction[2] could have permitted anyone to go anywhere in the world. But Huang never showed them the slightest tolerance. He was transferred to censor of the Shantung bureau.

Since the time of Emperor Shen-tsung,[3] the court officials had been divided into two parties, gentlemen and small men. Each had its turn as winner or loser, without ever ceasing to fight against the other party. In the beginning of the T'ien-ch'i period (1621–27), the small men gained ascendancy. The eunuch Wei Chung-hsien joined the royal governess K'o in order to control the young sovereign and gathered for themselves all power inside the palace.[4] They wanted to find help among the circles outside the court, while the small men among the officials also wanted to take advantage of this occasion to catch in one net the gentlemen of the world. The two groups (eunuchs and small men) needed one another but had not yet joined together. Huang Tsun-su warned those gentlemen who shared his lofty ambitions: "Brothers may quarrel within the walls, but they will oppose insult from without.[5] Let us not continue this internecine strife and invite outside insult."

Not long after, Juan Ta-cheng was head of the supervising office for personnel and was on unfriendly terms with Tso Kuang-tou and Wei Ta-chung.[6] Juan wanted to resign from office in an effort to start the fight. Huang persuaded Juan not to leave office, and Juan also gradually changed his mind, though Huang was powerless to control the behavior of Tso Kuang-tou, who shunned Juan. When the minister of personnel, Chao Nan-hsing, without asking for counsel, moved Tsou Wei-Lien[7] to the ministry of personnel, Tsou's fellow provincials serving as censors and supervising secretaries started a dispute over the issue of authority [asking why they had not been consulted]. Huang acted as a mediator, causing the officials from Kiangsi to say that he himself had been responsible for recommending Tsou to the minister of personnel. He was therefore blamed for these two matters.

The supervising secretary Fu K'uei had been like a brother to Fu Ying-hsing, the adopted son of the traitorous eunuch (Wei Chung-hsien) and feared privately that he would not be tolerated by the pure discussion circles *(ch'ing-yi)* of the gentlemen. Some adventurers then baited him with gambling for the credit of being the first [to attack the men of the Tung-lin party], by making use of the case of the central drafting secretary Wang Wen-yen to impeach Tso Kuang-tou and Wei Ta-chung. Wei Chung-hsien personally took charge of the case, using it to start a big persecution. Huang advised Liu Ch'iao, the judge in the Imperial Guard Prison, what to do and was able to settle the case [and save Tso and Wei from punishment]. But after that came the memorial of the vice censor-in-chief Yang Lien, who accused [Wei Chung-hsien] of twenty-four crimes. When it was about to be submitted, Yang told his friends [of Tung-lin]: "Wei Chung-hsien is for the small men, like the god of the city and of the earth. To stuff the cave and smoke the rat out is not as good as to make the city fall and change the altar of the god of the earth." Huang said, "No. He who wishes to clean up the ruler's sur-roundings must have inside help to succeed. Have you got it or not? To miss your first stroke will lead to much misfortune and calamity." But the memorial went in. Yang was rebuked for it, while Wan Ching, bureau director of works, as well as the censor Lin Ju-chu, were punished with a beating at court for the purpose of intimidating the other ministers. Huang told Yang, "As long as you remain at court, Wei will feel insecure, and the affairs of state will only deteriorate. It would be better for you to leave office and so diminish the calamities that might arise." Yang agreed, but hesitated before making a decision.

When Wei Kuang-wei rose to the position of grand secretary[8] through the favor of Wei Chung-hsien, he feared that this might become known to the public, leading scholar officials of north China (his fellow provincials) to become ashamed of association with him. On the occa-sion when he failed to be present at the autumnal sacrifices to the impe-rial ancestors (1626), Wei Ta-chung planned to impeach him. Huang said, "Better not. Now that we have lost power, if we desist from mak-ing too clear a distinction between gentlemen and small men, then the latter might be more hesitant and so leave a little opening for us to escape." But Wei Ta-chung was determined to attack the outside sup-porter of Wei Chung-hsien (Wei Kuang-wei), considering this as a fol-low-up to Yang Lien's efforts to attack Wei Chung-hsien himself. So he did not approve of Huang's advice. Wei Kuang-wei sighed, saying, "These men are forcing us into real danger. How can I hold a knife and not use it?" So he marked off on a copy of the list of government office-holders the names [of Tung-lin members] and passed it to his "kins-man," Wei Chung-hsien, saying, "These are men of the Tung-lin party, who are making difficulties for you." Wei Chung-hsien regarded that as a holy book. All during the reign of Hsi-tsung (1621–27) he used this list to execute and kill the gentlemen.

When the people of Shansi fought over the appointment of a governor, Huang told Chao Nan-hsing, "The people of Shensi, Shansi, Honan, and Kiangsi are like men in the same boat. Since you appointed Tsou Wei-lien, you alienated the men of Kiangsi. For criticizing the posthumous honors to Nan Shih-chung, you offended the men of Shensi. If you now make enemies of the men of Shansi, the situation will become quite impossible." Sure enough, the censor Ch'en Chiu-ch'ou impeached Wei Ta-chung for recommending his examiner (Hsieh Ying-hsiang) for governor of Shansi, and, as a result, no worthy man was left at court.

All Huang's worries and considerations were farsighted and served to remedy the deficiencies of the plans made [by the Tung-lin party]. His precautions were all for the assurance of success.

Huang impeached Wei Chung-hsien three times in all. His first memorial preceded Yang Lien's. His second followed Yang's, while his third one was submitted after Wan Ching was beaten at court. By his pure words and strong arguments, he stirred fear in the breasts of those belonging to the eunuch's party. But he said that he did all within the duties of a censor and not for the sake of building up his own reputation. In 1625, he left the capital. Then he was criticized by Ts'ao Ch'in-ch'eng and removed from the official register. That winter, rumors were rampant that the gentlemen of the Soochow area were planning to return to power. Huang used the eunuch Li Shih[9] to perform a role, as Chang Yung had done in the past, in a secret plot that struck fear in the heart of Wei Chung-hsien when he heard of it. His spies were sent in four groups to the region south of the Yangtze but found no sound or shadow [of any rebellion]. The one-time vice-minister of justice, Shen Yen, wanted to give himself credit and sent in a memorial. Wei then said, "We have found traces of the plot." So he gave Li Shih a scolding and snatched from Li the memorial. On this pretext, the seven gentlemen [of the Tung-lin party][10] were arrested. For when Wang Wen-yen first examined the case in prison, the wicked men plotted at once to involve Tso Kuang-tou and Wei Ta-chung and have both put into prison. They did not know that Huang was able to free them. So they feared Huang above all the others, regarding him as their greatest enemy. Because of this, they had also started some false rumors. On July 4, 1626, Huang expired after composing a last poem. He was then forty-three years old.

Huang never held an instructor's chair. At the assembly held in the capital, he once said to Tsou Yüan-piao, "To have worthy men and traitors together may not be helpful to government." Of the men whose characters he approved, Liu Tsung-chou, Kao P'an-lung, and Wei Ta-chung stood out. He traveled the distance of ten thousand *li* in order to go to prison. Liu Tsung-chou saw him off with tears. Huang was still regretting not being able to help the situation. Huang regarded the practical business of starting things and accomplishing missions as his learning, and the safety of the world as his own safety. Should a man's ambition be other than to resolve the difficulties of state and society, should he smugly select subjects for discussion in an effort to acquire a reputation, Huang would despise such a man as an unworthy and small person. At the time, the court officials lacked scholarship, using rote memory as their prompt book, without attending to the study of the classics. In one memorial, a reference was made to Jao Ch'ao's whip.[11] A famous official asked Huang about it. He explained that the reference was to the story of [Shih-hui], who fled from Ch'in to Chin but was sent back through a ruse (612 B.C.). Whenever a passage was quoted at random from the Five Classics, Huang was able to recite at once the relevant commentaries and subcommentaries, so quick and decisive were [his judgments and gifts], resembling the onrush of water when the dikes are crushed.

(MJHA 61:1a–2a)

NOTES

1. This is Huang Tsung-hsi's account of his father's life, and for this reason included in the translations. See also *MS,* ch. 245.

2. The two factions are explained in note 45 to the translation of Ku Hsien-ch'eng's biography in this volume.

3. Reference to the factional struggles that took place under Emperor Shentsung (r. 1572–1620). See the latter's biography by Charles Hucker, *DMB,* v. 1, 324–38.

4. See *MS,* ch. 22 and the biography of Emperor Hsi-tsung by George Kennedy, in *ECCP,* 190.

5. Reference to the *Book of Poetry.* See J. Legge, trans., *The Chinese Classics,* v. 2, 251.

6. Tso Kuang-tou was also called T'ung-ch'eng after the name of his native place, and Wei Ta-chung was also called Chia-shan. They were prominent scholars of the Tung-lin movement. See Tso's biography by Charles Hucker, *DMB,* v. 2, 1305–8.

7. Tsou Wei-lien, *hao* Hsin-ch'ang. Before making an appointment, the minister of personnel usually asked the candidate's fellow provincials in Peking about his qualifications.

8. Wei Kuang-wei, *hao* Nan-lo, was regarded as a kinsman of Wei Chung-hsien.

9. Li Shih appears to have been a eunuch. Chang Yung was a eunuch who had helped Yang Yi-ch'ing in Yang's difficulties with the powerful eunuch Liu Chin, eventually making possible Liu's arrest and execution (1510). He also rendered important service to Wang Yang-ming, after Wang had captured the rebel, Prince Ch'en-hao. See his biography by Richard Chu, *DMB,* v. 1, 111–13.

10. The seven gentlemen were Tso Kuang-tou, Yang Lien, Wei Ta-chung, Ku Ta-chang, Yüan Hua-chung, Chou Ch'ao-jui, and Huang Tsun-su himself.

Six of them died in 1625, a year before Huang, and are usually referred to as the "six gentlemen." See Yang Lien's biography by George Kennedy, *ECCP,* 893.

11. Jao Ch'ao was minister in the state of Ch'in. The story refers to the flight of Shih-hui, minister of Chin, to Ch'in, and the successful effort on the part of Chin to force him to return. When that happened, Jao Ch'ao gave him a horse whip as a parting gift, at the same time asking for his pardon, because Jao had not been able to persuade the ruler of Ch'in to prevent Jao's departure. See *Annals of Tso,* thirteenth year of Duke Wen of Lu (612 B.C.) in J. Legge, trans., *The Chinese Classics,* v. 5, 262–63.

17. The Chi-shan[1] School

The scholars of today usually acclaim Kao P'an-lung and Liu Tsung-chou as two great Confucians. This is undoubtedly correct. Now when Kao's *Surviving Writings* were first published, I was attending to my [now] deceased Master [Liu Tsung-chou] in the boat during our voyage from the River Ho (Yu-yao) to Hangchow. We spent whole days reading these writings. My master frequently showed me selected passages manifesting Buddhist influences. Later, I read a letter in which my master was discussing learning. It was addressed to Han Wei. Said he: "Both Chu Hsi[2] in the past and Kao P'an-lung today were influenced by Ch'an Buddhism." Then I read Kao's *San-shih chi,*[3] where he said that Buddhist sūtras differ from the teachings of the sages on very minute points, but that the Confucians already have all the subtle insights of Buddhism, which could be summed up in two words: *wu-chi* (Non-Ultimate). As to the defects of Buddhism, these have all been pointed out by the earlier Confucians and could all be summed up in two other words: *wu-li* (without principle). He seems to emphasize the word *wu* (nothingness). And this is why Buddhists are Buddhists. Even the words Kao said when he committed suicide, that there was originally neither life nor death, were Buddhist words. That was why my teacher (Liu Tsung-chou) corrected him by saying, "Kao's mind was one with the Way. He lived to fulfill the Way; he died to fulfill the Way. That is the meaning of 'transcending life and death.' It is not what the Buddhists call transcending life and death (i.e., *nirvāṇa*)." Kao P'an-lung did not teach a Buddhist doctrine, although he could not avoid being somewhat influenced by Buddhism. This is to say that there was a small flaw in his generally correct teachings. By comparison, my teacher (Liu) represents the most correct teaching. People in later ages would certainly be able to distinguish between them.

In 1668, I spent about half a year with Yün Jih-ch'u in Shao-hsing. He was a close disciple of the master and was then compiling the *Liu-tzu chieh-yao.* At the time of our parting, near the river's edge, Yün held my hand and said: "There is no one else [outside of us] who knows our master's philosophy. So the two of us must teach the same things. Where it regards what the deceased master meant by 'intention' we ought to harmonize more."[4] I did not then offer an answer. When his book was printed, he wrote to me, saying: "You know the master's teaching. You must write a preface for this book." Alas, am I the one who knows the master's teachings?

I read what Yün has said about the correct learning of Kao P'an-lung and Liu Tsung-chou: "Kao acquired his learning from enlightenment, yet his whole life gave witness to cultivation. This was like heavenly knowledge *(ch'ien-chih)* controlling earthly ability *(k'un-neng)*. My deceased master, Liu Tsung-chou, acquired his learning from cultivation but later on reached a stage that may be called the enlightenment arising from understanding *(chieh-wu)*.[5] This is like using earthly ability to prove heavenly wisdom. For Heaven's *ch'i* is called *Ch'ien* and Earth's *chih* (substance) is called *K'un*. *Ch'i* must be condensed to become *chih;* *chih* cannot become dispersed except as *ch'i*. The two are really one thing. To have heavenly wisdom and not earthly ability is to have the wisdom of the eccentric. To have earthly ability and not heavenly wisdom is to cultivate oneself blindly. How can there be an order of hierarchy between the two? The people who know of Kao's experience of enlightenment in an inn consider that he acquired his learning from enlightenment. This is the path of Ch'an Buddhism and is not related to the teaching of the sages."

But in teaching vigilance in solitude *(shen-tu)*,[6] if our master is not discerning between nature *(hsing)* and ultimate reality *(T'i)*, what would he be vigilant about? One may say from this that Yün did not even understand the master's teachings. If he did, he should have been able to penetrate into the master's intended meaning. For this reason, I did not write a preface to the *Liu-tzu chieh-yao*. Unfortunately, at the time, I did not pursue the discussion with him and so have not been fair to my good friend. Now I shall record here [selected writings] from the master, all according to the order given in his original writings. Although the master has written very much, I present here the selections giving his important doctrines, so that students need not regret not having seen the original works.

NOTES

1. Chi-shan is the place of retreat in Chekiang where Liu Tsung-chou stayed.

2. See *Liu-tzu ch'üan-shu*, 19:42a. The text, however, mentions by name Yang Chien (1141–1226) rather than Chu Hsi, and since the entire letter discusses Yang's relation to Lu Chiu-yüan, the mistake was probably Huang Tsung-hsi's in substituting Chu Hsi for Yang Chien. I think that he wrote and quoted frequently from memory and was therefore prone to such occasional errors.

3. See *Kao-tzu yi-shu,* 3:16a. This is taken from the essay *K'un-hsüeh chi,* rather than from the *San-shih chi* (10:36b–48a) as Huang Tsung-hsi states. Again, his memory is playing him false here.

4. See the Author's Preface, ch. 11. The two accounts do not tally exactly. Notice, for example, the difference in the year and in Huang's response to Yün.

5. The term, enlightenment coming from understanding *(chieh-wu),* is especially associated with Wang Chi's teaching. See the biography of Wang Chi by Julia Ching in *DMB,* v. 2, 1349–55.

6. Vigilance in solitude constitutes Liu's central doctrine.

Liu Tsung-chou

Liu Tsung-chou, *tzu* Ch'i-tung, *hao* Nien-t'ai (1578–1645),[1] was a native of Shan-yin in Shao-hsing (Chekiang) and a *chin-shih* in 1601. He was made an emissary (in the office for the transmission of imperial messages). He submitted a memorial on the subject of the root of the country,[2] saying that the Tung-lin party included many gentlemen and should not be attacked. For a while he returned home, after requesting leave, and was later raised to secretary in the ministry of rites. He impeached the eunuch Wei Chung-hsien and the royal governess Madame K'o.[3] He was transferred to assistant minister in charge of the imperial seal and vice-minister in the court of the imperial stud. He requested permission to resign but such permission was not granted. Later he asked for leave on the basis of sickness and returned to his native place. When promoted to vice-commissioner in the office of transmission, he once more begged for leave. The court then commented upon his disagreeable behavior, in desiring to refrain from serving society by feigning difficulties, and reduced his status to that of a commoner.[4] In 1629 he was once more elevated to prefectural governor of Peking.

At that time, the emperor was attempting to verify his ministers' performance of duties, and the many ministers dared take no leisure in covering their defects. Liu considered that such penal practices could not be employed in governing the world and counseled the teaching of benevolence and righteousness. The emperor regarded that as impractical and old-fashioned. When the capital was placed under martial curfew, the emperor suspected the court ministers to be lacking in loyalty toward the country and began to confide in eunuchs. Liu said that the exigency of the day was first to display a sincere mind as the basis for remedying a difficult situation. He thought that if the emperor were to favor the ministers of the outer court with the same mind with which he favored the ministers of the inner court and to esteem the civil officials with the same mind as that with which he esteemed the military officials, then the task of establishing great peace could be accomplished with one stroke.

At that time, mediocre men wanted to make good use of the occasion to reopen the case of the traitors (i.e., Wei Chung-hsien, etc.)[5] and so associated those who were under suspicion with the men of Tung-lin. Liu said that the men of Tung-lin had already been known for their loyalty and righteousness, that right and wrong had already been settled. Why should one therefore stir up the old storms and thus obstruct the paths by which worthy men might attain office? After martial law had been revoked, he submitted a memorial in which he begged Heaven to continue its mandate forever. He argued that Heaven respects the people's lives and that punishments ought to be diminished. He begged for the suppression of the Imperial Guard Prison, declaring too that since Heaven places importance upon the people's livelihood, old taxes should be lowered and new taxes abolished. He also said that high ministers should not start large penal cases, nor unduly praise wealth and prosperity. When the emperor asked him how military expenditures were to be defrayed, he answered that the original manpower, as well as resources, was always there. The emperor still considered him impractical and old-fashioned.[6]

Liu requested home leave and returned to his native place. But the emperor thought of him once more. While searching for candidates for appointment to the Grand Secretariat, he issued an edict summoning Liu to the Wen-hua Palace for an audience. There, the emperor asked him questions on three issues: the recruitment of talent, the need for military supplies, and the problem of the roving bandits. Liu replied, "The world does not lack men of talent, but, owing to impatience for good government, Your Majesty himself has tried out and dismissed the scholars of the world too flippantly. Thus, while talented men are available, you are unable to make good use of them. Besides, the surtaxes for military use have been excessive, and the penalties for failing to produce are severe. The bureaucracy is going from bad to worse. Since the people are unable to meet their needs of livelihood, they turn to banditry, which in turn has led to a shortage of military funds. But since the roving bandits were originally children of the court, if they were properly handled and pardoned, they would once more become the people of the land."

The emperor then asked him about military affairs. He replied, "I hear that the best defense is rooted in a good internal government. That was why [Shun] defeated the Miaos after the court dances of shields and feathers.[7] So Your Majesty need only model yourself upon [the sages] Yao and Shun." At this the emperor turned to [the Grand Secretary] Wen T'i-jen and said: "How impractical and old-fashioned are Liu's words!" But he used him as senior vice-minister of works. Liu took the occasion to reiterate instances of recent bad government, saying "Your Majesty need merely issue an edict explaining the reasons for the rise of bandits, and your own intention of not abandoning these people, and your plan to send court ministers with court funds to tour the provinces throughout the country as envoys asking for their surrender, in order to win back the innocent and those who had run away. Your Majesty should deploy troops to strategic places and wait until the rebels have been reduced to great straits. When the situation becomes impossible, they will be forced to surrender themselves to the court. So, apart from the leaders, no one would be killed and the campaign can be concluded." The emperor read this and was enraged. He became calmer after a long time and gave instructions saying that when a high official submitted opinions on affairs, he ought to consider well the state of the country and the needs of the time and refrain from imitating small officals, who, in wanting merely to gain a few steps, blamed everything wrong on the court. Liu then said, "Your Majesty possesses the mind of Yao and Shun; however, where it concerns the mind of man and the mind of Tao, there is always the need for interdependence. Thus, when [an intention] that comes forth from the mind of man, either in excess or defect [of harmony] is applied to the affairs of government, then even if one desired good government too much, one might injure the order of government. I beg Your Majesty to pay careful attention." After three memorials begging for leave, the emperor granted the request.

On his way home, Liu stopped at Tê-chou, where he once more submitted a memorial, saying, "Today's crisis is the result of all that has happened since 1629. The calamity yet to come is being prepared for by all that is happening at present. In the incident of 1629,[8] those involved were enemies to those in power and could therefore be punished without much difficulty, as they indeed were submitted to severe penalties. In the incident of 1636, right now, however, those involved are protégés of those in power, so that superiors and inferiors easily hide the truth from each other, and the judgments meted out are quite different. Since antiquity, small men have always been agreeable to eunuchs, and there are always small men in the world who ally themselves with eunuchs, but no small men who agree well with gentlemen; while there are always gentlemen who could use small men, but no gentlemen who would ally themselves with eunuchs. Now who has been in control of the country during these eight years [between 1629 and 1636]?—I am unable to explain the conduct of our grand secretary, Wen T'i-jen."[9]

An edict then reduced his status to that of a commoner (1636). But the emperor was unable to forget Liu Tsung-chou and sighed in court, saying, "Liu Tsung-chou was a high official who was not corrupt and dared to say the things on his mind. No court minister could quite emulate him." In 1642, he was promoted to senior vice-minister of personnel.

Liu regarded the problem of finding order in the world as irresoluble

apart from the Way and anything touching on external accomplishments and profit as leading to opportunism. On his way he submitted a
memorial to make manifest the learning of the sages. Before arriving in
his office, he was promoted to senior censor-in-chief and summoned to
an imperial audience. The emperor asked him what he considered to be
his responsibility. He answered, "The chief censorate has an office, the
correction of oneself for the sake of the correction of the hundred officials. It is necessary to have something as a norm, in the middle, in
order that one might face the sovereign and father above and question
the scholars and officials of the world below. Only then could the hundred officials model themselves upon such an exemplar. As to duties, I
regard the inspection of the different regions to be his first duty. If the
right person were entrusted with such inspection, the bureaucracy
would become clean, and with this the people could be secure in their
livelihood."[10]

When another curfew was imposed, he submitted a memorial saying:
"Your Majesty desires with your whole heart to become the ruler of
Heaven and Earth, of spirits and men. Calmness in order to establish
greatness and peace in order to prepare for change are the first principles of such an endeavor. As to the steps for applying such, they include
lauding Lu Hsiang-shen and executing Yang Ssu-ch'ang."[11] The emperor said: "You are right to rebuke my mind. But of what good to military strategy are posthumous rewards and executions?"

He was then summoned for an audience at the Chung-tso Gate. The
censor Yang Jo-ch'iao was discussing firearms. Liu rebuked him,[12] saying, "The censor's words are mistaken. Recently our frontier officers
have not spoken of the policies of securing peace and of resisting aggres-
sion, and the methods of war and defense, of stationing and feeding the
troops. Rather, they regard firearms to be the life of the troops, relying
not on people but on things. This is the reason the country continues to
lose its might." The emperor discussed the issue of keeping or dismissing governors. Liu requested that this begin with the officer Fan Chih-
wan: "Fan had charge of three frontier posts.[13] In the days of peace, he
made no preparation, allowing enemies to enter the realm. Now he uses
the [Manchu] intrusion in the south as a pretext to run away from the
enemies. From henceforth the passes will present no obstruction to enemies, and things have gone from bad to worse." The emperor said: "To
go south to help was his order. Why should you call this an attempt to
run away from the enemies?" Liu replied, "For fifteen years, Your
Majesty has not properly handled the question of rewards and punishments, until we find ourselves in such dire straits today. Unless you
trace the calamity back to its sources and change your ways of governing, any policy of appeasing the situation could only provide momen-
tary respite and is no substitute for permanent government." The

emperor's expression changed, and he said: "The past cannot be recaptured. Where is the plan for rehabilitation today?" Liu answered, "The first principle for the day is for Your Majesty to show your sincerity to everyone, in order to resolve suspicion, declaring to the world what you consider to be good and bad. Then I believe you will have achieved more than half of what you can." The emperor said: "The country is already in a very bad state. How can one repair it?" Liu replied, "Recently those who offer counsel have only discussed people of talent and reputation without going into moral character. They do not know that the real talent of the world comes from the real moral character of the world. From the time of antiquity on, there were never men who were careless of their moral character and yet dared to come forth to serve in time of danger, just as there were never men without moral character who could command the respect of the soldiers." The emperor said, "In a time of crisis, talent comes before character." Liu said: "The more critical the times, the more urgent is character. For example, Fan Chih-wan is defective in character; he accepts bribes in his filling of vacancies. For this reason the troops have disintegrated and are unwilling to fight with their lives. From this viewpoint, can one not believe that character is essential?" At this, the emperor began to calm down.

Liu continued, "Your Majesty recently issued an edict asking for advice. Now the supervising secretary Chiang Ts'ai and the assistant director of the office of emissaries Hsiung K'ai-yüan have been punished for offering advice and placed in the Imperial Guard Prison. But Your Majesty has a surpassing capacity for tolerance, so that a minister like myself who has often said crazy things has been spared the executioner's axe, while your other minister Huang Tao-chou[14] has also been pardoned for his foolish but outspoken words. Why should these other two ministers not also experience your benevolence?" The emperor said: "Huang Tao-chou is a man of both learning and character. How could the other two ministers be compared to him?" Liu answered, "Truly, the two ministers could not be compared to Huang. But the court should regard censors with propriety. Even should they be guilty of real crimes, they ought to be sent to the proper judicial office for judgment. Placing them in the Imperial Guard Prison is an injury to the honor of the country." The emperor said angrily, "If I punish one or two censors, why should that be an injury to the honor of the country? Suppose there had been crimes of bribery and other transgressions of the law, of deception of the sovereign and insult of a superior, should all these not be investigated?" He answered: "Even when Your Majesty wishes to investigate into cases of bribery and transgression of the law, of deception of the sovereign and insults to a superior, you still ought to send these cases to the appropriate judicial offices." The emperor was furious and said: "How partial you are to those of your own party! How can you fulfill the duties of censor? You may await an edict of punishment." Liu then apologized, while the civil and military officials at court took turns begging for mercy on his behalf. So he was relieved of his office and sent back to his native place.[15]

After the capital was moved to the south (Nanking), Liu was once more restored to his original position. He submitted a memorial saying: "Today, the dynasty's greatest task lies in repulsing the bandits in vengeance. Nothing outside of this can express Your Majesty's desire to cross the Yangtze [and recover the lost territories]. And no action outside of Your Majesty's personal decision to lead the campaign can arouse the morale of the faithful ministers and brave men of the world. The left bank of the river (Yangtze) does not provide a base for a temporary moment of respite. I beg that you advance over to the north of the river. The city of Feng-yang has been called the central capital. To the east, it controls the rivers Hsü and Huai; to the north, it controls Honan; to the west, it is not far from Nanking in the south. The troops under your personal command could be stationed in Feng-yang. And when the patterns of government have been established, one can begin to speak of policies."[16]

At a time of disorderly government, Liu did not refrain from offering critical advice. Among the grand secretaries, he singled out for criticism Ma Shih-ying; among the nobility, he especially criticized Liu K'ung-chao, and from among the four military commanders, Liu Tse-ch'ing and Kao Chieh. He had originally no intention of leaving his place of retirement, saying, "At court, the talk of factionalism is rife. What free time can there be for recovering the north from the enemy? The plans for establishing the foundations of the country are already lax. How can one discuss the strategies of resisting the aggressors?"[17]

At that time, the traitorous officials who did not esteem Liu were ashamed of being unable to reach him and of forcing him to come out of retirement. Ma Shih-ying said that Liu had a high reputation in the world but called himself a minister in retirement, without writing out his new rank, which clearly showed his insubordination. Chu T'ung-lei said that in asking the government to move its base to Feng-yang, a place with a high walled prison, Liu was desirous of treating the emperor as a criminal. The four military commanders all said that Liu wanted to execute a coup d'état, intending to depose the emperor and enthrone someone else in his stead. When Liu was at a Buddhist monastery in Tan-yang, Kao Chieh and Liu Tse-ch'ing sent several assassins after him. Liu sat erect all day with no weariness of expression. The assassins left him in admiration. Only after repeated urging by the emperor did he accept the offer to serve at court. And then, when Juan Ta-cheng was named vice-minister of war, Liu said: "With the advancement and retirement of Juan is associated the fate of the entire left bank of the river." The court commented, asking if this was his mature judgment. He sent memorials begging for leave and was given permission to go home with an escort. As he left the capital gates, a crowd of old and young gathered there sighing, knowing as they did that Nanking would not long remain intact.

When Chekiang fell, Liu wept, saying:[18] "It is now time for me to complete my life." His disciples told him the stories about Wen T'ien-hsiang, Hsieh Fang-te, and Yüan Lang.[19] He told them: "At the time of the fall of Peking (1644), I could have died, but I also did not have to die, since I have been removed from the official register. At the fall of Nanking (1645), which occurred because the emperor himself [the prince of Fu] abandoned his realm, I was arriving at my post and could still say that I could choose between dying and not dying. But now that Nanking (Kiangsu) and Chekiang have fallen, what can an old man like me do? One may say that I am not holding office and need not die with the city, but should I not die with the land itself? For this reason, the former prime minister Chiang Wan-li[20] died (1274?). If there is no prime minister running away from death, should there be a censor running away from death? The ruler-minister relationship is actually decided upon human feeling. To speak of righteousness outside of feeling is not righteousness. The father-son relationship could not be resolved by the mind; the ruler-minister relationship also should not be resolved by the mind. I can now say that I am dying without having to die, that I am dying with a proper expectation, and that dying is a closer duty than not dying. Should I now run away, I would only be a fellow who is attached to his own life and fearful of death." So he fasted for twenty days and then died. This was on July 30, 1645, at the age of sixty-eight.[21]

Liu began life as an orphan, studying first with his maternal grandfather, Chang Ying. When he grew up, he became a disciple of Hsü Fu-yüan and had as friends, urging him on in matters of nature and destiny, Liu Yung-cheng, Ting Yüan-chien, Chou Ying-chung, *tzu* Ning-yü, my deceased father Huang Tsun-su, and Kao P'an-lung.[22] Although, in later life, Liu shared the instructor's chair with T'ao Shih-ling[23] and together with him called the assembly of Cheng-jen Hui, their teachings were not the same. T'ao's disciples all studied Buddhism, meeting separately on Mount Po-ma, and got into such things as causation and retribution.

I (Huang Tsung-hsi) once heard T'ao teach. He said that a famous minister was changed into a horse, citing his sickness as proof of this statement.[24] I did not like what T'ao said, so together with Wang Yeh-hsün and Wang Yü-ch'i I gathered together some forty choice scholars of the time, to become Liu's disciples. But although these forty or more people liked to attack Buddhism, they did not have much foundation for their learning and remained superficial. Thus they only provided excuses for those who studied Buddhism to do so. Liu was anxious about this. As the two factions mocked each other, there were only one or two persons who really transmitted his teachings.

Liu's teaching[25] considers as its essential doctrine vigilance in soli-tude *(shen-tu)*. The Confucians all speak of vigilance in solitude, but only Liu acquired its truth. What fills Heaven and Earth is *ch'i*. In the mind of man, the process of *ch'i* penetrates all things and returns to its beginnings, dividing naturally into joy, anger, sorrow, and pleasure. The names of benevolence, righteousness, propriety, and wisdom all issue from this. Without the ordering of character, one could naturally avoid transgressing their norms, which is the meaning of the harmony of the Mean. That is what one possesses at birth and is common to all. Hence it is also called the goodness of nature, which is without any excess or deficiency. Now nature-in-itself is naturally in process, with-out injuring the virtue of the harmony of the Mean. Students need only attest the distinctness of nature-in-itself, and adhere to it constantly, in order to practice what is called vigilance. The effort of vigilance consists only of [self]-mastery. Our consciousness has a master, which is called intention. To be one step removed from the root of intention is illusion and therefore not solitude. So the more one is recollected, the more one's [intention] is also extended. But mastery does not refer to resting in one place. It is always present in the process itself. That is why one says: "How it passes, without the difference of night and day."[26] For there is no *li* separate from *ch'i*, no nature separate from mind. The Buddhists say:

> There is something before Heaven and Earth;
> Without shape, and originally quite alone.
> It can be master of the myriad phenomena;
> It does not decay with the four seasons.[27]

This is their real treasure and cannot be taken away from them. But why should Confucians also say that *li* produces *ch'i?* Where is this infinitesimal difference [between Buddhism and Confucianism]? When one seeks only to interest the self and to profit the self, one cannot gov-ern the country and the world; and when one abandons this difference, differentiations between ruler and minister, father and son, all become quite arbitrary. Would not these people become the laughingstock of the Buddhists?

In pointing all this out, Liu Tsung-chou has traced out the differences between the southern carriages and the northern tracks quite clearly. Since the time of Sung, there has been nothing like this. Those who knew [how to read the skies] say that when the five planets gathered around the K'uei, Chou Tun-yi, the Ch'eng brothers, Chang Tsai, and Chu Hsi had emerged. When the five planets gathered around Shih, the teachings of Wang Yang-ming became prominent. And when the five planets gathered around Chang,[28] the master Liu's way penetrated the world. Has this not been the work of Heaven? Has this not been the work of Heaven?

(*MJHA* 62:2a–5a)

NOTES

1. See his *Chronological Biography* by Tung Yang, in *Liu-tzu ch'üan-chu* (Complete Works of Liu Tsung-chou) (abbreviated as *LTCS*), 1822 ed., ch. 40, pt. 1. See also Huang Tsung-hsi's account of his life, ibid., ch. 39. For an English account, see Earl Swisher's biography, *ECCP,* 532–33.

2. *LTCS* 10:3a–18b. For the memorials, see ch. 10–18.

3. Ibid., 10, pt. 1, 19b–20a.

4. Ibid., 10, pt. 1, 25a.

5. Ibid., 10, pt. 1, 35a–42b.

6. Ibid., 15:27b–30b.

7. Reference to the *Book of History.* See J. Legge, trans., *The Chinese Classics,* v. 3, 66–67. The moral is that virtue can move Heaven to bestow an effortless victory.

8. Reference to the punishment meted out to Yüan Ch'ung-huan.

9. *LTCS* 40:12a–b.

10. Ibid.

11. Ibid., 40:14a–15b. Both Lu and Yang had commanded troops against the Manchus.

12. Ibid., 17:48a–50a. Liu was against the government's reliance on Adam Schall, the Jesuit missionary, and his firearms.

13. The three frontier defense posts were Ning-yüan, Shan-hai-kuan, and Chi-chen. However, when the Manchus intruded southward into Shantung, Fan used the pretext of going to the aid of the south and left the three posts without adequate defense. For this incident (1642–43), see T'an Ch'ien (1594–1658), comp., *Kuo-ch'üeh* (Shanghai, 1958), 5947–52.

14. For Huang Tao-chou, see his biography by J. C. Yang and Tomo Numata, *ECCC,* 345–47. See also *MJHA,* ch. 56.

15. *LTCS* 18:13a–15a.

16. Ibid., 40:39b–40a.

17. Ibid.

18. Ibid., 40:42b–49a.

19. Wen T'ien-hsiang (*hao* Wen-shan), late Sung scholar and prime minister, was a captive of the Mongol invaders and attempted suicide by fasting, giving up after eight days, while he was still alive. As he refused to transfer his loyalty, he was finally executed in 1289. See *Sung-shih,* ch. 418. Wen left behind a poem explaining his understanding of Confucian loyalty and became famous as an exemplary patriot-martyr. Hsieh Fang-te (*hao* Liu-shan), also a late Sung scholar and official, died of fasting after refusing to transfer his loyalty (1282). See *Sung-shih,* ch. 425. As for Yüan Lang, little is known except a mention of him as an official in the history of the latter Han dynasty (25–220 A.D.). See *Hou Han-shu,* ch. 83.

20. Chiang Wan-li, late Sung prime minister, committed suicide as an act of loyalty to the dynasty in 1274. See *Sung-shih,* ch. 418.

21. *LTCS* 40:45–49.

22. Liu Yung-cheng (*hao* Ching-chih), *MJHA* 60:6a–b, was a scholar of the Tung-lin movement, as was also Ting Yüan-chien, *hao* Ch'ang-ju (*LTCS* 22:42a). As for Chou Ying-chung, *tzu* Ning-yu, see *LTCS* 39:35b.

23. T'ao Shih-ling, *hao* Shih-liang, younger brother of T'ao Wang-ling. See *LTCS* 23:43b. *MJHA*, ch. 36. See also *Liu-tzu ch'üan-shu yi-p'ien,* 24:35b.

24. The reference appears to be to Buddhist belief in transmigration, although the story is difficult to understand unless the sickness referred to was a terminal illness.

25. This is Huang Tsung-hsi's account of Liu's teachings.

26. Reference to *Analects* 9:16.

27. This affirmation of a metaphysical absolute is the burden of the *Book of Chao,* the well-known work of the Chinese Buddhist monk (fl. 400 A.D.), a disciple of Kumārajīva. See Walter Liebenthal, trans., *Chao Lun* (Hong Kong, 1968), pts. 1–2, 46–63. See especially p. 48, where Confucius' saying (n. 26) on the fleeting character of life is quoted and a commentary given regarding the apparent change and underlying immutability of things. The quotation, however, comes from the monk Fu Hsi, also known as Tsui-hui (fl. 530 A.D.), in his *Fu ta-shih tsui-hui shuo-fa,* in *Zokuzōkyō,* v. 129, 13a.

28. The five planets are Jupiter, Mars, Saturn, Venus, and Mercury. The reference here is to the motion of the planets and its astrological significance. The K'uei refers to the 15th constellation, the Shih to the 13th constellation, and the Chang to the 26th constellation. See J. Needham, *Science and Civilisation in China,* v. 3, 390–408.

Part Three
Epilogue

Epilogue

IT is a pleasure and a relief to have brought a selected translation of this scope to conclusion. Huang Tsung-hsi's *Ming-ju hsüeh-an* is a big book, which integrates historical information with discussions of subtle, even elusive, philosophical ideas. If translated in toto, it could become a five-volume work in English.[1] Indeed, it could only have been planned, structured, and compiled by a man with a passion—a passion for life, as this is reflected in his selected biographies. For Huang, biographies, like history itself, have a didactic function, philosophically as well as otherwise, since personal integrity is the touchstone for the validity of philosophical claims. This is a logical corollary to the conviction, voiced especially by Wang Yang-ming, that knowledge and action are one.

Of course, Huang Tsung-hsi was not venturing into entirely unknown territory, since the broad genre of intellectual history had been known to Chinese scholars for some time.[2] For example, the early texts, such as *Chuang-tzu* and *Hsün-tzu,* all contain chapters discussing similarities and differences among various schools of thought. Huang's book is however much closer to Chu Hsi's *Yi-Lo yüan-yüan lu,* an anthology of the teachings of the important Neo-Confucian philosophers of the Sung dynasty. But that anthology is not intended to be a biographical one, even though it gives brief biographical information on the thinkers included. Chu Hsi himself is the author also of two biographical records of famous officials of the Sung dynasty, in which he relates their words and deeds.[3] As Huang himself acknowledges, his more recent models are the works of Chou Ju-teng and Sun Ch'i-feng, which also combine biography with philosophical discussions. But Huang Tsung-hsi was conscious of the fact that he himself had improved on his models in the *Ming-ju hsüeh-an,* which is more comprehensive in scope and more selective and critically incisive in scholarly judgment than the two previous works. In that sense, Huang actually created a new genre, one which has been used time and again after him.

The vast scope and the comprehensive nature of the book are such that Huang Tsung-hsi has effectively produced a small encyclopedia of Ming intellectual history, with its advantages and disadvantages. In preparing a selected version of the book for Western readers, the editors and contributors have discovered many mistakes made by Huang Tsung-hsi, such as erroneous dating, misplaced quotations, and the like. Whenever they have appeared important, we have pointed out and corrected these mistakes in the footnotes. Besides, Huang Tsung-hsi seems frequently—and exasperatingly—elliptical, in his use of allusive language. This could sometimes be condoned because of the controversial nature of the questions he dealt with, even if it has made our task more difficult.

As is obvious, Huang Tsung-hsi was personally involved in certain discussions and activities described by the book, particularly those discussions and activities in which members of the Tung-lin school, including his own father, Huang Tsun-su, participated. The biographies of Ku Hsien-ch'eng (d. 1612) and Kao P'an-lung (d. 1626) are among the longest in the book. For Huang Tsung-hsi, these were not merely historical figures he had read about. He also heard about them from his father and from his teacher, Liu Tsung-chou. Thus, the later biographies—particularly those of Huang Tsun-su and Liu Tsung-chou—are eyewitness accounts by a man whose whole life was marked and shaped by the events that led to the fall of the Ming dynasty. He was himself a scholar of the late Ming and early Ch'ing times, brought up and educated by those same scholars and thinkers who were also heroes and martyrs, who lived and died, literally, for their philosophy—for the love of wisdom and in witness to truth.

Huang Tsung-hsi's personal involvement in the controversial discussions of his time is evidenced as well by many references to academic gossip in his biographies and by the many brusque comments with which he sometimes ends his accounts. His self-styled disciple and posthumous collaborator, Ch'üan Tsu-wang, points out a certain partisan spirit[4] with which Huang covertly protects the followers of the Yang-ming school while overtly criticizing them, just as he covertly attacks the school of Hsüeh Hsüan, a follower of the Ch'eng-Chu school, while making an overt show of approval. However, in hindsight, we realize that Huang was obliged to pay some lip service to the Ch'eng-Chu orthodoxy, although his heart was with their rivals. And we remain in Huang's debt for the passionate account of personal encounters and philosophical debates which he has left us.

In the *Ming-ju hsüeh-an*, we find a union of historical and biographical scholarship with philosophical discussions and moral judgments. It has unfolded for us a panorama of Ming intellectual history. We witness its humble beginnings in the lives and dreams of Wu Yü-pi[5] and Ch'en Hsien-chang. We rejoice with Wang Yang-ming in his discoveries and regret—as did Huang Tsung-hsi—that he had not lived longer. We learn about the vicissitudes of the Yang-ming school with its many branches, the spread of the doctrine of *liang-chih,* the debates over the Four Positives and the Four Negatives, the assemblies held to discuss controversial interpretations of the Four Sentences (or Four Maxims). These included the assembly at Ling-chi Temple, Peking (1554), presided over by Ou-yang Tê, and the Nanking meetings (between 1595 and 1598) organized by Hsü Fu-yüan and Chou Ju-teng, at which Hsü queried Chou on the teachings of the Four Sentences with his *Nine Inquiries (Chiu-ti)* and Chou replied with his *Nine Explanations (Chiu-chieh).* Here, Huang Tsung-hsi sides with Hsü Fu-yüan, Liu Tsung-chou's teacher and opposes the doctrine of the Four Negatives propagated by Wang Chi and his followers, especially Chou Ju-teng.

But the *Ming-ju hsüeh-an* is more than a history of Ming thought. It is also an expression of Huang Tsung-hsi's own *Weltanschauung.* In his General Preface, Huang speaks of the dynamic mind *(hsin)* as that which fills the universe and manifests itself under myriad forms. He gives his approval to the kind of philosophical pluralism that is represented by the many schools of Ming thought, each striving to reflect certain manifestations of the one truth and wisdom. Here, as well as in the *Fa-fan,* he places emphasis on *tzu-te,* acquiring insights for oneself, rather than mouthing the wisdom of others, while he also takes some pains to trace intellectual lineages to show the collaborative nature of the quest for truth. Throughout the pages of the book, he reveals himself not only as a recorder of events and ideas, but also as an active thinker himself. As a philosopher, he strongly affirms the unity between *ch'i* and *li,* as well as between mind and nature. He also seeks to reconcile the two directions of "honoring virtuous nature" *(tsun te-hsing)* and "following the path of knowledge and inquiry" *(tao wen-hsüeh)* that have represented the Lu-Wang and Ch'eng-Chu schools. This shows that although he admits himself to be sympathetic to Wang Yang-ming's philosophy, he maintains a mediating position between two potentially extreme tendencies. From this position, he has been able to interpret and criticize all the schools of opinion included in his book in an involved and yet discerning manner. He has also performed a polemical function, defending Wang against those critics who attacked the doctrine of absence of good and evil for having opened the road to moral indifferentism. Instead, he insists that the Buddhistic overtones of the Four Sentences have been exaggerated by Wang Chi. And he offers an alternative interpretation, harmonizing the Four Sentences with his own understanding of the *Doctrine of the Mean*—of the equilibrium of consciousness prior to the rise of emotions *(wei-fa chih chung)* and of the harmony of due proportions posterior to their rise *(yi-fa chih ho).* He argues for a proper balance between the former, which stands for stillness and meditation (Nieh Pao and Lo Hung-hsien) and the latter, symbolizing commitment in action (Tsou Shou-yi and Ou-yang Tê).

Is Huang Tsung-hsi correct in his interpretations? Has the *Ming-ju hsüeh-an* given the final answer to the controversy over the teaching of the Four Sentences? Or might one, on the other hand, maintain—with all due respect for Huang's judgments—that the question remains an open one?

In my opinion, Huang Tsung-hsi, heir to the Tung-lin and Kan-ch'üan schools by personal and intellectual lineage, has been loyal to the legacy of the whole of Ming thought. He has pointed out the central position of Wang Yang-ming's contributions; and he has indicated the controversial nature of Wang's legacy. Besides, he shows how the efforts of the Chiang-yu, Kan-ch'üan, and Tung-lin schools counterbalance the excesses of the T'ai-chou school and work toward a reconciliation of Wang's teachings with those of Chu Hsi. But he has perhaps overemphasized Liu Tsung-chou's closeness to Wang Yang-ming, and he has insisted on the quietistic side of Ming thought *(kuei-chi)*, beginning the book with Wu Yü-pi, a Confucian hermit, and ending it with Liu Tsung-chou, a man whose thought is centered on the realm of inner consciousness. Interestingly, although Huang himself was a man of action, a fighter, and a patriot, a philosopher of the dynamic *hsin,* he was prevented from participating in government by the dynastic changes, which freed him for the activities of prolific scholarship—a life of retirement spent in compiling such books as the *Ming-ju hsüeh-an.*

The Japanese scholar Okada Takehiko makes this point in his book on Wang Yang-ming and the thinkers of the late Ming.[6] He regards Tsou Shou-yi and Ou-yang Te as the most faithful interpreters of Yang-ming's philosophy. He says that Nieh Pao and Lo Hung-hsien, with their emphasis on stillness, represent a rightist return to the principles of Ch'eng Yi and Chu Hsi, in contrast to Wang Chi and Wang Ken, whose emphasis on spontaneity in action represents a leftist development of the Yang-ming school.[7]

The *Ming-ju hsüeh-an* remains an indispensable work, even for those who delve into the collected writings of the Ming thinkers themselves. The reasons are obvious. Collected writings, although remaining necessary and primary sources for students of intellectual history, represent only the authors' point of view and offer little assistance in evaluating his contributions against a wider perspective. The other historical sources, such as the Ming dynastic history, offer very scanty information on the content of the thought itself. The *Ming-ju hsüeh-an* remains the best guide and companion for the students in question, encouraging them and assisting them in their readings of the individual thinkers' collected writings and permitting them thereby to develop their own points of view in dialectical interaction with the individual thinkers as well as with Huang Tsung-hsi himself.

We have pointed out in the Introduction the difference between the

Chinese philosophy of mind *(hsin-hsüeh)* and the understanding of this in Western analytical philosophy, a difference based very much on the meaning of the word *hsin* (mind-and-heart). We might also point out that the discussions of inner consciousness and of a certain transcendental principle in this consciousness, called *chu-tsai* or *pen-t'i,* carry resonances that bring to mind Husserl's phenomenology, with its concept of the transcendental ego. Besides, the constant reference to a continuum between life and thought represents a similar commitment to a *Lebenswelt,* a consciousness of lived experiences. But the texture of thought—especially when the text is seen against its total context, cultural as well as linguistic—remains very different. By and large, Ming thinkers show no preoccupation with the demands of the logical method. Their preference is for intuition, although this is an intuition that should not be described as irrational, and they offer the fruits of insight that come from their entire lives—as these are directed to a quest for wisdom, for the Tao, for *pen-t'i.*

There is no simple key to understanding Chinese philosophy as a whole or the history of Ming thought in particular. The student must combine philosophical reflection with personal realization: practicing the principles exemplified in the thought itself, balancing interior knowledge with exterior exertions.[8]

The many dimensions of Ming thought reflect the many dimensions of life itself: life as it was lived several centuries ago in one particular cultural area, with lessons, nevertheless, for those of us who have arrived late on earth and who find a universe vastly transformed. In the midst of the flux, of the ebb and flow of human consciousness, much has changed, but much remains also the same.

NOTES

The Epilogue is written by Julia Ching, after discussion with Chaoying Fang.

1. We wish to point out that thirteen biographies included in this translation are not found in either *DMB* or *ECCP,* although these include important figures such as Nieh Pao, Lo Hung-hsien, and Hsü Fu-yüan. We hear that a Japanese translation of the *Ming-ju hsüeh-an* is in preparation at the University of Kyushu, Fukuoka, but we do not know whether it will be a full or selected translation, or when it will appear. We already have, in Goto Motomi, ed., *Yōmeimonka,* part 2, (in the *Yōmeigaku taikei* series) Yamanoi Yū's introductory essay on Huang Tsung-hsi (pp. 59–69) and an annotated Japanese translation of certain sections from the book. These include two versions of the General Preface (the second one was written before the first one, but was superseded by the latter), the Introductory Remarks *(Fa-fan),* and the prefaces to all the individual records (pp. 294–339). See *Yōmeigaku taikei,* v. 7. Another volume of this same series, v. 12 *(Yōmeigaku benran),* has been very useful as it provides detailed lists of names of all the figures included in the *Ming-ju hsüeh-an,* with various cross-references as well as tables of scholarly lineages.

2. On this subject, see also Yüan Chin-shen, "Hsüeh-an t'i-ts'ai yüan-liu ch'u-t'an" (Preliminary Study of the Evolution of Intellectual History [*hsüeh-an*] as a Genre), in *Shih-yüan,* 2 (October, 1971), 57–76. The term *hsüeh-an* was first used by Huang Tsung-hsi to designate the genre.

3. The reference here is to the two biographical anthologies compiled by Chu Hsi: the *Wu-ch'ao ming-ch'en yen-hsing lu* and the *San-ch'ao ming-ch'en yen-hsing lu.* They have been published together as one book, *Sung ming-ch'en yen-hsing lu* (On Famous Sung Officials), with a supplement by Li Yu-wu *(Sung-shih chih-lui ts'ui-pien,* first series, compiled by Chao T''ieh-han) (Taipei, 1967).

4. See the short record of Ch'üan's answer to his students on the subject of Huang Tsung-hsi's scholarship, in his *Collected Writings, Chieh-ch'i-t'ing chi,* Supplements *(Wai-pien),* 44:14b–16a.

5. Chaoying Fang is fascinated with Huang Tsung-hsi's selection of Wu Yü-pi to head the *Ming-ju hsüeh-an.* Wu was not the earliest Ming scholar included in the book, not even the best known among the earlier ones, but Huang has recognized his special contributions. If Huang were compiling today a *Record of Contemporary Scholars,* he might surprise many people by the selection of scholars and the relative importance he would assign to them.

6. Okada Takehiko, *Ō Yōmei to Minmatsu no Jugaku* (Tokyo, 1970), especially ch. 3. See also his other book, *Sō-Min tetsugaku jusetsu* (Introduction to Sung-Ming Philosophy) (Tokyo, 1977). The latter seeks to compare and contrast Sung and Ming thought, with discussions that extend not only to classical scholarship but also to examples drawn from art history.

7. Okada means nothing political by words like "leftist" and "rightist." In the People's Republic of China, however, Huang Tsung-hsi is assessed politically. He is usually praised for his political critiques and criticized for his philosophy of mind. See Ren Jiyu, ed., *Chung-kuo che-hsüeh shih* (A History of Chinese Philosophy) (Peking, 1979), v. 4; Sun Shu-ping, *Chung-kuo che-hsüeh-shih kao* (A Draft History of Chinese Philosophy) (Shanghai, 1981), v. 2, pt. b, ch. 9. Ren's book (p. 25) points out the interesting fact that although Huang Tsung-hsi's philosophy is that of the unity of *li* and *ch'i,* Huang actually affirms the existence of a supreme and personal deity, who transcends *li.* See Huang's essay on *Shang-ti* (Lord-on-high) in *P'o-hsieh lun* (Against Perverse Theories) in *Li-chou yi-chu hui-k'an* (Shanghai, 1910), 2a–b.

8. This appears to be the burden of Huang Tsung-hsi's own message, expressed in his judgments of those scholars who failed, in his view, to acquire wisdom or, in his words, to "see the Tao."

The Schools of Ming Thought
According to Huang Tsung-hsi

A. Till Wang Shou-jen (Yang-ming)

Ts'ung-jen (Kiangsi) 崇仁	Po-sha (Kwangtung) 白沙	Ho-tung (Shansi/Shensi) 河東	San-yüan (Shensi) 三原	Yao-ching (Chekiang) 姚江
Wu Yü-pi (1392–1469) 吳與弼		Hsüeh Hsüan 薛瑄 (1389–1464)		
Lou Liang (1422–91)—Hu Chü-jen (1434–84) 婁諒　　胡居仁	—Ch'en Hsien-chang 陳獻章 (1428–1500)	Lü Nan 呂柟 (1479–1542)	Wang Shu 王恕 (1416–1508) Wang Ch'eng-yü 王承裕 (d. 1538)	Wang Shou-jen 王守仁 (1472–1529)

B. Wang Shou-jen's Disciples

Che-chung (Chekiang) 浙中	Chiang-yu (Kiangsi) 江右	Nan-chung (South Kiangsi) 南中	Ch'u-chung (Hunan/Hupei) 楚中	Pei-fang (Shantung/Honan) 北方	Yüeh-Min (Kwang-tung/Fukien) 粵閩 Fukien
Hsü Ai 徐愛 (1487–1517)	Wang Chi 王畿 (1498–1583)	Ch'ien Te-hung 錢德洪 (1497–1574)		Tsou Shou-yi 鄒守益 (1491–1562)	Ou-yang Te 歐陽德 (1496–1554)
				Nieh Pao 聶豹 (1487–1563)	Hu Chih 胡直 (1517–85)
				Lo Hung-hsien 羅洪先 (1504–64)	Tsou Yüan-piao 鄒元標 (1551–1624)
Huang Hsing-tseng 黄省曾 (1490–1540) T'ang Shun-chih 唐順之 (1507–60?)	Chiang Hsin 蔣信 (1483–1559) (also a disciple of Chan Jo-shui) 湛若水	Mu K'ung-hui 穆孔暉 (1479–1539)		Hsüeh K'an 薛侃 (fl. 1517)	

C. Wang Shou-jen's Disciples and Others

Chih-hsiu 止修

(Tsou Shou-yi)

Li Ts'ai
李材
(fl. 1562)

T'ai-chou (Kiangsu) 泰州

(Wang Shou-jen)

Wang Ken
王艮
(1483–1541)

Hsü Yüeh
徐樾
(fl. 1532)

Keng Ting-hsiang
耿定向
(1524–96)

Lo Ju-fang
羅汝芳
(1515–88)

Keng Ting-li
耿定理
(1534–77)

Ho Hsin-yin
何心隱
(1517–79)

Chiao Hung
焦竑
(1540–1620)

Chou Ju-teng
周汝登
(1547–1629?)

Kan-ch'üan 甘泉

(Ch'en Hsien-chang)

Chan Jo-shui
湛若水
(1466–1560)

T'ang Shu
唐樞
(fl. 1526)

Hsü Fu-yüan
許孚遠
(1535–1604)

Feng Ts'ung-wu
馮從吾
(fl. 1589)

Li Chih
李贄
(1527–1602)

Chu-ju* 諸儒

Fang Hsiao-ju
方孝孺
(1357–1402)

T'sao Tuan
曹端
(1376–1434)

Lo Ch'in-shun
羅欽順
(1465–1547)

Wang T'ing-hsiang
王廷相
(1474–1544)

Lü K'un
呂坤
(1536–1618)

Hao Ching
郝敬
(1558–1639)

Tung-lin 東林

(Ou-yang Te)

(Hsüeh Ying-ch'i)
薛應旂

Ku Hsien-ch'eng
顧憲成
(1550–1612)

Kao P'an-lung
高攀龍
(1562–1626)

Sun Shen-hsing
孫慎行
(1565–1636)

Huang Tsun-su
黃尊素
(1584–1626)

Chi-shan 蕺山

Liu Tsung-chou
劉宗周
(1578–1645)

Huang Tsung-hsi
黃宗羲
(1610–95)

*The scholars grouped here are independent, and not disciples of one another.

Glossary of Technical Terms

THE following terms, both single words and expressions, have been selected for discussion because of their frequent occurrence in this study, and also because they often illustrate for us the richness of thought contained in *The Records of Ming Scholars*. Attention is called to the interpretations of the Sung masters, especially Ch'eng Yi and Chu Hsi, and of the great Ming master, Wang Yang-ming, whose philosophy dominates *The Records of Ming Scholars*. The words are usually used in a multivalent sense, i.e., on different levels of meaning at the same time, including cosmological, metaphysical, psychological, moral, and spiritual. Alphabetical order is followed.

This glossary includes some Chinese terms with Buddhist associations and Sanskrit equivalents.

Ch'eng 誠
　Literally, sincere, sincerity.
　a. In the *Doctrine of the Mean* (ch. 20–26), it refers to perfect virtue, the virtue of the sage, and is given cosmic qualities, as "the beginning and end of things," and the man of sincerity is described as "co-equal to Heaven and Earth."
　b. The Sung thinker Chou Tun-yi uses the term in this sense in his *T'ung-shu*. The Ming thinkers, especially Wang Yang-ming and Liu Tsung-chou, speak often of *ch'eng-yi* (sincerity of intention), making it the core of their teaching. Liu relates it to *shen-tu* 慎獨 (vigilance in solitude), another term from both the *Doctrine of the Mean* and the *Great Learning*.

Cheng-hsin 正心
　Usually translated as "rectifying the mind-and-heart." It may be said that whereas Chu Hsi gives greater importance to *ko-wu* and *chih-chih*, Wang Yang-ming prefers the second two and explains all in terms of *ch'eng-yi* and *cheng-hsin*.

The glossary in Julia Ching, *To Acquire Wisdom: The Way of Wang Yang-ming*, appendix V, has been consulted in the compiling of this expanded glossary.

Ch'eng-yi 誠意

Usually translated as "making the intention sincere." The word *yi* 意 refers to both thought and intention.

Chi 寂

Literally, solitude, loneliness.

This term carries a Buddhist resonance. It is used by many Ming thinkers, especially Liu Tsung-chou, and refers to silence and solitude as a spiritual discipline. In this sense, it is very close to *ching* 靜 (tranquility or stillness). *Kuei-chi* 歸寂 (return to stillness) is a term used by those later Ming thinkers after the time of Wang Yang-ming who seek to return to the teaching of silence and meditation of the Chu Hsi school. In their view this teaching had not been given enough emphasis by disciples of the Wang Yang-ming school who preferred to emphasize the dynamic unity of knowledge and action.

Chi 機

Origin, origination, usually in the context of insight or inspiration. *T'ien-chi* 天機 refers to creativity, "the creativity of nature," or "heavenly mystery."

Ch'i 氣

Literally, breath, ether, vital force, matter-energy.

a. It is found in the Appendix to the *Book of Changes* and especially in Wang Ch'ung's *Lun-heng*.

b. Chu Hsi considers it to be the concrete, material, differentiating principle of things, that which together with *li* constitutes all beings, that which gives life to things.

c. For Wang Yang-ming, *li* and *ch'i* represent not distinct principles, but the rational and moral versus the irrational and vital manifestations of the same human nature or of nature at large.

d. Huang Tsung-hsi insists on the inseparability of *li* from *ch'i,* calling *li* the *"li* of *ch'i."*

Chih 知

Literally, knowledge, wisdom.

For Wang Yang-ming, moral knowledge is united to action and experience. *Chih-chüeh* 知覺 refers to consciousness.

Chih-chih 致知

Usually translated as the extension of knowledge.

a. For Chu hsi, knowledge is extended especially through the investigation of the essences or meanings *(li)* of things.

b. For Wang Yang-ming, the only knowledge to be "extended" is *liang-chih,* "knowledge of the good" or wisdom. Since this knowledge is regarded as being somehow both innate and acquired, this extension involves not merely development and increase, but also realization—the passing from potentiality to actualization.

Ching 敬

Literally, respect or reverence.

a. The word appears frequently in the Confucian Classics, especially the *Book of History,* where ancient sage-kings are described as reverentially obedient to the decrees of the Lord-on-high or Heaven.

b. In *Analects* 12:19, Confucius exhorts his disciples to be "reverent" in the carrying out of their daily actions.

c. In the Great Appendix to the *Book of Changes,* we can find the formula, "reverence to straighten the inner [life], righteousness to square the outer [life]." It is a formula that the Ch'eng-Chu school is fond of using.

d. In Buddhism, the word *ching* (reverence) has a religious meaning, associated, for example, with the observance of ritual.

e. The Ch'eng-Chu school teaches a dual formula for moral and spiritual cultivation: abiding in reverence, and pursuing principles exhaustively. The word *ching* here refers to an inner disposition of composure and moral alertness, which is to pervade one's whole life. It is not the same as its homophone, *ching* 靜 (tranquility), which has a narrower meaning. *Ching-tso* 靜坐 (quiet-sitting), for example, refers to meditation. *Ching* (reverence), however, is an attitude which should be present both in and out of meditation, in activity as well as tranquility.

f. Chu Hsi emphasizes the importance of such reverence, and uses this concept to interpret the *Great Learning.* Wang Yang-ming considers such an interpretation to be an artificial one, imposed by Chu Hsi on the text itself. This does not mean that Yang-ming himself is opposed to the doctrine of reverence, but only that he opposes an interpretation that is alleged to be derived from the text, which is actually imposed from outside of it. Besides, Yang-ming prefers a more dynamic unity between knowledge and action and finds the doctrine of reverence inadequate because it tends to divide the inner life from the outer.

Chu-tsai 主宰

Literally, master or lord, to lord over.

It refers to a controlling principle, in the universe or in human consciousness. In the *Ming-ju hsüeh-an,* it is more often used with reference to consciousness or to spiritual cultivation.

Chüan 狷

Literally, rash, but often the opposite.

In *Analects* 13:21, it is the opposite of *k'uang* 狂 and refers to a personality that is cautious or obsequious—slow, careful, but also committed to the quest for sagehood.

Chung 中

Literally, the middle, the Mean.

In the *Doctrine of the Mean* it refers to the state of equilibrium that governs the person's dispositions before his emotions have been stirred or aroused.

Chu Hsi speaks much of the importance of equilibrium as the characteristic of *hsing-chih-pen-t'i* 性之本體 , i.e., of "pure nature" as such.

Chung-hsing 中行

Literally, walking or acting according to the middle or the Mean.

a. In *Analects* 13:21, it refers to the perfect. Confucius does not expect to find many perfect persons and expresses contentment with finding the "ardent" and the "cautious."

b. In the *Ming-ju hsüeh-an*, the two types of *k'uang* and *chüan* are frequently used to describe the personalities and the thinking of the scholars, such as in the cases of Ch'en Hsien-chang and Hu Chü-jen, Liu Tsung-chou and Kao P'an-lung.

Erh-ch'eng 二乘

Literally, the two vehicles.

This term is found in Chiao Hung's biography, and refers to the two vehicles of the *śrāvakas* (the hearers) and the *pratyekabuddhas* (holy hermits): two degrees of saintship among those followers of the Buddha who believe in attaining salvation for oneself rather than forgoing one's salvation in order to save others, as with the Bodhisattvas of Mahāyāna Buddhism. In this sense, there is a pejorative connotation.

Fa or *Fo-fa* 法/佛法

Literally, law, doctrine, principles of Buddhism. Sanskrit, *dharma*.

Ch'üan-fa 權法 means contingent doctrine.

Fo 佛

The Buddha or Buddhism.

Ju-lai-fo 如來佛 or *Tathāgata,* the "Thus Arrived," the highest epithet of the Buddha.

Ho 和

Literally, harmony, peace.

a. In the *Doctrine of the Mean,* it refers to the state of harmony that, ideally speaking, should govern the person's dispositions after his emotions have been stirred or aroused.

b. Chu Hsi emphasizes the importance of acquiring a "harmonious" disposition, as close as possible to that of one's prestirred equilibrium. He later developed the doctrine of uniting activity (*tung* 動)

and stillness *(ching)* by permeating one's life with the spirit of reverence *(ching)*.

   c. Wang Yang-ming makes no distinctions between equilibrium and harmony, or even between activity and stillness, since he says that the work of extending *liang-chih* unites these states of the mind.

Hou-t'ien 後天

Literally, after Heaven or Nature.

The term refers to the artificial as opposed to the natural, or the conscious as opposed to the preconscious.

Hsien-t'ien 先天

Literally, before Heaven or Nature.

The term refers to the natural, the preconscious or prereflective.

Hsin 心

Literally, mind, or mind-and-heart.

It is used to translate the Sanskrit (Buddhist) term *citta*—the discriminating mind. Actually, in general Chinese philosophical usage, *hsin* refers to the principle of both thinking and feeling.

   a. Mencius considers *hsin* to be the principle of all human activity. "He who completely develops his heart (or mind) knows his nature."

   b. In Ch'an Buddhism, it refers to the undifferentiated First Principle.

   c. For Chu Hsi, it is composed of both *li* and *ch'i* and is inferior in importance to *hsing* 性(nature), which is full of *li*. It is the active principle, which controls both *hsing* (nature) and *ch'ing* 情(emotions) but is less important than *hsing,* the tranquil principle, full of *li* (being and goodness).

   d. For Lu Chiu-yüan, *hsin* and *hsing* are identical. There is only one principle of both activity and stillness. It is full of *li* and possesses the capacity of transcending itself, because it is somehow greater than itself, one with the universe. In this regard, he speaks also of *pen-hsin* 本心 .

   e. Wang Yang-ming adopts Lu's understanding of *hsin.* More clearly than Lu, he explains that *hsin* is the principle in man that is capable of self-determination and self-perfection, which hides, within itself that greater than itself, the Absolute. It is also identical with *liang-chih.*

Hsing 行

Literally, to walk, to act.

For Wang Yang-ming, every conscious and voluntary human act that proceeds from the mind-and-heart and is united to the knowledge of the morality of the act in question.

Hsing 性

Literally, natural, human nature.

a. Mencius speaks of human nature as being originally good.

b. Chu Hsi regards *hsing* as the source and principle of moral and ontological goodness in man and in things and as that which is full of *li,* while he takes *hsin* to be that which contains both *li* and *ch'i* and so is morally ambivalent. In the case of human nature, the distinction is frequently made by the Ch'eng-Chu school between *T'ien-hsing* 天性 (Heaven-endowed nature) or *Pen-jan chih-hsing* 本然之性 (nature as such) and *Ch'i-chih* 氣質 (physical nature) or *Ch'i-chih chih-hsing* 氣質之性 .

c. Lu Chiu-yüan and Wang Yang-ming understand *hsing* and *hsin* to represent one and the same reality, considered in its source and principle, as that by which man shares in *T'ien-li* and, considered in its more dynamic aspect, as that which directs all human activity, that is, the given nature of man as well as that which is to be acquired through experience and action.

d. The Lu-Wang school is frequently referred to as *hsin-hsüeh* 心學 (school of mind) and the Ch'eng-Chu school as *hsing-li hsüeh* 性理學 (school of nature and principle).

Hsing-ch'a 省察

Literally, to examine, to watch over.

It refers to self-examination, the examination of one's thoughts and intentions, words and conduct, to make sure that the rules of morality are observed. As such, the expression occurs frequently in the *Ming-ju hsüeh-an.*

Hsiu-shen 修身

Usually translated as "cultivating the self."

It is a term that is found in the *Great Learning* and refers to moral and spiritual cultivation.

Jen 仁

Literally, kindness, benevolence, humanity, goodness, love.

a. In Confucian philosophy, the perfect and universal virtue, that which makes the perfect human being.

b. Ch'eng Hao and other Sung philosophers have given this word a metaphysical as well as cosmic, life-giving connotation, making it that power or virtue by which man becomes one with Heaven and Earth and all things and shares in the creative processes of the universe. Wang Yang-ming also identifies *jen* with the *pen-t'i* of *hsin,* that is, with the mind-in-itself, the Absolute.

c. *T'i-jen* 體仁 refers to realizing perfect virtue or experiencing the metaphysical nature of *jen.*

d. *Jen-t'i* 仁體 refers to the substance of *jen,* or *jen*-in-itself.

Ko-wu 格物

This comes from the text of the *Great Learning,* and is usually translated as "investigation of things."

a. For Chu Hsi, it refers essentially to "investigating the meanings (*li*) of things," that is, the word *ko* is understood mainly as "reaching" and the word *wu* is understood as "things."

b. For Wang Yang-ming, it refers to "rectifying the mind-and-heart," especially through the acts in which man's mind-and-heart is engaged; that is, the word *ko* refers to "rectifying" and the word *wu* refers to "affairs" (*shih* 事) more than to things or objects.

K'uang 狂

Literally, mad, crazy.

In *Analects* 13:21, Confucius describes two types of personalities: the *k'uang* (translated by Legge as "madly ardent") are those eager to find sageliness, even to the point of showing impatience about their eagerness.

K'ung 空

Literally, emptiness. Sanskrit, *śūnya.*

A Buddhist term, indicating the illusoriness and unreality of all phenomena.

Chen-k'ung 眞空, true emptiness. It is paradoxically identified with *miao-yu* 妙有 (mysterious being). Such an idea came from Nāgārjuna's (2nd cent. A.D.) philosophy. In China, it was propagated especially by the monk Seng Chao in his essay, the *Chao-lun.*

Kung-an 公案

Literally, a judicial case. Japanese, *koan.* No Sanskrit equivalent.

A paradox or riddle, in the Ch'an Buddhist technique of using riddles to arrest discursive thought and induce sudden enlightenment.

Kung-fu 工夫

Literally, work and effort.

a. In Ch'an Buddhism, it refers to self-exertion, ascetic or spiritual effort, including that of trying to resolve a riddle (*kung-an*).

b. Confucians, including both Chu Hsi and Wang Yang-ming, also use the term to refer to self-exertion and spiritual effort.

c. Wang Yang-ming speaks frequently of *pen-t'i* and *kung-fu,* explaining the latter as the simple effort of being always attentive and watchful over one's self, i.e., of extending *liang-chih.* He equates *pen-t'i* and *kung-fu,* signifying that wisdom is to be discovered in its own quest, and especially that, for the enlightened, this quest is characterized by spontaneity.

Li 理

Etymologically, the veins in jade, or polishing jade.

In both ordinary and philosophical language, it signifies meaning,
pattern, reason, truth, discernment, analysis. It is translated as principle, meaning, or essence.

a. It is found in the *Book of Mencius,* the *Book of Rites,* and the Appendix to the *Book of Changes,* where it assumes greater importance.

b. In Hua-yen Buddhism, *li* refers to the realm of noumena as
opposed to *shih* (the same word as that for "affairs"), which refers
to the realm of phenomena. It also refers to ultimate reality, or
Sanskrit *Tathatā.* But *li* and *shih* are also said to interpenetrate,
representing the dialectical unity of noumena and phenomena.

c. For Chu Hsi, it is being, reality, the principle of organization, that
which is full of truth and goodness, the transcendent and norma-
tive principle of moral action. It is usually opposed to *ch'i* and yet
inseparable from *ch'i.* And, just as *li* is attributed to human nature
and explains its original goodness, so too *ch'i* is attributed to the
mind or heart *(hsin)* and suggests its more physical nature and its
association with emotions *(ch'ing).*

d. Lu Chiu-yüan and Wang Yang-ming both consider *li* as being and
goodness, perhaps stressing the latter. And since they regard the
mind and heart, *hsin,* as somehow one with nature *(hsing),* they
also regard *hsin* as full of *li* or goodness. In this way, their views
diverge from Chu Hsi's.

Liang-chih 良知

Literally, good knowledge, knowing the good.

The word *liang* contains also the meaning of "innateness," a reason
for the term to have been translated sometimes as "innate knowledge." But this translation is avoided as it is too much associated in
Western philosophy with Cartesian "innate ideas."

a. In the *Book of Mencius* (7A:15), the expression refers to man's
inborn capacity to know the good.

b. For Wang Yang-ming, it is that in man which enables him to discern between right and wrong, an inborn capacity to know and do
the good, a capacity to be developed as well as a goal to be
attained, since the perfect development of *liang-chih* signifies sagehood. He places the word *chih* (extend, develop), taken from *chih-
chih* 致知 ("extending knowledge," from the *Great Learning*) before
the term *liang-chih* to express his "Way" of acquiring sagehood and
wisdom. Yang-ming also speaks of *liang-chih* as the principle of vital
consciousness in man. He identifies it with *hsin,* especially by
speaking interchangeably of *hsin-chih pen-t'i* and of *liang-chih pen-t'i,*
i.e., the mind-in-itself and *liang-chih*-in-itself. In this context, he
gives it a metaphysical importance, as being-in-itself, identifying it
with *T'ai-hsü* (Great Void), which for him signifies in negative

terms the Absolute. Wang Yang-ming also understands *liang-chih* in man as that which possesses the ultimate authority for its own decisions, intentions, and actions. In the Four Sentences, he speaks of *hsin-chih-t'i* 心之體 also as being "without good and evil," another negative manner of attributing to it absolute qualities (First Sentence). Yet he returns in the Third Sentence to *liang-chih* as that which discerns between good and evil. Instead of showing mental confusion, this indicates that the term contains for him a multivalence of meaning on different levels.

   c. The *Ming-ju hsüeh-an* relates the philosophical controversies surrounding the discussion of the Four Sentences, especially of *wu-shan wu-ô* 無善無惡 (absence of good and evil), among the many branches of the Yang-ming school, as well as among Ming thinkers not directly descended from the Yang-ming lineage. The members of the T'ai-chou school (Wang Chi, Hsü Yüeh, Keng Ting-hsiang) speak of *hsien-ch'eng liang-chih* as that in us which is already perfect and so absolves us from the need of making efforts at spiritual cultivation.

Liu-hsing 流行

Literally, to flow, or flowing, as in the case of water moving and flowing. It is translated as process or the flow of process.

   a. The allusion is to *Mencius* 2A:2, where Confucius is quoted as referring to the "flow of virtue."

   b. In the *Ming-ju hsüeh-an,* it may describe either the flux or flow of nature or the stream of human consciousness—frequently the latter.

   Liu-hsing-chih-t'i 流行之體 refers to that which is in flux, in the "flow of process," either regarding cosmic change, or more often, the ebb and flow of inner consciousness.

Nieh-p'an 涅槃

Chinese transliteration of Sanskrit *nirvāṇa.*

   Nirvāṇa literally means "extinction," but refers in Buddhist contexts to release from the cycle of rebirth.

   In Sanskrit the cycle is called *saṃsāra,* a term with the literal meaning of rotation and popularly rendered in Chinese as *lun-hui* 輪廻. It is also transliterated into Chinese as *sheng-ssu* 生死 (literally, life and death), a term which sounds close to *saṃsāra.*

Nien 念

Literally, thought.

   It is frequently the Chinese Buddhist translation of the Sanskrit *smṛti,* which refers more to the power of memory.

Pen-t'i 本體

Usually translated as "original substance."

a. Wang Pi explains ultimate reality, called *pen-wu* 本無 or original nothingness, in terms of *pen-t'i,* in which *t'i* and *yung* are united.

b. In Ch'an Buddhism, it refers to the Absolute, which is usually described in negative terms, e.g., as emptiness *(śūnyatā).*

c. The Sung and Ming thinkers speak often of *pen-t'i.* Chu Hsi speaks especially of *hsing chih pen-t'i,* i.e., nature-in-itself.

d. Wang Yang-ming speaks interchangeably of *pen-t'i* (i.e., ultimate reality), *hsing chih pen-t'i,* and *liang-chih.* In his usage, *pen-t'i* refers to the true self or the true mind, as opposed to the self or mind which is affected by selfishness or passion.

e. In the *Ming-ju hsüeh-an,* it refers frequently to the mysterious and elusive ultimate meaning or reality that is being sought, as in the case of Kao P'an-lung.

San-chieh 三界

Literally, the three regions or realms. Sanskrit, *trilokya* or *trailokya.*

The Buddhist custom is to divide a universe into three philosophical-psychological categories: of desire, form, and formlessness.

Shou-lien 收斂

Literally, to gather together or to collect.

It refers to gathering one's self, one's inner faculties, together, keeping composure of mind and heart. It may be translated as "to recollect oneself," in the less-used sense of the English word "recollection," as found in the literature of spirituality (*not* as remembering). It is the opposite of *fa-shan* 發散 (to disperse), which refers sometimes to the dispersal of emotions or a generally distracted state of mind and heart.

Ssu-tuan 四端

Literally, the Four Beginnings.

In the *Book of Mencius* the term refers to the Four Beginnings of Virtue which are found in human nature.

T'ai-chi 太極

Literally, the Great Ultimate.

The term is found in the Great Appendix to the *Book of Changes* and in the *Lao-tzu,* in each case having a connotation close to that of the cosmic principle from which all things come to be.

a. For Chou Tun-yi, it represents the source and principle of all being and goodness, the ground of being, the One behind the Many, the fullness of *li.* As such, it is a kind of cosmic principle.

b. Chu Hsi identifies it with the *T'ien-li* of the Ch'eng brothers, the embodiment of all truth, wisdom, and virtue. He thus internalizes Chou's *T'ai-chi,* describing it as immanent not only in the whole of the cosmos, but in each individual being as well.

c. Wang Yang-ming seldom refers to it, and then usually as the source and principle of moral goodness.

T'ai-hsü 太虛

Literally, the Great Void.

a. For Chang Tsai, it is full of *ch'i* (matter-energy?), the shapeless stuff that makes up the universe.

b. Wang Yang-ming speaks of *liang-chih* as being somehow one with *T'ai-hsü*, thus endowing the latter not only with life and vitality but also with consciousness and a certain intelligence and spirituality. He speaks, for example, of *Liang-chih pen-t'i* as *T'ai-hsü*, describing it as a self-transcending state of mind-and-heart.

Tao 道

Literally, the "way" by which we travel.

It has the extended meaning of "reason." In philosophical usage, *Tao* is sometimes opposed to *ch'i* (literally, "utensil"), i.e., the concrete object. In this sense, it represents the metaphysical as versus the physical, the abstract as versus the concrete.

a. In Taoist philosophy, it refers to the nameless and ineffable or ultimate reality.

b. In Taoist occultism, it refers to the secret of life and the art of prolonging life.

c. In Buddhism, it refers to the meaning of life, ultimate reality, or Buddhahood.

d. In Confucianism, it refers to the way of life, especially the moral observance of the five relationships. It can refer as well to the meaning of life and to ultimate reality.

e. For Chu Hsi, the term refers to all the above meanings, as well as to the correct or orthodox knowledge of an ultimate reality or of the Absolute, as understood in the school of Confucius. This is held to be the understanding transmitted to posterity by the Ch'eng brothers and by himself, after the interruption that occurred with the death of Mencius.

f. For Wang Yang-ming, it refers to all the above meanings, including the meaning given by Chu Hsi, with the exception that for Wang Yang-ming, the *Tao* is identified with *hsin* as well.

Tao-hsin 道心

Literally, the "mind of Tao" or the "moral mind."

a. In the movement of thought called *Tao-hsüeh* 道學 as represented by the Ch'eng-Chu and Yang-ming schools, but especially by the former, it refers to the sacred legacy that is transmitted by the sages. As such, it is opposed to *jen-hsin* 人心 (literally, the "mind of man" or "human mind," with the "human" connoting frailness and fallibility). This usage alludes to a passage from the chapter of "Counsel of Great Yü" from the *Book of History*.

b. Ch'eng Yi explains *jen-hsin* as the mind-and-heart that is affected by *jen-yü* 人欲 (human passions or selfish desires) and *Tao-hsin* as the mind-and-heart that is full of *Tien-li* 天理 .

c. Chu Hsi explains *jen-hsin* as man's mind-and-heart, considered the seat of consciousness, composed of blood and "matter-energy" *(ch'i)*, and *Tao-hsin* as the same mind-and-heart, considered the source of moral discernment.

d. Wang Yang-ming regards *jen-hsin* as the mind-and-heart contaminated by passions and so prone to error, and *Tao-hsin* as the pure mind-and-heart, without passions or selfish desires and identical with *liang-chih*.

Tao wen-hsüeh 道問學

Literally, the path of inquiry and learning.

a. In the *Doctrine of the Mean* (ch. 27), it is given, together with *tsun te-hsing* 尊德性 (literally, to honor virtuous nature), as the gentleman's way of life: namely, to honor virtuous nature and follow the path of inquiry and learning, and in that order of priority.

b. With Sung Neo-Confucianism, the two expressions came to represent separate priorities. The school of Chu Hsi is often described as giving more priority to inquiry and learning, while the school of Lu Chiu-yüan is represented as giving more importance to honoring virtuous nature, that is, more concerned with moral than with intellectual values. This characterization continued to be used in Ming times.

T'i/yung 體用

Literally, "body" and "use," usually translated as substance and function. The problem arising therefrom is that the English word "substance" has a philosophical connotation of being immutable.

a. The words come from Wang Pi's commentary on the *Lao-tzu* (ch. 4) and refer to two cosmic states, the latent *(t'i)* and the manifest *(yung)*.

b. The Buddhist Seng-chao (384–414) describes the cosmos in terms of *hsin* (mind), referring to *t'i*, the "within" *(nei)*, and to *yung*, the "without" *(wai)*, that is, the manifestations of Mind. Through meditative trance *(samādhi)* one can unite with Mind and so acquire wisdom *(prajñā)*.

c. T'ien-t'ai Buddhism regards the Absolute, *Chen-ju (Tathāgata-garbha)* as *T'i* and its manifestations as *yung*.

d. Among the Sung and Ming thinkers, *T'i/yung* sometimes retains its metaphysical meanings, inherited from Neo-Taoism and Buddhism, and sometimes takes on a simpler meaning, as the "essential" or "basis" or "theory" *(t'i),* and as "function," "application," or "practice."

    e. Wang Yang-ming follows the Sung and Ming thinkers' usage, but more frequently refers to the metaphysical meaning. He often speaks of *t'i/yung* in terms of *pen-t'i* and *kung-fu.*

T'ien 天

Literally, Heaven or "sky."

    a. In the *Book of History,* it is synonymous with *Shang-ti* 上帝 ,the Lord-on-high, i.e., God.

    b. In the *Analects,* it refers especially to the Supreme Being.

    c. For Mencius, it refers sometimes to the Supreme Being, sometimes to the ultimate truth of the universe, or to the fullness of goodness, and sometimes to fate or destiny.

    d. For Hsün-tzu, it refers especially to the physical heaven, i.e., the sky, or to nature.

    e. For Tung Chung-shu, it refers sometimes to nature at large, to which he attributes qualities of intelligence and spirituality.

    f. The Sung and Ming thinkers sometimes speak of *T'ien-ti* 天地 , i.e., Heaven and Earth, as representing the whole universe, and sometimes speak of *T'ien* alone, as representing the whole universe, or the fullness of being and goodness.

    g. Yang-ming identifies *T'ien* with *Tao,* with *hsin,* and with *liang-chih.*

T'ien-li 天理

Literally, heavenly reason, principle of Heaven, principle of nature.

    a. It is found in the *Book of Rites,* chapter on music, where it refers to the moral law of Heaven, in which all men share by their reason, and as such is opposed to *jen-yü* (passions).

    b. The two Ch'engs speak of *T'ien-li* as the fullness of being and goodness, innate in human nature as well as in all things, and also oppose it to *jen-yü.*

    c. Chu Hsi follows this interpretation and identifies *T'ai-chi,* a term derived from the *Book of Changes* and given importance especially by Chou Tun-yi, as source and principle of being and goodness, to *T'ien-li.* Thus he internalizes this concept, describing it as immanent not only in the whole universe but also in each individual being.

Ting 定

Literally, fixity, calm. Sanskrit, *samādhi.*

    It refers to perfect tranquility, a state of deep peace attained in meditation.

Tung/Ching 動靜

Literally, activity and stillness or tranquility, movement and quiescence. They may refer to activity and contemplation.

a. The *Great Learning* mentions *ching;* the Appendix to the *Book of Changes* mentions both *tung* and *ching,* as does the *Book of Rites'* chapter on music.
b. The Sung and Ming thinkers often identify *tung* with *yi-fa* and *ching* with *wei-fa.*
c. In the *Ming-ju hsüeh-an,* the terms refer sometimes to action and contemplation as two ways of life or, even more, as two options to pursue in the quest for sagehood.

Wei-fa/Yi-fa 未發巳發

Literally, "aroused" and "not yet aroused."
a. In the *Doctrine of the Mean,* the words refer to two successive states of consciousness, which prevail before and after the emotions are aroused.
b. Chu Hsi speaks of *wei-fa* in terms of *chung* (equilibrium) and recommends that it be restored and preserved.
c. Wang Yang-ming regards the terms as referring to two aspects under which *liang-chih,* always active and yet always the same, can be understood.
d. In the *Ming-ju hsüeh-an,* *yi-fa* and *wei-fa* are sometimes used to represent action and contemplation, commitment to moral action and to quietude and meditation.

Wu 悟

Literally, awakening. Sanskrit, *bodhi;* Japanese, *satori.*

Another Chinese word, *chüeh* 覺, has the same meaning. It refers either to that intelligence or knowledge by which a person becomes a Buddha or to just a transient mystical experience bringing some illumination.

Wu/Hsiu 悟修

Usually translated as enlightenment and cultivation.
a. The idea of sudden enlightenment (*tun-wu* 頓悟)is prominent in Chuang-tzu. The teaching of sudden enlightenment (*tun-wu*) is especially attributed to the monk Tao-shen (c. 360–434) and to the Ch'an patriarch Hui-neng (638–713). Discussion gradually evolved regarding the relationship between enlightenment and cultivation (*hsiu*).
b. The word cultivation (*hsiu*) is found in the *Great Learning,* where it refers to self-cultivation. In this context, it is frequently spoken of by Sung and Ming thinkers. Chu Hsi's teaching contains elements suggesting the importance of enlightenment. Wang Yang-ming speaks of it openly, especially in his Four Sentences.
c. In the *Ming-ju hsüeh-an,* Huang Tsung-hsi likes to speak of *wu/hsiu,* sometimes as paths followed by personalities he represents as *k'uang* and *chüan* respectively.

Wu-sheng wu-ch'ou 無聲無臭

Literally, without sound or smell.

a. The expression comes from the *Book of Poetry* (III. i. Ode 1, stanza 7), where the workings of Heaven are described as imperceptible, "without sound or smell."

b. This is quoted in the *Doctrine of the Mean* (ch. 23). However, in the earlier classic, it referred historically to the overthrow of the Shang dynasty. Here, it is quoted in the context of a discourse on virtue.

c. Neo-Confucian philosophers frequently use this expression to refer to Heaven, the Absolute, or that transcendent goal they seek. This is Kao P'an-lung's usage in his autobiographical account in the *Ming-ju hsüeh-an*. It is another proof of the spiritual and transcendent dimension of the Neo-Confucian movement, as well as of the mysticism it developed.

Wu-wang wu-chu 勿忘勿助

Literally, neither forgetting nor helping.

This is an allusion to *Mencius* 2A:2, where cultivation of the mind is discussed as that which should be undertaken with proper seriousness (i.e., without forgetting) and also with proper detachment (without helping), or without forcing oneself. According to this passage, one otherwise acts like the man who pulled up his corn in order to help it to grow. (*Chu-chang* 助長 means "help to grow.")

Yü 欲

Literally, desire, passion. Sanskrit, *rajas, kāma*.

Wu-yü 物欲 refers to the desire for material things or creature comforts; *Wu-yü* 無欲 refers to having no desire, i.e., desirelessness.

Selected Bibliographies

The division of sources into various categories is made mainly to facilitate finding the works listed. Bibliographical information is also given according to the genres of the works themselves and scholarly usage. For works that are better known by their titles than by their authors or compilers, or for which authorship is composite or in dispute, only the title and the edition (or the collection) are listed. One example is *Chuang-tzu;* others are the Dynastic Histories. For works from the Buddhist canon, only the titles of the sūtras are given (in Sanskrit whenever possible), followed by their title numbers in the *TSD.* In the case of local histories or gazetteers, only titles and dates of publication are given. For other primary sources, such as collected works in Chinese, the author and title are given, and the date of publication (as noted in the book's preface) is listed wherever possible. In those cases where the books used belong to a series, the series name is given in abbreviation.

The following bibliographical information concerning certain large series of books may be useful:

Chin-lin ts'ung-shu. This collection was published by Wen Ch'ang-sheng and Chiang Kuo-pang between 1914 and 1916.

CYTC. This series of mainly Neo-Confucian texts was compiled and published by Chang Po-hsing, with subsequent additions by Tso Tsung-t'ang (1866–70).

ESWS. The Twenty-five Dynastic Histories series was originally published in Shanghai, by Kaiming Press, in 1935.

Han-fen lou mi-chi. This collection was first published in Shanghai, by the Commercial Press (1916–26).

Hsüeh-hai lei-pien. This collection was compiled by Ts'ao Jung (1831) and published in Shanghai by Han-fen lou (1920).

Kuang-li-hsüeh pei-k'ao. This collection of mainly Neo-Confucian texts was compiled and published originally by Fan Hao-ting (1825).

SPPY. This series was originally published by Chung-hua shu-chü, Shanghai (1927–36). It includes over two thousand volumes of books selected from the Imperial Four Libraries series (1773–83).

SPTK. This came out originally during the years 1919–22, with additions in 1929 and 1936. The publisher was the Commercial Press, Shanghai. Many of the books were earlier in the Han-fen-lou series. It includes over eleven thousand volumes, also selected principally from the Imperial Four Libraries series.

Ssu-k'u ch'üan-shu. The Four Libraries or the Imperial Four Libraries series represents the largest collection of Chinese books. It was collected and copied by imperial order of Emperor Ch'ien-lung and under the directorship of Chi Yün and other scholars (1773–83). It includes 79,070 *chüan*. The National Central Library selected some of the rare books for photographic reprint (1935) by the Shanghai Commercial Press. Subsequently, more appeared under the auspices of the Commercial Press in Taipei (1971–76).

TSCC. This mammoth collection of about 20,000 thin volumes was published by the Shanghai Commercial Press (1st series, 1935–37). It is a heterogenous collection of over two thousand books considered rare and useful.

TSD. The Taishō edition of the Buddhist canon was brought to print by a group of leading Japanese scholars, including Takakusu Junjirō and others, with a publishing company bearing the same name as the collection (1924–27). Taishō is the name of the reign period of the then Japanese emperor. It includes mainly Chinese translations of Buddhist works from Pali and Sanskrit, as well as Chinese and Japanese commentaries, and has become recognized as the standard edition.

Yü-chang ts'ung-shu. This collection was originally published by T'ao Fu-lü (1890).

Yüeh-ya-t'ang ts'ung-shu. This was collected and published by Wu Ch'ung-yao of Nan-hai, Kwangtung (1850–75).

I.   Primary Sources and Other Older Works

A.   Chinese Works

Avataṃsaka Sūtra (*Hua-yen ching* 華嚴經). *TSD*, no. 278.

Chan Jo-shui 湛若水. *Kan-ch'üan wen-chi* 甘泉文集. 1886 ed., microfilm copy.

Chan-kuo-tse chiao-chu 戰國策校注. SPPY ed.

Chang Po-hsing 張伯行 comp. *Cheng-Yi-t'ang chüan-shu* 正誼堂全書 1866–70.

Chang Tsai 張載. *Chang-tzu ch'üan-shu* 張子全書. SPPY ed.

Chao-lun 肇論. *TSD*, No. 1858.

Ch'en Chien 陳建. *Huang-Ming tzu-chih t'ung-chi* 皇明資治通紀. 1551 ed., NLP microfilm no. 979–80.

———. *Po-sha-tzu ch'üan-chi* 白沙子全集. 1612 ed., Taipei reprint, 1973.

Ch'en Ting 陳鼎, ed. *Tung-lin lieh-chuan* 東林列傳. 1711 ed., Taipei, Commercial Press, 1975.

Ch'eng Hao 程顥 and Ch'eng Yi 程頤. *Erh-Ch'eng ch'üan-shu* 二程全書 incorporating *Yi-shu* 遺書, *Wai-shu* 外書, *Ming-tao wen-chi* 明道文集, and *Yi-ch'uan wen-chi* 伊川文集, SPPY ed.

Chi Yün 紀昀 et al. *Ssu-k'u ch'üan-shu tsung-mu t'i-yao* 四庫全書總目提要. Shanghai, Commercial Press, 1933.

Ch'i-sung 契嵩. *Ch'uan-fa cheng-tsung chi. 傳法正宗紀. TSD*, no. 2078.

Chiang Hsin 蔣信. *Chiang Tao-lin wen-ts'ui* 蔣道林文粹. NCL microfilm copy.

Chiao Hung 焦竑. *T'an-yüan chi* 澹園集. *Chin-ling ts'ung-shu* 金陵叢書.

———. *Kuo-ch'ao hsien-cheng lu* 國朝獻徵錄 NCL Rare Books, Taipei reprint, Hsüeh-sheng, 1965.

Ching-te ch'uan-teng lu 景德傳燈錄. SPTK ed.

Chou Ju-teng 周汝登. *Sheng-hsüeh tsung-chuan* 聖學宗傳. Preface 1606.

———. *Tung-yüeh tseng-tao lu* 東越證道錄. 1605 ed., Taipei reprint, 1970.

Chou Tun-yi 周敦頤. *Chou-tzu t'ung-shu* 周子通書. SPPY ed.

Chou-yi cheng-yi 周易正義. SPPY ed.

Chu Hsi 朱熹. *Chu-tzu ch'üan-shu* 朱子全書. 1714 ed.

———. *Chu-tzu yi-shu* 朱子遺書. Taipei, Yi-wen Press, 1969.

———. *Chu-tzu yü-lei* 朱子語類. 1473 ed., Taipei reprint, Cheng-chung shu-chü, 1970.

———. *Chu Wen-kung wen-chi* 朱文公文集. SPPY ed.

———. *Hsiao-hsüeh chi-chu* 小學集注. SPPY ed. (Also *Hsiao-hsüeh chi-chieh* 小學集解, ed. by Chang Po-hsing in CYTC series.)

———. *Ssu-shu chi-chu* 四書集注, incorporating *Ta-hsüeh chang-chu* 大學章句, *Chung-yung chang chu* 中庸章句, *Lun-yü chi-chu* 論語集注, and *Meng-tzu chi-chu* 孟子集注. SPPY ed.

———. *Sung ming-ch'en yen-hsing lu* 宋名臣言行錄 with Supplement by Li Yi-wu 李幼武 in *Sung-shih chih-liao ts'ui-pien* 宋史資料粹編 (Selected Anthology of Sung Historical Materials), comp. by Chao T'ieh-han 趙鐵寒. First series. Taipei, Wen-hai, 1967.

———. *Yi-lo yüan-yüan lu* 伊洛淵源錄. CYTC series.

——— and Lü Tsu-ch'ien 呂祖謙. *Chin-ssu lu chi-chu* 近思錄集注. SPPY ed.

Ch'üan Tsu-wang 全祖望. *Chieh-ch'i-t'ing chi* 鮚琦亭集. 1804 ed. and 1872 ed.

Chuang-tzu 莊子. SPPY ed.

Fang Hsiao-ju 方孝儒. *Fang Cheng-hsüeh chi* 方正學集. CYTC series.

Fu Hsi 傅翕. *Fu Ta-shih tsui-hui shuo-fa.* 傅大士 *Zokuzōkyō.* 續藏經 v. 129.

Han Yü 韓愈. *Han Ch'ang-li ch'üan-shu chiao-chu* 韓昌黎全書校注. Taipei, 1972.

Han-shu 漢書, comp. by Pan Ku 班固. *ESWS* series.

Hou Han-shu 後漢書, comp. by Fan Yeh 范曄. *ESWS* series.

Hsieh Chao-che 謝肇淛. *Tien-lüeh* 滇略. Imperial Four Libraries Collection Rare Books series, Taipei, 1972.

Hsin-T'ang shu 新唐書, comp. by Ou-yang Hsiu 歐陽修. *ESWS* series.

Hsü Hsien 許獻, ed. *Tung-lin shu-yüan chih* 東林書院志. 1881 ed.

Hsü Hsüeh-mo 徐學模. *Shih-miao shih-yu lu* 世廟識餘錄. Taipei reprint, 1965.

Hsü Hung 徐紘. *Huang-Ming ming-ch'en wan-yen lu* 皇明名臣琬琰錄. NCL microfilm copy.

Hsü K'ai-jen 徐開任. *Ming ming-ch'en yen-hsing lu* 明名臣言行錄. Preface 1681.

Hsüeh Hsüan 薛瑄. *Hsüeh Ching-hsüan hsien-sheng chi* 薛敬軒先生集, in *Kuang li-hsüeh pei-k'ao* 廣理學備考 series.

―――. *Tu-shu lu* 讀書錄, and *Hsü-lu* 續錄. 1827 ed.

Hsüeh Ying-ch'i 薛應旂. *Fang-shan chi-shu* 方山紀述 in *Hsüeh-hai lei-pien* 學海類編, v. 31.

―――. *Hsien-chang lu* 憲章錄. 1573 ed.

Hsün-tzu 荀子. SPPY ed.

Hu Chih 胡直. *Hu-tzu Heng-ch'i* 胡子衡齊, in *Yü-chang ts'ung shu* 豫章叢書 series.

―――. *Heng-lu ching-she hsü-kao* 衡廬精舍續稿 incorporating the *K'un-hsüeh chi* 困學記, 1902 ed.

Hu Chü-jen 胡居仁. *Chü-yeh lu* 居業錄. CYTC series.

―――. *Hu Ching-chai chi* 胡敬齋集. CYTC series.

Hu Kuang 胡廣 et al., comp. *Hsing-li ta-ch'üan* 性理大全. 1597 ed.

Huang Chi 黃驥. *Pen-ch'ao fen-sheng jen-wu k'ao* 本朝分省人物考 (1622). Taipei, 1971.

Huang Tsun-su 黃尊素. *Huang Chung-tuan kung yi-chi* 黃忠端公遺集, comp. by Huang Pin-hou 黃炳垕. 1887 ed. (Appended to this is Huang Tsung-hsi's *nien-p'u* 年譜, also compiled by Huang Pin-hou.)

————. *Shuo-lüeh* 說略, in *Han fen-lou mi-chi* 涵芬樓秘笈, v. 13.

Huang Tsung-hsi 黃宗羲. *Huang Li-chou wen-chi.* 黃梨洲文集. Peking, Chung-hua shu-chü, 1959.

————. *Huang Tsung-hsi ch'üan-chi* 黃宗羲全集 ed. by Shen Shan-hung 沈善洪 and others. Vol. 1. Hangchow, Chekiang Ku-chi ch'u-pan-she, 1985.

[————.] *Hung-kuang shih-lu ch'ao* 弘光實錄鈔, 4 *chüan*, appended to Ch'ien Shih 錢𮊙, *Chia-sheng ch'uan-hsin lu* 甲申傳信錄. 1951 ed. Shanghai reprint, 1982.

————. *Li-chou yi-chu hui-k'an* 梨洲遺著彙刊, ed. by Hsüeh Feng-ch'an 薛鳳昌, in *Ming-Ch'ing shih-liao hui-pien* 明清史料彙編, comp. by Shen Yün-lung 沈雲龍. Taipei, Wen-hai, 1969.

————. *Ming-ju hsüeh-an* 明儒學案. SPPY ed., and selected editions by Liang Ch'i-ch'ao 梁啓超 (Shanghai, 1906), Miao T'ien-shou 繆天綬 (Shanghai, 1933), and Li Hsin-chuang 李心莊 (Chungking, 1945).

————. *Ming-yi tai-fang lu* 明夷待訪錄. Taipei, Kuang-wen, 1965.

————. *Nan-lei wen-an* 南雷文案. Shanghai, Shih-chung, 1910; also in Shen Yün-lung, *Ming-Ch'ing shih-liao hui-pien*, comp. by Shen Yün-lung, 1969.

————. *Nan-lei wen-ting* 南雷文定. Shanghai, Shih-chung, 1910.

————. *Nan-lei wen-yüeh* 南雷文約. Shanghai, Shih-chung, 1910.

————. *P'o-hsieh lun* 破邪論. Shanghai, Shih-chung, 1910.

————, et al. *Sung-yüan hsüeh-an* 宋元學案. Taipei, Shih-chieh, 1966.

Huai-nan-tzu 淮南子. SPPY ed.

Huang Wan 黃綰. *Ming-tao pien* 明道編. Peking reprint, 1959.

Kao P'an-lung 高攀龍. *Kao-tzu yi-shu* 高子遺書 ed. by Ch'en Lung-cheng 陳龍正. 1746 ed.

Keng Ting-hsiang 耿定向. *Keng T'ien-t'ai hsien-sheng wen-chi* 耿天臺先生文集. 1598 ed. Taipei reprint, 1970.

Ku Hsien-ch'eng 顧憲成. *Ku Tuan-wen kung yi-shu* 顧端文公遺書. ca. 1698 ed., 1877 reprint, incorporating *Hsiao-hsin-chai cha-chi.* 小心齋劄記. Taipei, Kuang-wen, 1975.

————. *Ching-kao ts'ang-kao* 涇臯藏稿. 1847 ed.

Ku Yen-wu 顧炎武. *Jih-chih lu chi-shih* 日知錄集釋. SPPY ed.

Ku Ying-t'ai 谷應泰. *Ming-shih chi-shih pen-mo* 明史紀事本末. TSCC ed. 1st series.

Kuo T'ing-hsün 郭廷訓. *Pen-ch'ao fen-sheng jen-wu k'ao* 本朝分省人物考. 1622 ed. Taipei, Ch'eng-wen, 1971.

(*Leng-chia-ching* 楞伽經). *TSD*, no. 670.

Lao-tzu 老子. SPPY ed.

Liu Tsung-chou 劉宗周. *Liu-tzu ch'üan-shu* 劉子全書. 1822 ed.

———. *Liu-tzu ch'üan-shu yi-pien* 劉子全書遺編. 1850 ed.

Liu-tsu ta-shih fa-pao t'an-ching 六祖大師法寶壇經 (Platform Scripture). *TSD*, no. 2007.

Lo Ch'in-shun 羅欽順. *K'un-hsüeh chi* 困學記. CYTC series.

———. *Lo Cheng-an hsien-sheng ts'un-kao* 羅整庵先生存稿. CYTC series.

Lo Hung-hsien 羅洪光. *Nien-an Lo hsien-sheng chi* 念庵羅先生集. 1586 ed.

Lo Ju-fang 羅汝芳. *Hsü-t'an chih-ch'üan* 盰壇直詮. n.d. Taipei reprint, Kuang-wen, 1967.

———. *Lo Chin-hsi hsien-sheng ch'üan-chi* 羅近溪先生全集. 1618 ed.

———. *Lo Chin-hsi tzu chi* 羅近溪子集. 1606 ed.

Lu Chiu-yüan 陸九淵. *Hsiang-shan ch'üan-chi* 象山全集. SPPY ed.

Lü K'un 呂坤. *Ch'ü-wei-chai wen-chi* 去偽齋文集 in *Lü-tzu yi-shu* 呂子遺書. 1936. This collection includes the *Kuei-fan t'u-shuo* 閨範圖說.

Lü Liu-liang 呂留良. *Lü Wan-ts'un hsien-sheng wen-chi* 呂晚村先生文集. Taipei reprint, 1967.

Mahāparinirvāṇa Sūtra. *TSD*, no. 374.

Mao Te-ch'i 毛德琦. *Po-lu shu-yüan chih* 白鹿書院志. 1795 ed.

Ming-shih 明史., comp. by Chang T'ing-yü 張廷玉 and others. *ESWS* series.

Ming shih-lu 明實錄 comp. by Hu Kuang and others. Huakang, Taiwan, Academia Sinica, 1960–62.

Mo-tzu 墨子. SPPY ed.

Nieh Pao 聶豹. *Shuang-chiang Nieh hsien-sheng wen-chi* 雙江聶先生文集. 1572 ed.

Ou-yang Hsiu 歐陽修. *Ou-yang Wen-chung kung wen-chi* 歐陽文忠公文集. SPTK ed.

Ou-yang Te 歐陽德. *Ou-yang Nan-yeh hsien-sheng wen-hsüan* 歐陽南野先生文選. Preface 1569.

Saddharma-puṇḍarīka (Lotus Sūtra). *TSD*, no. 262.

San-kuo chih 三國志, comp. by Ch'en Shou 陳壽. *ESWS* series.

Shao Yung 邵雍. *Huang-chi ching-shih shu* 皇極經世書. SPPY ed.

Shih-chi 史記, comp. by Ssu-ma Ch'ien 司馬遷. *ESWS* series.

Shui-ching chu 水經注, comp. by Li Tao-yüan 酈道元. Shanghai reprint, 1958.

Ssu-ma Kuang 司馬光. *Hsin-chiao Tzu-chih t'ung-chien* 新校資治通鑑. Taipei, Shih-chieh, 1969.

Sun Ch'i-feng 孫奇逢. *Li-hsüeh tsung-chuan* 理學宗傳. 1666 ed. Taipei, Yi-wen, 1969.

Sung-shih 宋史, comp. by T'o-t'o 脫脫. *ESWS* series.

Sūraṅgama Sūtra (*Lun-yen ching* 楞嚴經). *TSD*, no. 945.

T'an Ch'ien 談遷. *Kuo-ch'ueh* 國榷. Shanghai reprint, 1958.

T'ang Chien 唐鑑. *Ch'ing hsüeh-an hsiao-shih* 清學案小識. 1845 ed.

T'ang Shun-chih 唐順之. *Ching-ch'uan hsien-sheng wen-chi wai-chi* 荊川先生文集外傳. SPTK ed.

Tao-shih 道世, comp. *Fa-yüan chu-lin* 法苑珠林. SPTK 1st series.

T'ao Wang-ling 陶望齡. *Hsieh-an chi* 歇庵集. Taipei reprint, Wei-wen, 1976.

Teng Yuan-hsi 鄧元錫. *Huang-Ming shu* 皇明書 1606 ed.

Ts'ao Tuan 曹端. *Ts'ao Yüeh-ch'uan hsien-sheng chi* 曹月川先生集. This work includes *Yeh-hsing chu* 夜行燭. *Kuang li-hsüeh pei-k'ao* series.

Tsou Shou-yi 鄒守益. *Tung-kuo hsien-sheng wen-chi* 東郭先生文集. 1538 ed. NLP microfilm no. 1003.

Tu Mu 杜牧. *Fan-ch'uan wen-chi* 樊川文集. SPTK 1st series lithograph ed.

Wang Ch'ang-ling 王昌齡. *Wang Ch'ang-ling shih chiao-chu* 王昌齡詩校注. Taipei, 1973.

Wang Chi 王畿. *Wang Lung-hsi hsien-sheng ch'üan-chi* 王龍溪先生全集. 1822 ed. Taipei reprint, 1970.

Wang Ch'ung 王充. *Lun-heng* 論衡 SPPY ed.

Wang Ken 王艮. *Wang Hsin-chai hsien-sheng ch'üan-chi* 王心齋先生全集. 1846 Japanese ed. Taipei, Kuang-wen, 1975.

Wang Shou-jen 王守仁. *Wang Wen-ch'eng kung ch'üan-shu* 王文成公全書. SPTK 1st series lithograph ed.

Wang Shu 王恕. *T'ai-shih Wang Tuan-yi tsou-yi* 太師王端毅奏議. NLP microfilm no. 42.

Wu Yü-pi 吳與弼. *Wu K'ang-chai wen-chi* 吳康齋文集. Imperial Four Libraries Collection Rare Books series.

Wu-men-kuan 無門關. *TSD*, no. 2005.

Yang Lien 楊廉. *Huang-Ming ming-ch'en yen-hsing lu* 皇明名臣言行錄 1541 ed.

Yang Shih 楊時. *Kuei-shan chi* 龜山集. Imperial Four Libraries Collection Rare Books series. Taipei, 1973.

Yin Chih 尹直. *Chien-chai so-chui lu* 謇齋瑣綴錄 in *Ming-tai shih-chi hui-k'an* 明代史籍彙刊 ed. by Ch'ü Wan-li 屈萬里. Taipei, Hsüeh-sheng, 1969.

Yü Hsien 俞憲. *Huang-Ming chin-shih teng-k'o k'ao* 皇明進士登科考, in *Ming-tai shih-chi hui-k'an.* ed. by Ch'ü Wan-li. Taipei, Hsüeh-sheng, 1969.

Yüan Hao-wen 元好問. *Yüan Yi-shan hsien-sheng ch'üan-chi* 元遺山先生全集. 1881 ed.

Yüan-chüeh ching 圓覺經. *TSD*, no. 842.

B.   Local Histories (Gazetteers)

An-fu hsien-chih 安福縣志. 1872 ed.
Ch'ang-chou fu-chih 常州府志. 1884 ed.
Ching-shan hsien-chih 京山縣志. 1882 ed.
Chekiang t'ung-chih 浙江通志. 1934 ed.
Hunan t'ung-chih 湖南通志. 1934 ed.
Jao-chao fu-chih 饒州府志. 1872 ed.
Kuang-hsin fu-chih 廣信府志. 1873 ed.
Shao-hsing fu-chih 紹興府志. 1586 ed., microfilm copy.
Yünnan t'ung-chih 雲南通志. 1894 ed.
Yüyao hsien-chih 餘姚縣志. 1899 ed.

C.   Translations and Anthologies

Book of Changes (Yi-ching). The Yi King. Trans. by James Legge. *SBE,* v. 16. Oxford, Clarendon, 1892. Delhi reprint, 1966.

Book of Historical Documents (Shu-ching). Trans. by James Legge with introduction, critical and exegetical notes, and indexes. *The Chinese Classics,* v. 4, parts 1 and 2. Oxford, Clarendon, 1893. Hongkong reprint, 1960.

Book of Rites (Li-chi). The Li Ki, an Encyclopaedia of Ancient Ceremonial Usages, Religious Creeds and Social Institutions. Trans. by James Legge. The Sacred Books of the East series, v. 27–28. Oxford, Clarendon, 1885. New edition by Ch'u Ch'ai and Winberg Chai. New York, University Books, 1967.

Chu Hsi. *Reflections on Things at Hand.* Trans. by Wing-tsit Chan. New York, Columbia University Press, 1967.

Ch'an and Zen Teachings. Comp. and trans. by Charles Luk. 3rd series. London, Rider, 1962.

Chuang-tzu. *The Complete Works of Chuang-tzu.* Trans. by Burton Watson. New York, Columbia University Press, 1968.

Confucian Analects (Lun-yü). Trans. by James Legge with introduction, critical and exegetical notes, and indexes. *The Chinese Classics,* v. 1. Oxford, Clarendon, 1893. Hongkong reprint, 1960.

Doctrine of the Mean (Chung-yung). Trans. by James Legge. *The Chinese Classics,* v. 1. Oxford, Clarendon, 1893. Hongkong reprint, 1960.

Great Learning (Ta-hsüeh). Trans. by James Legge. *The Chinese Classics,* v. 1. Oxford, Clarendon, 1893. Hongkong reprint, 1960.

Han Fei Tzu: Basic Writings. Trans. by Burton Watson. New York, Columbia University Press, 1964.

Hui-neng. *The Platform Sutra of the Sixth Patriarch: The Text of the Tun-huang Manuscript.* Trans. with introduction and annotations by Philip B. Yampolsky. New York, Columbia University Press, 1967.

The Laṇkāvatāra Sūtra, Mahāyāna Text. Trans. by Daisetz T. Suzuki. London, Routledge, 1932. 1959 reprint.

Lao-tzu: Tao-te-ching. Trans. by D. C. Lau. Harmondsworth, Penguin, 1963.

Liu Hsiang, comp. *Chan-kuo ts'e.* Trans. by J. I. Crump, Jr. Oxford, Clarendon, 1970.

[*The Lotus Sūtra*] *Scripture of the Lotus Blossom of the Fine Dharma.* Trans. by Leon Hurvitz. New York, Columbia University Press, 1976.

Mencius. Trans. by D. C. Lau. Harmondsworth, Penguin, 1970. Also, *The Works of Mencius.* Trans. by James Legge. *The Chinese Classics,* v. 2. Oxford, Clarendon, 1895. Hongkong reprint, 1960.

Mo Tzu: Basic Writings. Trans. by Burton Watson. New York, Columbia University Press, 1963.

Seng-chao. *Cho Lun: The Treatises of Seng-chao.* Trans. by Walter Liebenthal. Peiping, Catholic University, 1948. 2nd revised edition. Hongkong University Press, 1968.

A Source Book in Chinese Philosophy. Comp. and trans. by Wing-tsit Chan. Princeton, Princeton University Press, 1963.

Spring-Autumn Annals (Ch'un-ch'iu) and Annals of Tso (Tso-chuan). The Ch'un Ts'ew with the Tso Chuan, parts 1 and 2. Trans. by James Legge with introduction, critical and exegetical notes, and indexes. *The Chinese Classics,* v. 5. Oxford, Clarendon, 1893. Hongkong reprint, 1960.

The Sūraṇgama Sūtra. Trans. by Charles Luk. London, Rider, 1966.

Tao-yüan. *The Transmission of the Lamp.* Original Teachings of Ch'an Buddhism, selected from the Transmission of the Lamp. Trans. by Chang Chung-yuan. New York, Pantheon, 1969.

Vajrāccedika Prajñāpāramitā (Buddhist Wisdom Books: The Diamond Sutra and the Heart Sutra). Trans. by Edward Conze. London, Allen and Unwin, 1958.

Wang Shou-jen (Wang Yang-ming). *Instructions for Practical Living and Other Neo-Confucian Writings.* Trans. by Wing-tsit Chan. New York, Columbia University Press, 1963.

————. *The Philosophical Letters of Wang Yang-ming*. Trans. and ann. by Julia Ching. Canberra, Australian National University Press & University of South Carolina Press, 1972.

II.   Other References

A.   *Miscellaneous Chinese and Japanese Works*

Aoyama Sadao 青山定雄. *Chūgoku rekidai chimei yōran* 中国歴代地名要覧 (A Directory of Important Chinese Historical Place Names). Tokyo, first ed., 1933; third ed., Taiwan, 1965.

Araki Kengo 荒木見悟. *Minmatsu shūkyō shisō kenkyū* 明末宗教思想研究 (Religious Philosophies of the Late Ming). Tokyo, Sōbunsha, 1979.

Araki Kengo, Okada Takehiko 岡田武彦 et al., *Yōmeigaku benran* 陽明学便覧 (A User's Guide to the Yang-ming School), v. 12 of *Yōmeigaku taikei* 陽明学大系 (A Compendium of the School of Wang Yang-ming). Tokyo, Meitoku, 1974.

Chan, Wing-tsit 陳榮捷. "Lun *Ming-ju hsüeh-an* chih *Shih-shuo,*" 論明儒學案之師說 (On the "Teacher's Sayings" in the *Records of Ming Scholars*). *You-shih* 幼獅 Monthly, v. 48 (1978), 6–8.

Ch'en T'ieh-fan 陳鐵凡. *Sung-Yüan-Ming-Ch'ing Ssu-ch'ao hsüeh-an so-yin* 宋元明清四朝學案索引 (Index to the Records of Scholars of the Four Dynasties: Sung through Ch'ing). Taipei, Yi-wen, 1974.

Ch'ien Mu 錢穆. *Chung-kuo che-hsüeh ssu-hsiang lun-chi. Sung-Ming P'ien* 中國哲學思想論集宋明篇 (On the History of Philosophical Thought in China: Sung through Ming Times). Taipei, Tung-ta, 1976–77.

————. *Chung-kuo chin-san-pai-nien hsüeh-shu shih* 中國近三百年學術史 (A History of Chinese Scholarship of the Last Three Centuries). 2 v. Shanghai, Commercial, n.d. Taipei reprint, 1967.

Fan Hsi-tseng 范希曾. *Shu-mu ta-wen pu-cheng* 書目答問補正 (Revised and Enlarged Edition of Chang Chih-tung's Handbook on Bibliography). Peking reprint, Chung-hua, 1963.

Fung Yu-lan 馮友蘭. *Chung-kuo che-hsüeh shih* 中國哲學史. (A History of Chinese Philosophy). Shanghai, Commercial, 1935.

————. *Chung-kuo che-hsüeh-shih hsin-pien* 中國哲學史新篇 (A Revised History of Chinese Philosophy), v. 1. Peking, Jen-min, 1980.

————. *Chung-kuo che-hsüeh shih shih-liao hsüeh ch'u-kao* 中國哲學史史料學初稿 (A Draft Introduction to the Sources of the History of Chinese Philosophy). Shanghai, Jen-min, 1962.

Goto Motomi 後藤基己, Okada Takehiko, Yamanoi Yū 山井湧 et al., ed.

Yōmeimonka 陽明学門下 (Yang-ming's Disciples). *Yōmeigaku taikei*, v. 7. Tokyo, Meitoku, 1974.

Hsieh Kuo-cheng 謝國楨. *Huang Li-chou hsüeh-p'u* 黃梨洲學譜 (An Intellectual Biography of Huang Tsung-hsi). 1932 ed., Taipei reprint, Commercial, 1967.

Hu Ch'iu-yüan 胡秋原. "Wei-ta ai-kuo che-hsüeh ho ssu-hsiang chia *Huang Li-chou*" 偉大愛國哲學和思想家黃梨洲 (Huang Tsung-hsi, the Great Patriot Philosopher), *Chung hua tsa-chih* 中華雜誌 5 (1967), 19–25.

Huang Chien-chang 黃健彰. *Ming-Ch'ing-shih yen-chiu ts'ung-kao* 明清史研究叢稿 (Studies on Ming and Ch'ing History). Taipei, Commercial, 1977.

Huang Chin-shing 黃進興. "*Hsüeh-an t'i-ts'ai ch'an-sheng te ssu-hsiang pei-ching*" 學案體裁產生的思想背景 (The Emergence of a Historical Genre: the Background to the 'Philosophical Records') *Han-hsüeh yen-chiu* 漢學研究 (Chinese Studies) 2 (1984), 201–21.

Huang K'ai-hua 黃開華. *Ming-shih lun-chi* 明史論集 (Essays on Ming History). Taipei, Ch'eng-ming, 1972.

Huang Kung-wei 黃公偉. *Chung-kuo Fo-chiao ssu-hsiang ch'uan-t'ung shih* 中國佛教思想傳統史 (A History of the Transmission of Buddhist Thought in China). Taipei, Shih-tzu hsün tsa-chih, 1972.

Jung Chao-tsu 容肇祖. *Ming-tai ssu-hsiang shih* 明代思想史 (A History of Ming Thought). First published, 1941. Taipei reprint, Kaiming, 1962.

Ku Ch'ing-mei 古清美. *Huang Li-chou chih shen-p'ing chi ch'i ssu-hsiang* 黃梨洲之生平及其思想 (The Life and Thought of Huang Tsung-hsi). Taipei, Taiwan University Press, 1978.

Liang Ch'i-ch'ao 梁啓超. *Chung-kuo chin-san-pai-nien hsüeh-shu shih* 中國近三百年學術史 (A History of Chinese Scholarship of the Last Three Centuries). Shanghai, Chung-hua, 1941.

Liu Shih-p'ei 劉師培 "Nan-pei Li-hsüeh pu-t'ung-lun" 南北理學不同論 (On the Differences between the Neo-Confucianism of the North and That of the South), *Liu Sheng-shu hsien-sheng yi-shu* 劉申叔先生遺書 (Surviving Works of Liu Shih-p'ei). n.p., 1936, v. 15.

Lo Kuang 羅光. "Ming-ch'ao ch'u-yeh che-hsüeh ssu-hsiang" 明朝初葉思想 (Philosophy in the Early Ming Dynasty), *Che-hsüeh yü wen-hua* 哲學與文化 8 (1981), 2–8.

Mai Chung-kuei 麥仲貴. *Ming-Ch'ing ju-hsüeh-chia chu-shu sheng-chu nien-piao* 明清儒學家著述生卒年表 (A Chronological Table of the Lives and Works of Ming and Ch'ing Dynasties). 2 v. Taipei, Hsüeh-sheng, 1977.

Mou Tsung-san 牟宗三. *Ch'ung Lu Hsiang-shan tao Liu Chi-shan* 從陸象山到劉蕺山. Taipei, Hsüeh-sheng, 1979.

Okada Takehiko. *Ō Yōmei to Minmatsu no Jūgaku* 王陽明と明末の儒学 Wang Yang-ming and Late Ming Confucianism). Tokyo, Meitoku, 1970.

————. *Sō-Min tetsugaku jūsetsu* 宋明哲学序説 (Introduction to the Philosophy of the Sung and Ming Dynasties). Tokyo, Bungensha, 1977.

Ono Kazuko 小野和子. *Ko Sogi* 黄宗羲. Tokyo, Jinbutsu Oraisha, 1967.

Ren Jiyu 任繼愈, ed. *Chung-kuo che-hsüeh shih* 中國哲學史 (A History of Chinese Thought), v. 4. Peking, Jen-min, 1979.

Shimada Kenji 島田虔次. *Chūgoku ni okeru kindai shii no zasetsu* 中国に於る近代思惟の挫折 (The Breakdown of Modern Thought in China). Tokyo, Chekuma, 1949.

Sun Shu-ping 孫叔平. *Chung-kuo che-hsüeh-shih kao* 中國哲學史稿 (A Draft History of Chinese Philosophy), v. 2. Shanghai, Jen-min, 1981.

T'ang Chün-i 唐君毅. *Chung-kuo che-hsüeh yüan-lun. Yüan-chiao pien* 中國哲學原論・原教篇(An Inquiry into Chinese Philosophy. Section on Doctrines). Part 2. Taipei, Hsüeh-sheng, 1977.

Wang Shou-nan 王壽南, ed. *Chung-kuo li-tai ssu-hsiang chia* 中國歷代思想家 (Chinese Historians of Thought), v. 7. Taipei, Commercial, 1978.
Wen Hsien-hsin 翁咸新. "Huang Li-chou te shen-p'ing chi ch'i hsüeh-shu ssu-hsiang" 黃梨洲的生平及其學術思想 (The Life and Thought of Huang Tsung-hsi), *Tung-fang tsa-chih* 東方雜誌, v. 9–11 (1976), pts. 1–2, 30–37, 50–56.

Yamamoto Makoto 山本命. *Minjidai Jugaku no rinrigaku teki kenkyū* 明時代儒学の倫理学的研究 (The Study of Confucian Ethics in the Ming Dynasty). Tokyo, Risosha, 1974.

Yamanoi Yū. *Ko Sogi*. Tokyo, Kodansha, 1983.

————. "Minjugakuan no shikōteiyō ni kansuru nisan no mondai" 明儒学案の四庫提要に関するの問題 (On Some Problems Regarding the *Ming-ju hsüeh-an* Entry in the *Ssu-k'u t'i-yao*), *Tokyō Shinagakuhō* 東京支那学報 12 (1966) 75–95.

————. *Min-Shin shisōshi no kenkyū* 明清思想の研究 (A Study of the History of Ming and Ch'ing Thought). Tokyo, Tokyo University Press, 1980.

Yamashita Ryūji 山下龍二. *Yōmeigaku no kenkyū* 陽明学の研究 (A Study of the Yang-ming School). 2 v. Tokyo, Gendai juhosha, 1971.

Yang T'ing-fu 楊廷福. *Ming-mo san ta ssu-hsiang-chia* 明末三大思想家 (The Three Great Thinkers of the Late Ming). Shanghai, Ssu-lien, 1954.

Yü Ying-shih 余英時. *Fang Yi-chih wan-chieh k'ao* 方以智晚節考 (Fang I-chih: His Last Years and His Death). Hongkong, New Asia College, Institute of Advanced Chinese Studies and Research, 1972.

Yüan Chih-sheng 阮芝生. "Hsüeh-an t'i-ts'ai yüan-lui ch'u-t'an" 學案體裁淵源初探 (Preliminary Study of the Evolution of the Intellectual History [*Hsüeh-an*] as a Genre), *Shih-yüan* 史源 2 (1971), 57–76.

B.   Western Language Works

Atwell, William S. "From Education to Politics: The Fu-she," *The Unfolding of Neo-Confucianism,* ed. William Theodore de Bary. New York, Columbia University Press, 1975, pp. 333–68.

Balazs, Étienne. *Political Theory and Administrative Reality in China.* London, University of London, School of Oriental and African Studies, 1965.

Berling, Judith. *The Syncretic Religion of Lin Chao-en.* New York, Columbia University Press, 1980.

Busch, Heinrich. "The Tung-lin Academy and Its Political and Philosophical Significance," *Monumenta Serica* 14 (1949–55), 1–63.

Chan, Wing-tsit. *Neo-Confucianism etc.: Essays by Wing-tsit Chan.* Comp. by Charles K. H. Chen. New Haven, American Oriental Society, 1969.

Chang, Yü-ch'üan. "Wang Shou-jen as a Statesman," *Chinese Social and Political Science Review* 23 (1939–40), 30–99, 155–252, 319–75, 473–517.

Ch'en, Kenneth. *Buddhism in China.* Princeton, Princeton University Press, 1964.

Cheng, Chung-ying. "Consistency and the Meaning of the Four Sentence Teaching in the *Ming-ju hsüeh-an,*" *Philosophy East and West* 29 (1979), 275–94.

Ch'ien, Edward. *Chiao Hung and the Restructuring of Neo-Confucianism in the Late Ming.* New York, Columbia University Press, 1986.

Ching, Julia. "Chu Shun-shui, 1600–82: A Chinese Confucian Scholar in Tokugawa Japan," *Monumenta Nipponica* 30 (1975), 177–91.

———. "The Records of the Ming Philosophers: An Introduction," *Oriens Extremus* 23 (1976), 191–211.

———. *To Acquire Wisdom: The Way of Wang Yang-ming.* New York, Columbia University Press, 1976.

de Bary, William Theodore. "Chinese Despotism and the Confucian Ideal: A Seventeenth Century View," *Chinese Thought and Institutions,* ed. by John K. Fairbank. Chicago, University of Chicago Press, 1957, pp. 163–204.

———. *Neo-Confucian Orthodoxy and the Learning of the Mind-and-Heart.* New York, Columbia University Press, 1981.

————, ed. *Principle and Practicality.* New York, Columbia University Press, 1979.

————, ed. *Self and Society in Ming Thought.* New York, Columbia University Press, 1970.

Dimberg, Ronald. *The Sage and Society: The Life and Thought of Ho Hsin-yin.* Honolulu, University Press of Hawaii, 1974.

Franke, Herbert, ed. *Sung Biographies.* 2 v. Wiesbaden, Steiner, 1977.

Fung Yu-lan. *A History of Chinese Philosophy.* Trans. by Derk Bodde. 2 v. Princeton, Princeton University Press, 1976.

Goodrich, L. Carrington; and Chaoying Fang, ed. *Dictionary of Ming Biography.* 2 v. New York, Columbia University Press, 1976.

Handlin, Joanna F. *Action in Late Ming Thought: Reorientation of Lü K'un and Other Scholar-Officials.* Berkeley, University of California Press, 1983.

Hucker, Charles O. "Governmental Organization of the Ming Dynasty," *Harvard Journal of Asiatic Studies* 21 (1958), 1–66.

Hummel, Arthur. *Eminent Chinese of the Ch'ing Period.* Washington, United States Government Printing Office, 1943.

Kim, Ha-tai. "The Religious Dimension of Neo-Confucianism," *Philosophy East and West* 27 (1977), 337–48.

Lu Kuang-huan. "The *shu-yüan* Institution Developed by Sung-Ming Neo-Confucian Philosophers," *Chinese Culture* 9 (September 1968), 98–122.

Mori Masao. "The Gentry in the Ming Period—An Outline of the Relations Between the *Shih-ta-fu* and Local Society," *Acta Asiatica* 38 (Tokyo, 1980), 31–53.

Needham, Joseph. *Science and Civilisation in China,* v. 2–3. Cambridge, Cambridge University Press, 1959.

Shryock, John. *The Origin and Development of the State Cult of Confucius.* New York, Paragon, 1966.

Stace, Walter Terence. *Mysticism and Philosophy.* London, Macmillan, 1960.

Struve, Lynn A. "The Concept of the Mind in the Scholarship of Huang Tsung-hsi," *Journal of Chinese Philosophy* 9 (March 1982), 107–29.

————. *The Southern Ming: 1644–1662.* New Haven, Yale University Press, 1984.

Taylor, Rodney L. "The Centered Self: Religious Autobiography in the Neo-Confucian Tradition," *History of Religions* 17 (1978), 266–83.

————. "Journey into Self: The Autobiographical Reflections of Hu Chih," *History of Religions* 21 (1982), 321–38.

Tu, Wei-ming. *Neo-Confucian Thought in Action: The Youth of Wang Yang-ming.* Berkeley, University of California Press, 1976.

Watters, T. *A Guide to the Tablets in a Temple of Confucius.* N. p., 1879.

Yen, Maria. "Philosophie der Erziehung des Pai-sha-tzu." Dissertation. University of Hamburg, 1981.

Glossary of Transliterations

An-shen	安身
Cha Tuo	查鐸(子警・毅齋)
Chai Luan	翟鑾
Ch'ai Feng	柴鳳
Chan Jo-shui	湛若水(元明・甘泉)
Chang Ch'i	張綮(士儀・本靜)
Chang Ch'ien	張騫
Chang Chü-cheng	張居正
Chang Chung	張中
Chang Fu-ching	張孚敬
Chang Hsü	張詡(廷實・東所)
Chang Hsüeh	張鷽
Chang Hsün-shui	張洵水
Chang Ken	張覬
Chang Kuei	張璜
Chang Kun	章袞
Chang Mao	張茂
Chang Mou	章懋
Chang Shih	張栻
Chang Shih-ch'e	張時徹
Chang Shih-luan	章時鑾
Chang Tsai	張載
Chang Tso	張佐
Chang Ts'ung	張璁
Chang Wei	張位
Chang Wei	張惟
Chang Ya-tzu	張亞子(梓童)
Chang Yi	張儀
Chang Ying	章穎
Chang Yüan-chen	張元禎(延祥・東白)
Chang Yüan-lo	張原洛
Chang Yüan-pien	張原忭

Chao Chen-chi	趙貞吉
Chao Chih-kao	趙志皐
Chao K'o-huai	趙可懷
Chao Nan-hsing	趙南星
Chao Po-lou	趙白樓
Chao Shih-ch'un	趙時春
Chao Wen-hua	趙文華
Chao Yung-hsien	趙用賢
Chen-chi	眞機
Chen-ju	眞如
Chen-k'ung	眞空
Chen-t'i	眞體
Ch'en (Lady)	岑
Ch'en Chen-sheng	陳眞晟(剩夫)
Ch'en Chien	陳建
Ch'en Chiu-ch'uan	陳九川(明水)
Ch'en Chü	陳矩
Ch'en Feng	陳奉
Ch'en Fu-liang	陳復良
Ch'en Hsi-ku	陳錫嘏(介眉)
Ch'en Hsien-chang	陳獻章(公甫・石齋・白沙・文恭)
Ch'en Hsüan	陳選
Ch'en Jui	陳瑞
Ch'en Shih-chieh	陳世傑
Ch'en Ting	陳鼎
Ch'en Tseng	陳增
Ch'en Yi-ch'üan	陳一泉
Ch'en Yu-nien	陳有年
Ch'en Yü-pi	陳宇陛
Cheng Chen	鄭溱
Cheng Ch'eng-en	鄭承恩
Cheng Chu	鄭燭(景明)
Cheng Hsing	鄭性
Cheng Liang	鄭梁
Cheng Shan-fu	鄭善夫
Cheng Ts'ai	鄭材
Cheng Yi-ch'u	鄭一初(朝朔)
Cheng Ying	鄭寅
Cheng-hsin	正心
Ch'eng	誠
Ch'eng, King	成王
Ch'eng Hao	程顥(明道)
Ch'eng Hsüeh-po	程學博
Ch'eng Hsüeh-yen	程學顏(二蒲・後臺)

Ch'eng Ming-chen	程敏政（篁墩）
Ch'eng Mo	程默（子木）
Ch'eng Shih-chieh	程世傑
Ch'eng Ta-pin	程大賓（汝見・心泉）
Ch'eng Wen-te	程文德（松溪）
Ch'eng Yi	程頤（伊川）
Ch'eng-yi	誠意
Chi (name)	季
Chi (stillness)	寂
Chi (creative beginning)	機
Chi Pen	季本（明德・彭山）
Chi Yüan-heng	冀元亨（惟乾・闇齋）
Chi Yün	紀昀
Chi-shan hsüeh-an	蕺山學案
Ch'i	氣
Ch'i Hsien	戚賢（秀夫・南元）
Ch'i Kun	戚袞（補元・竹坡）
Ch'i-chih / ch'i-chih chih hsing	氣質／氣質之性
Ch'i-sung	契嵩
Ch'i-yün	氣運
Chia Jen	賈潤（若水）
Chia P'u	賈樸（醇菴）
Chiang Hsin	蔣信（卿實・道林）
Chiang Kuo-pang	蔣國榜
Chiang Li	姜里
Chiang Pao	姜寶（廷善）
Chiang Shih-ch'ang	姜士昌
Chiang Ts'ai	姜埰
Chiang Wan-li	江萬里
Chiang-hsüeh	講學
Ch'iang-tzu	腔子
Chiao Hung	焦竑
Chieh, King	桀王
Chieh-ts'ai	解才
Chieh-wu	解悟
Chieh-yüan	解元
Ch'ien Lin	錢林
Ch'ien Neng	錢能
Ch'ien Te-hung	錢德洪（洪甫・緒山）
Ch'ien T'ung-wen	錢同文（懷蘇）
Ch'ien Yi-pen	錢一本
Ch'ien	乾
Ch'ien-chih	乾知
Chih	知

Chih	志
Chih-chih	致知
Chih-chüeh	知覺
Chih-hsiu	止修
Chin Li-hsiang	金履祥
Chih-t'i	知體
Chin Ying	金英
Ching	敬
Ching	靜
Ching-ch'a	京察
Ching-feng	靜峯
Ching-tso	靜坐
Ch'ing	情
Ch'ing-yi	清議
Ch'iu Chün	邱濬
Chou, Duke of	周公
Chou, King	紂王
Chou Ch'en	周忱
Chou Chi	周積(恭節)
Chou Ch'ao-jui	周朝瑞
Chou Ch'ung	周衝(道通)
Chou Hui	周蕙(小泉)
Chou Ju-teng	周汝登(繼元・海門)
Chou Liang-yin	周良寅
Chou Meng-hsiu	周夢秀
Chou Ning-yü	周寧宇
Chou T'an	周坦
Chou Tun-yi	周敦頤(茂叔・濂溪)
Chou Wen	周文
Chou Yen-ju	周延儒
Chou Yi	周怡
Chou Ying	周瑛(翠渠)
Chou Ying-chung	周應中
Ch'ou Chao-en	仇兆鼇(滄柱)
Ch'ou Luan	仇鸞
Chu Ch'ang-hao	朱常浩(瑞王)
Chu Ch'ang-lo	朱常洛(福王)
Chu Ch'en-hao	朱宸濠(寧王)
Chu Ch'i-chen	朱祁鎮(英宗)
Chu Ch'i-ch'üan	朱祁銓(淮王)
Chu Ch'i-yü	朱祁鈺(景帝)
Chu Chien-shen	朱見深(憲宗)
Chu Ch'un	朱純
Chu Hou-chao	朱厚照(武宗)

Chu Hou-ts'ung	朱厚熜（世宗）
Chu Hsi	朱熹（元晦・晦庵）
Chu Hsin-hsüeh	朱心學
Chu Keng	朱賡
Chu Kuo-chen	朱國禎
Chu Lung-hsi	朱龍禧
Chu Shu	朱恕（光信）
Chu Te-chih	朱得之（近齋）
Chu Ti	朱棣（成祖）
Chu Tsai-hou	朱載垕（穆宗）
Chu Tsai-jui	朱載壑（莊敬太子）
Chu T'ung-lei	朱統鑨
Chu Yi-chün	朱翊鈞（神宗）
Chu Yi-liu	朱翊鏐（潞王）
Chu Ying	朱瑛
Chu Yu-chiao	朱由校（熹宗）
Chu Yu-chien	朱由檢（思宗・毅宗）
Chu Yüan-chang	朱元璋（太祖）
Chu Yün-chen	朱蘊鍪
Chu Yün-wen	朱允炆（惠宗）
Chu-chang	助長
Chu-tsai	主宰
Ch'ü P'ing	屈平
Ch'u-shih	楚石
Chüan	狷
Ch'üan Tsu-wang	全祖望
Ch'üan-fa	權法
Chuang-tzu	莊子
Chuang Ch'ang	莊㫤（定山）
Chüeh	覺
Chung Ch'eng	鍾城
Chung	中
Chung-hsing	中行
Chung-yung	中庸
Erh-ch'eng	二乘
Fa/Fo-fa	法／佛法
Fa-ch'u	法初
Fa-shan	發散
Fa-yen	法言
Fan Chih-wan	范志完
Fan Huan	范瓛（廷闓・栗齋）
Fan Yin-nien	范引年（半野）

Fang Hsiao-ju   方孝儒 (希直・遜志・正學・文正)
Fang Hsien-fu   方獻夫 (叔賢・西樵・文襄)
Fang K'o-ch'in   方克勤
Fang Ts'ung-che   方從哲 (德清)
Fang Yü-shih   方與時 (湛一)
Feng Ching-ti   馮景第
Feng En   馮恩
Feng Ts'ung-wu   馮從吾
Feng (Fung) Yu-lan   馮友蘭
Fu, Prince   福王
Fu Hsi   傅翕
Fu-hsi   伏羲
Fu K'uei   傅櫆
Fu Ying-chen   傅應禎
Fu Ying-hsing   傅應星
Fu Yüeh   傅說

Han Chen   韓貞 (以中・樂吾)
Han Ching   韓敬
Han Fei Tzu   韓非子
Han K'uang   韓爌
Han Pang-ch'i   韓邦奇 (苑洛)
Han Shih-chung   韓世忠
Han Wei   韓位
Han Yü   韓愈
Hao Ching   郝敬 (仲輿・楚望)
Ho   和
Ho Chi   何基 (北山)
Ho Ch'ien   何謙
Ho Ch'i-ming   何起鳴
Ho Ch'in   賀欽 (醫閭)
Ho Feng-shao   何鳳韶 (汝諧)
Ho Hsin-yin   何心隱
Ho T'ing-jen   何廷仁 (善山)
Hou-t'ien   後天
Hsia Ch'un   夏醇 (惟初・復吾)
Hsia Yen   夏燮
Hsiao Ch'iao   項喬 (甌東)
Hsiang Ying-hsiang   項應祥
Hsiao Liang-kan   蕭良幹 (以寧・拙齋)
Hsiao Yen   蕭彥 (念渠・定菴)
Hsieh Chao   謝昭
Hsieh Fang-te   謝枋得 (疊山)
Hsieh Tuo   謝鐸 (鳴涸)

Hsieh Ying-fang	謝應芳
Hsien, Prince of Shu	蜀獻王
Hsien-ch'eng liang-chih	現成良知
Hsien-t'ien	先天
Hsin / hsin-chih-t'i	心／心之體
Hsin Tzu-hsiu	辛自修
Hsin-hsüeh	心學
Hsin-t'i	心體
Hsing	性
Hsing	行
Hsing, Prince	興王
Hsing Jang	邢讓
Hsing Tuan	邢端
Hsing-ch'a	省察
Hsiu-shen	修身
Hsiung K'ai-yüan	熊開元
Hsü	虛
Hsü Ai	徐愛(曰仁·橫山)
Hsü Chang	許璋(半圭)
Hsü Chieh	徐階(存齋)
Hsü Ch'ien	許謙
Hsü Chün	許俊美
Hsü Fu-yüan	許孚遠(孟仲·敬菴)
Hsü Hsi	徐墀(孺子)
Hsü Hsüeh-mo	徐學模
Hsü Hung	徐鈜
Hsü P'eng	徐鵬
Hsü Pin	許彬(道中)
Hsü San-li	許三禮(酉山)
Hsü T'ai	許泰
Hsü T'ien-ch'üan	徐天全
Hsü Yu-chen	徐有貞(天泉)
Hsü Yüeh	徐樾(子直·波石)
Hsü Yung-chien	徐用檢(魯源)
Hsüan-chüeh	玄覺
Hsüeh	學
Hsüeh Chen	薛貞
Hsüeh Ching-chih	薛敬之(思庵)
Hsüeh Feng-ch'ang	薛鳳昌
Hsüeh Hsüan	薛瑄(德溫·敬軒·文清)
Hsüeh K'an	薛侃(尚謙·中離)
Hsüeh Shang-hsien	薛尚賢
Hsüeh Ying-ch'i	薛應旂(方山)
Hsüeh-an	學案

Hsüeh-p'u	學譜
Hu An-kuo	胡安國
Hu Chih	胡直(正甫‧廬山)
Hu Chü-jen	胡居仁(叔心‧‧敬齋)
Hu Hung	胡宏
Hu Kuang	胡廣
Hu San	胡珊(鳴玉)
Hu Ta-shih	胡大時(季隨)
Hu T'ien-feng	胡天鳳
Hu Tsung-chen	胡宗正
Hu Tsung-hsien	胡宗憲
Hua Yün-ch'eng	華允誠(鳳超)
Huan, Duke of Ch'i	齊桓公
Huang Chi	黃驥(德良)
Huang Chia-ai	黃嘉愛(懋仁‧鶴溪)
Huang Ch'ien-ch'iu	黃千秋
Huang Hsing-tseng	黃省曾(五岳‧勉之)
Huang Hung-kang	黃宏綱(洛村)
Huang Kan	黃幹
Huang K'uei	黃夔(子韶‧後川)
Huang P'ei-fang	黃培芳
Huang Po-chia	黃百家
Huang Tao-chou	黃道周(石齋)
Huang Tso	黃佐(泰泉)
Huang Tsun-su	黃尊素
Huang Tsung-hsi	黃宗羲
Huang Tsung-hui	黃宗會
Huang Tsung-ming	黃宗明
Huang Tsung-yen	黃宗炎
Huang Wan	黃綰(宗賢‧久庵)
Huang Wen-huan	黃文奐(吳南)
Huang Wen-kang	黃文剛
Huang Yüan-fu	黃元釜(丁山)
Hui-neng	惠能
Hung-jen	弘忍
Hung Yüan	洪垣(覺山)
Huo Tao	霍韜(文敏)
Jan Po-niu	冉伯牛
Jao Ch'ao	繞朝
Jen	仁
Jen-hsin	人心
Jen-t'i	仁體
Jen-yü	人欲

Ju	儒
Ju-lai-fo	如來佛
Ju-lin	儒林
Juan Ta-cheng	阮大鋮
Juan Yüan	阮元
Kao Chiao	高校
Kao Chieh	高傑
Kao Ku	高鵠
Kao Kung	高拱
Kao Ming	高明
Kao P'an-lung	高攀龍(存之・景逸・忠憲)
Kao Shih	高時
Kao Ts'ung-li	高從禮
Kao Wen-chih	高文質
Kao-tzu	告子
Keng Chiu-ch'ou	耿九疇
Keng Ting-hsiang	耿定向(在倫・天臺)
Keng Ting-li	耿定力(叔臺)
Keng Ting-li	耿定理(楚倥)
Ko-wu	格物
K'o (Madame)	客
Ku Hsien-ch'eng	顧憲成(叔時・涇陽)
Ku Hsüeh	顧學
Ku Ta-chang	顧大章
Ku Yen-wu	顧炎武
Ku Ying-hsiang	顧應祥(箬溪)
Ku Yün-ch'eng	顧允成(涇凡)
Kuan Chih-tao	管志道(登之・東溟)
Kuan Chou	管洲(子行・石屏)
Kuan Chung	管仲
Kuan Yü	關羽
K'uang	狂
Kuei Ô	桂咢
Kuei-chi	歸寂
Kuei-ku-tzu	鬼谷子
K'un	坤
K'un-neng	坤能
Kung	公
Kung An-kuo	貢安國
Kung Mao-hsien	龔懋賢
Kung-an	公案
Kung-fu	工夫
K'ung	空

K'ung Jung	孔融
Kuo Ching	郭景
Kuo Hsün	郭勛 (武定侯)
Lan Tao-hsing	藍道行
Li	理
Li / Chen	利/貞
Li Chih	李贄
Li Chung	李中
Li Fu-yang	李復陽
Li Hsien	李賢 (德遠)
Li K'o-shao	李可灼
Li Ling	李齡
Li Meng-yang	李夢陽
Li Mou	李茂
Li San-ts'ai	李三才
Li Shih	李實
Li Shih-lung	李士龍
Li Sui	李遂
Li Tao	李道
Li T'ing-chi	李廷機 (九我・晉江)
Li Ts'ai	李材
Li T'ung	李侗
Li Wen-hsiang	李文祥
Li Yu-tzu	李幼滋 (義河)
Li Yüan-yang	李元陽 (中溪)
Liang Ch'i-ch'ao	梁啓超
Liang Ch'o	梁焯 (日孚)
Liang Fang	梁方
Liang Ju-yüan	梁汝元
Liang-chih	良知
Liang-hsin	良心
Liang-neng	良能
Liao Yung	廖鏞
Lin Ch'iao	林墧
Lin Ch'un	林春
Lin Chün	林俊 (見素)
Lin Han	林釬
Lin Hsi-yüan	林希元
Lin Hsin-chang	林心章
Lin Ju-chu	林汝耆
Lin Kuang	林光 (緝熙)
Liu Chi	劉吉
Liu Chi	劉基

Liu Ch'iao	劉墧
Liu Ch'i-tsung	劉起宗
Liu Chin	劉瑾
Liu Hsiang	劉向
Liu Hsien-te	劉獻德 (重陽)
Liu Kai	劉概
Liu Kuan-shih	劉觀時
Liu K'ung-chao	劉孔昭
Liu Pang-ts'ai	劉邦采
Liu Pei	劉備
Liu Pi	劉濞
Liu T'ai	劉臺
Liu T'ing-lan	劉廷蘭
Liu Tse-ch'ing	劉澤清
Liu Shih-chen	劉世珍
Liu Tsung-chou	劉宗周 (起東・念臺)
Liu T'ung	劉侗
Liu Tsung-yüan	柳宗元 (子厚)
Liu Wen-ming	劉文敏 (兩峯)
Liu Wen-t'ai	劉文泰
Liu Yang	劉陽 (三五)
Liu Yung-ch'eng	劉永澄
Liu-hsia Hui	柳下惠
Liu-hsing	流行
Liu-hsing chih-t'i	流行之體
Lo Ch'in-shun	羅欽順
Lo Hsün	羅循
Lo Huai-chih	羅懷智
Lo Hung-hsien	羅洪先 (達夫・念庵)
Lo Ju-fang	羅汝芳
Lo Lun	羅倫 (一峯)
Lo Mao-chung	羅懋忠
Lo Ts'ung-yen	羅從彥
Lo Wan-hua	羅萬化
Lou Ch'en	婁忱
Lou Hsing	婁性
Lou Liang	婁諒
Lu Ch'eng	陸澄
Lu Chiu-yüan	陸九淵 (象山)
Lu Pao	魯保
Lu T'ang	盧鏜
Lü Huai	呂懷
Lü Kuang-tsu	呂光祖 (五臺)
Lü K'un	呂坤

Lü Liu-liang	呂留良
Lü Nan	呂柟
Lü Pao-chung	呂葆中
Lü Ts'ui-ming	呂粹明(古樵)
Lü Tsu-ch'ien	呂祖謙
Lü Yen	呂岩(純陽・洞賓)
Lun-hui	輪廻
Lung Ch'i-hsiao	龍起霄(正之)

Ma Ming-heng	馬明衡(子莘)
Ma Shen	馬森
Ma Shih-ying	馬士英
Ma Ssu-ts'ung	馬思聰
Ma Tzu-ts'ai	馬子才
Ma Wen-sheng	馬文升
Ma Yüan	馬援
Mei Shou-te	梅守德(純甫・苑溪)
Meng Ch'iu	孟鰍(我疆)
Meng Hua-li	孟化鯉(雲浦)
Mi Wan-ch'un	米萬春
Miao-yu	妙有
Min Tzu-ch'ien	閔子騫
Mo Chieh	莫階
Mo Chin	莫晉
Mo-tzu	墨子
Mu Ch'ao-pi	沐朝弼
Mu K'ung-hui	穆孔暉

Na Chien	那鑑
Na Hsien	那憲
Nan Shih-chung	南師仲
Nan Ta-chi	南大吉(元善・瑞泉)
Nieh Pao	聶豹(文蔚・雙江・貞裏)
Nieh-p'an (nirvāṇa)	涅槃
Nien	念
Nien-t'ou	念頭
Niu Yü	牛玉

| Ou-yang Hsiu | 歐陽修 |
| Ou-yang Te | 歐陽德 |

Pen-hsin	本心
Pen-jan	本然
Pen-jan chih hsing	本然之性
Pen-lin	本領

Pen-wu	本無
P'eng Shao	彭韶
P'eng Tse	彭澤
P'eng Tsung-ku	彭宗古
Pin	賓
Pin-hsing	賓興
Po Yen-hui	薄彥徽
Po-yi	伯夷
Pu-ch'i-yi	不起意
Pu-jung-yi	不容已
Pu-tuan-mieh	不斷滅
San-chieh	三界
Shang-ti	上帝
Shao Chu-feng	邵竹峯
Shao Yung	邵雍
Shen	身
Shen Chia-ho	沈嘉禾
Shen Ch'ung	沈寵
Shen Li	沈鯉
Shen Pu-hai	申不害
Shen Ssu-hsiao	沈思孝
Shen Shih-hsing	申時行
Shen Yen	沈演
Shen Yi-kuan	沈一貫
Shen-tu	慎獨
Shih	事
Shih (monk)	石和尚
Shih Chien	石簡
Shih Heng	石亨
Shih San-wei	石三畏
Shih-shuo	師說
Shou-lien	收歛
Shu-ch'i	叔齊
Shun	舜
Shun-yü K'un	淳于髡
Ssu	私
Ssu-ma Ch'ien	司馬遷
Ssu-ma Kuang	司馬光
Ssu-tuan	四端
Ssu-wu / Ssu-yu	四無 · 四有
Su Ch'in	蘇秦
Su Shih	蘇軾
Su Ts'an	蘇瓚
Sun Ch'i-feng	孫奇逢(鍾元)

Sun K'uang	孫絋(月峯)
Sun Lung	孫鑨(清簡)
Sun P'ei-yang	孫丕陽(福平)
Sun Shen-hsing	孫慎行(聞新・淇澳)
Sun Ying-k'uei	孫應奎(文卿・蒙泉)
Sung Lien	宋濂
Ta-chi	大計
Ta-chang-fu	大丈夫
Ta-lang-chang	大郎長
Tai Hsien	戴銑
Tai Shih-heng	戴士衡
Takakusu Junjirō	高楠順次郎
T'ai-chi	太極
T'ai-chia	泰甲
T'ai-hsü	太虛
T'ang Chien	唐鑑
T'ang Nai	湯鼐
T'ang Pin	湯斌(潛庵)
T'ang Pin-yin	湯賓尹
T'ang Shu	唐樞(一菴)
T'ang Shun-chih	唐順之(應德・荊川)
T'ang Yen	唐演(汝淵)
Tao	道
Tao-hsin	道心
Tao-hsüeh	道學
Tao-shen	道生
Tao-t'ung	道統
Tao wen-hsüeh	道問學
T'ao Chung-wen	陶仲文
T'ao Fu-li	陶福履
T'ao Shih-ling	陶奭齡
T'ao Wang-ling	陶望齡
Te	得
Teng Hao	鄧鶴(太湖・豁渠)
Teng Yi-tsan	鄧以讚(汝德・定宇・文潔)
Teng Yüan-hsi	鄧元錫
Ti-erh-yi	第二義
Ti-yi-yi	第一義
T'i-jen	體仁
T'i / Yung	體用
T'ien-hsing	天性
T'ien-li	天理
T'ien-min	天民

T'ien-ming	天命
T'ien-ti	天地
T'ien-tse	天則
Ting	定
Ting-ching	定靜
Ting Chi	丁璣
Ting Tz'u-lü	丁此呂
Ting Yu-wu	丁右武
Ting Yüan-chien	丁元薦
Ts'ai	才
Ts'ai Ching	蔡京
Ts'ai Ching	蔡清
Ts'ai Ju-nan	蔡汝南
Tsang Wen-chung	臧文仲
Ts'ao Chi-hsiang	曹吉祥
Ts'ao Ching-tsu	曹敬祖
Ts'ao Lung	曹龍
Ts'ao Ta-hsien	曹大咸
Ts'ao Ts'ao	曹操
Tsao-hua	造化
Ts'ao Tuan	曹端(正夫・月川)
Ts'ao Ying-ju	曹胤儒
Tseng Chih	曾直
Tseng Kung	曾鞏
Tseng Tien	曾點
Tseng-tzu	曾子
Tso Kuang-tou	左光斗
Tso Tsung-t'ang	左宗棠
Tso-hsia	坐下
Tsou Chih	鄒智(立齋)
Tsou Hsien	鄒賢
Tsou Shan	鄒善
Tsou Shou-yi	鄒守益(東廓)
Tsou Te-han	鄒德涵
Tsou Te-yung	鄒德泳
Tsou Te-p'u	鄒德溥
Tsou Ying-lung	鄒應龍
Tsou Yuan-piao	鄒元標(南皋・忠介)
Ts'ui Ch'eng-hsiu	崔呈秀
Ts'ui Hsien	崔銑(後渠)
Ts'ui Luan	崔鸞
Tsun te-hsing	尊德性
Tsung-chih	宗旨
Tu Mu	杜牧

Tu-chih	獨知
Tuan Chien	段堅
Tuan-ni	端倪
Tung	動
Tung Yün	董澐
Tun-t'ien	屯田
Tuo-ch'ing	奪情
Tzu-hsia	子夏
Tzu-jan	自然
Tzu-kung	子貢
Tzu-ssu	子思
Tzu-te	自得
Wan Ching	萬爆
Wan Piao	萬表
Wan Ssu-t'ung	萬斯同
Wan Ssu-nien	萬斯年
Wan T'ing-yen	萬廷言(思黙)
Wan Yen	萬言(貞一)
Wang An	王安
Wang Chen	王振
Wang Chi	王畿(汝中・龍溪)
Wang Chia-p'ing	王家屏
Wang Chih-ts'ai	王之采
Wang Chih-yüan	王之垣
Wang Ching	王敬
Wang Ch'iung	王瓊
Wang Chuan	王篆
Wang Ch'ung	王充
Wang Chün	汪俊
Wang Hsi-chüeh	王錫爵(婁江)
Wang Fan-ch'en	王藩臣
Wang Hua	王華
Wang Hung	汪鋐
Wang Ken	王艮
Wang Kuo-kuang	王國光
Wang Mang	王莽
Wang Ming-huo	王鳴鶴
Wang Pi	王璧(順宗・東厓)
Wang Po	王柏
Wang Shen-chung	王慎中(道思)
Wang Shih-chen	王世貞(弇州)
Wang Shih-huai	王時槐(塘南)
Wang Shou-jen	王守仁(陽明・文成)

Wang Shu	王恕
Wang Tao	王道
Wang T'ing-hsiang	王廷相
Wang Tsao	王藻
Wang Wen	王文
Wang Wen-ming	汪文鳴(應奎)
Wang Wen-yen	汪文言
Wang Wen-yüan	王文轅(司輿)
Wang Yang-hao	王養浩
Wang Yeh-hsün	王業洵
Wang Yi	王翊
Wang Yü-ch'i	王毓蓍
Wang Yün	王雲
Wang Wei-shan	王維善
Wei	微
Wei Chang	魏璋
Wei Chiao	魏校(莊渠)
Wei Ch'un	魏純(希文)
Wei Chung-hsien	魏忠賢
Wei Kuang-wei	魏廣微(南樂)
Wei Ta-chung	魏大中
Wei Yün-chung	魏允中
Wei-fa / yi-fa	未發/已發
Wei-fa chih-chung	未發之中
Wen, Duke of Chin	晉文公
Wen, King	文王
Wen Ch'ang-sheng	翁長森
Wen T'i-jen	溫體仁
Wen T'ien-hsiang	文天祥(文山)
Wen-t'ung	文統
Wen-jen Ch'üan	聞人銓(邦正・北江)
Wu/Hsiu	悟・修
Wu Ch'eng	吳澄
Wu Chih-yüan	吳志遠(子往)
Wu Ch'ung-yao	伍崇曜
Wu Jen	吳仁
Wu P'u	吳溥
Wu Shih-lai	吳時來
Wu T'i	吳悌(疏山)
Wu Tsung-yao	吳宗堯
Wu Yü-pi	吳與弼
Wu-chi	無極
Wu-li	物理
Wu-hsin	無心

Wu-ting	武丁
Wu-shan wu-ô	無善無惡
Wu-sheng wu-ch'ou	無聲無臭
Wu-wang wu-chu	勿忘勿助
Wu-yü	無欲
Wu-yü	物欲
Ya-ch'ien	牙籤
Yang Chi	楊驥(仕德)
Yang Chi-sheng	楊繼盛(忠愍)
Yang Ch'i-yüan	楊起元(復所)
Yang Chien	楊簡(慈湖)
Yang Chu	楊珠
Yang Chu	陽朱
Yang Chüeh	楊爵(斛山)
Yang Hsi-yen	楊希顏(仕鳴)
Yang Hsiung	揚雄(子雲)
Yang Jo-ch'iao	楊若僑
Yang Jung	楊榮
Yang K'o	楊珂(秘圖)
Yang Lien	楊漣(月湖)
Yang Po	楊博(襄毅)
Yang P'u	楊溥(文定)
Yang Shih	楊時(中立・龜山)
Yang Shih-ch'i	楊士奇
Yang Shih-ch'iao	楊時喬(止菴・端潔)
Yang Ssu-ch'ang	楊嗣昌
Yang T'ing-ho	楊廷和
Yang Wei	楊巍
Yang Ying-su	楊應宿
Yang Yüeh	楊杓(介誠)
Yao	堯
Yao Ju-hsün	姚汝循
Yao Kuang-hsiao	姚光孝
Yeh Hsiang-kao	葉向高
Yen Chün	顏鈞(士農)
Yen Shih-fan	嚴世蕃
Yen Sung	嚴嵩(分宜)
Yen Yüan	顏淵
Yi-ch'i	意氣
Yi-ch'ieh p'ing-shih	一切平實
Yi-fa-chih-ho	已發之和
Yi-nien	一念
Yi-pen wan-shu	一本萬殊
Yi Yin	伊尹

Yin Chih	尹直
Ying Mai	殷邁(時訓・秋溟)
Yu Shih-hsi	尤時熙
Yü Ch'ien	于謙
Yü Hsien	俞憲
Yü Shen-hsing	干愼行
Yu-chu	有主
Yü-ping	寓兵
Yüan Ch'ung-huan	袁崇煥
Yüan Hao-wen	元好問
Yüan Hua-chung	袁化中
Yüan Lang	袁閬
Yüeh Cheng	岳正(季方・蒙泉・文肅)
Yüeh-ch'üan	月泉
Yün	運
Yung	庸
Yün Jih-ch'u	渾日初(仲昇)
Yung-chia Hsüan-chüeh	永嘉玄覺

Index

▥ Production Notes

Composition and paging for this book were
done on the Quadex Composing System and
typesetting on the Compugraphic 8400 by the
design and production staff of University of
Hawaii Press.

The text and display typeface is Baskerville.

Offset presswork and binding were done by
Vail-Ballou Press, Inc. Text paper is Writers RR
Offset, basis 50.

Compiled in the seventeenth century, *The Records of Ming Scholars* is one of the finest examples we have of a Chinese history of thought. It presents a compelling account of the many different schools of Ming Confucianism and the lives and teachings of representative thinkers and scholars, all organized around the principal school of the time, that of Wang Yang-ming.

Huang Tsung-hsi (1610–95), the author of the *Ming-ju hsüeh-an,* was a famous scholar, philosopher, historian, Ming loyalist, and resistance fighter against the Manchu invaders. Reflecting his ardent character, Huang's *Records* are not of armchair philosophers but of men living in difficult circumstances who were sometimes called to heroic self-sacrifice.

The central topics of discussion are the nature of wisdom and how to acquire it. For these scholars of the Ming dynasty, wisdom was understood to be inseparable from a life of virtue. Their lives and teachings disclose an intense spiritual quest for the Absolute or, in Chinese terms, for the Tao, and the record the book unfolds is one of impressive intellectual and spiritual vitality.

This selective translation of *The Records of Ming Scholars* will be an indispensable source for students of Chinese philosophy, religion, and intellectual and social history. In addition, since many of the scholars were active government officials, the book provides interesting insights into the political events of the time.